MEXICAN AMERICANS
AND THE CATHOLIC CHURCH, 1900–1965

THE NOTRE DAME HISTORY
OF HISPANIC CATHOLICS IN THE U.S.

General Editor: Jay P. Dolan

Volume One
Mexican Americans and the Catholic Church, 1900–1965

Volume Two
Puerto Rican and Cuban Catholics in the U.S., 1900–1965

Volume Three
Hispanic Catholic Culture in the U.S.: Issues and Concerns

Mexican Americans and the Catholic Church, 1900–1965

Edited by

Jay P. Dolan

and

Gilberto M. Hinojosa

UNIVERSITY OF NOTRE DAME PRESS

Notre Dame   London

Library of Congress Cataloging-in-Publication Data

Mexican Americans and the Catholic Church, 1900–
1965 / edited by Jay P. Dolan and Gilberto M.
Hinojosa.
    p.   cm. — (The Notre Dame history of His-
panic Catholics in the U.S. ; v. 1)
  Includes bibliographical references and index.
  ISBN 0-268-01409-4 (alk. paper)
  1. Mexican American Catholics—History.
2. Catholic Church—United States—History—20th
century. I. Dolan, Jay P., 1936– II. Hinojosa,
Gilberto Miguel, 1942– . III. Series.
BX1407.M47 1994
282'.73'0896872—dc20   94–14003
                                   CIP

CONTENTS

ACKNOWLEDGMENTS

The Notre Dame History of Hispanic Catholics in the U.S. began in 1989 when the Cushwa Center for the Study of American Catholicism at the University of Notre Dame and its director, Jay P. Dolan, together with Mary Ewens, O.P., at that time the associate director of the Cushwa Center, began to design a plan for the study. An essential component of this phase of the project was an advisory committee made up of individuals who were engaged in various aspects of Hispanic studies. Allan Figueroa Deck, S.J., Gilberto M. Hinojosa, Michael J. McNally, Moisés Sandoval, Anthony M. Stevens-Arroyo, and Olga R. Villa Parra comprised this committee and have guided the study throughout the four years that it took to complete it. We are truly grateful for their assistance. Also making an important contribution to the study was Jaime R. Vidal, who replaced Mary Ewens at the Cushwa Center in 1990. He served as an important liaison between the Cushwa Center and the numerous scholars involved in the study. Another key person was the secretary of the Cushwa Center, Delores Dant Fain. She took care of a myriad of details and was mainly responsible for administering what proved to be a very complex project. We are very grateful for all her work on behalf of the study.

A special word of thanks must go to Jeanne Knoerle, S.P., and Fred L. Hofheinz of the Lilly Endowment. They continually encouraged us throughout the four years of the study; without their support the study would not have been possible.

Mexican Americans and the Catholic Church, 1900–1965 is only one part of the study. Another volume in this history is *Puerto Rican and Cuban Catholics in the U.S., 1900–1965*. The third and final part of the study is *Hispanic Catholic Culture in the U.S.: Issues and Concerns*. All of these books are available from the University of Notre Dame Press. Together they comprise the Notre Dame History of Hispanic Catholics in the U.S., a landmark study of a people too long neglected by historians of American Catholicism.

INTRODUCTION

With the advent of the twenty-first century the face of the United States and the American Catholic Church will change dramatically. By the year 2010, Hispanics—Mexican Americans, Puerto Ricans, Cuban Americans, and other Latinos—will comprise the nation's largest minority and possibly more than half of the Catholics in the United States. Hispanics bring to the Catholic Church spiritual and communal traditions which are very different from those of other Catholics whose origins lie in Anglo-Saxon and Eastern European cultures. The challenges presented to the United States Church by the large numbers of Hispanics will be formidable. The expectation of these and other Catholics that the Church respond to their spiritual gifts and needs and more fully integrate their cultural traditions into the ecclesial community will test the ability of the institutional Church to respond to the needs of the people. Indeed, the diversity among Hispanics and even within each group, while contributing to the richness of Catholic culture, often perplexes Church officials. Nevertheless, if the past has set the foundation for the future, the Catholic Church, whatever its shortcomings, will embrace the new challenge Hispanics present in the twenty-first century.

Among Hispanics, Mexican Americans are by far the most numerous and the ones with the longest legacy within the American Church. Like other Latinos, Mexican Americans have a heritage with extensive roots in Native American, Spanish, and to some extent African peoples and cultures. That *mestizo* (racially and culturally mixed) background combines sometimes conflicting traditions that, in turn, have blended and contrasted with those of the United States Church when it took over jurisdiction of the once Indian-Spanish-Mexican faith communities of the Southwest.

The new synthesis in the United States has not been free of conflict and turmoil any more than the earlier *mestizo* Mexican Church. A major source of conflict in the nineteenth-century American period was the people's understanding of the Church as community. For Mexican Americans the Church was *their* Church—*el pueblo's*

1

(the people's) Church—as much as it was the clergy's, and membership was determined by their commitment to it rather than by some other official criteria such as regular church attendance. When ecclesiastical leadership no longer emerged from the immediate or extended community after the mid-1800s, the institutional Church often appeared alien and at times adversarial.

The line separating popular and official religiosity was often unclear, but it was unquestionably there. Despite their independence from institutional structures in certain areas, most Mexican-American faith communities did not exist without official leadership before their incorporation into the United States Church and thus they did not generally oppose or reject the new ecclesiastical direction. Though there were currents of anticlericalism and even separatism, the great majority of Mexican Americans always professed a strong loyalty to the official Church. The commitment to that institution, however, did not mean full compliance with specific regulations and prescriptions or acceptance of priests and bishops who appeared to defend the groups that exploited *el pueblo*.

Today the loyalty of Mexican Americans is threatened not only by the competition of other churches but also by the seemingly opposing forces of acculturation and marginalization in United States society. On the one hand, many Mexican Americans are being transformed by the secular agents of cultural change that enter their daily lives: the schools, the workplace, and the ever-present entertainment industry. On the other hand, just as many, if not more, Mexican Americans have been relegated to an underclass bereft of human dignity and hope. In these circumstances the age-old faith communities are being tested more severely than ever before and the institutional Church faces a daunting challenge.

But before the Church, as institution and as people, can respond to the current crisis and devise a strategy for the future, it needs to reflect upon the past and understand the Mexican-American faith communities, their pre-twentieth-century roots, and their more recent development. This volume addresses that experience. Part I, authored by Gilberto M. Hinojosa, examines the Mexican-American Catholic communities in the Southwest. Part II, written by Jeffrey M. Burns, focuses on the California experience. And Part III, by David A. Badillo, traces the history of the Catholic Church among Mexican Americans in the Midwest, an aspect of the story that is less familiar because of its more recent development.

The essay by Gilberto M. Hinojosa in Part I includes a chapter entitled "Antecedents to the Twentieth Century," which presents a brief view of the Indian heritage and the Spanish colonial and Mexican past, as well as a review of the later nineteenth-century experience under the United States Church. This look at pre-twentieth-century developments provides an important background for the study of Mexican Americans in the Church not only in Texas, New Mexico, and Arizona but also in the regions examined by the other authors in the volume. Chapters Two and Three cover the Mexican-American faith experience within pre- and post–World War II contexts.

Hinojosa's thesis is that in order to understand the historical relationship between Mexican Americans and the Catholic Church one must first look at the faith of the communities and their popular ritual expressions and secondly at their response to and participation in official ecclesial initiatives and worship. While popular and official religiosity are not necessarily separate from one another or in opposition to one another, as appears to have been the case at times, in the Mexican-American experience elements of those two aspects of religiosity did not always blend. What conflicts there were centered around profoundly religious internal convictions and fervent external faith expressions of Mexican Americans that did not always reflect official teachings or conform to regulations laid down by the clergy.

Thus, several priests cited by Hinojosa decried the Mexicans' ignorance of their religion, their failure to obey Church rules, and their lack of support of the official Church. Yet priests also expressed great admiration for the people's faith, even to the point of demonstrating surprise that a vibrant and intense spirituality existed in the day-to-day lives of people who were not "properly" educated in Church doctrine and sometimes distant from the sacraments. The United States Church, of course, incorporated through certain devotions and celebrations some of the Mexican religiosity. In some instances Church officials led the community by promoting popular spirituality. But they were not beyond vigorously condemning what appeared in opposition to the faith or what they could not control.

Hinojosa also distinguishes the Church as an institution and as a community. As institution, the Church is described as being more concerned at times with permanence and prominence than with serving the Mexican-American faith community. But the official Church also contributed significantly to supporting and deepening the faith of the community. Many priests and men and women religious left legacies of service and dedication that reflect intimate bonds with *el pueblo*. Promoting institutional concerns and living out the gospel are not necessarily contradictory goals, since the Church is in this world but not of it. But in balancing those two objectives the institutional Church did not always work for the optimum benefit of Mexican Americans.

In Part II Jeffrey M. Burns grapples with the same dilemma in the context of California. In California, the links with the earlier Spanish and Mexican faith communities are not as evident as in Texas, because the rapid expansion of the United States economy and population seemed to eclipse the earlier society. That apparent "disappearance" (actually, marginalization, according to Burns) of the Mexican community soon resulted in the official Church all but completely ignoring the spiritual needs of Mexican Americans for several decades. Still, the earlier foundations survived the nineteenth-century changes and by the early 1900s Los Angeles once again became the center of the *"México de afuera"* (the exiled Mexican) community that became the nucleus of California's Mexican Americans.

Family traditions and self-help community societies, according to Burns, were at the heart of the Mexican-American community's survival and progress. These traditions and organizations were instrumental in enabling the Mexicans to endure the dislocation of immigration and the demoralization that resulted from their being used as a labor commodity in California's large-scale agricultural concerns. The name of San Jose's barrio, *Sal Si Puedes* (Get Out [of Here] If You Can), captured both the sufferings of Mexican Americans and their aspiration to improve their lives.

The California Catholic Church did not sit idly by when challenged by the numbers of Mexican immigrants and their economic plight. Charitable and educational efforts contributed significantly to improving the lot of the newcomers. While officially disapproving of ethnic parishes, the Church founded barrio "missions" that grew into *de facto* Mexican parishes. The charitable and educational endeavors as well as the establishment of parishes were not without controversy. This was mostly about whether or not the Church was ignoring Mexican traditions and promoting "Americanization" and to what extent the Church failed to address economic ills of the people. Nonetheless, it is clear that the Church did not ignore its responsibility toward Mexican Americans.

Burns also takes up the matter of Mexican spirituality. Along with analyzing the issues examined by Hinojosa, Burns also examines the role of national and international politics and the cultural response of the United States clergy to the challenge presented by the increasingly larger Mexican community. Both accommodation and inflexibility were demonstrated by Church leaders. Despite mutual distrust and personal conflicts, the American Church was able to find ways of incorporating aspects of Mexican spirituality into the worship and life of the Mexican-American faith communities.

The major theme in the post–World War II period is the Church's efforts to promote both the Americanization of the newcomers and the formation of group consciousness. The context of those seemingly contradictory processes was the emergence of a Mexican-American generation. As American-born youngsters matured and broke away from their parents, they experienced a cultural gap that complicated how the Church would respond to "the Mexican problem." The Church's answer was to form youth organizations and expand the Catholic school system, thereby reaching out to the new generation without alienating the older churchgoers.

Ministry to migrant laborers proved a greater challenge. Taking the sacraments to the thousands of temporary workers in California's vast agricultural hinterland proved difficult, if not impossible. But many priests, particularly those in the Spanish Mission Band, took the Church's institutional presence out to the fields rather than wait for the farmers to truck their workers into the towns. Contact with the *braceros* inspired many priests to encourage organized labor to fight the agribusiness concerns that profited from the exploitation of those workers. The Church's work on behalf of the farm workers included a spiritual revival called the Cursillo movement which contributed to a new identity among Mexican Americans. Clerical involvement with the unions angered growers, some of whom were Catholic and Church supporters and strongly protested the work of the activist priests to the hierarchy. Despite some hesitation, the Church strongly supported the cause of social justice.

In Part III of this volume David A. Badillo examines the Mexican-American faith communities in the American Midwest. Badillo begins by tracing the Mexican migration away from the border region along the railroad lines and describing the establishment of the first Hispanic communities outside the Southwest. The early settlements quickly attracted workers who went there directly from Mexico in search of a better life. Simultaneously, the religious conflicts ignited by the Mexican revolution forced many Mexican clergymen and religious to emigrate to the United

States. Immigrant lay people together with churchmen and women founded the pioneer Mexican-American parishes from which later faith communities emerged. The newcomers did not always find the American environment hospitable, but they adjusted nonetheless. Catholic Church officials, who often saw themselves in competition with Protestant sects for the hearts and souls of the immigrants, also established missions and parishes in the barrio.

To counteract Anglo-American nativist charges of a foreign community, bishops launched an "Americanization" campaign. But Mexicans resisted acculturation, insisting instead on retaining their cultural-religious traditions. The clergy also opted to build on Mexican devotions rather than eradicate them, and the sheer numbers of immigrants who needed spiritual solace weakened the resolve to Americanize the newcomers. Bishops therefore welcomed exiled Mexican clergymen and concentrated on the administration of the sacraments. In fact, the clergy together with Mexican and Mexican-American community leaders promoted ethnic identity and unity in a variety of ways, including creation and support of mutual aid societies.

Post-1930 developments in Mexico and in the United States introduced many changes in the Mexican-American communities in the Midwest. The settling of religious controversies south of the border encouraged the return of the persecuted clergy to their native land. Mexican repatriation efforts lured some of the newcomers back home, while a mounting anti-immigrant campaign drove many others to return to Mexico. Ironically, while this was going on, a new wave of Mexicans were arriving in the Midwest. Disillusioned Mexican labor leaders and political radicals were leaving their country and heading to the American heartland. Also, in the late 1930s and early 1940s Mexican Americans from Texas began migrating as far north as the Dakotas and east into Ohio. Eventually, as the military draft depleted labor pools in the United States, Mexican nationals, as braceros or as undocumented workers, made the trek northward to many of the Hispanic communities.

The post–World War II period ushered in a diversity of immigrant, ethnic, and religious experiences. The acculturation process accelerated, Protestant sects made greater inroads, and Puerto Ricans began to move into previously all-Mexican neighborhoods or establish enclaves of their own. The institutional Church response was different too. In some ways it was stronger, with more organized and concentrated efforts and greater tolerance for ethnic religiosity in some areas and with greater encouragement for mixed

parishes in others. The national programs promulgated by Archbishop Robert E. Lucey, of San Antonio, are also examined in the
midwestern context.

In tracing the history of Mexican Americans in the United
States Catholic Church, these three essays utilize wherever possible a common periodization and treat recurring themes. Both
Hinojosa's and Burns's essays begin by placing twentieth-century
developments within the perspective of the community's Spanish
and Mexican pre-1836/48 roots. The American takeover of the area
and the incorporation of the faith communities into the United
States Church presented new challenges for both Mexican Americans and the Church as they adjusted to each other. There were
cultural clashes as well as a coming together of spiritual traditions.
The conflict and confluence of cultures and interests resurfaced
between 1910 and 1930 and then again in other decades of heavy
Mexican immigration. The clashes stemmed from a variety of factors. Mexicans and Mexican Americans possessed a religiosity that
at times appeared very different from that of other Catholics in the
United States and seemed to exist apart from current institutional
leadership and control. Many Mexicans and Mexican Americans
did not speak English and there were few non-Hispanic priests
who spoke Spanish or understood Mexican and Mexican-American
culture. Influential Church authorities favored the Americanization
of the immigrant, while pastors drew upon Mexican traditions to
revive the faith of the newcomers. The Church's pro–social justice
tradition was stalled once European immigrants who had been
beneficiaries of that tradition were included among the exploiters
of the Mexicans. Even in the distribution of its own resources
the Church favored Anglo-American parishioners over Mexican
Americans. Only after World War II, once the process of economic
and social integration into this country's socioeconomic structure
was well on its way, did the official Church assume important
leadership on behalf of equality. It is at this point that Mexican-
American vocations emerged, reflecting greater acceptance of el
pueblo by the institutional Church.

Despite its failings, the Church ministered to Mexicans and
Mexican Americans with great dedication and sacrifice. In all of the
periods under study many European and Anglo-American priests
and men and women religious spent their lives working among
el pueblo, sometimes making the sacraments and education more
available than it had been in their Mexican homeland. After a century of assimilating various Mexican religious traditions into the

Church's devotional worship, the official Church in its support of the Cursillo movement in the 1960s backed the involvement of lay people in the preaching of the gospel, thus further incorporating into its mission Mexican-American culture and spirituality.

The process of making Mexican Americans fully a part of the United States Church was by no means complete at mid-century, however, and a subsequent volume in this study examines ongoing conflicts and areas where the official Church and el pueblo have remained distant from one another. Nevertheless, the Church of the mid-1900s that attempted to merge the institution and the faith communities by involving Mexican Americans in the proclamation of the gospel was very different from the earlier Church. Before, non-Hispanic priests as well as men and women religious saw themselves as reviving and educating the "dormant" faith of the Mexican. Occasionally, they adopted Mexican devotions, sometimes for the power of grace that worked through them, but most often merely as a means to draw Mexicans and Mexican Americans more fully into the official Church. The Church of the 1960s, by contrast, affirmed the richness of the faith in Mexican-American communities and accepted the leadership that emerged from the people. Many problems remained, to be sure, but for the first time many Mexican Americans began to feel at home in the United States Catholic Church.

Gilberto M. Hinojosa
Jay P. Dolan

PART I

Mexican-American Faith Communities in Texas and the Southwest

Gilberto M. Hinojosa

PROLOGUE

In the summer of 1992 a woman praying at the shrine of Our Lady of Guadalupe in San Antonio's Mexican-American West Side noticed that a statue of the Blessed Mother was "weeping." Word spread quickly through the barrio, and soon hundreds began filing past the statue to witness the miracle and to pray. A week or two later, across town in a North Side Anglo-American church, a priest giving a homily on the central role of Christ in the salvation of humanity, a very appropriate theme for that day's feast of Corpus Christi, decried the "weak faith" of those streaming by the statue. For Mexican Americans in the barrio, however, the phenomenon was no less than an incarnational event, a manifestation of God's presence on earth. *La Virgen* was crying for her people and their community, which was enduring a rash of senseless gang slayings and drive-by shootings. Just a few days before the statue had begun "weeping," a young man had been killed in a public housing project only a few blocks from the church. To most middle-class North Siders, those deaths were merely headlines in the newspapers and the tearful statue a curiosity of Mexicans* of little "true" faith. To Mexicanos, the Blessed Mother's "weeping" was a sign that she shared their pain. Moreover, some of the faithful would claim, her tears were not shed in vain, for in the following weeks the violence slacked off. La Virgen helped them through this crisis, as she had assisted them in the past.[1]

While most Mexican Americans in San Antonio did not flock to venerate the weeping statue, the incident and the North Side priest's reaction to it are poignant reflections of the contradictions in the Mexicano faith experience. The Catholic Church has always played an important role in the Mexican-American faith community. Some of the sacraments and traditional Catholic devotions have contributed significantly to the spiritual lives of many Mexicanos. Bishops, priests, and women religious have

---

*I will use "Mexicanos," "Mexicans," and "Mexican Americans" interchangeably. References to "Tejanos" and "Nuevo Mexicanos" refer specifically to Hispanic Texans and Hispanic New Mexicans. Anglo Americans are sometimes referred to as "Americanos."

11

served generously, some heroically. But like the priest in the North Side parish, the Church has not always understood the Mexican-American community. Because at times the Church has been overly concerned with doctrine, regulations, institutional goals, it has not responded adequately or equitably to the spiritual and temporal needs of Mexican Americans. Indeed, at times the goals of Church authorities have been in conflict with those of the Mexican-American community.

The incident of the weeping statue also reflects the strength of popular religiosity and the Church's ambivalent attitude. The pastor at the Guadalupe church did not promote the devotion; neither did he discourage it or close down the church. On other occasions, the official Church has nurtured popular beliefs and found a place for them within traditional doctrine and rituals. For their part, Mexican Americans have for centuries integrated the supernatural with the joys and tribulations of their worldly society through their belief system. Their faith has been closely linked to institutional religion and is nourished by it, but Mexicano religiosity has also been independent of official structures.[2]

However ambivalent, the relationship between the Church and Mexicanos and their religiosity has given rise to a faith community. Members of this community sometimes formulate a set of beliefs and devise rituals that do not follow the standard Church traditions. *El pueblo*, the people, also propose their own norms, virtues and sins. Most importantly, they support one another in the faith, irrespective of the Church's sometimes helpful, sometimes hindering role. The mutual support among the people sustains the community through change and adversity.

Part I of this volume examines the nature of the relationship between the Mexicano faith community and the Church in the Southwest. While the most detailed overview is of Texas, other areas of the Southwest, particularly New Mexico, are also treated. Selected parish case histories exemplify the vitality of the Mexican-American faith communities.

1

Antecedents to the Twentieth Century

The Mexican-American faith community is heir to Indian and Spanish religious legacies. It has also been shaped by the process of Spanish expansion into what is now the American Southwest in the seventeenth and eighteenth centuries, and by the developments related to the area's transition from Spanish to Mexican sovereignty in the early 1800s, and then to United States control at midcentury. Early contact between Native Americans and Spaniards revealed that certain aspects of the Indian traditions lent themselves to blending with the faith of the newcomers. Nevertheless, as in central Mexico, the encounter of Indians and Spaniards in New Spain's northern frontier involved conquest and ongoing conflict in the social, political, and religious spheres of daily life. Yet some resolution was achieved as lasting Hispanic communities were organized and certain traditions and a common faith contributed to bringing together disparate segments of society: Indian and Spanish, rich and poor, first settlers and newcomers. Mexico's independence movement disrupted those communities in the northern frontier, but the social bonds among the people and their unity in the faith helped them to survive the turmoil of war and institutional change.

Still greater upheaval awaited Mexicanos when the area came under American rule and they faced new social, economic, and cultural adjustments. Faith communities found themselves in transition as ecclesiastical authority was transferred to bishops in the United States. The American Church responded to the spiritual needs of Mexicanos by assigning priests to the area in greater numbers than had been present there before. Numerous women religious also served in the Southwest, and funds poured in from European and American Catholics. Yet the Church often fell short of fully integrating itself with the Mexicano community and showed greater commitment to institutional goals than to the service of Mexicanos.

THE INDIAN BACKGROUND AND
SPANISH-MEXICAN FOUNDATIONS

For Mexican Americans in the Southwest, faith and community have been interrelated for centuries. Long before the Europeans arrived on this continent, some of the Native Americans had established permanent villages in which they found survival and security. Members of these communities were held together through interdependence and through the exchange of gifts and favors, a reciprocity that bound family, friends, and mere acquaintances and held factionalism in check. In addition, social rifts and the potentially disruptive forces of nature were allayed through rituals that sought to provide harmony and reiterated their reliance on the Creator and Provider of all. The economic, social, and ceremonial roles of all members of the community, male and female, were essential for preserving the unity that gave the Indian village substantial security.[1]

Among nomadic bands that seemed to lack formally prescribed social structures, strong family bonds and a link to nature helped them survive famine and external threats. Many bands scoured the semiarid Southwest countryside, living off small animals and fruits, nuts, and roots and surviving only through the mutual assistance found in their close-knit extended family units. Deer hunt and peyote ceremonies, celebrated with drums, gourd rattles, and flutes, united the participants to the animal and supernatural world around them, upon which they depended. Medicine men, or shamans, cured physical and spiritual ills with prayers and herbs, while gift-giving among all in the community promoted loyalty and assurance of survival for times of scarcity.[2]

When missionaries from Spain introduced the Catholic faith in the Americas, many of the natives of central Mexico embraced it because certain aspects of Christian spirituality, particularly the faith communities of the Gospels, resembled and complemented their worldview. As Spaniards, *mestizos* (mixed-bloods) , mulattoes, and Hispanicized Indians increased in numbers and moved into New Spain's northern frontier, they planted missionary-Indian, soldier-settler, and civilian towns (missions, *presidios*, and *villas*) that incorporated in varying degrees the indigenous peoples' and Hispanic socioeconomic and spiritual concerns. The resulting synthesis contributed to the towns' ability to adjust to various changes in sovereignty and to become beacons for several waves of immigrants from the Mexican core.[3]

Expansion into the Southwest by Hispanic peoples had begun shortly after the fall of the Aztec empire in the early sixteenth century. Inspired by their findings in central Mexico, Spanish conquistadors entered the vast semiarid north in search of similar treasures but found little that attracted them. Rumors of cities of gold, however, eventually brought the newcomers to the northern reaches of the Rio Grande by the mid-1500s. Franciscan missionaries came along with the conquistadors hoping to convert the natives. The New Mexico natives did not accept Christianity immediately, but the padres were encouraged by discovering that the Indians lived in settled villages (*pueblos*) resembling the towns in the Mexican core. Given these circumstances, the missionaries came away optimistic, expecting great success for the new religion.

The introduction of Catholicism in the late sixteenth century, nonetheless, often required the use of force and caused disruption in Pueblo society. The ministers of the new faith tried to take the place of religious-civic leaders of the Indian society and, like other Spaniards, made too many demands for Indian labor. This disruption led, in 1680, to a major revolt during which the newcomers were killed or expelled from northern New Mexico. The refugees fell back to the El Paso community, where they established new mission towns. Eventually, however, Spaniards returned and reestablished social and religious control, but instead of trying to eradicate native traditions, sought greater social and cultural compromise than before.

New Mexico's society in the post-Reconquest era remained divided between Indian and Spanish, but several factors helped blur some of the differences and allowed for a greater cultural and religious interchange than before. The two societies, for example, were ministered to spiritually by the same Franciscan friars. Also, as some Indians (Pueblos as well as others) and Spaniards interacted, a racially mixed *mestizo* society emerged locally and blended with the growing number of mixed bloods migrating into the area from the Mexican core. Developments in the Church, too, brought unity and cohesion to New Mexican communities. As early as 1730 a secular priest represented the bishop of Durango as vicar for the region, and by the time of Mexican independence in the early nineteenth century several pastorates were staffed by secular (diocesan) priests native to New Mexico or to other northern provinces of New Spain. The rise of a local clergy contributed greatly to the local "ownership" of the Church, wherein social and faith concerns and expressions were integrated.[4]

In Texas, evangelization began in the early 1700s through a different process. On that frontier seminomadic natives were "reduced" (gathered) into missionary-Indian towns for the purposes of acculturation and conversion. By midcentury, these Franciscan-led missions became rather efficient economic enterprises. Extensive irrigation systems carried water to fields that yielded vast crops, with surpluses for the *presidios*, soldier-settler town garrisons, and for new missionary ventures beyond the edge of the settlement. In addition, each missionary-Indian town managed vast horse, cattle, and sheep herds from distant ranching stations along the San Antonio River Valley. The productivity of the missions freed numerous laborers to build impressive complexes, including substantial granaries, imposing church structures, and extended stockades. The need to manage a large work force, however, compelled the padres to divert their energies from the intended acculturation of the natives that was the prerequisite for conversion. Thus, the number of Hispanicized and Christianized Indians in the missions was relatively small when compared to the effort expended.

The goals of the Franciscans were thwarted in other ways as well. The Indian population in the missions dwindled because of disease and the drop in new recruits toward the end of the eighteenth century. At that time, the once predominantly Indian towns came to be inhabited increasingly by workers from the nearby Hispanic settlements hired to maintain minimal operations in hope of better days. This demographic transformation had important social and political consequences. The missionary-Indian towns, which had functioned as autonomous communities with a strong tradition of racial/ethnic and legal exclusivity, merged with the more populous soldier-settler and civilian towns into the Villa de San Fernando de Béxar (later, San Antonio). The missions were then "secularized," that is, they ceased to exist as separate corporate entities directed by the missionaries.

In San Antonio, as elsewhere, city officials and Church leaders joined hands to promote the social moral order and the common good. Local vocations to the priesthood emerged as an elite class developed and as the dominance of the Franciscans, who had previously served the Hispanic community but remained outsiders, faded or was overcome. The parish structure and Church rituals provided the vehicles for unity among various groups within the towns—Indians and Hispanics, first settlers and newcomers, rich and poor.[5]

The Church played a similar role in the towns along the Rio Grande. Towns there were established in the mid-1700s through the settlement expedition led by José de Escandón. This enterprise did not include the founding of missions, but the natives of the area were nonetheless incorporated into the various communities as *indios agregados*, attached Indians. Religious-order clergy and, later, secular priests attended to spiritual needs of the natives as well of the Hispanic settlers. As in San Antonio, the Church in the Rio Grande towns functioned as a critical force in the molding of the community.[6]

While Hispanic civil (non-religious, non-military) towns played a central role in the development of Texas and New Mexico, the military and mission communities were the focus of settlement in colonial Arizona and California. Those two frontier regions stemmed from expansionary thrusts on New Spain's northwestern flank. At first, the settlement of Arizona, which was adjacent to other northern settlements, seemed more promising than the occupation of distant California, but warring natives and the barren environment prevented the flourishing of missionary-led Indian and Hispanic towns. Nonetheless, the missions established in the central desert frontier survived, and the soldier-settler towns founded there in time attracted civilians. Once a sea link was established with California, the province prospered rapidly because of the large numbers of Indians amenable to missionization. As elsewhere, Californian presidial and civilian settlers organized in separate, autonomous towns competed with the padres for land and the labor of Indians and, as in Texas, eventually merged into one community.[7]

Frontier society was fragmented by rank, class, and race. *Ricos* (rich) and *pobres* (poor); "Spanish," mestizos, mulattoes, and Indians; *primeros pobladores* (first settlers) and recent arrivals all held clearly defined places in the community. Relative status could be identified by racial designations, by titles (such as *don* or *doña*), by official position, and by place of residence. In this divided society, the group with the most power attempted to monopolize the scant resources of land and Indian labor. Yet certain traditions softened the friction between groups. The ricos sometimes baptized members of the lower classes, be they poor or racially distinct, forming *padrino-madrina* (godparent) and *compadrazgo* (co-parent) relationships with friends and neighbors and their children. Intermarriage across class and racial/ethnic lines extended important familial ties that blunted prejudice and assisted social mobility.

Indeed, these processes served as vehicles for racial "passing" so that mulattoes and mestizos could become "Spaniards."[8]

A shared faith also played a role in holding together the disparate parts of society. While State and Church officials quarreled over subsidies, land, and Indian labor, there was also cooperation and mutual support based on the centrality of religion. Being a member of the society meant being a member of the Church. Even captive Indian youths who worked as house servants or field laborers until maturity often were baptized by their masters and received the latter's surnames, thus opening the way for their full incorporation into the community later on. Building the town church was an expression of both community and faith. Church feasts were celebrations of community as much as they were religious acts of worship and piety. To be sure, the arrangement was not without its problems. The *diezmo*, or tithe, for example, became another government tax that was farmed out to a collector who might use intimidation and force. Still, the faith seemed as much the people's as it was that of the civil and Church officials.[9]

The official, structural support for the faith began to weaken during the period of Mexico's War of Independence from Spain, a revolt by the provinces on the fringe of the colony against the center. Far removed from the seat of authority, *criollos* ("Spaniards" born on this continent) in the remote provinces had developed interests that clashed with imperial concerns. As war and its accompanying turmoil quickly expanded to the north, many residents on the frontier were drawn into the conflict. Like their fellow northerners, some clergy in the outlying provinces sided with insurgents. The ecclesiastical hierarchy, however, defended the goals of the Crown, undermining the Church's position in postwar independent Mexico.

More damaging still for the institutional Church was the liberal ideology that inspired the independence movement. This philosophy held that the individual was the primary basis for the social contract and that corporate rights, such as those held by the Church and Indian communities, undermined the state and the nation's economic expansion. As liberalism gained ground, cracks appeared in the Church's sociopolitical foundation, and division and chaos replaced unity and order.

On the northeastern frontier, including Texas, the War of Independence from Spain disrupted the communities and undermined the traditional leadership role of the Church. Civic leaders who joined the insurgents were imprisoned and executed by loyalist forces, and their properties were confiscated. Family members were pitted against one another. The local church, which had formed the bonds unifying the communities, was thrown into disarray. Because of diplomatic problems between Mexico and the Vatican, bishoprics remained vacant when the ordinaries, usually Spaniards, abandoned their dioceses or died and were not replaced. The tithe was not imposed and, in order to survive, parish priests turned to their own or their families' ranches or enterprises.[10]

Still, despite such problems, most pastors on the frontier did not neglect their flocks and continued to administer the sacraments, sometimes at great personal sacrifice. While they lacked the resources available to them before, priests continued to be linked to local families and exercise leadership in their communities. Religious ceremonies remained at the center of town life and identity, and though the institutional Church no longer had the same official role in society as before independence, the life of faith continued to be important.[11]

The American Church: Institutional Change in the Southwest

While Hispanic Catholic communities in the northern frontier maintained their faith traditions in the wake of Mexican independence, the official Church faced a whirlwind of change. After the Texas Revolution (1835–36) and the U.S. War with Mexico (1846–48), ecclesiastical jurisdiction in Texas and New Mexico passed to the American Church, which at the time drew heavily on European-born clergymen. Almost as soon as the new bishops arrived on the frontier they removed most of the old-time pastors, some of whom were quite popular because they had led the resistance by Mexicanos against the recently installed American political order. In Texas, Bishop Jean-Marie Odin made a cursory investigation of the work of the native-born Refugio de la Garza and his Mexican compatriot José Antonio Valdez and then evicted them, alleging neglect and scandal. Whether justified or not, Odin's actions won favor with the officials of the new Republic of Texas for getting rid of leaders believed to be still loyal to Mexico. In New Mexico, Bishop Jean Baptiste Lamy alienated the faithful by

excommunicating the well-regarded Father José Antonio Martínez, who was alleged to have taken part in the rebellion against the new American governor.

Making matters worse, the bishops and the new French clergy they recruited often did not understand or respect their Mexican parishioners and their traditions. Texas's Bishop Odin stirred an unnecessary controversy in San Antonio when he refused to allow the customary ringing of the church bells on civic occasions, including the death of a leading citizen who happened to be Protestant. Bishop Lamy ordered the *retablos* (folk art painting of saints) taken down from the churches and replaced with blond French statues. He also declared war on the Penitente brotherhood. This religious society for the laity had gained ground during the period of turmoil following Mexico's War of Independence and the U.S. War with Mexico. Penitente rituals expressed the deep desire of Nuevo Mexicanos to keep their village cultural-religious traditions even as the world around them changed with the arrival of the American capital-intensive economy.

Bishops Odin and Lamy and the clergy they recruited found themselves in a very complex situation. In order to strengthen the faith among Mexicanos, they sought to continue and give new life to Hispanic religiosity, which in many ways was quite similar to their own devotional heritage. They felt threatened by Protestant proselytism and outright anti-Catholicism, all of which they associated with the increasingly pervasive American culture in the Southwest. Yet they accepted the inexorable expansion of the new American political and economic system and were convinced the Church's prospects lay with the new order.

Some clergymen may have seen the Church's role as one of assisting Mexicanos in the transition. To this end, Bishop Lamy ordered that all churches celebrate the American centennial in 1876 with Te Deums and High Masses. He also played an important part in the expansion of the railroad system that linked New Mexico with the nation. These economic and political changes fostered economic development that ultimately would benefit all Nuevo Mexicanos. Immediately, however, they favored a few Hispanic *ricos* (wealthy elites) and the Anglo-American newcomers. The majority of Nuevo Mexicanos' lives, however, were disrupted as the villages lost their communal land holdings and the previous shareholders became salaried day laborers. American ecclesiastical leaders observed this without public protest or comment.[12]

Identifying with the American future, bishops, priests, and women religious set out to secure a permanent role for the Church in the Southwest communities now dominated politically and economically mostly by Anglo Americans. Accordingly, the Church sent numerous priests and Sisters into the area and acquired substantial outside funds which were dedicated to building impressive church structures, schools, and hospitals that served mostly the well-to-do. These endeavors also required the backing of prominent local civic leaders, Catholic and Protestant, who directed the introduction of the new economic system. Some spaces were reserved in the schools for those who could not pay tuition and some free health care and orphanages were also available for the poor. But the primary goal was to gain the trust and support of the elites, not to serve the Mexicanos.[13]

Mexicano areas shared in the resources secured by the American Church, but funds going to predominantly Mexican-American dioceses invariably soon began to lag behind those invested in Anglo-American sections. In Texas the pattern of treating Mexicans as second-class status Catholics began when Bishop Odin selected Galveston instead of San Antonio as the seat of the first Texas diocese. Odin himself had worked in "western" Texas for some time and he made San Antonio and Brownsville important ecclesiastical subcenters, but the ministry to Mexicanos was not his top priority. The long-range survival of the Church lay in establishing a solid foundation in and around Galveston, the biggest city in Texas and the gateway for American and European immigrants, even though this was not the district with the largest number of Catholics.[14]

Favoring the urban areas and Anglo Americans proved to be a good decision for the Church as an institution, but, as the table below demonstrates, by the end of the century the dioceses of Galveston and Dallas, which served mostly European immigrants and Anglo Americans, received disproportionately more attention than did the Mexican dioceses of Brownsville, Santa Fe, and Tucson.

According to these figures, in 1890 the Mexicano vicariate of Brownsville and the Anglo-American diocese of Galveston had about the same Catholic population (45,000 and 41,000, respectively), but the Galveston see had more than twice as many priests and six times as many churches. Rapid population growth in the nineties required the creation of the Dallas see from the Galveston territory. Together, these two dioceses reported 62,000 faithful, approximately the same number as in the Brownsville district, yet they listed five times as many priests and churches. The mostly

Priests and Churches Relative to Faithful
in Selected Dioceses/Vicariates, 1890–1900

Diocese	N of Faithful	N of Priests	Ratio to Faithful	N of Churches	Ratio to Faithful
Galveston					
1890	41,000	48	1–854	60	1–600
1900	40,000	64	1–718	42*	1–1,095
Dallas 1900	22,000	44	1–500	32*	1–687
Brownsville					
1890	45,000	21	1–2,142	10	1–4,500
1900	60,000	22	1–2,727	13*	1–4,615
Santa Fe					
1890	128,000	64	1–2,000	49	1–1,020
1900	133,000	61	1–2,180	38*	1–3,500
Tucson					
1890	35,000	19	1–1,842	16	1–2,187
1900	40,000	25	1–1,600	16*	1–2,500

Source: *The Official Catholic Directory* (New York: P. J. Kenedy, 1890, 1900)
*Churches with resident priests

Mexicano dioceses of Santa Fe and Tucson served twice as many Catholics as Galveston and Dallas, but had ten fewer churches and twenty-two fewer priests. Apparently, higher Church authorities in the United States or at the Vatican did not consider these disparities worthy of their attention.

The poverty of Mexicanos probably discouraged clergymen from seeking pastorates in South Texas. In fact, one bishop, the Rev. Dominic Manucy, decried his assignment to the Brownsville vicariate as the most severe sentence anyone could receive for the worst of crimes. Manucy's lament and that of others notwithstanding, the priests in charge of the few established Mexican-American parishes reported that these were largely self-supported. But Mexicanos could have been better served had Church agencies from outside Texas and the United States sent their aid to the dioceses with the most Catholics and most financial need.[15]

Despite the effort of Mexicanos to support their clergymen, the American Church developed a historical legacy that downplayed

Nuevo Mexicanos, thus, had more time to reinforce community bonds and to adapt to the new political system. They preserved certain village traditions, particularly those related to honor, to family, and to their protectors, the local saints. They adapted their sheep industry to the new markets and turned to cattle grazing and agriculture as well. Their world, however, was not without discrimination. In fact, to deal with this, Nuevo Mexicanos adopted various strategies, including shifting their identity to "Spanish Americans" with romantic overtones in order to fare better in an Anglo-American world that looked down upon "Mexicans."[21]

By reintroducing and strengthening Mexican cultural traditions and by their sheer numbers, immigrants from Mexico in the mid- and late-1800s helped revitalize the old southwestern communities and established new ones. The boundary set by the Treaty of Guadalupe Hidalgo at the conclusion of the U.S. War with Mexico reconfigured political entities and controlled the crossing of goods, but not of people. Not until the second decade of the new century was there any attempt to regulate immigration. For over half a century, then, Mexicans came and went across the border without any formalities. At times they followed earlier patterns, moving into the former Mexican frontier states to work in the traditional occupation of farming and cattle raising. More often immigrants now came as a response to new enterprises such as building of *el traque* (the railroad) as far north as Kansas, mining in Arizona, New Mexico or Colorado, or cotton farming in the Nueces Valley and in East Texas.

While these attractions "pulled" the immigrants into the United States, dislocations in Mexico "pushed" them north. The economic policies of President Porfirio Díaz (1874–1910) opened the border to trade, and new enterprises disrupted local Mexican economies. The availability of export markets for agricultural products encouraged investors to take over Indian *ejidos* (common village lands). Dispossessed, the peasants moved to the cities and then northward to the United States on the railroad networks built for the international trade. Sometimes the immigrants, usually young single men, came only to get a head start and returned to their homeland, but just as often they stayed behind, finding cultural affinity with Mexican Americans in the old or new communities.[22]

The Mexican immigrants fared better in the United States than they had in their homeland, but they nonetheless found themselves in yet another caste system in which they lacked security, permanence, and upward mobility. A seemingly trivial matter brought before the city council in Brownsville, Texas, in the 1890s reveals the condition of Mexican laborers. At issue was a proposal that the city market close at six o'clock rather than later, as was customary. Opponents to the measure argued that if the market closed early the majority of the Mexicans would not be able to purchase what they would eat that day. Apparently workers were paid at the end of the day, and they received only enough to stay alive for the morrow.[23]

The immigrants were also not allowed to become a part of the new society. On the excuse that Mexicans were all transient laborers, immigrants and settlers alike were not admitted as full, participatory members of the various communities. The earlier patrón-peón hacienda system had also been unjust, but it had at least provided some sense of security and belonging through personal relationships. The new, capitalist system offered no such assurances. Yet Mexican immigrants continued to be attracted by the opportunities in the Southwest, and many made their homes there despite difficult adjustments.[24]

The experience of Mexicanos in the United States inevitably resulted in cultural change, some of it not for the best. French-born Bishop Granjon noted that the traditional strengths in Mexican culture were weakened by contact with Americans. One could ask any favor of a friend, including the use of one's home:

> The home is perhaps only a miserable hut, a *jacal*, there is inside only a crust of bread, and for sleeping only an old sheepskin spread on the ground. No matter; all is yours, the *jacal*, the crust, and the sheepskin. . . .
>
> Contact with the whites, it is true, tends to make disappear, from day to day, this beautiful urbanity, completely natural and so gracious. The selfish manners of the "invader," as they call the American in their ballads, are not without a disturbing influence on the naturalness which formerly gifted the ancient inhabitants of these regions so well.[25]

Another cleric remarked that "wherever he [the Anglo American] has [entered], conditions have changed and these people have lost much of their integrity and honesty."[26] Clearly, the new political and economic order disrupted traditional culture.

MEXICANO/HISPANIC NINETEENTH-CENTURY FAITH COMMUNITY

Some of the turmoil resulted from population shifts as economic development attracted Mexican immigrants into the United

States. In 1836 the number of Mexican Catholics in what is now Texas came to about 9,000. Twenty-five years later, the diocese of Brownsville in South Texas alone reported 30,000 Catholics, almost all Mexicans and Mexican Americans. Hispanics also accounted for a significant percentage of the 40,000 Catholics enumerated in the San Antonio see in 1870. Forty years later, in 1910, the bishops of Brownsville and San Antonio reported 82,000 and 85,000 Catholics in those two dioceses. Thus, by the turn of the century Hispanics made up from one-third to a half of all Catholics in the state.

Elsewhere in the Southwest, growth was relatively slower but just as impressive. When New Mexico became a part of the United States in 1848, it had approximately 70,000 in population, of whom some 60,000 were Hispanic, that is, not Indian. By 1890, the Catholic population, which constituted the vast majority of Nuevo Mexicanos, totaled 128,000. Other Catholics in the region numbered 50,000 (mostly Anglo Americans) in the diocese of Denver and 35,000 (mostly Hispanics) in the vicariate of Arizona, which included southern New Mexico and El Paso. Twenty years later, in 1910, the Santa Fe see listed 127,000 faithful; Denver, 56,112; and Tucson, 47,324.[27]

While immigrants revitalized the Mexican-American communities, so did the Church. Because the American Church received substantial external support from various sources (money from the Society for the Propagation of the Faith, and priests and women religious from American and European dioceses and religious orders) the sacraments and instruction in the faith were more available than before. Priests now visited the faithful scattered across the Southwest more frequently than before, this despite the formidable challenge presented by the vast unsettled areas. At one point (in 1880), for example, there was one priest for every 10,000 square miles in Arizona. Typically *padres* rode into those isolated settlements at the end of the day, gathered the *rancheros* and their families for some devotion, instruction, and confessions, and then celebrated Mass the following morning before saddling up for a day's ride to the next *rancho*. Other priests and Sisters opened and staffed schools, hospitals, and orphanages in the towns.[28]

Some of the priests and women religious became folk heroes of sorts. In South Texas, for example, there was the beloved "santo padre Pedrito" (Father Pierre Yves Keralum, O.M.I.). He had designed and directed the building of a Gothic church in Brownsville, Texas, but actually spent most of his priestly years riding on horseback taking the Good News to Mexicanos living on isolated ranchos. In the fall of 1872 he set out on his usual rounds, but he never returned. El santo padre Pedrito, with his dedication and endurance, had been a legend in his own lifetime; his disappearance added more color and a good bit of mystery. One story that circulated had him dying at the hands of bandits. The reality was less dramatic but more meaningful. In 1883, vaqueros working near Mercedes were hacking a path through a brush thicket to free some animals when they discovered a saddle and a chalice along with other items carried by the missionaries on the rancho circuit. The cowboys also found the remains of the elderly priest. In all probability he had lost his way or was tired or ill and set his horse free as he rested. He may have suffered a heart attack or been bitten by a snake. In any case, El santo padre Pedrito had died as he had lived, in the chaparral country on his way to a rancho, taking the Gospel and the sacraments to Mexicanos.[29]

In the San Antonio area, the Sisters of Charity of the Incarnate Word had taken up teaching in eleven schools and two orphanages while continuing to carry out their original mission of providing health care. The superior of the congregation, Mother St. Pierre Cinquin, was known for her dedication to serving the poor, especially her much-loved orphans, even as she built up and managed the Santa Rosa Infirmary and the other substantial establishments her group had founded.[30]

In some instances, too, churchmen continued the traditional unity between the faith and the community. Such was the case in Laredo, where the French priests assigned there in the early 1850s eased the transition into the new ecclesiastical order and with the newcomers, some of whom were European-born. The priests took on Spanish names, retained the old sacristan, and encouraged the continuation of earlier Mexican traditions. Later, in the 1890s, the bishop of the South Texas diocese, Rev. Pedro Verdaguer de Prat, a Spaniard, chose to make Laredo, rather than Corpus Christi, the episcopal see because it was larger and probably because Laredo was more Hispanic. Bishop Verdaguer was a true missionary. He rode the rancho circuit often and challenged his priests to make the sacrifices necessary for the faithful on this frontier. A man of no pretensions, the bishop liked to be called simply "Padre Pedro."[31]

In New Mexico, Bishop Lamy recruited many holy and dedicated priests and women religious. Among the clergymen was Jean Baptiste Ralliere, who arrived in the village of Tomé in 1857 and remained there until his retirement in 1911. El Padre Juan, as he was known, bought a *ranchito* in the area, quarreled with his neighbors over water rights like everyone else, and became a part of people's lives in Tomé, Adelino, La Constancia, Valencia, Peralta, Casa Colorada, and other surrounding villages. He also visited more distant points like Puerto de Luna and Ft. Sumner. Ralliere made sure some Mexican traditions, such as the Passion Play during Holy Week, were not lost. He loved music so much he purchased an organ for each village and even one that could be lent out so the singers could practice at home. He put together a brass band and acquired string instruments for his parishioners.

Father Ralliere also preserved Spanish-language hymns with the publication of *Cánticos Espirituales Recogidos por el Padre Juan B. Ralliere*, a small book republished several times and used well into this century. His leadership was critical in organizing relief during the great flood of 1884. His school taught a variety of crafts, including carpentry, blacksmithing, and whip, belt, and rope making, along with the three Rs, which were taught in Spanish in his school. As "Father *John* B. Ralliere," he often interceded for his community with the larger Anglo society and in this capacity became superintendent of schools in the area. In retirement, Father Ralliere grew a full white beard, so the people who knew and loved him changed his name from "el Padre Juan" to "el Padre Eterno," because his new look reminded them of a church image of God the Father.[32]

From Our Lady of Guadalupe parish in Conejos (later part of Colorado), Father Salvatore Persone, S.J., made the rounds of the *plazas*, or villages, in the San Luis Valley. His frequent visits inspired the *vecinos* (town dwellers) to build chapels, where "el Salvador de Conejos," the Savior of Conejos, reintroduced and preserved various traditions: First Communions; the celebration of Corpus Christi, replete with triumphal arches for the procession and veneration of the Blessed Sacrament; Christmas festivities that included the *luminarias* (at that time, torches or small bonfires on two-foot-tall triangular racks that lined the walkway to the church); the adoration of the Infant Jesus at midnight mass; and the elaborate ceremony connected the with feast of Our Lady of Guadalupe. Father Persone was known for treating rich and poor alike and for being, like his assistant, "Italian in his birth and Mexican in his heart."[33]

Dedicated and heroic as these priests and Sisters were, they did not integrate themselves to the Mexican-American community, particularly in Texas, in a manner to inspire many Mexicanos to join the priesthood or the religious orders. The sometimes controversial Bishop Lamy did ordain some native Nuevo Mexicanos, but his counterparts in Texas and in the religious orders did not deem Mexicanos worthy of the calling to the priesthood. This attitude, coupled with the turmoil of the economically and politically troubled society in which Mexicanos lived, prevented the emergence of Mexican-American candidates to the priesthood for close to a hundred years.[34]

The Church's role among Mexicanos in the post–Mexican War Southwest was negative in other ways. The United States bishops generally tended to replace the local Mexicano clergy with French priests who were more concerned than their predecessors with full compliance with Church laws. Bishops, priests, and women religious elected to serve primarily the local elites, mostly Anglo Americans, whether Catholic or non-Catholic, in order to secure permanence for the Church once outside funds stopped flowing into Texas dioceses. In their attempts to shield the Church from the attacks of the antiforeign, anti-Catholic nativists, churchmen and women seemed to be more preoccupied with having the Church become a part of the establishment than with serving Mexicanos. Thus, at times the Church appeared distant or removed from the Mexican-American community.

But, as we have seen, the Church did not neglect Mexicans and Mexican Americans altogether and in fact offered them many services. Priests took the sacraments to remote ranchos and, together with men and women religious, made religious instruction more accessible than ever before. In addition, the Church provided Mexicanos with some social services, such as schooling and health care, which, limited though they were, assisted some on the fringes of the new economic system. Culturally, too, the Church bridged the old and new. At the same time that it sought to preserve Spanish-Mexican spiritual traditions, the Church introduced Mexicanos to their new homeland. In keeping with this role of the Church, the beloved Father Ralliere translated "America" for his students and required its singing (to the original melody) at the beginning of the school day. In its own way, the Church also bolstered the Indian-Spanish-Mexican communities buffeted by the mid-eighteenth-century American expansion into the Southwest. In sum, the Church was, at one and the same time, a part of the conquest and a vehicle of strength for the Mexicano communities.[35]

2

The Immigrant Church, 1910–1940

No sooner had Mexicanos and the American Church adjusted to each other than new waves of immigrants from Mexico swept across the Southwest during the early decades of the new century. Their presence in the United States posed a new challenge to the Church because of their sheer numbers and because of the interest Protestant groups demonstrated in their proselytization. As before, the Church strove energetically to meet the spiritual needs of the newcomers but again exhibited a lack of full commitment to them and did not serve them as well as it did Anglo-American Catholics.

In the immigrants the Church encountered a group with a vibrant popular religiosity and a very distinct spirituality that did not always conform to traditional Church standards. Still, as the parish case histories attest, the uprooted newcomers welcomed the Church's nourishing of the faith and its assistance in their efforts to reestablish their communities in the new homeland. Whatever its shortcomings, the Church formed a genuine bond with the Mexicanos.

The crisis of the Depression presented the Church with yet another set of challenges: how to counter the economic exploitation of Mexicanos and how to promote their assimilation into the mainstream as Mexican Americans. In its response to these dilemmas, the Church was both timid and courageous, realistically political and prophetic. It led, and it followed. It both opposed and supported the Mexicano labor activists. It proposed solutions to economic problems, and it incorporated the leadership and direction offered by the rising Mexican-American middle class. As before, there was no single Church response to the needs of Mexicanos, and as before, the Church both assisted and failed them.

Immigration and Repatriation, 1910–1939

The immigrants that arrived in the Southwest in the early twentieth century came because of the great havoc in Mexico created by the 1910 Revolution against the regime of Porfirio Díaz. The major

31

fighting ended by 1917, but guerrilla warfare continued among different factions for two decades after that. More than a million Mexicans died in those civil wars, and millions more suffered great economic deprivations as investment, trade, and subsistence farming were disrupted. No region was spared the chaos. Most immigrants came from the war-torn regions deep in the interior of Mexico, but at times residents of Mexican border towns sought escape from the cross fire or even execution by running to the American side.

As the disruptions drove Mexicans northward into the United States, developments in the Southwest attracted them to the thousands of jobs created by technological change in agriculture. Giant pumping stations along the Rio Grande and other rivers and deep water wells were then converting semiarid regions into veritable gardens. Despite the new machinery available to clear the range and plow the fields, thousands of workers were needed to cultivate and harvest the fruits and vegetables and to pick the cotton. To meet this need, labor contractors recruited laborers in Mexico or waited for the immigrants at bridges and entry points, snapping them up for work far beyond the border.[1]

Early twentieth-century national legislation and population movements in the United States resulted in labor shortages that indirectly abetted Mexican immigration. The Immigration Act of 1917, which began the legislative process of setting quotas for newcomers from certain European countries, for example, placed constraints on the overall availability of workers. The draft law passed about the same time to raise troops for the war in Europe also tightened the labor supply. Furthermore, an exodus of Americans to the cities made the general shortage of workers more acute in farm areas.

The status of Mexicanos in the United States was not affected by the legal developments. The 1917 immigration act exempted Mexicans from the new quota restrictions for fear that economic growth of the Southwest would wither without the laborers, and the World War I draft law targeted only citizens, not all residents. Thus, given the circumstances, American officials espoused what was basically an open-border policy for Mexican immigrants who flocked to the new farms of the Southwest.[2]

At the same time that agricultural work beckoned the immigrants, the hundreds of small and large towns that sprang up across the Southwest also needed Mexican laborers. Generally, the smaller towns provided housing for the farm workers and supplied the hinterland with the trucks, tractors, other farm equipment, and consumer goods. Workers in these towns baled the cotton and processed the fruits and vegetables in preparation for shipment. Larger cities functioned as hubs for receiving and redistributing goods sent from the manufacturing and larger shipping centers. Builders in the cities hired hundreds of laborers as central business districts erected new office, banking, retail, and government structures.[3]

Mexican immigrants came by the thousands to U.S. farms, towns, and cities. Federal enumerators in 1920 counted 651,596 Mexican-born residents in the United States, up over 400,000 from a decade before. Significant as this figure is, it probably represents an undercount. Some estimates, in fact, place the number of Mexicans residing in the United States at about a million, while the ebb and flow of workers at the border may have brought the figure up to two million.

The largest number of immigrants came in during the 1920s. The census at the end of the decade reported 1,422,533 Mexicans in the United States. That figure included the Mexican-born as well as those of Mexican parentage. This second group amounted to well over half the "Mexican" population, suggesting the presence among the immigrants of large numbers of families with several children and, in turn, the fact that increasingly Mexicans came to stay.

Immigrants went to twenty-six of the forty-eight states, mostly to the Southwest, but also as far east and northeast as Mississippi and New York. In 1930 Texas reported 683,000 Mexican-born residents, almost twice as many as California. Arizona had a relatively impressive 144,173; New Mexico, 59,340; Colorado, 57,676; Illinois, 28,906; Kansas and Michigan, 19,150 and 13,336, respectively. While most immigrants declared their intention to live and did, in fact, live in states near the border, the newcomers did not limit themselves to the traditional Spanish-Mexican home region.[4]

Most of the immigrants were poor, but some of those who came to Texas were from the middle and upper classes displaced by the political and social chaos of the revolution. Some estimates put the number of Mexican political refugees in San Antonio in 1913 at 25,000. They were joined in the following decade by religious refugees, who came as a result of the Cristero War between Church-backed groups and the government (1926–29). At first, these immigrants saw their stay in the United States as temporary. They used their money and professional skills to argue their positions in newspapers like San Antonio's *La Prensa*, which was distributed across the Southwest and northern Mexico. But as the disturbances in Mexico continued, some of these elites lost hope of ever returning to Mexico and set their roots in this country. They took some interest in the Mexican-American community, analyzed the socio-economic problems facing Mexicans and Mexican Americans, and began the protest movements that would characterize the decades from 1930 to 1960.[5]

In some respects the experience of the refugees was not unlike that of most immigrants. For the most part, all yearned to return to Mexico, but as the years passed they realized this would not happen. They then began buying their homes whenever possible and sending their children to the public schools where English was taught. When the Depression struck, many went back to their ancestral lands or were sent back by the trainload, but well over half remained in what was to become their homeland.[6]

The immigrants established their new communities in ethnic neighborhoods called *Mexiquitos* (little Mexicos). The newcomers settled there in part because property covenants or prices restricted their buying or renting *en el lado Americano,* on the American side of town. Immigrants and Mexican Americans also formed their own communities, because Mexicans, like other immigrants, had never been fully welcomed by Anglo Americans. In the Mexiquitos, some joined *mutualistas* (mutual aid societies) that provided inexpensive burial insurance and allowed the newcomers to reestablish the community bonds disrupted by the migration. Often those societies also served as patriotic clubs that organized the community festivities on the *Diez y Seis de Septiembre* (September 16, Mexican Independence Day) and the *Cinco de Mayo,* the anniversary of the defeat of the French invasionary troops on May 5, 1862. The festivities included parades with marching bands hired for the occasion from schools south of border. Mutualista members also marched as a corps, each participant in his Sunday best, including some in suits, and all wearing a *distinctivo,* a ribbon with the Mexican tricolor and the organization's initials. Final ceremonies were held at *la placita,* a town square set aside by the developer or the city, with sidewalks and benches and a kiosk, from which leaders gave the *Grito,* a reenactment of the call for independence made by Miguel Hidalgo on September 16, 1810. These observances among Mexican Americans evoked Mexico's, and now the *barrio's* (the neighborhood's), yearnings for autonomy and self-determination.[7]

Leaders usually emerged from the middle-class exiles who managed to leave with money or from members of old-time ranchero families. Among the leaders were some professionals, including teachers and lawyers, but also small merchants and restaurateurs from the Mexican end of downtown. The professionals and merchants extended credit to the workers, thus gaining their loyalty and at the same time wooing them from businesses and services provided by Anglo Americans. The leaders brokered political arrangements that secured a few lower-rank jobs, such as constable and justice of the peace, for Mexicanos and some, very limited, public services for the barrio. The Mexicano politicians held rallies at la placita, urging those who could vote to do so and others to obtain their citizenship and help out in the struggle. Yet, despite their endeavors on behalf of Mexican Americans, these leaders could not prevent the very clear segregation that existed, the exploitation, and the occasional harsh treatment that Mexicanos received.[8]

Most of the immigrants worked as farm workers and the towns, or at least the Mexiquitos, served as camps for agricultural laborers. Every morning, save Sunday, *troqueros*, crew leaders who were lent trucks by the farm owners, picked up the laborers—men, women, and children—and transported them to the fields, where they worked until sundown. In the towns the workers lived in paper-thin wood frame houses built around a central courtyard. Most often they rented their homes, but sometimes they bought them through contracts of sale that did not accumulate equity for the purchaser. The developers often cut expenses by providing water lines only to the center of the block, where two or three spigots were placed. Sometimes drainage lines were extended to the central courtyard for the common toilets; more rarely even some common bathing rooms were built.

Neither did Mexicanos receive public services. Their neighborhoods were situated on the slope at the end of town. Thus, barrio lots and homes were often flooded and drainage lines—culverts in the Anglo American side, but open canals in the Mexican town—carried sewage to lakes just beyond the barrio. Needless to say, the stagnant pools of water and the sewage canals and lakes contributed to the poor health of the residents. Mexiquitos could not boast any paved streets, save maybe a highway cutting through the barrio. There was no street lighting. Schools were inferior to the ones across town, and the Mexican children were taught by teachers who would rather have been assigned to the Anglo schools.

Used textbooks from those schools received an extended life in the "Mexican school."[9]

Educating the children of the immigrants was one of the first issues identified as a serious problem for the local and state communities. In Texas, only approximately 30 percent of school-age Mexican children (*vs.* 78 percent for Anglos) attended school in the 1920s. Responsibility for educating these youngsters fell first to the local school districts, which for all practical purposes were autonomous. But this "Mexican problem," civic leaders and educators soon realized, was a statewide one. While Mexicano children were concentrated in South Texas, they were in fact attending schools in all but eight of the 252 counties in the state. Overall, by 1922, the number of school-age Mexican children was growing at a rate five times that of Anglos and nine times that of blacks. But many school districts across the state made no provision whatsoever to accommodate Mexican children. Sometimes the districts refused to spend tax dollars for a separate school and yet did not admit Mexicano youngsters into the existing schools, arguing the lack of room. Often Anglo-American educators simply were unprepared to teach these children, most of whom could speak little or no English. It was all too easy to agree with those who considered the Mexican "uneducable" or with the farmers who did not see any need to provide schools for these children. By the same token, some Mexicano parents could not be persuaded to send their children to school because they were needed in the fields.[10]

Mexican children who attended school faced problems related to language and to the quality of the education they received. Regarding the use of English in the schools, this requirement came not from the backers of an Americanization movement, but from those who considered Mexicanos as disloyal to the United States because of their "obstinacy" in maintaining their language and culture. To remedy this, in 1918 the Texas legislature required English-only instruction in public schools. Pressure to apply this law to all schools was finally successful in 1923. But because enforcement proved practically impossible, grade schools in the border counties were exempted. In a similar manner, officials hardly ever enforced the compulsory school attendance law for Mexicanos. Educational "experts" calmed any misgivings expressed by some community leaders about the inadequacy of schools for the Mexicans, arguing that the recently devised IQ exams showed Mexicanos to be intellectually inferior to Anglo Americans. Accordingly, school boards spent little money on Mexican schools, and when they did, the curriculum was watered down. This met with approval from the farm owners, who worried that if Mexicans received an education they would no longer be available to work in the fields.[11]

Schooling was in fact out of the question altogether for the thousands of Mexicanos who resided in the countryside. There, Mexicanos who planted cotton in sharecropping arrangements (often for as little as one-fourth of the crop) could not afford to transport their children to the schools or to have them board in the towns. Families in the work crews were herded from one farm to another, living in tents or make-shift huts, with their family's movement restricted through a system of passes enforced by the local sheriff and the state police. These families and the many laborers in the work gangs could hardly concern themselves with schooling or, for that matter, with other benefits of living in communities.[12]

The introduction of Mexican laborers upset the delicate structures worked out by Mexican Americans in the older settlements. In northern New Mexico, for example, village life of the Spanish-Mexican era had changed, but the transformation of villages to regional communities had been gradual, because in the late 1800s immigration had been slow. As the economy expanded, the men in the villages migrated to work in neighboring fields and mines, while women stayed at home and provided continuity and stability in the villages by carrying out a variety of domestic and public duties that gave those communities a certain autonomy and protection from outside influences. The introduction of new enterprises and large numbers of workers in the twentieth century, however, quickly destroyed the village-and-region structure and reduced everyone, including village women, to "Mexicans," that is, marginal day laborers. Thus the gradual incorporation into the American economy and society of the previous century ended as workers in the 1900s came to be considered a commodity more than ever before.[13]

Changes in the cities were also disruptive. While Mexicanos were welcomed as cheap labor by the employers, immigrants were not necessarily well received by all. A 1941 economic report for San Antonio noted that only the presence of a large Mexican population was impeding the city's growth:

Replacement of 35% of the Latin Americans by an equivalent number of economically independent families [meaning, Anglos] would transform San Antonio, socially, politically, economically, and in health. It would increase its tourist and convention business. It would help attract industry. It would raise the whole standard of living.[14]

Branding Mexicans as inferior justified their exploitation, segregation, and discrimination across the state. Lighter-skinned Mexicans fared better than most until the prospective employers realized they were dealing with a Spanish-surnamed person. Many restaurants, barbershops, and entertainment establishments outright refused service to Mexicans. In the schools, teachers sometimes not only sat the Mexican children separately and otherwise segregated them during lunch, play periods, and transportation, but also kept their names on different pages in the grade books. Mexicanos were often victims of police brutality and could not expect to get a fair trial if the victim was an Anglo. The inflexibility of segregation and degree of mistreatment varied in different areas of the state—reputedly it was more common in the German counties and in West Texas—but all Mexicanos in Texas faced discrimination.[15]

THE CHURCH AND THE IMMIGRANTS

The large numbers of Mexican immigrants arriving in the Southwest tested the ability of all institutions, including the Church, to serve the Mexicano community. The magnitude of the challenge was reflected in ecclesiastical censuses. Deep in South Texas (Brownsville/Corpus Christi) the number of faithful soared from 82,000 in 1910 to 248,000 in 1930. In San Antonio the figures for the same years rose from 85,000 to 182,000; in El Paso they went from a few thousand to 108,000. Immigrants also streamed into the Galveston diocese, which included the Houston area, accounting in part for the increase from 57,000, previously almost exclusively Anglo-American or European-descent Catholics, to 135,000.

In New Mexico, the Catholic population of the archdiocese of Santa Fe jumped from 50,000 in 1890, to 133,000 a decade later. Reported increases in the early twentieth century were much smaller (143,000 was the total for 1930). In Colorado, the diocese of Denver listed 60,000 in 1900 and 133,000 in 1930. Dramatic increases also occurred in nearby Arizona, which still included southern New Mexico. In 1900 Arizona reported 25,000 Catholics, and almost twice as many in 1930. The Church clearly faced a daunting challenge across the Southwest, especially since the figures no doubt undercounted the faithful.[16]

As a response to such demographic changes, the Church sent more priests and religious into the Southwest, opening parishes and missions throughout the area. In the educational sphere, Catholic religious communities already in Texas and the Southwest extended their work to the immigrants. New orders and congregations also arrived in the state to serve the increasing Catholic population. Among those serving Mexicans were the Ursuline Sisters, the Sisters of Charity of the Incarnate Word, the Congregation of the Incarnate Word and Blessed Sacrament, the Sisters of Divine Providence, the Sisters of the Holy Cross, the Sisters of Mercy, the Congregation of the Holy Cross, the Sisters of Loretto at the Foot of the Cross, the Jesuits, the Franciscans, the Basilian Fathers, the Oblates of Mary Immaculate, the Claretians, the Vincentians, the Marist Brothers, the Carmelites, the Brothers of Christian Schools, and the Salesian Sisters of St. John Bosco, and others. In time, the secular clergy also increased in number.[17]

Yet the Church did not serve the immigrants to the same extent that it ministered to Anglo Catholics. Statistics in the table below reveal this failure. As this table demonstrates, relatively fewer priests were serving in South Texas than in Anglo-American dioceses, probably because of the lack of adequate funds, both internal and from other Church sources, for their livelihood. In 1920, for example, the Mexicano diocese of Corpus Christi in South Texas reported 7,000 more Catholics than Galveston and more than twice as many as Dallas. Yet despite a doubling of the number of clergymen from the previous decade, the Corpus Christi see could provide only about half as many priests as either of the other two Texas dioceses. A decade later, in 1930, Corpus Christi listed approximately 113,000 more faithful than Galveston, and over five times as many as Dallas. Yet Corpus Christi had only three-fourths as many priests as Galveston and the same number as Dallas.

The ratio of churches with resident priests to the number of Catholics suggests the Church's lack of full commitment of capital investment, most of which was made with outside monies. On this issue, there seems to be a clear pattern, with of course some exceptions: the initial wave of Mexican immigrants, those who arrived in the decade of the 1910s, elicited a strong response from the Church across the board. The second wave, arriving in the 1920s, was larger than the first, and the Church may have been unprepared for the large numbers thrust upon it. Hence, in 1930 in the

Number of Priests and Churches with Resident Priests
Relative to Faithful in Selected Dioceses/Vicariates
1910–1930

Diocese	N of Faithful	N of Priests	Ratio to Faithful	N of Churches w Res. Priests	Ratio to Faithful
Corpus Christi*					
1910	81,917	20	1-4,095	15	1-5,461
1920	91,977	45	1-2,043	30	1-3,065
1930	247,769	86	1-2,881	46	1-5,386
Galveston					
1910	57,000	82	1-695	48	1-1,187
1920	85,000	110	1-772	60	1-1,416
1930	135,045	144	1-937	72	1-1,875
Dallas					
1910	60,000	92	1-652	55	1-1,090
1920	37,027	94	1-394	60	1-617
1930	45,933	82	1-560	56	1-800
Sante Fe					
1910	127,000	66	1-1,924	45	1-2,822
1920	141,573	80	1-1,769	46	1-3,077
1930	142,934	104	1-1,374	56	1-2,552
Tucson					
1910	48,500	36	1-1,347	21	1-2,309
1920	50,000	68	1-735	34	1-1,470
1930	95,472	80	1-1,193	39	1-2,448
Denver					
1910	99,485	148	1-672	64	1-1,554
1920	112,637	181	1-622	93	1-1,211
1930	132,887	229	1-580	111	1-1,197

Source: *The Official Catholic Directory*, 1910, 1920, 1930
*Previously the diocese of Brownsville

border dioceses of Corpus Christi and Tucson the ratio of churches with resident priests to the number of faithful was the same it had been two decades earlier, before Mexicanos started coming to the United States in large numbers. Since personnel allocations reflect available funds, the statistics suggest that, as before, the proportion of money invested in those Mexicano dioceses continued to be minuscule when compared to outlays in Anglo-American dioceses (Galveston and Dallas). There are also indications, as we shall see, that parish-by-parish allocations for staffing and for buildings in the dioceses with mixed populations reflect similar inequalities.

Not surprisingly, the predominantly Anglo dioceses had more Catholic schools and more children attending. In 1900 Galveston could boast of two colleges for boys, five academies for girls, and twenty-seven parish schools. About 4,000 children attended these institutions. At the same time Brownsville listed one college for boys, five academies for girls, but only seven parishes with schools, and only about a thousand children in attendance. Thirty years later, in 1930, South Texas had three colleges for boys, six academies for girls, and twenty-seven parish schools, all of which were attended by some five thousand youngsters. Galveston, with 100,000 fewer Catholics than Corpus Christi, had the same number of colleges and academies, but listed over four times as many parish schools (118) and over seven times as many children attending (37,000). Santa Fe, with about as many Catholics as Galveston, had only thirty-five parish schools with 6,000 children in attendance. As with churches, personnel and investment for schools was considerably greater both in absolute numbers and proportionately in the wealthier dioceses than in Mexicano areas.

Underlying the inequality was the uneven support by the national Church. By 1930, the Anglo-American diocese of Dallas with 46,000 Catholics received almost as much money ($211,000) from the Catholic Extension Society as Corpus Christi, which listed eight times as many faithful (428,000), most of whom were Mexican Americans. The same dioceses each received $3,000 from the Mission Students' Endowment Fund for training of priests, even though the ratio of priests to faithful in each was disproportionate: one priest for 2,881 faithful in Corpus Christi, one for 560 in Dallas. Apparently, despite the crisis created by the immigration of thousands of Mexicanos, the Church continued the late nineteenth-century pattern of institution-building as a priority over serving Mexicans.[18]

THE PROTESTANT CHALLENGE

Limited though it was, the Church's response to the newcomers was motivated in part by the fear that Protestant proselytizing would sweep the barrios. Various Protestant groups had been gaining ground in Mexico since the 1870s, ever since Church rights had been curtailed by President Benito Juarez's reforms. During the regime of Porfirio Díaz (1874–1910), Protestants enjoyed a policy of religious tolerance that was agreeable to the United States. As a consequence, various Protestant denominations established churches and seminaries that trained native ministers. But their work in Mexico was slowed by the revolution, which disrupted church communications, the deployment of American missionaries, and the shipment of money and goods into that war-torn country. However, the waves of immigration in the early twentieth century facilitated the Protestant evangelization of Mexicans, since they were now north of the border. Many immigrants, then, already had some exposure to Protestantism before arriving in the United States; if they had not, they were soon to hear the gospel preached to them by churchmen other than priests. To this end Protestant missionaries were sent into the Southwest, to be joined by some Mexican ministers.

Protestantism had some appeal to Mexicanos. Rituals, of course, were in the vernacular and often involved greater participation than traditional Catholic worship. Many of the Protestant groups also had strong commitment to community values that Mexicanos admired. In the smaller congregations members knew and were called to help one another. Because of the lighter educational requirements for the ministry, local Mexicanos could and did emerge as religious leaders of their own congregations. Protestantism, too, preached the American work ethic, and it made some sense for Mexicans to emulate the Anglo Americans in their choice of religion.[19]

Despite such inducements, Mexicanos by no means left the Church in droves. Not all Protestant sects accepted lower-class Mexicans. Certain Protestant groups, too, required behavioral codes that appeared overly strict to many Mexicans. And then there were the austere aspects of many denominations—the absence of elaborate rituals, attractive symbols, and colorful ceremonies—that left most Mexicans feeling unsatisfied. Indeed, some fundamentalist sects also were more rigid in their demands for orthodoxy than the Catholic Church, which often incorporated popular religiosity in its rituals.[20]

Given the links between Catholicism and Mexican culture, conversion was a drastic step, even for lax Catholics or those with anticlerical sentiments, for it implied a rejection of heritage, culture, and even family. Indeed, because the Catholic faith was closely linked to community, conversion often required not only conviction but the willingness to accept condemnation by family and friends. One New Mexican, Gabino Rendón, described his father's reaction to his (Rendón's) conversion:

> "I have known for a long time," he [the father] said, "that the Protestants are right. Yet I don't want you to be one. You are sure to be hated. I saw what happened to Don Ynez Perea. He suffered insults by the dozen. Small wonder he has gone to work elsewhere. I know what happened to Rafael Gallegos. His eagerness to preach is not the only reason he left Las Vegas."
>
> "Now you will be *aborrecido* (despised) because you are a Protestant, and I will be despised because I am the father of a Protestant. I tell you, I don't want that to happen."
>
> . . . My Father was right about (my) being despised for becoming a Protestant. Men friends and girl friends alike begin to ignore me. Even Father Fede, my former teacher, refused to speak to me when I met him once in a doctor's office. That hurt me, but I was fond of him just the same.[21]

It is not surprising, therefore, to see that at most only some 5 percent of the Mexicans and Mexican Americans converted to Protestantism.[22]

Undaunted by the many cultural and social obstacles, Protestants nevertheless launched an intensive proselytizing campaign. In New Mexico, Methodists and Presbyterians were the most active, setting up over sixty schools between 1879 and 1891 alone, often in areas that did not receive strong support by the Catholic Church. Both Protestant groups also actively recruited, trained, and subsidized Hispanics in the ministry. Given their commitment to the word, written and spoken, Protestants launched various newspapers, including *El Metodista*, *El Abogado Cristiano*, *La Revista Evangélica*. These and other efforts attest to the commitments of several Protestant churches to evangelize the Mexicano.[23]

The Church's Response to the Protestant Challenge

Catholics responded in various ways to the threat of losing Mexicanos to the Protestants. In New Mexico, the Jesuits published *La Revista Católica*, which fought against the attacks and countered the theological arguments in the Protestant journals as well as the

anti-Catholic assaults in the secular press. The Church strengthened its position by recruiting more clergy and women religious,
by increasing its work in the education field, and as the various
printings of the *Cánticos Espirituales* attest, by renewing efforts to
incorporate Hispanic culture. With such new endeavors and with a
decline of interest in New Mexico on the part of Protestant leaders
with headquarters in the northeastern United States, the number of
conversions dwindled somewhat, at least in New Mexico. This may
also have taken place, ironically, because some of the preachers decided to follow a more Christian strategy, namely, fewer attacks on
Hispanic Catholicism and a greater emphasis on the proclamation
of the gospel.[24]

Overall, however, the Protestant challenge remained and created a sense of urgency among Catholic Church leaders. But there
was also among churchmen and women a genuine desire to meet
the spiritual needs of the recent arrivals. Accordingly, the Church
organized parishes in the Mexiquitos of South and West Texas and
in the villages and barrios of New Mexico previously served only
by visiting priests. Often Anglo-American Catholics in the various
towns donated the town lots and contributed substantially to the
construction of the church building and school. Start-up monies
were also secured from the Catholic Extension Society and from
the faithful in the Northeast. Religious congregations drew from
their own resources to support clerical and religious personnel,
to buy land for churches and schools, to pay for teachers, and to
acquire fixtures and supplies.[25]

But Mexicano parishioners did their part as well. Despite their
poverty, they contributed in the Sunday collection and in special
campaigns, while their organizations allocated part of their dues to
support the parishes. Local church-goers sponsored *obras teatrales*,
plays, and *jamaicas*, Church-community festivals that also provided
entertainment. Altar societies kept the churches clean and laun-
dered the liturgical linens.

Relationships between Mexican-American and Anglo-American Catholics were harmonious at times and at times not. Many
towns could barely afford to support one parish, and in those
circumstances the pastor preached in Spanish at one Mass and
in English at another. Sometimes the sermon was delivered in
both languages. Not everything worked out so neatly, however.
Anglo donors were accorded a certain deference, such as reserved
pews, and when parallel organizations were not formed, Anglo

parishioners were often assigned leadership roles. In short, the Church went along with the social order.[26]

To a large extent, the bishops agreed with the view that blamed the Mexicans for their conditions. Church leaders accepted the stereotypes of the immigrant as "childlike, ignorant, superstitious, improvident, long-suffering, unwilling to contribute financially to the Church, indifferent to the education of their children, and recognized as having a claim only on the Church's charity." Preparing the Mexican for a college education was "too preposterous to even think about," according to one bishop. Local prelates, of course, did not contradict the official papal pronouncements on social justice, but they did not try to carry them out because to do so would have involved confrontations and impositions on the farm and business owners. It was, indeed, easier for the Church to focus on personal, individual virtues rather than on social injustice. To have taken the side of Mexicanos would have pitted the Church against those who viewed it as un-American or as against the rising Catholic well-to-do. To be sure, the Church often did provide a nucleus for the reestablishment of the Mexicano communities, but it had great difficulty becoming the advocate of social change in behalf of the immigrant.[27]

POPULAR RELIGIOSITY

The local Church's reluctance to grapple with the social issues deterred many Mexican immigrants from reaching out to the Church and making it the center of their community in the way other immigrants had. Instead, the Church had to reach out to the Mexicanos. But for what it had to offer them, mostly solace and comfort in the spiritual realm, Mexicanos had other sources besides the Church, since their heritage included a strong, personally supportive popular religiosity.[28]

The Mexican spiritual tradition included *rezadores/as*. These were men and women who prayed over others or led the community in prayer in private homes and officiated in the absence of the priest, sometimes in the churches and chapels. Often elders in a household also carried out the role of rezadores with the family or with neighbors who gathered in front of little home altars to favorite saints, to the Virgin Mary, or to a popular *Cristo*. Incorporating popular Indian practices into Spanish Catholic spirituality, Mexican Americans developed their own rituals and traditions.[29]

There were also *curanderos*, or healers. Probably the most popular was don Pedrito Jaramillo, the Curandero de Los Olmos. As a young man growing up in Mexico, don Pedrito had worked as a goat herder, one of the lowliest occupations. When he received the gift of healing, he moved to Los Olmos Ranch in South Texas from which he served the Mexicano community for the rest of his life. Don Pedrito's cures were simple: He would pray over the sick person and then specify prayers to be said by the patient while he or she bathed or washed. Sometimes he prescribed herbs and even passed out some "pills." Don Pedrito cured not in his own name, but in God's, and those he could not cure he would gently advise to bear their ailments with resignation as a cross. He never asked for money for his healing, and the donations he received he spent to buy food for those who had come to see him and waited for days at Los Olmos while he was away on his tours of mercy.

Don Pedrito's intercessory powers of healing, some contend, have continued to be effective even after his death in 1907. The shrine in his honor at Los Olmos has been rebuilt several times to accommodate the many who go there to pray for his assistance. Votive candles with his image may be acquired in every barrio grocery or religious store. In don Pedrito's lifetime, devotees to whom a favor had been granted named their children after him. This tradition continues, and many Mexican Americans still speak of the Curandero Los Olmos, who greeted people and prescribed his cure "en el nombre de Dios"—"in the name of God."[30]

Don Pedrito's use of herbs and water with prayers reflected the special relationship between the people and the land. As one farm worker put it:

> Man is born from the earth and each man is a temple of Jesus Christ. Cristo comes and gathers the bodies and souls of those who belong to the earth. Every one of us, like each little plant, belongs to the earth. Today the world has changed a lot. There are so many things that do not belong to the earth. That is why the world is so strange today.[31]

As practiced by don Pedrito and other curanderos, Mexicano religion also brought together the extended family, by blood and by social contract (compadres), and the community. It did so describing in very practical and specific terms the particular roles individuals were to assume in the community. More importantly, religion "protected the culture . . . from the worst of all failures: the loss of the people's confidence in their way of life."[32]

The Immigrants' American Crisis

But neither priests nor curanderos healed social ills, such as peonage, deportations, and violence at the hands of brutal sheriffs, and Mexicano society lacked a united front to confront the powers that be on this earth. In the older Texas towns, such as San Antonio, Laredo, Brownsville, and El Paso, the Mexican-American upper-class families that survived the nineteenth-century American economic expansion were too few and perhaps too frightened to do anything. Many of these landed elites had worked out a "peace arrangement" with the newcomers in order to retain some of their properties as well as some influence in the political process. By the same token, many of the middle- and upper-class immigrant leaders, who provided new leadership in the communities, were at first very committed to returning to Mexico once the Mexican Revolution ended and their positions of importance were restored. Thus they, too, were not disposed, at least for some time, to respond to the exploitation in the barrio. The very poor, of course, were preoccupied with earning their daily bread and hence powerless to launch a serious protest.

But Mexicanos were not without any recourse. Some Mexican Americans had participated in labor union protests in the late 1800s. In the early twentieth century, activists joined the international labor movement inspired by the efforts of Ricardo Flores Magón and his anti-Díaz Partido Liberal Mexicano. Flores Magón and other labor leaders had stayed in South Texas for several months before moving to St. Louis, Missouri, where they could be beyond the long reach of Díaz's agents. While in Laredo and San Antonio, Flores Magón and his followers joined Mexican Americans from organizations which advocated social justice and cultural autonomy. The Flores Magón connection provided the hope of an alternative, just order; it brought in secular beliefs and values that would support a new system and justify the overthrow of the old; and it had the organization necessary to bring this about. The favorable reception Mexican Americans across the Southwest gave the Mexican labor activists reflects the pre-1910 origin of some immigrants and the close ideological links between them and Mexican nationals who were dissatisfied with the negative aspects of American capitalist expansion. The Flores Magón activities injected a radicalism among labor organizers and others that would eventually spark serious protests against the condition of Mexicanos in the United States.[33]

A variety of other organizational vehicles also served to demand justice for Mexican Americans. From the mutualista and masonic groups emerged *ligas protectivas*, protective associations, that protested exploitation and discrimination and demanded more schools and the right to retain Mexican culture. These associations appealed to altruistic, quasi-religious values. Their efforts received extensive public notice in Texas with the convocation in Laredo of a statewide meeting, el Congreso Mexicanista of 1911. But new organizations became necessary as conditions changed radically in the following two decades when the huge waves of immigrants reached the Southwest. The presence of such large numbers of newcomers engendered a substantial anti-Mexican backlash. Mexican Americans reacted by forming the Sons of America, an organization that encouraged the immigrant to learn English and acquire citizenship. Such a strategy, it was hoped, would gain acceptance for Mexican Americans and mitigate the widespread discrimination from which they suffered. The accommodationist efforts existed side by side with the Mexican patriotic movement among the immigrants and did not get much support at first from Mexican Americans.[34]

Despite their organized endeavors, Mexicanos continued to lack access to power, as was clear when the Depression worsened in the 1930s. During that decade those who had been welcomed—and indeed brought over from Mexico by labor agents—were no longer needed or wanted and therefore were driven back to their homeland. Charitable organizations sometimes cut off assistance to Mexicans in hope that many would leave the country. And they did, in caravans. At one point, some 400 Mexicans were leaving each day from San Antonio. Mexican-American bakers in Laredo took turns feeding the waves of *repatriados*, or returnees, who streamed through that border town. Other Mexicanos were rounded up and sent back to Mexico by the newly created Border Patrol. In the 1930s, officials from that agency began to enforce the entry rules, such as the possession of a passport, that had been enacted earlier but had previously been waived for Mexicans.[35]

But many Mexicans had already made their homes in the United States and chose to weather the Depression rather than return to their old homeland. They had acquired property in the United States and were part of well-organized communities. More importantly, their children had been born north of the border and were U.S. citizens. Those immigrants were here to stay. Indeed, they and their children often called themselves "Mexicanos de acá de este lado"—"Mexicans from over here, from this side."

Instead of returning to Mexico, immigrants and Mexican Americans flocked to the larger cities, where relief provided by charitable organizations and the government was more likely to be available. This was particularly the case for migrants and for those in work crews. Without a home base, farm laborers suffered the most when the depression extended into agriculture. The owners turned to subsistence farming for themselves and left the workers to their own devices, much as they had done before, during the off seasons. In the 1930s, however, the work cycles did not come back for years. So Mexicanos headed for the cities, where they got assistance and, later, jobs.[36]

But life in the big cities was by no means easy. In fact, the poverty there was more inhuman. One observer thus described the Depression-era Mexican barrio of San Antonio:

There it stretched, dismal and dirty . . . sweltering in the midsummer heat—block after block of flimsy shacks, thrown together with rotting lumber and rusted pieces of tin picked up on the dump pile of the city. Over all hung the stench that comes from disease and death, from the filth that is born of complete lack of sanitation. And over all lay the heavy hand of poverty and human suffering. In one square mile 12,000 men and women and children were stuck like struggling flies caught in the sticky mess that is fly-paper. Here thousands of God's children's lived in squalor and died in wretchedness.[37]

Another visitor remembered the area in these terms:

[The Guadalupe District] was especially repulsive to me. A huge mass of humanity emerging out of little shacks wrung my heart. Those shacks were built facing dirt roads which became impassable with mud when rain fell. Pale, emaciated faces of the children playing in the dust without laughter in their hearts or on their lips haunted me at night. And the women! They were bent with weariness; and their faces were etched with the hopelessness of long years of struggle against sickness and hunger. Their husbands lingered about without jobs and without hope of jobs that would alter their pitiful existence. When I left San Antonio, I was more than glad.[38]

Mexican-American women were, indeed, among those who suffered the most from the Depression. They had the lowest wages, and because of their nationality or even their appearance, were subject to deportation. The few jobs available to women included meat packing, food processing and preparation, commercial laundry, and home sewing. Piece work was very poorly paid. To make this point, one observer remarked that it took several members of the household—sisters, daughters, aunts, grandmothers—to earn more than what was spent on shoe leather walking to and from the factories. The worst paid were the pecan shellers, whose sole advantage was that they were not closely supervised on the consumption of pecans. Under the leadership of Emma Tenayuca, among others, from this group emerged an organized labor movement that challenged the system with protests and strikes in San Antonio. Charged with being driven by Communist influence, the protestors were jailed en masse by Sheriff Owen Kilday, whose family was closely linked to the political establishment and the local Catholic Church.[39]

Although the archbishop had condoned the roundup of the pecan shellers, the Church worked with rising middle-class Mexican Americans to save the working class from starvation and death and from the worst aspects of discrimination. The Church and the middle class would also be instrumental in forging a new definition of *el pueblo*, the Mexican-American community. Their actions and outlook would be a bridge between the new immigrants and the Mexican-American generation. But before telling that story, let us examine the parish histories that vividly portray the Mexican faith communities of the early twentieth century.

CASE HISTORIES OF FAITH COMMUNITIES:
SAN BENITO, TEXAS

From the view of the men and women on the front line of the ministry meeting the spiritual needs of the many new souls was a crisis by itself. A missionary in the Texas Lower Rio Grande Valley, a semiarid desert transformed almost magically by irrigation, described the challenge in the early 1920s:

Besides the town of San Benito, the Oblate Fathers [Oblates of Mary Immaculate] of this Parish have to attend to the spiritual needs of thousands of Catholics living in the surrounding country. Rev. Father J. B. Haas attends the mission north of the Arroyo, including Harlingen, La Feria, Lyford, Raymondville and many miles around these places. The undersigned [Father Isidro Chateau] attends to the missions south of the Arroyo, including Sta. Maria, Las Rucias, Ranchito, Rio Hondo and all the San Benito plantations [labor camps] and a number of ranches east of here in undeveloped land. There are about 7,000 or 8,000 souls belonging to the Catholic religion living in my missions.[40]

At first the priests ministered to their flock by horse or horse and buggy. Occasionally, until the parish could afford an automobile, a well-to-do Anglo drove them to the outlying missions. Later the Extension Society provided the priests with a "chapel car," a motorized home-and-altar van, christened "the St. Peter." The vehicle was something of a monstrosity for the times, and it often was more of a headache than a convenience because it constantly needed repairs and, when it rained, became hopelessly stuck in the mud roads. When the St. Peter was working and conditions were right, however, it was an eye-catcher. In fact, the sight and sound of its approach on the horizon called for the *vaqueros* (cowboys) to mount and form an appropriate entourage to accompany its entry into the small towns and ranchos.[41]

The home base for the St. Peter was San Benito, one of the many little towns across South and West Texas and New Mexico that sprang up at the turn of the century. The city was the creation of the San Benito Land and Water Company. Like dozens of other similar firms across Texas and the Southwest, this one had purchased hundreds of acres of farm land, brought in irrigation, and subdivided the area for resale to midwestern farmers looking for investments. At the center of the development was the town of San Benito. It serviced the hinterland in various ways, including housing the Mexican laborers, who lived in a sectioned-off barrio. In the case of San Benito, Sam Houston Boulevard was the line of demarcation between the Mexican and Anglo-American sides of town; in other towns, the railroad tracks served as the residential boundary line. Near the barrio, accessible to the workers, was the gin, the storage and packing sheds, and the garages that repaired the farm implements.[42]

Once the parish was organized, the church was built on the Mexican side, since most of the faithful lived there. Mexicanos in other towns were not always as fortunate, but in San Benito the church was close to their homes. The church served Anglo-American Catholics as well, and one of the first acts of the new pastor was to bless two statues, one of Our Lady of Guadalupe donated by the Mexicans and one of St. Ann with the Blessed Mother donated by the Anglos. A Mexican choir was formed shortly after the founding, and not much later an American group was organized. On some occasions, such as Christmas, both choirs participated at midnight Mass. Some of the church organizations were established exclusively for one group or the other.[43]

The Anglo Catholics were instrumental in building the church structure and the pastor referred to them with a certain respect. Like other parishes, San Benito's was named "St. Benedict" in English rather than in Spanish. But the Mexicanos there (some to this day) called their parish "San Benedicto." The overwhelming numbers of Mexicans and the obvious need to conduct most of the services in Spanish motivated the Anglos to ask for their own church. They therefore sponsored fund-raisers independently of the parish and rented a house for a chapel, which they named after St. Francis. The arrangement was opposed by one of the pastors, but the chapel was apparently used for worship nonetheless. Anglo Americans also purchased a lot across the main avenue, not very far from San Benedicto, for a permanent structure. Their church was never built there, however, presumably because the proximity would have pointed very dramatically to the ethnic crevice within the Church community. A brief note entered in the parish diary on the occasion of the Feast of Corpus Christi, 1931, speaks volumes of the divisions at San Benedicto: "For the first time [since 1911] the Children of Mary of the American congregation took part in a procession" along with the Mexicans.[44]

For all practical purposes, then, San Benedicto was the parish of the Mexicanos, who eventually became its sole supporters. One-third of the *padrinos* and *madrinas*, or sponsors, who pledged donations for the new church were Spanish-surnamed. Periodically, not just festivals but regular Sunday collections were used to reduce the parish debt. As time went on and Mexican Americans gained a modicum of security, they increased their contributions to the parish. They continued to support it even during the Depression, as is evidenced by a list of contributors for a special May collection in 1939. On that occasion various individuals donated sums ranging from one to sixteen dollars. Parish organizations— the choir, the sodalities, the schools—also took up collections or sponsored fundraisers. So did non-church social clubs. The largest contribution, $50 of the $313.54 collected, came from the "Señoritas Adela y Delfina González y Aficionados," a reference to an amateur night performance organized by those two dedicated ladies. At the bottom of the list, in large print, is a note from the pastor, Father J. W. Fritz, O.M.I., "Muchísimas gracias en nombre de la parroquia"—"Many thanks on behalf of the parish."[45]

The community supported their church, and some priests formed strong relationships with the townspeople. The pastors' long-term assignments in San Benito may have facilitated the bonding with the community. Then, too, many of the priests were very dedicated and put up with many hardships. One of the first pastors and the principal author of a parish chronicle, Father Isidro Chateau, slept in the sacristy for a long time. When his first assistant joined him in San Benito, Father Chateau ceded the sacristy and put his cot in the choir loft. Father Chateau moved to a room in back of the barn once that building went up, but when the first freezing "norther" blew in, he quickly went back to his spot next to the organ and stayed there until the priests' residence was constructed months later. Even after their house was built, the priests rarely ate their meals there and continued to take them "at a little Mexican lady's house" at the cost of fifty cents for three meals. His mixing with the people and his sacrifices endeared "el Padre Isidro" to the people as much as he was attached to them.[46]

But a strong relationship with the people did not mean that Mexicanos met the religious expectations of the pastors fully. Like other priests, Father Chateau was perplexed with the response he received from his parishioners. Given the sacramental role of the Church and the priesthood, the padres were somewhat frustrated that Mexicans were not careful to have their marriage unions blessed. While Father Chateau does not characterize Mexicans as prone to violate marriage vows, he is perturbed by their disregard for the value of the sacrament of matrimony. For Mexicanos, it seems, this sacrament was a mere technicality required for other Church matters, such as being sponsors at a baptism. Holy matrimony was also viewed as essential for legitimizing offspring. On one occasion, for example, a man in a common-law marriage for thirty years asked to be married in the Church, not to reconcile himself with God, but so his daughter would not have any problems collecting his life insurance. Father Chateau was shocked. He and other priests were also disturbed by the fact that Mexicans, particularly the men, shied away from confessing their sins and approaching the altar for Holy Communion.[47]

Father Chateau described the spiritual challenges in a lengthy essay:

most of them [the Mexicans to whom he ministered] are very far from being practical [practicing] Catholics. Many don't even know the first prayers of a Christian. The greater percentage of marriages are made by the civil law only, though a good many of them in the course of time are having their matrimonial unions blessed by the priest, that is to say, are married by the law of the church.

Perhaps half, if not more, of my Catholic Mexicans come from Mexico and it is easy to recognize the sad consequences of the 15 years of [anti-clerical] revolutions in that country, especially in those coming from [the state of] Tamaulipas. The only sacrament which is carefully looked for is baptism: with, say a few exceptions, all our Mexicans are anxious to have their children baptized: also to have them confirmed, if they have a chance to be near a place where confirmations are given.

Father Chateau continued:

Very few people keep up the practice of going to Confession and Holy Com[munion] even once a year. Occasionally a certain number of adults can be induced to go to confession & Holy Com., but out of themselves they would not do it, especially not men: and this way, those that live at a distance from church or from places where religious service is given, do not care at all to make their Easter duty and live for many years without the sacraments, but without feeling any remorse of not fulfilling this duty.[48]

Yet this pastor, like others, was impressed with Mexican spirituality:

Not withstanding the religious carelessness of our poor mexican catholics, they have a great religious mind in their own way. They do not despise their religion, they do not use blasphemies in their language, they respect the padrecito [a term of affection for a priest] and most of them have religious pictures in their homes, for which they have very often an exaggerated, superstitious confidence . . . [a practice attacked by] mexican ministers of protestant denominations [who] use [this argument] to avert our poor people from their faith. . . . [But] even the ignorant mexican, if questioned in the right way, will give you to understand that the favors he asks from "his saints" are obtained from the living saint in heaven and ultimately from God: so much so that they themselves have a proverb saying: When God does not want, the saints are powerless [*Si Dios no quiere, ni el santo puede*].

Another practice that shows the religious mind of the Mexicans is that they keep, most of them, very scrupulously certain festivals of the year: especially Holy Thursday and Good Friday. Just this very year on Good Friday I had to make a journey by train to Corpus Xti [Christi] to get the Holy Oils. And I was very much moved in my heart when I saw from the train mexican people dressed like [on] Sundays, not working, because it was the day our Lord died on the cross for us. And I said to myself: Certainly our Lord will deal leniently with many of these poor people['s] defects and faults when he sees them keeping holy the day of his suffering. After all God judges every one according to each one's individual conscience and many things that theoretically speaking are classed by theologians as mortal sins and habits or states of mortal sin are not mortal sins for our poor ignorant [uneducated] Mexicans who do not realize the gravity of sinful actions.[49]

This passage reveals, on the one hand, the intercessory role of the saints (and the Blessed Mother, as the discussion below indicates) with God the Father. There is a clear understanding that these intercessors carry their work out in heaven, where they reside. On the other hand, the reference to the observance of Good Friday by Mexicanos points to their homage to the suffering Christ. This devotion embodies the attraction to a down-to-earth hero who shares in human suffering and gives his life for others as he performs a saving act in which the people could participate vicariously. Interestingly, in San Benito, all the padrinos and madrinas of the images of the stations of the cross were Mexicanos. In New Mexico, the reenactment of the passion and death of Christ was the principal Penitente ritual. Mexicanos, whose lives were also filled with suffering, wanted their agony to be redemptive, as Christ's had been. Understandably, then, Good Friday was an important holy day for the Mexicans across the Southwest.[50]

The Mexicano belief system also involved ritual obligations, as Father Chateau observed:

I noticed also that very few of our Catholic Mexicans will knowingly eat meat on a [special] day of abstinence. . . . On ordinary Fridays they eat meat because it is allowed in Mexico. . . .

. . . [most Mexicans] even people who are married [only] by a judge or not married at all keep on saying their night prayers and [continue] keeping a nice altar in their home, and I met a good many [who], even after telling me that they did not know any prayer, were found never to begin their day's work without a little offering like "Be it done in the name of God" (En nombre sea de Dios) and to practice some little devotion at night when they go to sleep.

Our Mexican people hav[e] generally a very kind and devoted feeling towards the Blessed Virgin and they like the priest to give them a rosary service at night. In fact they assist much better at a rosary [than] they do at Sunday mass in the ranchos & they like to sing hymns.[51]

On the subject of sin, Father Chateau outlined the failings that troubled the Mexican conscience:

For him [the Mexican] only sins against the natural law seem to stir his conscience, like:

a) ill treating one's parents or friends, killing, slandering, blaspheming, breaking or not fulfilling promises made to God or to the saints,

b) [faults] against nationally *accepted customs*, like eating meat on nationally accepted fast days,

c) failing against one's *compadre* or *comadre*, [and]

d) going against superstitious beliefs (e.g., killing cats, spitting out on days one has received Holy Com.)[52]

Fundamentally, then, despite their lack of compliance with standard Church rules, Mexicans were very religious and had a clear sense of what was right and wrong. They exhibited a personal relationship with "their saints" and through them with their heavenly Father, to whom they entrusted their day and to whom they bid goodnight before resting. One immigrant's morning/night prayer reflected these close bonds with God the Father:

O Dios, alabo tu gran poder,
Que con el alma en el cuerpo
Me dejaste amanecer [anochecer],
Así te suplico y ruego
Me dejes anochecer [amanecer],
En honor y servicio tuyo
Y sin llegarte a ofender.

(Oh, God, I praise your power and might,
That with my soul in my body
You have granted me to see the morning light [night],
In the same way I pray and beseech you
To allow me to see the night [the morning light],

All for your honor and in your service
And without ever offending you.)[53]

Obligations accompanied this religiosity. Mexicanos kept holy certain feastdays, some determined by the universal Church, others by their national traditions. They also held sacred filial and other personal relationships, such as the compadrazgo, and fulfilled their commitments to their heavenly intercessors. Actions that harmed those relationships, i.e., breaking the rules that kept their world in order, were considered sinful. The priests admired this code and the religiosity from which it sprang. Indeed, they hoped to cultivate that spirituality and have it complement the orthodoxy they preached.

But Mexicano religiosity did not make up for the neglect to confess sins and receive communion or for their forgoing a church wedding. This last issue may have been related, for the priests, to authority and control. For decades anticlerical factions in Mexican politics had campaigned vigorously for compliance with the registering of births, marriages, and deaths with civil authorities as a means of weaning the people from their loyalty to the Church. Still, the Registro Civil obviously did not supplant the spiritual need among Mexicans for baptism and confirmation and also possibly for a blessing at death. But the anticlerical reformers did weaken the custom among Mexicans of receiving the sacrament of matrimony. The American clergy labored to bring the tradition back and restore what they apparently considered a very important bond between the people and the Church. The prominence of this issue in Father Chateau's essay—he laments this failure on the part of Mexicans even more than he laments their inattention to the "Easter duty" (yearly confession and Communion)—suggests that, despite their admirable religiosity, Mexicans were not the Catholics he wished or expected them to be.[54]

Underlying the dichotomy of a "very religious" people who did not follow the same important rules of the Church was the strong adherence to what anthropologists call "folk religion." Often branded by the Protestants as "pagan"—Father Chateau referred to the folk belief system more tactfully as "exaggerated, superstitious confidence" in "their saints"—popular religiosity did not demand the faithful to conform with the "many things that theoretically speaking are classed by [Church] theologians as mortal sins or habits or states of mortal sin." Rather, by definition, the people themselves determine the belief structure and set the moral code.

In communities where religion plays a central role, the official clergy cannot have control of all the tenets of faith. By insisting that religion permeate every facet of life, the clergy necessarily lose absolute direction of the belief system. In addition, if the official organization of the folk belief system is disrupted—as it was by the anticlerical currents of the independence movement, the liberal struggle for state control over the Church, and the Mexican Revolution—understandably the people assume greater control over their faith structure and moral code than before.[55]

This was particularly the case with some Mexican immigrants, as one scholar has noted: "The[y] . . . appear, indeed, to have come from precisely that population group in Mexico among whom [official] Catholic influence was weakest. They were unaccustomed to parochial schools, financial support of the Church, religious instruction, and regular attendance at Mass, all of which are important to American Catholics."[56] Unable to understand the Mexicanos' independence from the Church, some Anglo-American priests despaired, calling Mexicans a *massa damnata*, a people without hope of redemption, an attitude that probably justified the Church's lack of full commitment to Mexicanos.[57]

However, at the same time that the immigrants are described as irreligious, they are paradoxically said to have been susceptible to the anticlericalism of the Revolution. But anticlericalism would presumably find fertile ground only where Church control was overwhelming, not where there was ecclesiastical neglect. Consequently, the prevalence of anticlericalism among Mexicanos may reflect something else, possibly frustration with the Church for not serving them adequately. This may explain why some Mexicanos in South Texas appeared to be both "unchurched" and anti-Church at the same time.

The anticlerical wars in Mexico had an unexpected positive consequence in South Texas: they brought many of that country's prelates, priests, and religious women to South Texas. By August 1914, five Mexican archbishops and eight bishops were residing, albeit temporarily, in San Antonio alone. An entire Franciscan monastery was relocated to San Diego, in the heart of South Texas. At some point, more than one seminary moved to the area. A seminary was established in New Mexico for Mexican students for the priesthood. Indeed, almost every diocese in Texas, New Mexico, and Arizona housed clerical refugees well into the 1930s. Exiled priests said Mass and preached missions while nuns taught in schools.[58]

This assistance was welcomed by the people and by the pastors. Father Yvo Tymen recorded the work of two Mexican priests in San Benito:

Today [July 31, 1929]. Last mass said by Padre David in San Benito, where he has been since exiled by new wicked laws of [the] Mex. gov't against [the] Church. He arrived here in Feb. 1927 from Xuclenall [?] where he had been parish [priest] since his ordination in Guadalajara, i.e., 4 years. Father David helps . . . me in S. Bto. [San Benito] and its missions, having good spirit and generosity. He was well liked by the people, and so did he like the people, so that, in one way, he departed from us regretting he had to do so.

Father J. Castillo had left S. Bto. about two weeks before, going to take possession of his new parish in Nuevo Laredo. He also spent the greatest part of his exile in San Benito, having escaped with difficulties the "Gendarmes" of [Mexican President Elias Plutarco] Calles who traced him from Tampico to Laredo but missed him. The Lord bless them both in their hardships.[59]

Evidently, while Mexicanos did not bring their clergy with them, as other immigrants had, Mexican clergy in a sense accompanied them and assisted them, at least temporarily.

Father Chateau took Mexican religiosity and the historical circumstances into account, but he actually reverted to stereotypes to explain what seemed to him to be imperfections in Mexican religiosity: "According to my best observations the real root of the many shortcomings in the religious life of the Mexican is his easy going character or laziness (la desidia) which makes him shun everything disagreeable much as he can afford it, and look for everything agreeable as much as he can afford it: in religion as well as in every day life & business."[60]

Whatever the unworthiness of the faithful, the Church was there to serve, not only spiritually, but also by way of providing some cultural and social services. The priests in San Benito, for example, set the building of a school as a goal almost as soon as they erected the church. Wrote Father Chateau: "What is most needed here is a Catholic School. There are many boys and girls, but they are ignorant of their religion and likewise of their letters. And how are we going to get a School without property, nor a house, nor nuns?"[61]

To realize the goal of establishing a Mexican school a variety of forces had to be brought into line. The San Benito Land and Water Company donated a plot of land 100 x 150 feet near the resaca [a river outlet]. Some $150 were secured by selling an unneeded corner of land near the church. The Oblate missionary congregation guaranteed the salaries for the teachers; money was secured from the Extension Society; and the parishioners contributed to the construction of the wooden frame building. In September 1912 the school began classes with twenty-five students under the guidance of "la maestra Carmen" Martínez and her sister. By the end of September it had eighty children and by January, one hundred and fifty. Tuition amounted to fifty cents a month, *adelantados*, paid in advance, but children from poor families could attend free. Enrollment fluctuated because, out of pride, many parents chose to send their children to the public school rather than request that tuition be waived. Still, la Escuela Guadalupe did well and a few years later the building needed expansion. Eventually a second school, San José, was opened in another barrio in San Benito.[62]

In time, the Guadalupe school was rebuilt, and its blessing was a community affair. In the morning there was a solemn *misa cantada* (sung Mass) by special permission, in the open air. Then, Father Chateau writes,

> in the afternoon, the boys had a game, and then the "Danzantes" [Indian "Matachines" dancers] shocked us and continued down to 6 o'cl. dancing in the open air. At 8 p.m. a big crowd tried to find room in the old Guad. [Guadalupe] school bldg, transformed into a theater. Many had to go home [for] lack of place in the hall. This was the best crowd I ever witnessed in this place. The drama, nicely arranged by Sister Rose, was beautifully rendered.[63]

The San Benito players were popular with the audiences, creating demand for their performances in the bigger city of Brownsville. Indeed, a good number of San Benito residents apparently liked to be on stage, as is evident from the popularity of amateur "Noches Mexicanas."[64]

Community celebrations, even Church-sponsored ones, however, carried the risk of disorder. Apparently after the Mass at the opening ceremony a rosary was recited, and during that service "most of the young people were going around smoking cigarettes, without any attention to what was going on in front of them." On another occasion Father Chateau commented on public order: "Midnight Mass has been forbidden by the Bishop. Many padrecitos [popular familiar term for padres] are mad at it. Personally I thank the Lord and His Lordship for the restriction. Too many bad Mexicans had to be watched so to avoid scandals & disorders around and in the church."[65]

These problems notwithstanding, San Benedicto and la Escuela Guadalupe were linked to the community and promoted Mexican nationalism. In fact, Anglo Catholics did not send their children to the school, where classes were taught in Spanish and the students took part in the Mexicano community festivities, as Father Chateau noted: "Periodically there were celebrations in which the school children took part, but the grandest was the Cinco de Mayo, 1913, in which the boys and girls took part in the parade of floats and in singing patriotic songs at the altar of the Fatherland."[66]

The 400th anniversary of the apparitions of Our Lady of Guadalupe in 1931 called for special festivities:

> On the occasion a great parade lined up in the afternoon, including booths [floats?] representing the Landing of Christopher Columbus in the new continent, the different phases of the apparitions of O. L. of Guadalupe. The societies [were] in uniform, typical groups of Indians [representations of Indians from different regions], little boys and girls, young men and young ladies' group[s], 200 men, cars decorated nicely, [all] marched at the sound of the band from the church ground to the Guadalupe School. There, it was a beautiful spectacle to see, 2,000 people around the Virgen y Madre de [Virgin and Mother of] Guadalupe praying [and] singing. Later the Danzantes took care of the crowd. At 7:30 we had an open air Rosario [rosary] and then the beautiful play of "Las Apariciones de [The Apparitions of] la V. de Guadalupe."[67]

The celebration and the play, which had been organized by the Sisters and a dozen lay men and women, had strong Mexican nationalistic overtones. It confirmed to all that Mexicanos had not crossed the border; rather, the border had crossed them.

Yet the need for acculturation also became evident in the church and school community. Possibly at the request of some parents or to compete with the public school, an Anglo-American teacher was hired and a room next to the sacristy was set aside for a class taught in English. Throughout the decade some twenty-five to thirty Mexican-American children attended this class. Eventually the Sisters of the Sacred Heart staffed the school and taught mostly in English. La maestra Carmen opened her own private school and operated it through most of the 1920s and part of the 1930s with teachers brought from Mexico. But that school was closed when local school authorities threatened to sue for violation of the English-only legislation.[68]

Living in the United States brought about other changes beyond language; it altered the roles of women in the barrio society. Like la Escuela Guadalupe, Church organizations such as the Vela Perpétua del Santísimo Sacramento and the Hijas de María functioned as vehicles for cultural retention. By conducting their meetings and special devotions entirely in Spanish and by emphasizing purity and affective sentiments, members of these Church groups reinforced traditional roles and cultural values. But these societies also served the participants in nontraditional ways that addressed women's needs. Organizations like the Vela Perpétua and Hijas de María provided their members with "safe" interests outside the home, including opportunities to socialize with other women and to exercise leadership and management skills in a variety of church-related projects. Indeed, using those skills and great dedication, women in these groups became the financial pillars of the parish. Without intending it, Church societies encouraged the aspiration of freedom expressed by immigrant women, "Ah, tener 21 años y en Tejas!"—"Oh, to be twenty-one and in Texas!"[69]

Male participation in church activities and organizations was not absent, but it was considerably more limited. An entry for February 2, 1912, notes that in the evening "the church was crowded to the utmost. A kind of Pastorela [Christmas play] was given by mexican workingmen that had come to this place from the surroundings of Monterrey." Another Christmas play, this one put on by the school children, was so moving that it brought tears to everyone's eyes, including, the pastor noted, those of men. As we have seen, Father Chateau made it a point of providing an estimate of the number of men (200) attending the 400th anniversary celebration of the Guadalupe apparitions. But few men attended the regular rituals. Few participated in the mission revivals preached for them, and fewer still approached the altar for Holy Communion.[70]

Men did not perceive the Church to be on their side in the conflict they faced in the larger society. During the killings of 1914 in the Lower Rio Grande Valley, the Church did not take a stand. When principal canal projects were completed large numbers of Mexicans wandered through the area seeking other work. Violence erupted as they encountered especially rough treatment and resorted to retaliatory raids. Anglo Americans alleged that all the laid-off laborers were bandits and revolutionaries linked to the Plan de San Diego, a regional revolt against the American landowners. Valley officials then undertook a hunt that resulted in the deaths of hundreds of Mexicans and Mexican Americans.[71]

The San Benito pastor described the situation, but said nothing of Church condemnation:

> In July some bandits began to burn the railroad bridges, steal from stores—ammunition and horses. Five thousand American soldiers were placed on alert on several points across the "Magic Valley" (as they have named for some time the American lands irrigated by [water coming through] canals from the Rio Grande. *Rinches* [technically "Rangers," but often meaning "hired guns"] were wandering everywhere. Fear overpowered many folks, and there go bunches of families to Matamoros and to Mexico! Some at least stopped at Brownsville.
>
> Several ranches that we minister to were burnt down by the *rinches* alleging that the bandits hid out there. But even today the bandit leaders have not been caught.[72]

There is surprisingly little comment in the parish history about the social conditions of Mexicanos. One of the few references to the poverty of Mexicanos, other than the customary "our poor Mexicans," was made on Christmas, 1911:

> Midnight mass—muddy roads, rainy weather, nevertheless the church was pretty crowded. High mass on Xmas day: church overcrowded. Besides the crib there were 2 Xmas trees in the church and many Xmas gifts for poor mexican children. [These] were distributed Sunday afternoon the 24th and Monday afternoon the 25th (apples, oranges, sweets, toys, objects of piety, clothing) a collection for that purpose had been made by Mr. Andres Curan [an Anglo]. May God reward him for the good work.[73]

Some church organizations were dedicated to helping out the poor and some, like Acción Católica Juvenil, were actually dedicated to social action, but there is no mention of activities other than spiritual exercises. As for Church officials, they would not have led the efforts for social justice since often they maintained close ties with Anglo Americans who were the farm owners and the mid-managers or owners of the companies that ran the town.[74]

Even if these links had not been there, in San Benito, as in most other places, the Church saw its role primarily as a spiritual one. Its principal goal was to sustain the life of grace of the immigrants by dispensing the sacraments and to safeguard them from encroaching

Protestantism. In addition, through organizations and celebrations the Church played an important part in reestablishing community for uprooted immigrants and restoring the role of faith in that community. Certainly the priests saw their efforts as bearing fruit and expressed satisfaction with their work on behalf of the people.

Certain actions of the parishioners suggest that the relationship was in fact mutually satisfying. In 1957 a caravan of the faithful from San Benedicto traveled to Rio Grande City to help celebrate Father Yvo Tymen's Golden Jubilee as a priest. Father Tymen was one of San Benito's and the Valley's pioneer pastors. Indeed, he was the last survivor of the "Cavalry of Christ" that had made the ranch circuit on horseback. Two years later a busload of parishioners traveled to San Antonio to bid farewell to another beloved pastor, Father William Caldwell, at his funeral. The church was packed for the rosary for Father Frederick J. DeRoche, who had suffered a heart attack while at his post in San Benito in 1963. These priests had obviously responded well and generously to Mexicano spiritual yearnings. The fire of the faith community in San Benito had burned bright and had perdured.[75]

BEYOND SOUTH TEXAS

Not all the immigrants stopped in Valley towns like San Benito. Most, in fact, streamed past the border areas into the western and eastern sections of Texas and into northern New Mexico. They picked cotton around El Campo, worked in the mines near Bastrop, and crowded into Houston. They were drawn to the beet industry of Colorado and into the mines of Arizona and other southwestern states. They gathered in labor camps, in towns, and in the growing cities.

In Houston, by 1912, "el Segundo Barrio" (the Second Ward) had grown from a vacant area invaded by Mexican laborers. *Jacales* (stick-and-mud thatched-roofed huts), strengthened by tin, sheet iron, and other materials from nearby junkyards, flanked the deteriorating older homes of a once-fashionable neighborhood. Barrio residents, led by J. J. Mercado in the organization "la Agrupación Protectora Mexicana," a civil rights organization, took up local and regional Mexicano issues. These included safety, education, discrimination, and violence. A handful of other organizations offered mutualista-type insurance and provided Houston Mexicanos with a sense of a reestablished community through the observation of patriotic holidays.[76]

Still, Mexican Americans apparently lacked a central rallying point, and the Church seems to have served this purpose. One priest wrote:

> Not having a place to bring the Mexicans together, the priests would go around the various barrios in the City of Houston, celebrating wherever they could, [including] in private homes, the Holy Sacrifice of the Mass, and administering the holy sacraments of the Church, and continued in this manner until the opening of a church built for the exclusive use of the Mexican Colony.[77]

To meet this need, the Oblate Fathers, one of the groups in Texas commissioned to look after the spiritual needs of the immigrants, were allowed to use the facilities of Anglo-American Annunciation parish neighboring the barrio so that at least the feast of Our Lady of Guadalupe could be celebrated properly. There was a triduum (three-days) of devotions and a solemn Mass at the Anglo-American church on December 12. The ceremony that day included the blessing of the image, for which there were over 150 padrinos y madrinas, some *de honor* and others *sencillos* (special and ordinary sponsors). The pastor was very impressed by what he witnessed in his church.[78]

With this auspicious beginning, the priests continued to forge Houston's Mexican and Mexican-American faith community. They sponsored a dramatic-musical performance to raise funds for Mexicano victims of "the catastrophe" (flood?) of February 1912. The same circular that announced the event reminded barrio residents not to forget to contribute to the church building fund. Before construction could begin, the priests somehow got the city to truck in 1,500 loads of dirt to build up the site, which, like the entire barrio, consisted of a lowland marsh where drainage waters collected. Once the church was finished later that year, the bishop came to officiate at the solemn blessing. The ceremony began with a procession in which "a Mexican orchestra" participated. At last with a home, the Mexicano parish, under the patronage of Our Lady of Guadalupe, was serving nearly two thousand faithful by 1916.[79]

The Mexican population of Houston was growing rapidly in the first decades of the twentieth century. By 1919 the parish expanded to four Masses on Sunday, and because "huge numbers were flocking into Houston on account of the good salaries," at least one priest had to be at the church at all times to meet the spiritual needs of the people. In 1921, there were 7,000 communions; in 1922, 13,000; and in 1923, 25,000.[80]

As time passed the parishioners decided to build a new church and began to gather contributions. In May of 1923 the blessing ceremony for the cornerstone was described in the following manner:

> From the old chapel, in perfect order, the procession wound its way to the entrance of the new temple under construction, it [the procession] being made up of the leader with the crucifix, flanked by two acolytes carrying candles [and followed] by the Hijas de María, the Hermanas de la Vela Perpétua, the madrinas of the blessing, all with their ribbons/mementos, the youthful members of the San Luis Gonzaga Society, the Men's Society of the Sacred Heart, the padrinos of the ceremony, also displaying the organizational emblems, one dozen of altar boys, part of the city's clergy, and His Excellency [the bishop] with staff and miter. . . . a large crowd gathered around the construction site and followed the solemn ceremony of Benediction with attention and respect.[81]

A few months later an even greater crowd was on hand for the blessing of the new church, since the event had been announced in all the barrios of the city. Later, in December, the church was filled to capacity for midnight Mass. A school was added to the complex, with enrollments quickly reaching 460 students.[82]

Mexican workers in Houston were reportedly getting "good salaries." In actuality, they received only fifteen to twenty cents an hour, according to the Sisters Virginia and Liberata, of the Congregation of the Divine Providence. These women walked the barrio "with staff in their hands and lunch baskets on their arms" in their effort to catechize the Mexicans in a few available meeting rooms. The close contact with Mexicanos and their living conditions led Sister Benitia Vermeersch to conclude that teaching religion was not enough. She therefore requested permission to leave the classroom in order to provide basic services to the colonia residents. To this end, Sister Benitia launched a variety of programs that included distributing free lunches to children, teaching area residents gardening, and organizing outside groups to collect and distribute money and supplies in the barrio. The National Council of Catholic Women, for example, established a clinic in 1924 to deal with the rising infant mortality among Mexicanos. Sister Benitia herself collected donations from business firms and from individuals. Her work led, in 1930, to the creation of a new congregation of women religious, the Missionary Catechists of Divine Providence, who worked among the poor Mexicans and Mexican Americans in South Texas.[83]

Near Houston, in the labor camps that formed adjacent to the cotton fields, roamed the St. Peter, the chapel car now transported to East Texas from the Rio Grande Valley. The van caused a commotion wherever it went. In Austin, this "immense machine" even drew people away from a carnival. On one occasion, as the motor chapel approached one of the settlements, some African Americans ran to the road at the end of the cotton field to take a good look at the contraption. "Lordie, what's this?" asked one woman, to which another replied, "Lordie, if it ain't Noah's Ark!"[84]

To the priests embarking on a week-long mission in a mining camp near Bastrop, the St. Peter was "an immense battery [at the top of a hill] ready to fight the battle of God." Spiritually unattended for a long time, Mexican workers there were seen as a special challenge: "indifference born of ignorance, bad example, and human respect had destroyed in the hearts of many, fervent and devout in their younger days, the seed of virtue and piety sown there by loving and religious mothers."[85]

On the first week of this particular mission revival the sermon centered on the "great truths" of the faith; then, "with the ground being well prepared," the priest conducted discussions "on different topics, especially those attacked by the so-called Liberals." Obstacles were overcome, and the mission went well:

> From the start we realized the difficulty of the work we had undertaken: the men especially seemed to come to the mission only to kill time, because they had no other place to go. The attendance was small in the beginning. It increased gradually however and the sermons, the sacred hymns and most fervent prayers revived the dormant faith, until we could read in the faces of everyone the various feelings in their hearts, feelings that brought back, no doubt, to their memory beautiful days gone by, when in the beautiful land of their birth now torn by fratricidal war, they prostrated themselves before the altar of God and sang with infant voice these same hymns learned on their mothers' knees.[86]

Over fifty men and three times as many women and children received Communion. Also, "four marriages were rehabilitated and two concubinaries [sic] were separated." In the concluding ceremony, a member of the congregation read "a most touching act of consecration of the Blessed Mother" and then all sang a popular hymn:

> Adios, Reina del Cielo
> Madre del Salvador
> Adios, oh, Madre Mía
> Adios, Adios, Adios
>
> So long, ye Queen of Heaven
> Mother of the Savior
> So long, oh, my Mother
> So long, so long, so long[87]

The following morning, "Noah's Ark" pulled up anchor and sailed off to another camp.

On other missions, the motor chapel's clerical crew battled the Protestants. Like everyone else, they approached the car out of curiosity. "[A] close inspection, however, revealed its object, and time and again some bigots could not refrain from expressing their feelings." At one point an argument over religion ensued with "heretics" near the vehicle, but "the Fathers brought out their ignorance . . . and they [the Protestants] left wiser than they had come, amidst the laughter of all [the others]." The stops at the camps, the priests complained, were of necessity too short "to destroy prejudices deeply rooted by ignorance and the malicious work of the sectarians. . . ." Nevertheless, the missionaries reported, "The powers of darkness could not remain indifferent to our work and success and they tried to harass us," something which backfired and gained support for the priests. At the closing of one mission, amidst prayers and verses of the familiar "Viva María, Muera el Pecado" ("Long Live Mary, Death to Sin"), a bonfire consumed "all the bad books [probably religious tracts] and protestant Bibles." It was hoped that this too would encourage the faithful to detest sin and to persevere in their good intentions as Catholics.[88]

In El Paso, at the other end of the state, the growing number of Mexican immigrants taxed the resources invested there by the Church. One of the Sisters of Loretto, Sister Mary Berchmans García, who staffed the Sacred Heart School, objected to the criticism that the Church was not doing enough for the area's Spanish-speaking, since many in her congregation and the pastor, Father Carlos Pinto, S.J., had made so many sacrifices to get the parish and the school organized. Part of the criticism may have come from the cost of building two churches, one for the Anglo Americans, who were very few in number, and one for the Mexicans.[89]

The Mexican community seems to have actively participated in their parish. On one occasion parents complained to the pastor of the cost involved in Sister García's requirement that the children making their first communion in 1892 had to be perfectly attired. After some discussion and compromises, "la Sister Juanita" helped the parents complete the arrangements, and on the appointed day the children and their parents proudly presented themselves for the ceremony properly attired. Parishioners also cooperated generously, paying off the debt for the church building in a short span of seven years. New parishes were erected during the first three decades of the twentieth century as the Mexican population of the city soared.[90]

From the Jesuit headquarters at Sacred Heart parish, Father Carlos M. Pinto, S.J., the pastor, assisted in the expansion of the Church in El Paso for twenty-five years. At his funeral in 1919 crowds stood outside during the Mass and "a vast throng" accompanied the body to the cemetery, some in cars, some in old rickety horse-drawn wagons, and some on foot. For those he had served no other information was necessary than that provided by the gravestone, which simply read "Father Pinto."[91]

In areas of the Southwest with mixed Hispanic and Indian populations, the Church community observed the visit of the bishop in unique ways. In southwestern New Mexico, for instance, Rev. Henry Granjon, Bishop of Tucson, described the procession from the train station at Las Cruces to the church in 1902:

> I am seated in a cart with benches, and the parade begins: the women and children on foot, through the dust, and the men on horseback. Just in front of my carriage, which advances majestically at a walk, an entire tribe of Indians and squaws executes, as in the time of David, a sacred dance. There they are, heads bare, a row of men, a row of women, alternately, their faces decorated with red ochre, their bodies covered with furs of wild animals or cottons in bright colors, their feet covered with moccasins. A drum beats the rhythm. . . .
>
> We arrive at the plaza of the church. The Indian chorus installs itself at the entrance of the temple. . . . [Then, inside,] the good Indians, grave, impassive, with long, angular, beardless faces in which not a muscle moves, their gazes fixed before them upon the great altar all blazing with lights at the end of the nave, continue their choreographic cycles. . . . Good children of nature, the Lord will have contemplated favorably the sincerity of your hearts and the form, strange but deliciously naive, of its expression.[92]

Yet he feared the natives were doomed to extinction, just as Hispanic traditions were doomed to fade as the people adopted the
bad habits of the "invaders":

> upon contact with the white race, the indigenous races almost al-
> ways adopt its failing and ignore its virtues. . . . And generally,
> unless the Catholic ethic comes to regenerate these contaminated
> [with modern civilization] races and save them from themselves,
> they disappear. Farewell, ancient virtues, sane and simple customs;
> farewell, noble and proud sentiments, unselfish life, calm and gen-
> tle. The age of gold replaces the golden age.[93]

Bishop Granjon, as is apparent from this observation, was not
oblivious to the cultural and social consequences of the encounter
with capitalism, but he overlooked the violence that accompanied
the new order and blamed the Nuevo Mexicanos for maintaining
"a core of indolence and a habit of incurable improvidence" and
for not resisting exploitation more vigorously.[94]

But Rev. Granjon also praised Nuevo Mexicanos for their
strong family traditions. The bishop had gone to Las Cruces to
administer confirmation. He expressed surprise that rather than
young people he was confirming infants, as dictated by the custom
of Mexicans. The cries from the babies interrupted the sermon,
which he preached in both Spanish and English, although he observed that the vast majority of his audience were Mexican or
mestizos. "This was apparent from the tanned complexions, the
shining black eyes, the abundant ebony hair, and the brightly
colored outfits." The parents and children were accompanied by
the padrinos and madrinas who, the bishop said, were honored to
have been asked to be sponsors. From that day on, the padrino
or madrina would "be considered as member of the family, and
is treated as such until death." The bishop survived the crying of
babies during the lengthy ceremony and observed:

> When everything is finished, the mammas gather up the babies,
> calm their crying, and dry the little cheeks flowing with sweat and
> tears. The godfather and all the family return home joyful and con-
> tent, determined to celebrate "twice in twenty-four hours" [baptism
> and confirmation] the beauty and sweetness of *compadrazgo*.[95]

The Mexican traditions which the bishop admired were complemented by the work of his clerical countrymen:

What good and fine missionaries France has given these distant missions for the past half century! The Latin blood and Gallic character adapt perfectly to apostleship in Mexican lands. Were it not for the admirable work of these valiant apostles, the mestizos, left to themselves without guidance, would long ago have lost the faith and reverted to a near-savage stage.[96]

Their work was sustaining a faith planted by the Spanish missionaries which had "issued forth such great roots that the revolutions . . . have not succeeded in making a dent in it." To emphasize the devotion of Hispanics to the faith, the bishop quoted a "sublime" epitaph on a humble Mexican monument:

TO THE MEMORY

OF MY CHERISHED WIFE.

SHE HAS LEFT ME

LEAVING IN MY HEART THE PAIN

FROM WHICH SHE SUFFERED

AND FROM WHICH SHE DIED:

THE LONGING FOR THE CELESTIAL HOMELAND[97]

Along with the hope of eternal life, it was the bonding of the community, Bishop Granjon discovered, that enabled the people to endure life on the frontier:

Relations of all degrees, neighbors and acquaintances, make a rule of visiting the sick, to attending to the dying. Each one helps, and contributes from what is his. Should a young mother leave this world, the *compadres* take on the task of raising the young family. Orphans always find those who will adopt them, and it is not rare to see large families grow indefinitely by the acquisition of new wards: one more mouth in the house, posh, is that all! The job is, moreover, singularly simplified by the completely natural lifestyle, naked of pretense, where false needs are rigorously excluded. In many homes poverty is great, but no Mexican ever dies of hunger. . . . The spartan frugality of these fine people equals their endurance and blunts the sense of deprivation.[98]

Family and social relationships were particularly important in the new era, when Nuevo Mexicanos found themselves in crisis: "These multiple attachments, mostly between families, maintain the unity among the Mexican population and permit them to resist, to a certain extent, the invasions of the Anglo-Saxon race."[99] While the battle could not be won against the "invaders," victory was sought for the spirit.

In time the mission outpost of Las Cruces evolved into a faith community with a permanent pastor. With a head start provided by outside assistance, the proud parishioners of Las Cruces organized themselves in the 1920s to fund various projects and to help one another. Some women in the local chapter of the St. Vincent de Paul Society made clothes for the needy, while others ran an employment referral service. Other ladies used the rectory kitchen to teach American cooking to young girls so as to make them eligible for domestic service. Still others assisted the Sisters of Loretto in the school. The men organized a chapter of the Boy Scouts. An advertisement in the Extension Society magazine brought books for the local public library. Nearly all the project membership lists in the parish bear almost an equal number of Anglo and Hispanic surnames, attesting to cooperation not always present elsewhere.[100]

Church-community events in Tierra Amarilla in northwestern New Mexico were different in some respects from developments in the southern end of the state, but they also reveal the social and cultural changes introduced by the American economy. The celebration of Santiago (St. James) in 1916 in Los Ojos (Park View) included a procession that involved practically everyone in the community. Among the participants were some twenty young men mounted on the best steeds of the district "gaily decorated with pink, white and blue ribbons, and strings of small tinkling bells around the necks of the horses." The two hundred Apache Indians who had come from quite a distance added color to the occasion. The day was replete with events:

> After the religious celebrations of the morning, there were games, races, etc., in the afternoon, followed by dancing in the evening. We witnessed some of these races, [in which] the Indians and the Mexicans rac[ed] barefooted on the rough roads. They also had hurdle races as well as a baseball game, and on the following day there was horse racing.[101]

Reference to the hurdle races and to the baseball game reflects the extent of cultural change even in a rather isolated area with few Anglo Americans.

One prelate also observed race/class differences among Mexican Americans:

The Mexicans of this part of New Mexico are of the more refined class . . . it was quite an eye-opener, and indeed a consolation to note the refinement and geniality of a portion of these people.

Upon inquiry as to why these people seemed so much superior to the ordinary Mexicans found on the outskirts of our cities, [I] was informed that these were more of the Spanish type [probably meaning, lighter-skinned] and besides most of them had been born in New Mexico itself. . . . Then, too, there was another reason—they live alone [isolated], and own the land, raising sheep and cattle in abundance.[102]

Clearly, native-born "Spanish Americans" with land resources and established village traditions fared better than Mexican immigrants. The former were not completely unaffected by market forces, as the mention of sheep and cattle raising indicated, but they had a secure base, as compared to the immigrant who was uprooted by the larger capital-intensive system and driven across the Southwest, settling impermanently in slums in the outskirts of the region's cities.

The growing economy in Tierra Amarilla region during World War I and in the early 1920s permitted improvements to parish structures, but these were not carried out without some controversy. First, a large, sturdy new school was constructed. Then the parish debated over what to do with the old church, the roof of which was on the verge of collapsing. Some argued that a new building was needed, while others, possibly for sentimental reasons, urged that it be repaired. The latter won out, but only temporarily, because the church was eventually torn down. In its place a new rectory was built, and the community came together to celebrate the blessing of the structure.

But dissent broke out again when parishioners discovered that erecting the new church would entail the "desecration" of the old *camposanto* (cemetery). The Depression also stalled the building project but did not kill it. To save money, the men of the parish, including the pastor, el Padre Teodosio (Father Theodosius Meyer, O.F.M.), made over a hundred thousand bricks. An architectural solution was found to the problem presented by the old cemetery, and the church was constructed after the town recovered from the *año de la nevada*, the severe winter of 1931, and when the Depression had eased. When completed, the new structure was graced by the old stained-glass windows as well as some new ones imported from Germany. The church had "a harmony and beauty of color" beyond words. After the solemn Mass and blessing, Ignacio Torrez organized a dance held at the Mayflower Pavilion, where all parishioners, Mexican Americans and Anglos, celebrated the community's accomplishment. The cultural melting pot so evident in that final event characterized the mix of peoples and traditions in this corner of New Mexico.[103]

Mexicano faith communities in the metropolitan areas faced greater problems than those in established rural areas. In Dallas, for example, Mexican immigrants chronically suffered from tuberculosis, meningitis, and influenza, all aggravated by the lack of food and proper clothing. The newcomers had been brought to Dallas in the early 1900s by labor contractors who had recruited them in Mexico for employment in the Midwest but abandoned them in Texas when jobs farther north dried up. Fortunately, Mexicanos were served by the Daughters of Charity, who teamed up with the Vincentian Fathers to establish a settlement house (converted from an old warehouse) which included a free clinic. Volunteer doctors, nurses, and social workers from St. Paul's Hospital treated more than two thousand individuals in 1923 at the clinic. Those needing more medical attention were given further care free of charge at the hospital.

The Dallas Catholic Ladies League funded a kindergarten that provided education and served breakfast and lunch to the Mexicano children. Within months the kindergarten was expanded into a school, which opened in 1925 with about four hundred students. A new school went up two years later, built with Extension funds and other donations, and shortly thereafter a high school, providing a "commercial education" for girls, was constructed. At the blessing of the new structure, the "Hidalgo Band" added favorite Mexican hymns to the clergy's traditional "Veni Creator Spiritus."

The Church's work among Mexican Americans in Dallas was begun by exiled Mexican Vincentians, who had joined their religious brothers in that city. The priests first ministered to the immigrants in 1914, celebrating Mass in a store near the railroad switching yards. Within two years the Vincentians coordinated the building of a small church dedicated to Our Lady of Guadalupe that served the community until a bigger structure was erected in 1925. Besides providing for the spiritual and temporal needs of Mexicanos, the pastor of the immigrant flock battled Protestants and the work of the National Mexican Catholic Church. The latter organization had been created by the anticlerical President Plutarco Calles and was brought to Dallas by an ex-seminarian. As more immigrants arrived in the Dallas–Fort Worth area, various other congregations of religious men and women ministered to the newcomers.[104]

Mexican immigrants also lived in other parts of the Dallas diocese, such as the Texas Panhandle. Catholic Irish railroad workers had settled there in the late 1800s and were joined by German farmers who had been attracted to the area by the boosterism of the early twentieth century. As the region was converted from semiarid plains into agricultural fields, and as oil and natural gas were discovered in the region, Mexican laborers started moving in, and churches with names like "Sagrado Corazón" and "Nuestra Señora de Guadalupe" began appearing in the many small towns that serviced the hinterland.[105]

The presence of the Ku Klux Klan made race relations in nearby West Texas particularly bitter. In Abilene, Father Henry Knufer, who served the Mexicans of the area, was the target of the Ku Klux Klan on at least two occasions. The first time, he was told he would be shot unless he left town (Colorado City, Texas). On the second occasion, he received more than just a threat. Armed Klan members came looking for him in the middle of the night. With their car lights turned off, they drove up to the house of a Mexican parishioner with whom the priest was staying, entered, and searched every room. Father Knufer escaped their wrath only because, being bald and the night being very cold, he was wearing a nightcap, and the Klan intruder mistook him for the family's grandmother. His startled hosts probably did not recognize him either.

Mexicanos had come to West Texas with the first Anglo-American settlers in the late nineteenth century, but the Mexicans were nameless. A parish history lists the Irish, the German, and the Anglo Catholic families in Abilene in the 1880s and adds:

> Joining these early pioneers of old American and European stock at Sacred Heart were undoubtedly many Mexican families, most likely ranch hands and farm workers. Their traditional Catholic faith brought them to the parish for worship, for "doctrina" [catechism] for their children's religious education, and to mark the great moments in life, birth, coming of age, marriage, sickness and death.

The relatively low status of Mexicans in Abilene is indicated by the transfer of their children by public school authorities into a building previously occupied by black children, who usually fared far worse than whites but who in this instance had been moved into a new structure. Even one priest is supposed to have "boasted to a

Protestant that he [the pastor] would have nothing to do with Mexicans," thus explaining why the bishop was sending in religious missionaries. As in other agricultural regions, the economy of West Texas confined Mexicanos to a racial caste system that guaranteed the labor supply but provided little room for social mobility.

As cotton farming spread to the Abilene area, the numbers of Mexicans increased significantly, and there was a need in 1907 to have a missionary come from Dallas to minister to the migrant workers who flocked into the area. Eventually the Abilene parish assumed responsibility for this ministry. A chapel, St. Francis, was erected for the Mexicans with funds from the Extension Society. In time, the old Sacred Heart Church (for Anglo Americans) was moved to the barrio to serve the Mexicans. At Christmas the "new" church resounded with "hymns and *alabanzas* (songs of praise) in true Mexican style and devotion" accompanied by musicians with violins. A priest from Mexico served at St. Francis and in the Mexican missions within a wide radius of Abilene.

Exiled Sisters of Our Lady of Guadalupe ran a school in the barrio. After they returned to Mexico, a lay teacher was hired until the school was leased to the public school system. Shortly thereafter the school was rebuilt into a four-room structure "in order to come up to the requirements of a modern school and [accommodate] the great number of Mexican children." Eventually, the Sisters of Divine Providence took over the school.

In the outlying areas of the parish served by the assistant pastor, "faithful and pious Mexicans" sometimes traveled long distances to a mission to worship at a monthly Mass. They helped with "all that [was] in their power" for the construction of a church. At times they came into Abilene itself from thirty miles away to request a Mass in fulfillment of a *promesa*, an action taken in gratitude for a favor granted by a saint. On one occasion, a Mexican man came in from a distant farm because he was sick and wanted to go to confession and make his First Holy Communion. The pastor apparently thought he was preparing the gentleman for Judgment Day, but the priest later found out the man had only come for "the best medicine."[106]

In San Angelo, a growing Mexican-American population seemed to be inundating the old Immaculate Conception Church, upsetting Anglo Americans to the point that they adopted a new name, Sacred Heart, for *their* congregation. When a new church was erected in 1906, it was blessed as "Sacred Heart," probably with the expectation that eventually the Mexicans would build their own parish. In the meantime, Sacred Heart was to serve all Catholics, the bishop decreed, and a carefully balanced building committee was formed to supervise the construction. Peace between the two groups reigned for some two decades until there was need to rebuild the church. By that time, Mexicanos worshiped in a separate building but remained within the same parish organization. When the issue of building a new church arose, the two groups quarreled over who would get the new structure. Once again, the Mexicans lost out.[107]

Hispanics in Denver, Colorado, also faced discrimination within the church walls. Helen Quezada La Roe recalls that Mexicans were "allowed" to use the basement of St. Leo's, the Anglo-American parish, for Mass and other liturgies. Her brother, for example, was christened in the basement rather than in the baptistery upstairs. Also, not all Mexicano children were admitted into the parish school.

Eventually, a second church, St. Cajetan's, was built for the Mexicans, and it quickly became the center of barrio life. During World War II, "Every house had a picture of a soldier and a flag from the dime store, and every time a telegram would come [informing a family] that someone had died in action, the bell at St. Cajetan's would ring and ring, and everyone would go to church and pray."[108]

In San Antonio, in the heart of colonial Spanish and later Mexican Texas, the Mexican and Mexican-American population declined throughout the 1800s, but it soared in the first decades of the new century. In 1900 the population of the city was about 53,000. Of these some 14,000 (26 percent) were Mexicans, most of whom were Catholics. Within twenty years the number of San Antonians zoomed to 161,000, with the growth of the Mexicanos, who numbered 60,000, accounting for almost half of the increase and 37 percent of the total. By 1930, the city's population reached 231,000, of whom 82,000 were Mexicans.

In 1910 Mexicanos were being attended spiritually by the Claretians, who were in charge of San Fernando Cathedral on the edge of the Mexican West Side barrio. A second parish, Immaculate Heart of Mary, also ministered to Mexican Americans. A third, Sacred Heart, was in the process of changing from a German to a Mexicano parish. At the same time, nine other churches served the Germans, the Irish, the Poles, the African Americans, and the Anglo Americans who made up the remainder of the Catholics in the city. Ethnic and Anglo parishes had been established as European and

American immigrants entered the state in the nineteenth century. Most of these newcomers had come with enough money to get reestablished as farmers, craftsmen, and merchants, and many of them brought their own clergy. By initially separating the Mexicans in South Texas into one vicariate—which seemed reasonable because of the distances—the bishops in the other dioceses (San Antonio, Galveston, and Dallas) centered their attention almost exclusively, it seems, on the European and American immigrants. Mexicanos in those dioceses were not ignored altogether. However, their presence originally in small numbers obscured their gradual increase. Thus, in 1911, San Antonio's Bishop John William Shaw estimated the number of Mexicans in the city at 20,000 when, in fact, the number was closer to 30,000 and may have constituted between a third and a half of the Catholics under his care in San Antonio.

As the city grew and the Mexican barrio expanded westward, children who attended the San Fernando Cathedral School had a greater and greater distance to walk, and when it rained and a nearby creek flooded, they could not get to school at all. A decision was made to build a school in the heart of the colonia, and some ladies from the parish sponsored a *jamaica* (bazaar), in which they raised the sum of $50. The opening of the school in turn gave rise to aspirations to build a church. So the parishioners began years of fund-raising, which by a decade later had netted them $2,000. At that point they petitioned Bishop Shaw's successor, the Rev. Arthur Jerome Drossaerts, imploring that "the poor Mexican people of the West Side were longing to see a temple in this city erected in honor of their patron, La Virgen de Guadalupe; that they could find neither peace nor happiness until they could kneel down and pray at the feet of la Virgen de Guadalupe in her own church."[109] With the work of the faithful and funds from the diocese and elsewhere, the temple was built with the appropriate dedication:

LOS MEXICANOS

DE

SAN ANTONIO

A SU CELESTIAL PATRONA

LA VIRGEN DE GUADALUPE[110]

Bishops Shaw and Drossaerts were recognized by the Vatican for their hospitality to the priests and nuns who fled the anti-clerical movement of the Mexican Revolution. But the American bishops faced a bigger task than just accommodating these exiled churchmen and women. During Archbishop Drossaerts' tenure, 1918–1940, as we have seen, the number of Mexicans rose dramatically. Even in the 1930s, when San Antonio's population expanded slowly in comparison to the previous decade—it increased by only 25,000 (half as much as in the twenties)—Mexicans accounted for 80 percent of the Depression-era growth. The lack of jobs and relief in the hinterland had driven Mexican Americans into San Antonio literally by the thousands. Given the circumstances, the archbishop concluded that he had "a Mexican problem."[111]

Part of the problem was his view of "Church." This issue arose indirectly in connection with the difficulties the Church was experiencing in Mexico. For the exiled Mexican hierarchy, which was well represented in San Antonio, Church meant "community." More precisely, a *Mexican* national community, and one led by them, of course. Bishop Drossaerts argued their case forcefully in the local and regional press. He hoped to help create a national consensus that would lobby Washington to put pressure on the Mexican government on behalf of the Church. But when it came to Mexicanos in San Antonio, Archbishop Drossaerts had great reservations about the implications of fostering the "Church as community" among the immigrants.

The problem did not have an easy solution. The archbishop of Monterrey had advised him that, for the faith to flower amongst the newcomers, the Church in San Antonio needed to identify with the Mexican-American community as it evolved and sought to define itself. The Mexican Church was struggling for a new definition in revolutionary Mexico. The challenge was not any less difficult for the American Church, but it had to be faced nonetheless.

To create a "Church as community" for the Mexicanos in San Antonio, Archbishop Drossaerts had to take up the issue of social justice. He eventually did, because he had genuine empathy with the plight of the poor, but with great trepidation and some ambivalence. The principal source of his hesitation was the fear that working-class movements were influenced by communism, which he abhorred ideologically. Any Catholic support of organized labor, he thought, would risk the Church's position within the larger community.[112]

Another part of "the Mexican problem" involved addressing the religious needs of the immigrant. At first Archbishop Drossaerts opted to have the Church attempt to save individual souls, awakening their dormant religiosity by invoking the name of *María*

Santísima (Mary Most Holy). He had to do this, however, before the Protestants got to the Mexicans. At one point he had been lulled into believing those who claimed that Mexicans could never be lured away from the faith. But he was disabused of this when he saw hundreds marching in a religious parade singing Protestant hymns in Spanish and carrying a large, float-sized open Bible. Various sects were sponsoring numerous religious and social events and organizing clubs to reach Mexican youths. Protestants also set up relief programs that provided financial assistance for families. More importantly, the incorporation of Mexicans and Mexican Americans into the ministry was attracting many to the Baptist, Presbyterian, Methodist, and Lutheran faiths.

Archbishop Drossaerts sought to define the challenge as a *"national* problem." The resources of the San Antonio see were small when compared to the extent of the poverty, the "ignorance," and simply the numbers of Mexicans. Beyond that were other challengers: the "Protestant proselytizers," the Calles schismatics, and the Communists. Drossaerts pleaded for assistance from the national Church to combat poverty among Mexicans and coopt its challengers. In time he received the help he wanted.[113]

The San Antonio Church addressed the crisis in a variety of ways. It cooperated with the Protestants to provide relief and health care. With funds from several sources, the Catholic Charity Board of San Antonio disbursed $151 million for relief and health-care services between 1929 and 1931 alone through a number of clinics, parish "health days," and sanitation projects. The work continued through the Depression, and deaths due to tuberculosis were cut by almost a third between 1939 and 1944.

The Church also promoted parish and diocesan associations of various kinds in West Side churches to create a sense of belonging to the parish community. New life was breathed into what would become the Catholic Youth Organization, the Holy Name Society, the Children of Mary, the Christ the King Society, and a few other organizations that involved various segments of the parish population. In addition, the Church established and expanded the Catholic parish school system. While including religious dogma, values, and morality cherished by traditional Catholicism, church schools taught in English and introduced American sports activities. The Church sponsored English classes after school hours and outside the school for adults.

To meet other needs of Mexicanos, the Church encouraged government involvement in the resolution of certain problems, such as housing. As we shall see, this involved allowing activist priests like Father Carmelo Tranchese to lobby the New Deal administrators and even the president of the United States. A group of clergy and lay men established *La Voz de la Parroquia*, a West Side Catholic paper that would communicate directly with the laboring class. The newspaper preached the gospel, but it also emphasized racial/ethnic pride, self-improvement, and social action. The paper enthusiastically called for the implementation of the social doctrine of Pope Leo XIII. But when *La Voz* began to focus on specific issues and concrete solutions, appearing to support labor unions, the archbishop stepped in to control it. Thereafter, *La Voz* became an organ to battle communism.

As the saga of *La Voz* indicates, Church efforts were not always coordinated. Archbishop Drossaerts, for example, denounced the protests of the Mexicano pecan shellers who had gone on strike because of poor working conditions and low wages. Drossaerts dismissed the claims of the strikers, alleging that the confrontation with the employers was Communist-inspired. Yet some parish priests encouraged the strikers and found ways to feed and clothe their families during the walk-out and afterwards, when they were replaced by automation. On another occasion, Father Tranchese worked hard for the government acquisition of property for the Alazán-Apache Courts and other housing projects, while the archbishop sympathized with the complaints of the owners.

The mixed reaction on the part of the Church could also be seen on other issues. For example, *La Voz* often wrote on "official" doctrine and on popular religious traditions. The paper also took up social justice issues forcefully, at least for a time, while the archbishop remained conspicuously silent. On another front, Catholic schools simultaneously taught in English and encouraged traditional Mexican spirituality.[114]

Father Tranchese himself exemplifies the ambivalent response of the Church. On the one hand, he became the hero of the underprivileged Mexicanos, supporting the pecan shellers, organizing relief and health care, operating Our Lady of Guadalupe as a national parish despite official policy to the contrary, lobbying politicians, and preaching the social gospel. There were people who would have gone hungry if it had not been for Father Tranchese. He was maligned and threatened, and when asked if that bothered him, he replied that he was more grieved by the thirty-nine funerals, mostly of children, in which he had officiated that month. In cultural matters, he revived old traditions like *Los Pastores*, offering don

Leandro Granados Pérez encouragement as he rewrote this traditional play from memory. But when confronted by the archbishop, Father Tranchese put aside his militancy and turned to preaching against materialism and advocating traditional spirituality.[115]

Still, the Church's effort in San Antonio, as elsewhere in the Southwest, was very energetic. At the start of the century, the parishes had provided the vehicle for the reestablishment of the communities the immigrants lost in the migration from Mexico. The newcomers contributed to the construction of their churches and schools, celebrated the laying of their foundations and their blessing, and took pride in those structures, the sturdiest and most beautiful buildings in the barrio. Certain Church feasts and school functions reinforced their identity and pride as Mexicans while the Anglo-American world discriminated against them. Traditional Catholic devotions energized their spirituality and complemented their religiosity, assisting the faith community to survive exploitation and change.

The Church was also instrumental in the survival of the Mexicano community in the Depression era, when workers migrated from the fields of South Texas and the Southwest to San Antonio and other metropolitan areas. Relief, health care, the support by the activist priests for the organization of the poor, and the pressure to get government to respond demonstrated to Mexican Americans that the Church was on their side. *La Voz* in San Antonio and the parish festivities and religious celebrations there and in other cities also helped Mexicanos retain their culture.

These activities were not exclusively class- or ethnic group–oriented, however. The Church was, after all, also committed to the Americanization of the immigrant. It promoted parochial schools that would teach in English and teach more effectively than the public schools. The Church also made the image of the Mexican less threatening and more acceptable to the dominant Anglo society. It did this by muting the radical interpretation of the gospel and refusing to support the workers' struggles publicly. However, the Church also empowered Mexican-American leaders to organize their parish communities and to work within the American system. In a sense, then, the Church promoted Mexican Americanism.[116]

Though the Church promoted and utilized the new identity, it did not forge it single-handedly. Once the newcomers realized they were in the United States for good, they opted to join labor unions and political organizations to better their lives, just as Mexicanos in the United States had done in the previous era. As before, too, twentieth-century Mexican Americans looked beyond the Church. Parish organizations continued to be important, but in the 1930s Mexicanos were more active and in more positions of leadership outside the Church than when they first arrived in the United States. In doing so, Mexican-American communities were redefining themselves more independently than before.

3

The Mexican-American Church, 1930–1965

The new political boundaries and the expansion of the American economy into the Southwest in the mid-nineteenth century were destined to change the ways Tejanos, Nuevo Mexicanos, and other Mexican Americans saw themselves and their community. The transformation from Spaniards and Mexicans to Mexican Americans had actually begun in the early 1800s, one could say, even before the outbreak of fighting that separated the northern provinces from their Mexican heartland. As the full force of the American economy set in, the cultural impact became stronger. Certainly, the proximity of the area to Mexico and the constant arrival of immigrants from Mexico, especially the huge waves of newcomers in the early 1900s, delayed full acculturation. But the process of cultural change moved forward and gained great momentum with the experience of World War II and the movement to the cities. Indeed, the mid-twentieth-century developments were crucial for the development of a "Mexican-American" generation.

Of course, cultural change is seldom swift, uniform, or rational and logical in all respects. In the Southwest resistance and rebellion had existed side by side with the trends of accommodation and integration. Thus, while earlier the "bandits" had struck against the encroachment of the new American order that dispossessed Mexicanos of their land and disrupted the security of the old patrón-peón system, other Mexican Americans involved themselves in merchandizing and sent their children to American schools in order to compete more effectively in the new system. The poor adjusted, too, producing cash crops and competing in the new cattle markets wherever they could. Economic interaction, limited as it was, involved cultural exchanges. Thus, the participants in the Primer Congreso Mexicanista held in Laredo in 1911 at once denounced their children's loss of the Spanish language and Mexican traditions because of Americanization in the schools and at the same time called for a curriculum that would prepare the next generation more efficiently for life in the United States. This dialectic of sorts resulted in compromises that eased the difficult transition into the new society.

A New Generation and Americanization, the First Stirrings

The flood of new arrivals in the early twentieth century disturbed the adjustment that the settlers and earlier immigrants had worked out with the American system. The most troubling aspect of the new situation, as we have already seen, was the anti-Mexican backlash, the brunt of which long-time Tejanos and Nuevo Mexicanos were not spared. Previously those groups had been allowed some participation in the new economic and political system because their weak economic condition had limited their influence to certain localities. But the "hordes" of Mexicans that appeared on the scene in the 1910s and 1920s threatened to tear down the cultural and social boundaries set by the dominant Anglo-American group. New controls and greater repression then fell on all Mexicans.

Tejano, Nuevo Mexicano, and Mexicano leaders looked for new solutions to deal with this reaction, and they came upon a campaign to have Mexicans learn English and become citizens. In 1921 the principle proponents of this movement in South Texas founded the Organization of the Sons of America. The group's members hoped to exploit the clout that would result from the participation of Mexican Americans in the political process. Only a few years previously Tejanos had been disfranchised by new voting registration requirements (the poll tax law). But as the numbers of Mexicans grew, the possibility of their becoming politically active was very promising. The Sons of America splintered soon after its founding but regrouped at the end of the decade under the League of United Latin American Citizens (LULAC). The new organization dedicated itself "to develop within the members of our race the best, purest and most perfect type of a true and loyal citizen of the United States of America." With this goal, LULAC hoped Mexican Americans would gain respect for their culture, bring an end to segregation and discrimination, and secure equal participation in American political and economic life.[1]

Through a delicate balancing act, middle-class LULACers sought to integrate a "great" Spanish heritage with an equally admirable Indian tradition. They also spoke in glowing terms of American culture, achievements, and democracy, and of course stressed loyalty to the nation, beginning all meetings with the Pledge of Allegiance and the hymn "America the Beautiful." But the Americanization process was not uniform. Some members did not abide by the rule requiring the exclusive use of English at the meetings. Certain chapters, too, continued to celebrate the Diez y Seis and the Cinco de Mayo, and some LULAC publications carried stories that emphasized the uniqueness of Mexican-American barrio culture.[2]

There was, however, no ambiguity in the LULAC position on segregation. Leaders argued that since Mexican Americans were white there was no legal basis for excluding them from establishments open to the public, from juries, and very importantly from the schools. LULACers were persistent in their efforts to tear down barriers in these areas and were not beyond employing what were then considered to be radical tactics, such as leading school children and their parents in marches across town to register them in the better "Anglo" school. Amidst controversy over succumbing to "compensatory" tactics, LULAC also backed the establishment of "Little Schools of 400 [Basic English Words]," the precursor of the Headstart program, for Spanish-speaking preschoolers.[3]

Middle-class Mexican Americans carried on the fight in other arenas. The School Defense League of San Antonio pressed the school board for equality in educational facilities. Journalists decried police violence and highlighted social and health problems among Mexican Americans. Politicians engaged in machine politics in order to reap improvements for the barrio and to have access to higher offices. The battles were valiantly fought, but the system was so closed and the forces arrayed against the civil rights activists so great that they had few tangible victories. This absence of substantial breakthroughs, along with the tinge of elitism and racism on the part of the leaders, has obscured the sacrifices of the early struggles.[4]

In its drive for inclusion in the dominant society, the middle class tended to ignore the plight of the poor and to view the efforts of Mexican-American labor organizers as class strife unworthy of truly loyal citizens. The Depression had caused Mexicanos to doubt the efficacy of the much-touted American capitalist system, encouraging them to turn instead to a revitalized Communist party and to the tactics of confrontation, strikes, and even violence. A dual wage system—one salary for Anglo Americans and a lower one for Mexicanos—bred deep resentment among smelter workers in El Paso, for example. Those workers joined the Congress of Industrial

Organizations (CIO) and cooperated with the Confederación de Trabajadores Mexicanos to prevent strikebreakers from interfering in the labor protests. For the El Paso workers, class and ethnic solidarity, it turned out, were not incompatible with loyalty to the United States, as the middle class had alleged.

The same strategy proved to be a winning formula for Mexican-American mine workers in Arizona and Colorado who were organized under the banner of the Asociación Nacional México-Americana. Successful in labor conflicts, some union workers then proceeded to address other issues, such as the plight of undocumented workers, housing needs in the Southwest, education, political representation, youth work, police violence, and the promotion of Mexican-American culture.[5]

Part of their success was due to their relentless efforts and part to the changes wrought by World War II. The war changed American—and Mexican-American—society profoundly. Millions of American men and women left their homes to defend their country. To supply them and wage massive war on two continents, the government poured billions of dollars into defense industries, reviving a Depression-wounded nation and attracting thousands of farm families into the cities. When the GIs returned, they could draw on their families' savings from wartime earnings and, better still, they received veterans' benefits for education, health, and housing, allowing them to join the middle class.[6]

Mexican-American society also changed dramatically. Thousands of Mexican Americans had joined the armed forces out of a sense of duty and patriotism. Long derided as not being fully Americans, Mexicanos in the Southwest saw participation in the war as an opportunity to prove their loyalty to this country, their parents' new homeland. They fought valiantly, garnering more Medals of Honor than any other group. They also experienced a radically different environment in the armed forces. Not only were they pulled out of the isolated regions of the Southwest, but classified as "whites," they served in integrated units and were treated with far greater equality than they had received in the Mexiquitos.[7]

When the veterans returned home, they organized the American GI Forum to secure their rights. Not bound by middle-class "propriety," the new organization took up a stronger activist role than LULAC. The Forum gained notoriety in a number of protests, including the famous Three Rivers incident. Like other South Texas towns, Three Rivers had separate cemeteries for Mexicans and for Anglo Americans. In the case of Three Rivers, however, the Mexican cemetery was not actually in the town or on the outskirts but in another community nearby. The arrangement had gone unchallenged until the body of a Mexican-American World War II soldier was brought home for burial and the family insisted that it be interred in Three Rivers. When local authorities refused this request, the GI Forum came to the family's assistance. The ensuing controversy received national coverage, bringing attention to the discrimination and segregation Mexicanos were subject to in Texas. There were many other wartime confrontations and numerous complaints to officials and to newspapers that reflected how participation in the war had motivated Mexican Americans to change the communities in which they lived. Clearly, many hoped the war against Nazism would become a war against discrimination, but substantial changes had to wait for the men to come home.[8]

NEW MIGRATIONS AND NEW CRISES

For returning Mexicano GIs, "home" often was not where it had been when they had left. During the war a combination of forces had drawn Mexican Americans to the cities and indeed outside the Southwest altogether in great numbers. Defense installations and industries attracted thousands to metropolitan areas such as Corpus Christi, San Antonio, Houston, Dallas, and Austin; Albuquerque and Santa Fe, and Detroit and Chicago. At the same time, a government-to-government arrangement between the United States and Mexico (the Bracero Program), brought thousands of Mexican temporary guest workers into the Southwest. These laborers displaced Mexican Americans in agricultural work, and their reports of the money that could be made in the United States encouraged a new wave of legal and illegal immigrants from Mexico. Responding to these forces, many Mexican Americans flocked to the cities, where better jobs and greater opportunities for mobility could be found. In contrast to the socioeconomic structure of the agricultural areas, urban economies offered more occupational "steps" which skilled Mexican Americans could climb. Thus the postwar industrialization of the Southwest and the demise of segregation made some social mobility possible.[9]

Other Mexicanos, however, were caught in the trap of migratory labor. For the migrants, the cotton route extended from the Lower Rio Grande Valley north to Nueces County (Corpus Christi) and from there east to the Houston hinterland and north through San Antonio or Central Texas to West Texas, and then on to Colorado and the Midwest. Sometimes the trek was made by individual families driving in their cars alone or in caravans to help one another out with repairs. Most often, families rode in truck beds outfitted with benches and with a tarpaulin for cover. In order to make the trip worthwhile, contractors piled as many migrants into the trucks as possible.

The entire migration was an odyssey. Gas stations along the way would not let the travelers use bathrooms, and they rarely stopped at restaurants, since they had brought their own food to save money. In fact, stops were infrequent, since the truckers were in a hurry to get the workers to the fields. So many migrants made the journey north so often that it came to resemble life's pilgrimage, encompassing the joys and sorrows of the critical passages of birth, coming of age, marriage, and death.[10]

Once at their destination, families sometimes lived in abandoned barns or chicken coops, sleeping on barren floors or on sacks filled with hay. More critically, work was not always as available as the contractors and owners had promised. And when it was, the wages were very low. Two-thirds of the South Texas migrant families, according to a 1945 study, earned less than $400 a year, despite the comparatively large number of workers per family (3.8). Those traveling to Michigan for beet work fared only slightly better. Perpetuating the vicious cycle was the migrants' late return to the home base (end of September, early November) and early departure (end of April, beginning of May) that prevented the children from completing their academic year in school.

Tragically, the migrants fared better, at least in the short run, than those who stayed in South Texas, where unemployment was high in the off-season and health conditions were deplorable. In Texas counties where Mexican Americans were 20 percent of the population, the death rate from diarrhea among children under two years of age was 85.1 per 100,000 in the population, more than eight times higher than elsewhere in the state. In counties with 50 to 60 percent Mexicanos, the rate was 129.4 per 100,000. Zavala County (Crystal City) had the highest death rate for children under one year of age, 141 per 100,000 live births. The lowest rates were in cattle counties like Starr and Zapata, but even they were fifteen to twenty points above the almost exclusively Anglo-American counties like Dallas (36.7).

Conditions were not much better in cities like San Antonio. In the early forties, Mexican Americans comprised only 40 percent of the population but had approximately the same number of live births as Anglos. Stillbirths for Mexicanos were about twice those of others in the population. Maternal deaths related to childbirth were six to seven times higher; infant deaths were three to four times higher. The most shocking statistic is the ratio of deaths resulting from diarrhea. From 1940 to 1944 mortality rates due to diarrhea were fifteen to twenty times higher for Mexican Americans than for Anglo Americans. Refrigeration, clean water, properly covered sewage facilities and pipes, and generally healthy living conditions—factors that would have reduced the high death rates—were still not available in the San Antonio barrio.[11]

The health statistics do not distinguish between Mexican Americans, long-time Mexican immigrants, and recent arrivals, all of whom were increasing in significant numbers. Mexicanos already here had high birth rates, and newcomers, some with passports, most without, were arriving every day. The latter mixed in with braceros and with Mexican Americans and thus were not easy to identify and trace. But clearly the immigrants began the process of reestablishing communities and finding their identity in their new environment. They replenished the agricultural labor pool while contributing to the migration to the cities. The newcomers entered at the bottom of the economic ladder, giving the impression that Mexicans had not experienced any social mobility. In fact, however, a middle class had emerged, and it and certain segments of the laboring class were being culturally transformed into Mexican Americans.[12]

MEXICAN AMERICANS AND THE CHURCH

The formulation of the new identity required bridging the Hispanic past and the American present. Among the Mexican-American intellectuals who attempted this was Carlos Eduardo Castañeda, a very talented and prolific historian. In his seven-volume *Our Catholic Heritage, 1519–1950* and in several other books and articles, Castañeda described "the Spanish-speaking" as a people with deeper roots in this continent than the Anglo Americans. Castañeda did not intend, however, to exalt the "Mexican" over the "American." In fact, the thrust of his work was to present a synthesis: the merging of the Indian and the Spanish, the Mexican and the American. To be sure, there were conflicts between Mexicans and Anglo Americans, but according to Castañeda, these resulted from political and economic, rather than cultural, differences. If bias existed, it was due to a lack of understanding. This was being remedied, however, by the work of the Church, whose task had always been to create a universal family.

For Castañeda, the Church also provided the link between the Spanish past and the Mexican-American present. The Church was at the center of Texas's Spanish heritage, and it was the one institution from the pre-1836 period which could be reestablished and reinvigorated in the American era and which survived into the mid-twentieth century. Echoing the reports of the Spanish missionaries and of the first American ecclesiastics in Texas, Castañeda painted a glorious, romantic Catholic Spanish past dominated by the friars (but without any Indians or mestizos as contributing members of society), a wounded, disintegrating Mexican Church, and a triumphant Anglo-American Church. In his admiration of the Spanish Church, Castañeda overlooked conflicts between the friars and the Indians and the role the local Church played in the frontier communities. He also depicted a heroically dedicated American Church ministering to what appeared to be rather passive Mexicanos.

The challenge for Castañeda and his generation was to find a new definition of the emerging Mexican-American society. Because of his own historical training, which stressed the development of institutions, Castañeda selected the official Church, rather than the faith community, as the core of his definition. The Church was, after all, a stabilizing force and the only ally Mexican Americans had. From this perspective, then, Castañeda could not admit any wrongdoing on the part of the Church, although he himself recorded—uncritically, to be sure—some of the statistics that demonstrate how the Church favored Anglo-American parishioners. More troubling, however, is absence in Castañeda's work of any mention of the vital Mexicano religiosity when it was precisely that spiritual inheritance that led him and others in the Mexican-American middle class to look to the Church in time of crisis and change.[13]

Indeed, the rising middle class put great hope in the Church, participating from the 1930s through the postwar era in activities and organizations that furthered the Americanization of Mexicanos. Members of the middle class assumed leadership roles in parish societies. They established Mexican-American sports clubs and other organizations that were modeled on their Anglo-American counterparts. They joined the Knights of Columbus and the Catholic War Veterans rather than the remnants of the Mexican nationalist clubs their parents had formed. The men became Boy Scout leaders, bequeathing the patriotism of World War II to the next generation. Well versed in the official doctrine, they were pro-clergy and were more consistent than the laboring classes in church-going and in worshiping in the standard liturgy. Most importantly, they attempted to define not only what it meant to be Mexican American, but also what it meant to be a Mexican-American Catholic.[14]

SURVIVING MEXICAN NATIONALISM AND POPULAR RELIGIOSITY

Yet the cultural transformation from Mexican to Mexican American was far from uniform. The new wave of Mexican immigrants kept alive many of the old religious traditions, and the Church did not risk everything on the Americanization process. In fact, given the immigrants' sentiment of being in exile and the discriminatory treatment they received from Anglo Americans, some priests at times appealed to Mexican nationalism to strengthen spirituality as well as to unify the community. A hymn made popular during the Cristero Revolts against the anticlerical government of Calles was often used in Mexicano churches long after that conflict was settled. The lyrics included:

> Reine Jesús por siempre,
> Reine Su corazón
> En nuestra patria,
> Y en nuestro suelo.
> Qué es de María la nación!

> May Jesus reign forever,
> May His heart reign
> In our country
> And in our land.
> For the nation [Mexico] is Mary's!

And a hymn to Our Lady of Guadalupe proclaimed in the refrain that she was clearly mestiza:

Y era mexicano, y era mexicano
Y era mexicano Su porte y Su faz.

Her looks and her demeanor
Were Mexican, very Mexican.

In keeping with the promotion of a certain amount of Mexican
nationalism, the Church did not discourage informal traditional
devotions, and chapels not officially affiliated with the Church
continued to function as before. In San Antonio, the tiny "Chapel of
Miracles" on Ruiz Street attracted many who went there to ask for
a special favor or to thank their favorite saint. As in the churches,
worshipers at the chapel would leave photographs, small images
of arms or legs, crutches, or notes as testimonials of the healing
they received. Photographs of a relative in uniform would be left
there as reminders to the saint or to the Virgin that servicemen
needed protection.[15]

In South Texas, a small house in a tiny settlement near the
Rio Grande Valley city of Alamo became a shrine when its owner,
Mrs. Saenz, found a broken mosaic of la Virgen while working in
some fields nearby. Mrs. Saenz gave the image a place of honor in
her bedroom, but once word of this finding got out, her neighbors
dropped in to see the image. An observer described the shrine in
the 1950s in this way:

> Over the years the shrine has grown. New pictures have been
> added. Vigil lights have been lit. Candles have been set about the
> room. Tinsel and decorations have accumulated. Little altars have
> been placed around the central figure. So many gifts have been
> showered upon the Virgin that the original little mosaic is almost
> lost among them. . . .
>
> In the war years local citizens called to the [armed] service[s]
> brought offerings and parents came to pray for the safe return of
> sons. Veterans returned to give thanks and left their uniforms as
> gifts to the Virgin.
>
> Today the room is always crowded with humble worshippers
> and [is] truly the center of the village.[16]

Another common religious practice among Mexican Americans
was *la promesa*, a commitment made to a saint, la Virgen, or Christ
to perform a special act, such as the saying of a special prayer, the
wearing of a religious garb (a scapular or a religious habit or dress),
or the making of pilgrimage, in return for the fulfillment of a favor.

Keeping a promesa is a serious obligation, one that may involve an expense if it requires a pilgrimage. To cynics, making a pilgrimage sounded like a good excuse to take a trip, but fulfilling a promesa was a *manda*, a duty not to be taken lightly. Priests discouraged the faithful from taking vows of this kind but had little success in changing this tradition.[17]

Priests also preached against the curanderos, but Mexicanos nonetheless availed themselves of healers and folk medicine. Cures for a variety of ailments called for the use herbs and ointments administered with *oraciones* and *ensalmes* (prayers for healing), practices that continued to be employed, despite some improvement in health care in the postwar era. Unspecified "sickness," for example, could have been attributed to *el mal de ojo* ("the evil eye" or, better still, "sickness from the eye"). This illness originates when a person with "strong eyes" casts his/her sight on someone out of *envidia* (jealousy) or even admiration. When this is done out of admiration, the one casting the spell needs to protect that person by stroking or touching his or her face to prevent the sickness. Illness from the mal de ojo results, not from the spell, but from not performing the required cure, which involves the prayers and rituals of a curandero. Other ailments, such as *empacho* (an undefined stomach illness), *el mal puesto* (a curse resulting from envy), and *susto* (fright), are among various psychosomatic illnesses said to need special attention by relatives and healers. A "bad back" or spasm can be cured by the soothing skilled hands and prayers of the *sobador*, the barrio chiropractor/rezador.

These traditions were not new, or indeed unique, but were revived with the movement to the cities of more "traditional" rural workers and the arrival of a new wave of immigrants from Mexico. The Church inveighed against these practices as "superstitious," but it could not set out to eradicate them altogether without destroying the popular religiosity that inspired them, a spirituality the Church itself promoted in order to animate the faith. As before, in the postwar era, then, the Church enjoyed a central, but not exclusive, place in the faith communities.[18]

PROTESTANTISM

As before, too, the Church faced increased proselytizing by Presbyterians, Methodists, and the evangelical sects, which were establishing churches that formed small, close-knit communities. Protestant churches attempted to do more than save souls; they addressed a variety of social and economic needs of barrio residents. For their part, Mexican Americans gave the Protestant invitation an increasingly more positive response. Converting to a new religion at times became an expression not only of personal change, but of acculturation.[19]

This may not have been evident to the priests who were on the front lines of defense against new, more forceful proselytization. Indeed, the clergy tended to think Mexicanos converted because there was "something in it" for them. A McAllen priest described the conversion in this way: "There are a lot of Protestant churches which have sprung up around here. . . . They have a lot of money, and the people of little faith run to them for bread and candy and whatever else they will give them. But if one of them gets sick, they call for the priest right away."[20]

Priests also mocked Protestant ministers, calling them *ministrillos*, "little ministers," implying that they did not have the training and status that priests had. In fact, Mexicano ministers were not given the training that Anglo-American ministers received from their churches, nor were they paid as well. But Mexican-American ministers acquired leadership in the community, something which priests often did not have or chose not to exercise.[21]

The fight was not one-sided, however. Protestant proselytizers entered the barrio "with the gift of loose tongue," one priest wrote angrily. "They present themselves to their Mexican brethren in sheep's cloth to do their destructive work, with the Bible in one hand but in the other they hold the book of insults and calumnies against Holy Mother Church and lie and defame with venom-swollen lips." The accusation had some truth, but must be taken in context. In contrast to the priests, who were working with a constituency that was already Catholic, the Protestants preached a competitive gospel, one which required a rejection of old ways and old institutions. Sometimes that gospel was virulently anti-Mexican Catholic.[22]

Indeed, Protestant churches saw their role as one of remaking Mexicanos culturally and spiritually, that is, Americanizing and converting them. To do this, Protestants had to change cultural traditions related to leisure pursuits and to emphasize getting ahead in American society. One director of a Protestant settlement house said that members of his community were "very puritanical-minded. They are strongly opposed to beer-drinking and other 'loose habits' of the people of the community. [He himself] has to be careful what he does and where he is seen. If he goes into a *cantina* [bar] looking for someone he wants to see, he is sure to get back to the faithful *pronto*." This "puritanism" was deemed necessary to counteract the alleged "low morals" of the Mexicanos.[23]

In fact, stricter discipline was required of Mexicanos than was demanded of Anglo-American Protestants within the same sects. Leaders, thus, tended to keep the two groups apart, lest problems result from the double standard. If, for example, Mexicans would see the Anglo-American elders smoking, it was claimed that they would conclude that all the restraints were off. Then, one pastor explained, "the inevitable consequence would be drinking, dancing, and finally prostitution and adultery."[24]

The connection between conversion to Protestantism and social mobility was also clear in the minds of Catholics and Protestants alike. One scholar observed of a Mexican subject that "most of the members of his church are trying to get ahead and feel that it is necessary to raise the standards of the whole group to do this. He mentioned a little Methodist church nearby where 50% of the members are professional people, doctors, and lawyers primarily."[25]

Those who got better jobs or became professionals moved out of the barrio but often returned to attend church there. At work converts may have received better treatment from their Anglo coreligionists. It thus may be that conversion to Protestantism was perceived as a means of getting ahead. It stands to reason that, if for Mexicanos religion and community went hand in hand, some Mexican Americans who were redefining who they were may have seen joining Protestant churches as part of their new role in American society.

The Protestant communities, which were considerably smaller and often more homogeneous than the Catholic parishes, were able to meet the needs of their members and establish communal bonds more easily in a rapidly changing society. One priest suggested that to meet the Protestant offensive the Church needed to quit building large church structures and establish a parish every four to six blocks.[26] As evident and simple as that suggestion was, to implement it the Church would have had to redefine the role of the clergy and indeed to redefine the meaning of "Church." Some bishops and priests were in the process of doing just that, but this was not an easy challenge to meet.

THE CHURCH IN THE POSTWAR PERIOD

With or without a Protestant threat, the Church faced the serious challenge of the increasing numbers of Mexican and Mexican-American Catholics, as the Church censuses reveal. The number of Catholics in the diocese of Corpus Christi, which had declined to 161,000 in 1930, jumped to 454,000 in 1950 and to 525,000 in 1960. During the same period, the El Paso see reached 200,000, an increase of 80,000 since 1930. The diocese of Amarillo was created in the postwar period, in part out of the El Paso territory, and by 1960 it could boast of 91,000 faithful, mostly Mexican Americans. In San Antonio, the figures showed the faithful, both Anglo-American and Mexican-American, rising from 182,000 at the start of the Depression to 380,000 thirty years later in 1960. That year Catholics in the Galveston-Houston area, which had been receiving more Mexican Americans and Mexican immigrants than ever before, numbered 412,000, tripling the 135,000 Catholic population of 1930. Mexicano Catholics had also increased in the new diocese of Austin as well as in the Dallas–Fort Worth metroplex, which had reached 121,000 and 119,000, respectively, by 1960.

In the Santa Fe see the number of Catholics climbed slowly in the 1930s, going from 145,000 to 165,00 in 1940. Then it more than doubled during the forties, reaching 430,000 in 1950, and then jumped to 600,000 by 1960. These increases do not include the 200,000 Catholics in the Gallup diocese. The size of the neighboring Tucson see zoomed from 95,000 in 1930 to over 1.6 million in 1960.[27]

The Church's response at the parish and diocesan levels to the postwar demographic increases and to the work of Protestant sects included a continuation of early twentieth-century policies. Principal among these was increasing the number of priests and women religious to administer the sacraments and teach the faithful Church dogma. Ideally, instruction would take place in Catholic schools, but there was also great emphasis on catechizing public school children. Parish organizations were encouraged, and programs were expanded to included diocese-wide meetings and conferences.

Even greater emphasis was placed on the Catholic school system. The number of parochial schools in the Corpus Christi diocese, for example, went from twenty-seven in 1930 to fifty-seven in 1960, while the number of students climbed from 5,000 to 15,000. In New Mexico the number of schools rose significantly during this period, from thirty-five to sixty-two, and the number of students tripled, from 6,000 to 18,000. Yet at the same time the Confraternity of Christian Doctrine (CCD) system for educating children who did not attend Catholic school received considerable support. From 1950 to 1960 alone, the number of those receiving this kind of religious instruction jumped from 22,000 to 45,000 in the Corpus Christi diocese. In New Mexico the number soared from 12,000 to 48,000.[28]

Women religious played an important role in the field of education. As teachers in the classrooms of the Catholic schools and in the parish CCD programs, Sisters carried out their mission often without taking a salary from the parishes. Some, such as the Sisters of Loretto, taught in the public schools of New Mexico for many years and used their earnings to finance other evangelization endeavors. Elsewhere, the education provided by the Sisters was generally superior to that of the still largely segregated "Mexican (public) schools." Catholic schools produced students who went on to high school and college and contributed significantly to the numbers in the Mexican-American middle class. Increasingly, most orders and congregations of women religious recruited more Hispanic candidates. New emphasis was also placed on recruiting Mexican-American men for the priesthood and for the religious life.[29]

But, as before, outside funds continued to be distributed unequally. Between 1930 and 1950 the dioceses of Corpus Christi (Mexican-American) and Dallas (Anglo-American) continued to receive about the same amount of funds from the Catholic Extension Society, a sum total of some $250,000, despite great disparity in the numbers of Catholics: 454,000 in South Texas; 67,000 in the Dallas see. The Commission for Catholic Missions Among the Colored People and the Indians granted Corpus Christi and Galveston the same amount of money, although Galveston had less than half as many faithful.[30]

Inequalities were also evident *within* the various dioceses. As the table demonstrates, between 1925 and 1951 funds from the American Board of Catholic Missions were distributed disproportionately among members of different dioceses. While the bishop of the Austin diocese, where there were relatively fewer Mexicanos, was funneling substantial funds to Mexicano parishes, Church leaders in other areas were not. In the dioceses where serious crises existed with the presence of thousands of poor Mexicanos, Corpus Christi, El Paso, and Amarillo, the Church was spending twice—

sometimes four times—as much on Anglo-American Catholics as on Mexican Americans. In San Antonio, where the numbers of Mexicans had risen dramatically during the 1930s, Mexicanos were receiving considerably less than their fellow Anglo-American Catholics. Ironically, Mexicans were the ones criticized for not contributing to the support of their parishes. Anglo Americans were better off and could put more in collection baskets, it is true, but they were also getting larger amounts of outside funds to build and staff their churches and schools than Mexicanos received. The Church was not ignoring the needs of Mexicanos, as the case histories and other evidence will demonstrate, but its commitment to them was far from complete.

American Board of Catholic Mission Funds to Texas Dioceses
1925–1951

Diocese	Dollars alloted to English-Speaking Parishes	Dollars alloted to Spanish-Speaking Parishes
San Antonio	159,800	115,000
Amarillo	173,100	40,000
Austin	45,886	40,000
Corpus Christi	182,800	70,000
Dallas	146,000	30,000
El Paso	178,000	70,000
Galveston	95,000	25,000

Source: Annual Report of Board, C.A.T., cited in Casteñeda, *Our Catholic Heritage*, p. 204

CASE HISTORIES OF FAITH COMMUNITIES:
TEXAS'S LOWER RIO GRANDE VALLEY

For parishioners of San Benedicto, as well as for many of the faithful across South Texas, one of the first major events in the postwar period was the celebration in 1949 of the 100th anniversary of the arrival to the area and to Texas of the Missionary Oblates of Mary Immaculate. Other statewide Church-related centennial observations—the arrival of the first Vincentians to Texas (1938) and the creation of the first diocese (1947)—passed unnoticed in South Texas. A solemn Mass had been sung in front of the Alamo in 1936 as part of the festivities of the hundredth anniversary of Texas

Independence, but few, if any, Mexicanos had attended it. However, the centennial of the Oblates' arrival in Brownsville in 1849 was celebrated by the clergy and the Mexican-American laity in the Rio Grande Valley in a major way, with a parade, a field Mass, and many other events. Numerous priests and prelates, many civic officials, dozens of Church organizations, and thousands of Mexican Americans were in attendance. Each Oblate parish in the Valley prepared a float: San Benito's depicted a cleric kneeling before a statue of the Blessed Mother, Weslaco's portrayed a priest saying Mass surrounded by angels, and another float showed the Oblates in a ship arriving on the Texas coast. There were bands from the area's high schools and from institutions in the Mexican cities along the Rio Grande.

The festivities involved many celebrations. At the center, of course, was the arrival in the area of the American Church in the person of the Oblate Fathers. All the speeches and sermons made reference to the prior neglect of the people by the Mexican Church and to the dawning of the new era. The participation of a great many Protestant Anglo Americans attests to the celebration of the beginning of American rule, the "introduction of civilization" into this "once benighted" Mexican territory in 1848. Appropriately, the festivities were in Brownsville, a town founded by Anglo Americans immediately after the U.S. War with Mexico. For Mexicanos the occasion was also very meaningful. Most of the participants were first-generation Mexican Americans, and they had important roles in this celebration. Interestingly, the floats and decorations displayed Indian, Spanish, and Mexican themes in an attempt to define who Mexican Americans were as a people.[31]

A little over a decade after this celebration, in 1962, San Benito's parish commemorated its fiftieth anniversary. San Benedicto Church was packed on the day of the ceremony, and the civic center, rather than the parish hall, had to be used to accommodate the crowds on that freezing morning. The church service began with the usual procession as the choir and the clergy intoned the Te Deum, which was followed, symbolically for this new era, by the congregation singing "God Bless America." Bishop Adolph Marx "urged the people of San Benito to be conscious of the heritage of sacrifice and accomplishment of their forefathers." The children of the immigrant generation now made "St. Benedict" their community.[32]

The role of men among the new generation had changed in the faith community. St. Benedict's fiftieth anniversary brochure lists the members of the Catholic War Veterans and the Catholic Men's Club and board members of the Cofradía de Doctrina Cristiana (Confraternity of Christian Doctrine). The men apparently took pride in their participation in parish activities, as is evident from the photographs. Clearly men's associations had assumed an importance in parish life that they did not have before. There was also an acolytes' club, the only male group that listed any Anglo Americans. Interestingly, none of the men's organizations were celebrating a golden anniversary, but their presence nonetheless indicates a new role for men and boys in the faith community.

Women undisputedly played more important roles in the life of the parish than men did. The numbers of men are actually very small when compared to the long lists of names in the women's organizations. Young women, for example, overwhelmingly outnumbered the men among those receiving teaching certificates for the catechetical program. There were half a dozen women's groups dedicated to devotional activities, but those societies also fulfilled many social needs at different life stages. Pre-teen girls who joined the Junior Sodality of the Blessed Mother, for example, could later continue as Hijas de María, the organization for those who had not yet married. Beyond that, there were a number of groups for adult women, married or unmarried. The photographs suggest that certain organizations appealed to women at different ages and possibly different economic levels. Reflecting the still very Mexican character of St. Benedict's community, most of the groups had Spanish-language names. There were two notable exceptions, the Junior Sodality and "Las Damas Católicas—NCCW." Their names imply the acculturation of the school-age girls and the wider American affiliation (National Conference of Catholic Women) of the latter organization. Both of these groups listed one Anglo American each. As before, women evidently continued to use the Church as an important center for their activities outside the home. Those activities—devotional, fund-raising, social—remained very Mexican culturally, but even that was changing somewhat.[33]

Shortly after the Golden Anniversary of the parish's foundation, different associations, such as the Vela Perpétua, reached their fiftieth year. On the occasion of la Escuela Guadalupe's celebration a large crowd turned out for the unveiling of a picture of la maestra Carmen, the school's first teacher. A photograph of one of the festivities shows the aged "Padre Yvo" (Tymen) being escorted by Father Eugene Cañas, O.M.I., one of two Mexican-American

San Benito–born priests. After a century on the Rio Grande the American Church had become an integral part of el pueblo.[34]

These expressions of community did not imply absence of division between the clergy and the people. Some of the priests maintained that Mexicanos were not truly part of the Church. For one cleric in South Texas Mexican Americans did not meet the criteria set by the Church:

> There are about 10,000 Mexicans in McAllen. If we get 1,800 of them out to mass on Sunday we are doing very well. Everyone has the idea that when it comes to deep faith, nobody can beat the Mexican people, but it's just not true. Of course, we have a few whose faith is so deeply embedded that they will never lose it, but most of these people don't even begin to measure up to my idea of what faith should be. They tell me it's too far to come to mass if they live ten blocks away from the church, but that's ridiculous because they will go downtown every day, to the stores or to the movies. Yet they don't come to church because it's too far away.
>
> I get all kinds of answers when I talk to them about it. And they have very peculiar ideas of what faith is. One will tell me, *yo soy muy católica* [I am a very Catholic woman], and when I ask them when they were in church last, they say, *tres o cuatro años pasados* [three or four years back]. And yet they still believe they are *muy católicas*. Some say, *toda mi familia es muy católica* [my entire family is very Catholic], although none of them have set foot in the church in years.
>
> We are lucky if we reach 10% of the men and 25% of the women. I don't believe these people were ever very religious. They are so matter of fact about their faith.
>
> Most of them won't even feel that it's necessary to have a church marriage. I have had cases of people who came to me and asked me to tell them what the church marriage would be like. After I would explain it to them, they would say, well, we'll go get married by the judge because we're not satisfied with the church marriage. They think of it as two alternatives, either a church or a civil marriage, when actually there is no alternative, there is only the church marriage for those who believe. I think that most of those who do go through a church marriage just do it because they like the ceremony of it and want to be married in the church [building].[35]

For this priest, being *muy católico* was not good enough; the test of Catholicity was attendance at the liturgy and getting married in the

Church. For the Mexicano, "being" Catholic was a matter of identification, of "belonging" to the faith community, not necessarily
of complying with regulations.

But clerical leadership took up a new importance in the formation of the urban communities. In the postwar era, larger numbers
of Mexicano youngsters attended school and fewer worked in the
fields, presenting new kinds of challenges to parish priests. Minutes from a meeting of the District of Mercedes, a subdiocesan
unit which incorporated several South Texas towns, reveal the
dilemmas of the post–World War II era:

> The subject of youth work was discussed in the theological-pastoral
> conference. The comparatively recent growth of the CYO in the
> Valley was reviewed and it was generally agreed that all should
> cooperate in its program. Methods of reaching the sub teen-age
> groups were then discussed. The Boy Scouts, Boy's Brigade, inde-
> pendent parish youth clubs, the Junior CYO, etc., were all suggested
> as means of reaching the thousands of children [educated] outside
> the parish schools and who receive only the bare minimum of
> catechetical instruction. It was agreed that the problem will remain
> essentially the same: lack of parish school facilities, but that some
> substitute must be arrived at.[36]

In Mercedes, as elsewhere, the demographic explosion was met
head on with substantial resources invested in the youth and with
expectations that the strategy would benefit the entire parish:

> Much of the spiritual growth and development, particularly among
> the youth of the Parish, must be attributed to the immense program
> of the Confraternity of Christian Doctrine, officially erected in the
> Parish on May 3, 1953. Dedicated men and women give their time
> to the Christian Education of the children attending Public Schools,
> and today there are almost two thousand children of grammar and
> high school age under regular instruction twice a week. The work of
> the Parish Confraternity received a special impetus with the advent
> of the Catechist Sisters of Divine Providence who came to the Parish
> in September, 1955, and in a short time took the children to their
> hearts. Catechist centers are now to be found adjacent to each of
> the Public Schools, making it convenient for the children to attend
> as they leave school in the afternoon; a similar program is carried
> on in Santa Maria [a ranch community] and in every place in the
> surrounding countryside where a group of families reside. The net
> result is that over five hundred children each year have the privilege

of making their First Communion; in addition the children and adults being better instructed are more faithful in the practice of their religio[n].[37]

Unmentioned in all of the entries regarding the catechetical endeavors is the role of women as teachers. Lay women of different ages with different levels of education participated alongside the Sisters who directed the programs. Sometimes the lay women themselves filled the positions of directors of CCD, taught the classes, and cleaned the catechetical centers. In their dedication to the catechetical program, women were continuing to carry out their responsibility of passing from one generation to the next Mexicano culture and religion.

Religious education, of course, was also part of the continuing substantial effort made by the Church to establish Catholic grade schools. The entries for September 1943 in the McAllen, Texas, parish history describe the conditions of the school, the sacrifices of the Sisters, and spirit of community among the children and their parents:

> Our Parochial School opened with a registration of 180 children.
> The school buildings are in a deplorable state, the desks pitiful, the books scarce.
> We have six Sisters of Mercy teaching. Sister M. Alexis is Superior. The Convent is worse than deplorable—it's abominable! One must admire the virtue of these sisters who in such miserable living quarters go about their work so cheerfully. The home is a combination of two old houses. Army cots of the last war [World War I] take the place of beds. They [the Sisters] eat on the back porch (even in the winter) because there is no dining room. They have a small round table for six of them to study around. Most of them come from Irish families of Boston, Mass.—that explains their fine spirit. . . .
> With the purpose of buying new desks for the upper grades in the school, we have started a game among the children to collect half a mile of pennies. The kids are running wild around town to collect and beg pennies. The coppers are rolling in. One day last week there was a shortage of pennies in town. The bank phoned us to bring some in. [We had] $430.00 in pennies.[38]

The parish community was forged with the cooperation of priests and laity. In January of 1945, the merchants on Seventeenth Street in McAllen's Mexiquito met on their own initiative and unanimously decided to close their stores on Sunday in observance of the Lord's Day. During the Depression, they had opened them to better serve workers who no longer got Saturday off, though "the better of them [the merchants] were always sincere in their desire to remain closed." These were "very good Catholic men," from whom the priests had always "received their full [unsolicited] encouragement and assistance."[39]

A list of the principal actors in the McAllen parish in the mid-1940s reveals the humanity and spirituality of all involved:

1) Zenobio Cruz is sacristan and janitor. He is over sixty years of age, but the slowness with which he moves around gives you the thought of Methusalem. He has been sacristan since Sept. 1925. Honest as St. Peter. Faithful as Barnabas—but slow as molasses.

2) Ramon Guerra—business man and City Commissioner of McAllen—from one of the oldest families settled in McAllen, known for their respectability and deep Catholicity—has been a right hand man and an influential helper in all our projects.

3) Doña Vincenta Lopez—one of the old generation and for years a staunch helper in the Parish—is still going strong. Faithful as Sarah, Holy as Rebecca, Prayerful as Anna—she has the respect of all the Parish and can get other women to work. It is a pleasant sight when the women make a *cena* [a fund-raising supper] to see her in a chair holding the money box and occasionally sneaking a smoke. God bless her!

4) Father Gody, the best kind of an assistant any pastor could hope and pray for. Faithful, methodical, punctual and liturgically minded. Above all, a marvelous and zealous priest, working without stint.

5) Miss Trinidad De Leon—the fac totum of the Parish. Always ready to help in everything, Bazaars, etc., etc. A one-girl choir by herself. If she misses a service, it's an event. I wonder if she will ever get married?

6) Mrs. Lydia Guerra—a refined and intelligent woman, president of the Damas Católicas [Catholic Ladies], who never once refused to help in anything she was asked, and always has worked smilingly and cheerfully.

7) The Sisters of Mercy—the most cheerful and self-sacrificing and devoted group I have ever met. More than half of our work was done by them. They were indispensable in the care

of the children both of our school and the public schools and in the adornment, music, and other needs of the Church.[40]

As in all parishes, at Sacred Heart new societies were formed as the older organizations outlived the goals of their founders. One entry in the parish log for September 1955 notes the creation of the "Acción Católica," a group that functioned as an Altar Society to take care of cleaning the church and washing the altar linens. The parish historian added, with a bit of humor, that "an attempt was made to 'rejuvenate' the Damas Católicas (—the society, that is)."[41]

Not all aspects of parish life proceeded on an even keel. In the mid-1950s, declining vocations for the teaching orders of women religious created a crisis for Sacred Heart School. In 1958 the pastor described the troubled situation:

> Only have *three* Sisters of Mercy for the School this year. Sure discouraging! Beautiful school, beautiful convent—and no Sisters. And apparently no hopes in the foreseeable future of getting any more—and even these three are not guaranteed! If one of them got sick, there would be no replacement!

The explanation of the problem reveals racial issues among some groups within the Church:

> The Sisters of Mercy are crying about no vocations, but apparently they do not care about vocations of Mexican girls. That is the only thing I can see in it.
>
> In the last two years nine (9) girls from this parish (3 last year and 6 this year) have entered the Convents. All were graduates of Sacred Heart School—but none entered the Sisters of Mercy! Porque [Why]??[42]

The Mexican-American girls were probably joining the Missionary Catechists of Divine Providence, which was serving the larger Mexicano community in South Texas with catechetical instruction and social services. To meet those needs, the McAllen parish acquired property and buildings near the public schools so it could provide activities and religious education to the children in the late afternoon. Teenage clubs were also organized for social activities. A high school Bible class was started, and by the third meeting thirty-two students attended. Among these were three boys. "Qué milagro!" [What a miracle!], the pastor added.[43]

As the communities became more stable, and more Mexican Americans entered the middle class, more men participated in the ritual observances that were at the heart of parish life. Some traditional devotions, including the early morning *"Mañanitas"* [Morning Greetings], were occasionally not as well attended as expected. But processions and large open-air meetings continued to be popular, and they often included substantial participation by men. On occasion groups such as the Veteranos Católicos took part in citywide celebrations involving both Mexican-American and Anglo parishioners.

Religious fervor among the men had been visibly increasing since the introduction of the Cursillos, a movement that, as we will see later, employed psychological techniques that appealed to Mexican-American men. "We have almost thirty men . . . at *daily* communion," noted the parish historian. Indeed, the Cursillos revived the spiritual life of the entire parish. The six priests at McAllen were celebrating six Masses every Sunday in the main church and three at the parish mission. All the services were very well attended by their parishioners. "Don't know where to put them if any more came," confessed the pastor. Impressed with the fervor of the faithful, he remarked that there were "millions" of Communions. The Church had apparently touched the pulse of Mexicano religiosity.[44]

Middle-class Mexican-American men took up roles with their parishes similar to those of their Anglo counterparts. In October of 1955 the pastor organized eighty men to conduct a door-to-door census and pledge campaign to improve the Sunday collections. The process was systematized so that three years later the parish was divided into six districts, each with a captain and four workers who, on a given Sunday, fanned out throughout the city. Between Christmas and New Year, the parish's full supply of 1,200 boxes of Sunday envelopes were distributed and more were ordered.[45]

The rise of some Mexican Americans into the middle class obscured the continued poverty of others, a poverty sometimes overlooked by pastors, as demonstrated by an entry in the parish log for January 1962.

> The Valley was hard hit this month by the hardest and longest freeze on record. Looks very bad for all vegetables and fruit. Many trees have been ruined. Lots of people out of work. Sure a bad time to try to push for better collections to renovate the church.[46]

Indeed, social issues appear as interruptions to more important parish concerns. In November 1955 the bishop (Mariano Garriga, of Corpus Christi) ordered a clothes drive for the victims of a hurricane in Tampico, Mexico, and the pastor had to scurry around to find "a place to dump all the stuff." He was also upset that the bishop was sending some Mexican-American Sisters who would be engaged in "Social Work." Apparently, the pastor did not understand exactly what that involved, and Bishop Garriga did not explain. Garriga himself may not have known and was probably acting under pressure from Church leaders such as Archbishop Robert E. Lucey.[47]

It would take new leadership for social issues to be considered seriously, but not without resistance at the local level. The June 1966 entry describing the installation of the Rev. Humberto S. Medeiros as bishop of the recently created Brownsville diocese reveals the pastor's reluctance to be distracted from spiritual concerns:

> Archbishop Lucey did the installing & Bishop Drury of Corpus Christi gave the sermon. The talks from both sounded more like a union rally for "social justice" than the installation of a bishop.
>
> The Bishop [Medeiros] came to the diocese just as we are in the midst of a "strike" & march by the melon workers of Rio Grande City. They are seeking a minimum wage of $1.25 per hour for farm workers. Feelings are running high, pro & con. What a welcome for our new Bishop![48]

BEYOND SOUTH TEXAS

The Lower Rio Grande Valley of Texas was but one of the many centers for Mexican-American communities. El Paso, as we have seen, could boast of an even longer legacy and received many more thousands of immigrants. Communities there provided permanence for the Mexicano newcomers while the parish offered a sense of belonging. The most important day in the Santo Angel faith community, according to the pastor, was when the parishioners paid off the $46,000 loan for their church building on May 19, 1946. Their effort had begun in earnest during Lent eleven years earlier. After a parish mission for women, the ladies pledged to donate ten cents a week from the family budget to retire the debt. A decade later families were contributing ten dollars a month for this special project. The effort demonstrates the roles of women in the home, that is, as managers of the household budget, and in the Church as the financial supporters of the parish. It also reflects the pride of ownership in the parish.[49]

North of El Paso, in Las Cruces, New Mexico, the Great Depression brought Hispanics and Anglos at St. Genevieve's together. To save the parish money, the cleaning and repairs of the church were done by volunteers from both groups. The priest organized the unemployed men in the town to dig up mesquite roots for firewood, which was sold to the county. Special collections were taken up to buy medicine for a sick baby. There was even cooperation with the Methodists across the street. Periodically, the priest went out to the Civilian Conservation Corps camp for religious services.

The parish continued Mexican traditions, such as the Christmas *Posadas*, the procession with Mary and Joseph looking for a place in the inn, and the *Fariseos*, the guard at the Holy Sepulchre on Good Friday, now enacted with rifles instead of lances. But new traditions were also begun. On the Sunday after Easter, a play entitled "The Upper Room" was performed for both Spanish and English speakers. The work had been translated into Spanish by a Jesuit priest who had resided at Las Cruces. While the parish organized a boys choir, the school sponsored basketball teams for both boys and girls.

In the war years and in the 1950s, the parish exhibited some signs of full maturity. The pastor began to say Mass for residents at the other end of Las Cruces in a small chapel and catechetical center. This "mission" grew into Immaculate Heart of Mary parish in 1953. Four years later, the community celebrated the first Mass of Father David Viramontes, who had graduated from the parish's Holy Cross School. At the ceremony, "he looked quite sacerdotal in his gold vestments. . . . His father, José Viramontes, was in his Knights of St. Gregory uniform, and they had him assist in the ceremony as much as possible."[50]

Across New Mexico, as elsewhere in the Southwest, a strong tradition of home altars and *oratorios* (home chapels) continued into the twentieth century. The altars and chapels were usually built at the insistence of devout women of strong faith. Often they constructed these holy corners or rooms in their homes in appreciation for a favor granted by beloved *santitos*. The omnipresence of religious symbols in the home was also part of the transferal of culture and religious values from one generation to another, for which generally mothers were primarily responsible.[51]

The emergence of local clergy to some degree reflected the rise of a middle class among Mexican Americans by the 1950s. In San Antonio, West Side residents were moving out of the barrio to "mixed" areas, although many Mexicanos still attended Mexican parishes. This, despite Archbishop Lucey's prohibition against "national," or ethnic, parishes in favor of "territorial" parishes. San Fernando, Our Lady of Guadalupe, and other barrio churches continued to attract the faithful who had moved up into "nicer" residential neighborhoods. However, at some point, possibly when it came to time to send the children to school, loyalty to the old parishes began to wane.[52]

But poorer Mexican Americans continued to express their faith in traditional ways. The devotion to Our Lady of Guadalupe, for example, continued to hold great meaning for them. One observer remarked:

> The fact that the Mexican people, *la raza*, has had divine recognition, that the virgin would have bothered to cast her attention on the Mexican people—it's a great symbolic thing . . . there's nothing worse than being made to feel you're nothing, or that you're inferior. I think that's been a great source of consolation to many of these people, particularly the humble, who after all see that the Virgin took the shape of an olive-complexioned woman. In those churches (San Antonio) where the largest part of the congregation is the humble Mexican, a lot of emphasis is placed on the virgin, and you see the images of Our Lady of Guadalupe everywhere.[53]

Times had changed, and many Mexican Americans had improved their lot in American society, but continual immigration and an unjust social structure left just as many, if not more, in poverty.

The National Hispanic Faith Community: The Leadership of Archbishop Robert E. Lucey

Middle-class Mexican-American leaders of the post–World War II period, as we have seen, fought to bring about an end to discrimination in the schools and on juries, and members of labor unions battled specific employers, but few had the luxury to examine and analyze the economic condition of Mexican Americans from a national perspective. Across the Southwest, as elsewhere, the Church had encouraged the mainstream tactics of middle-class Mexican Americans when it recruited them to help save Mexicanos from the worst aspects of the Depression. This alliance had also preserved the traditional loyalty of Mexicanos to the ancestral faith. But poverty among Mexican Americans continued and was overlooked by many in the Mexican-American middle class and in the Anglo-American Church. In the postwar period, however, there emerged an ecclesiastical leader, the Rev. Robert Emmet Lucey, Archbishop of San Antonio, who would confront the Church and the nation with the economic sufferings of Mexicanos.

At an early age Lucey acquired identification with the working classes and he would never lose it. When Lucey was a little boy, his father had suffered a fatal accident while counting railroad cars by hopping from one to another, as required by "corporate tyranny" (unregulated companies). Lucey never forgot this, and later, after his ordination to the priesthood in 1916, he would take the cause of the poor to the public and to the Church hierarchy.[54]

As a young priest Lucey dedicated himself to furthering social justice. For example, he used the airwaves to explain *Rerum Novarum* and *Quadragesimo Anno*, the papal encyclicals that outline the principles of a just society, on the "Saint Anthony Hour," a program previously dedicated to devotional spirituality. When the radio show became too controversial for conservative Catholics and the bishop discontinued it, Lucey turned to endeavors that would reach the lower classes. At first he chose to promote the Confraternity of Christian Doctrine, a program of religious instruction directed at all children (including Mexicanos) who did not attend Catholic schools. Later he became a member of the ecumenical Ministerial Alliance in order to join forces with the Protestants in getting relief to the needy in the trying days of the Depression.[55]

In his first appointment as bishop, Lucey found Amarillo, Texas, a bitterly anti-Mexican and anti-Catholic town. Tensions there were such that, a few years before, while one priest preached to Mexicans, another cleric carrying a double-barreled shotgun guarded the church against attacks from an anti-Mexican crowd. This situation did not deter Lucey from creating a Bureau of Catholic Charities to assist poor Mexicanos or from insisting that Confraternity of Christian Doctrine programs in every parish reach the migrants. Lucey also established a diocesan newspaper in which he wrote a weekly column explaining social doctrine. He shocked pastors and parishioners when he ordered that all Church construction use union labor or at least pay union wages. He also urged Catholic editors in Texas and the nation to cease undercutting labor unions by implying that they were pawns of communism. Lucey startled his fellow bishops at national conferences by criticizing the American Church for espousing a spirituality based solely on individual virtues, exclusive of social justice. He advised the American Board of Catholic Missions that "a disordered economic system nullifies the best [evangelization] efforts of the Church and school." The Spanish-speaking, according to Lucey, suffered from a social order that was, in the words of the pope himself, "hard, cruel, and relentless in a ghastly measure."[56]

Because of his leadership in social justice on behalf of Mexicanos, Lucey was made Archbishop of San Antonio in 1941. True to his style, he launched an active Catholic Welfare Bureau that within a few years was sponsoring a maternity clinic, managed over $200,000 of health care for the poor at Santa Rosa Hospital, and handled over 400 relief cases. He called a two-week conference to educate the clergy on social justice. As one participant remarked, the presentations were "as far to the left as the thinking of the San Antonio Archdiocese had heretofore been to the right." Lucey also called another conference, which was attended by over 2,000 priests, Sisters, and laity, on the ideology and methodology of the Confraternity of Christian Doctrine. He believed that knowledge of the faith would move Catholics to action on behalf of the poor.

Lucey fought racism, calling segregation a "sin." He admonished a crowd at a rally for war bonds that the racism against which Americans were fighting abroad was alive and well at home, as evidenced by the anti-Mexicano and anti-black attitudes and unjust social structures that perpetuated poverty. Because of Lucey, San Antonio had a Catholic Interracial Council as early as 1945, one of the first such councils in the South. In 1954, six weeks before the Supreme Court handed down its famous decision, Lucey ordered the integration of Catholic schools in the archdiocese. He also supported the participation of priests and women religious from San Antonio in the civil rights marches of the 1960s. In addition the archbishop often composed letters to be read at Sunday Masses advising the faithful to vote in favor of certain social and economic issues and against others, bluntly explaining that promoting social justice was part of bringing about the kingdom of God.[57]

One of Lucey's favorite projects was the Confraternity of Christian Doctrine. For Lucey, the Confraternity program was the cornerstone of the edifice of Catholic social doctrine. Consequently, he sought to strengthen and promote the program in his own diocese and across the nation. In San Antonio he sponsored various training sessions for his priests so that they, in turn, would prepare the laity. He advocated home visits and neighborhood discussion groups. Beyond his archdiocese, he spoke at various national and international conferences on the need to establish the CCD. He invited Latin American prelates to examine the work of the Confraternity in San Antonio and subsidized instruction of their clergy on the establishment and operation of the program.[58]

Lucey also worked to increase the number of workers in the Lord's Mexicano vineyard. As archbishop, he supported the work of the Missionary Catechists of Divine Providence, helping Sister Benitia Vermeersch—whose ministry to Mexicanos began in Houston, as we have seen—to gain canonical (Vatican) recognition for the new organization. The Missionary Catechists came to be widely recognized for their success in merging the faith with Mexican culture. In addition, Lucey insisted that all his priests be fluent in Spanish so that all would be eligible to serve in Mexicano parishes. Those assignments had previously been viewed as undesirable. To prepare English-speaking priests for that ministry, the archbishop required them to take language courses, in which for a time he himself administered the final oral examination.[59]

Yet Lucey never fully appreciated the cultural differences between Mexicanos and Anglo Americans. In his eyes, for example, the Confraternity program was critical for Mexican Americans because the majority of this group attended public schools rather than Catholic schools. But he never addressed the issue of just how the CCD program would function most effectively among Mexicanos. He often insisted that CCD meant more than the rote memorization of the catechism and was not to be used solely for the preparation of the sacraments. Yet during confirmation ceremonies he quizzed the children in the traditional way. In one instance he walked out of the church without confirming a single Mexicano youngster, saying they had not been adequately prepared. For this and other slights, Mexicanos never came to view Lucey as a true pastor.[60]

Still, Lucey sincerely believed that the Confraternity program and his other endeavors would kindle the light of the gospel, which in turn would induce the powerful to end injustice and would arm the oppressed to secure their rights. To carry out those goals, he dedicated himself to working on the Bishop's Committee for the Spanish Speaking, which he chaired for over twenty years. At first he proposed the committee as a regional group and, later, as a national organization that would address the problems of Mexicanos in general and migrant workers in particular. He faced obstacles at every turn from other bishops who did not like his emphasis on the social needs of the faithful and who wanted the committee to work on strategies for outsmarting the Protestants.[61]

One bishop who presented innumerable objections to Lucey's endeavors for social justice was the Rev. Mariano Garriga from the neighboring, mostly Mexicano, see of Corpus Christi. When asked for a report on the scope of the Church's work among Mexicanos, Garriga claimed he made no distinctions between national/ethnic groups. The problem of migrants in his diocese, Garriga estimated, was minuscule and not worthy of special attention. Lucey fired back, pointing out that a state agency had enumerated 25,000 migrants in the Corpus Christi see. Garriga replied saying that he would attend to them only if Lucey provided information regarding their location.[62]

The archbishop of Los Angeles, John J. Cantwell, who had helped Lucey form the Bishops' Committee for the Spanish Speaking, disclaimed any problem in his diocese saying, "I cannot truthfully say that there exists here the discrimination that you describe in the Pastoral [Letter drafted for the National Catholic Welfare Conference]," which Cantwell and others refused to sign. Garriga and Cantwell, like other bishops, did not want any interference in their dioceses from an outside committee and were not as committed to helping Mexicanos as Lucey was.[63]

Still, the San Antonio archbishop continued to insist that the economic condition of Mexicanos was a regional, if not a national, problem. He pressed on and secured a committee less powerful than the one he envisioned, but one he thought would provide a fairly good vehicle for carrying out his agenda. But progress was slow, and the seventeen centers designated to attend to the needs of Mexican Americans tended to provide spiritual, rather than social, assistance. Nonetheless, Lucey's efforts did not go unnoticed by the Holy See, and the archbishop used that recognition (which he himself inspired) to pressure his reluctant brother bishops. Because of Lucey's efforts, the Committee for the Spanish Speaking drew public attention to the spiritual and economic plight of braceros and migrant workers. In 1942, the committee evolved into the Catholic Council for the Spanish Speaking, an organization with wider support and with links to the National Catholic Welfare Council. Lucey's ideas were also later incorporated into the National Council for the Spanish Speaking.[64]

None of those organizations succeeded in creating local diocesan offices that actively addressed the plight of poor Hispanics. Typically, those bureaucracies were not well-funded, encountered interference from bishops, and generally they were not open to suggestions from the people they served. Many of the directors and the episcopal board members themselves did not understand Mexican culture. Lucey himself admitted as much when he remarked to an assistant, "I'll never understand these [Mexican] people."

Despite his shortcomings, Lucey became the most ardent advocate for Mexican Americans among the Church clerics. He was a man of conviction and a determined administrator, although he lacked personal warmth. In the twenty-eight years of his episcopacy he toured the San Antonio barrio only once, shortly after his arrival. Thereafter, his forays were brief, only to churches where he was scheduled for confirmation, and then he preferred to send coadjutors rather than have to deal with Mexicans himself. Lucey's predecessor, Archbishop Drossaerts, had enjoyed walking through the West Side dispensing baskets of food to the hungry in the worst days of the Depression, but he had no idea of how to address the causes of poverty. Lucey, on the contrary, felt uneasy among the common people (some say with everybody), but he knew structural changes were necessary to eliminate poverty and drove himself and others to secure them. To the extent that he sought to end the exploitation of Mexicanos, he may have served them better than any of his predecessors since 1836.[65]

Lucey was the first prelate to examine the underlying problems of Mexicanos and admit the Church's complacency. He and a comrade in arms, Rev. Raymond McGowan, of the National Catholic Welfare Conference once drafted a pastoral letter that proclaimed:

> The greatest root of the trouble is that the first English-speaking people came here as conquerors and have tried ever since to rule as oppressors . . . instead of as brothers of the Spanish speaking in the development of a civilization that will bring both groups together. Yet the conquering attitude still prevails. Some of our English-speaking Catholics have accepted it against their Faith and against [the socially inclusive feast of] Pentecost. . . .
>
> Hardly anywhere in the United States is greater or more systematic injustice done to and suffered by the Spanish speaking of our dioceses. . . . The injustice done them is a disgrace. . . . [66]

Lucey and McGowan declared the crisis a challenge to all Christians: "So we [also] ask non-Catholics to pay and work for the health, education, economic welfare, civic betterment and incorporation into the community of the Spanish speaking people of our states."[67]

The problems were not resolved in the immediate postwar era—indeed, Lucey's fellow bishops refused to sign the letter—

but a new beginning had been made with a call to incorporate Mexican Americans into the Church and the national community.

A New Spirituality for a Transformed Local Community

The post–World War II urbanization experience created problems for the smaller, more personal Mexican-American community. While the cities offered new opportunities for economic mobility, life in the large urban areas militated against the social-cultural structures that had helped Mexicanos to survive major changes in the past. The anomie of the postwar city undermined the parish and barrio community, the compadrazgo, and the extended and nuclear family and placed a greater burden than ever before on the individual. Communal units did not, of course, disappear or become unimportant, but they would no longer play the exclusive and central role they exercised before.

The transformation was reflected in the emergence of the Cursillo Movement in the Church. Participants in this movement (at first, only men) underwent a three-day initiation of spiritual instruction ("Cursillo" means "small course"). The sessions were first presented in the United States by two laymen from Spain who happened to be in training in a Texas military installation in the 1950s, and soon the Cursillo movement spread like wildfire in South Texas. Hundreds of Mexicanos, many of them previously uninvolved in the Church, attended the retreat and returned to their parishes with a burning zeal for the faith, to the amazement—and to some extent the envy—of the pastors, the Mexican-American women who had been the pillars of the Church, and the Anglo-American middle-class churchgoers. The Cursillo was obviously providing something which the parishes were not.[68]

At the heart of the Cursillo were two critical elements: 1) strong lay involvement in the process, and 2) a deep personalization of the faith. Surprisingly, the movement offered little theological innovation, even though the Church was at that time being transformed radically by the theological reflection that led to the Second Vatican Council. In fact, Cursillo instruction repeated in very traditional terms the standard doctrine on morality, the basic tenets of the faith, the sacraments, the role of ordained ministers, and the authority of the Church. There was, however, critically important participation by laymen in teaching roles and a new existential perspective. The *rollos*, or lessons, were given by both priests and laypersons, and in both instances emphasis was on the meaning of the beliefs to the individual making the presentation rather than on abstract information. On one occasion, a bishop who was going through the Cursillo attempted to intervene during the reassessment conference at the end of the day in order to correct a doctrinal detail in one of the presentations. He was politely told that the conviction with which the point had been made far outweighed the issue of accuracy. To be sure, the participation of priest-leaders ensured fidelity to the core of Church teaching, but the Cursillo was not a catechism class.

The fact that ordinary men, not intellectuals or middle-class community leaders, were explaining what salvation and the sacraments meant to them had a powerful impact. Indeed, the personal testimonials of the Cursillo presenters encouraged what amounted to emotion-packed public confessions by the participants. The admission of serious sins to the Church community gathered at the Cursillo allowed the men to overcome the *machismo*, or male ego, that often prevented them from confessing to a priest. Indeed, baring their souls to other men made the telling of sins in the confessional much easier. By the same token, committing oneself to a new life before their fellow men became a matter of honor.

In an ingenious way, through the use of laymen, the Cursillo both sidestepped Mexicano cultural barriers and used tradition to strengthen the faith. It presented Christ as human and male as well as divine and called for commitment and loyalty to him and to the family and Church community, where his teachings were to be lived out. Thus, while the Cursillo emphasized individual conversion, something that resonated with post–World War II urban life, the movement urged the return of the Cursillista to the community.

The Cursillo validated the importance of ordinary men as individuals and as members of the community. In fact, the movement appealed to the poor and the common man. It also appealed to the ne'er-do-wells. On one occasion an individual turned down an invitation to make a Cursillo by declaring *"Yo no soy un borracho"* ("I am not a drunkard"). To be sure, the vast majority of the Cursillistas were not borrachos or outcasts but average Mexicanos struggling to make a living and to find meaning in their lives. The retreats provided Cursillistas with a powerful message which they took back to their towns and parishes, where they, simple men like the apostles, preached the message of salvation boldly, conveying the importance of the life of the Spirit for the revitalization of the individual and the community. Traditional middle-class leaders and pastors sometimes found the new converts obnoxious, yet they envied the energizing force they displayed. In time, the movement spread across class, gender, and ethnic lines, but it never had the impact on the middle class, on women, and on Anglo Americans that it had on working-class Mexicano males.

One observer claimed that the Cursillos were successful because "for the first time, instead of 'giving' us the faith, the Church recognized the life of God already within us, as individuals and as a people. The Cursillos called for the Church to go to the people rather than the people to come to the Church." Clergymen who viewed themselves as "bringing salvation" and middle-class Mexican Americans and Anglo Americans who saw themselves as the "leaders" were somewhat threatened by the assertiveness of the Cursillistas, who seemed oblivious of roles and of rank and distinction. To them, Christ's becoming a part of everyone's life gave equality to all.

Interestingly, the Cursillo predated both the Chicano movement and the Second Vatican Council, and the emergence of both of them appears to have undercut the Cursillo movement. The Chicano protests of the 1960s and early 1970s rose from the poor empowered by a variety of forces, including President Johnson's Great Society, and called for greater access to opportunity for all. Similarly, Vatican II emphasized the role of the People of God as the Church. In a sense, then, both the Chicano movement and the post–Vatican II Church were advocating visions similar to the one espoused by the Cursillo movement and both had wider acceptance than the Cursillo movement. Hence the latter's apparent "demise" in the 1970s and 1980s.

In any case, the Cursillo was never meant to become an organization like other parish or diocesan organizations and therefore it never created the structures that would ensure its continuation. As a "movement," it was destined to change. Yet it had a profound impact on the participation of Mexican Americans in "their" Church.

To the extent that the Cursillo called for an active participation in and "ownership" of the Church, it was a very modern movement. There were, to be sure, many traditional aspects to the program. The Cursillo, for example, appealed to Mexican-American men from the lower classes who did not appear to be assimilated into American society; it advocated traditional devotions; and the sessions and meetings were most often conducted in Spanish. But the movement did not espouse the type of Mexican cultural nationalism the Church had used in the past to revive the religiosity of the immigrants. Instead, the Cursillo addressed personal conversion, "giving witness" at work, and recruiting other devotees from among friends and acquaintances. It promoted individual leadership and encouraged parish and neighborhood organizations to animate the faith, endeavors that would eventually spill over into political activism. As such the Cursillo movement contributed to the transformation of the community from Mexican to Mexican American.

Summary and Conclusion

For over a century, from the time the American bishops accepted the responsibility of ministering to Catholics in the Southwest to the 1960s, Mexican Americans have maintained vibrant faith communities. The Church has nourished those communities by taking the sacraments to Mexicanos, sometimes in isolated ranchos, and instructing them in Church dogma. In towns where parishes were established, efforts were also made to provide schools. For decades priests tapped elements of the traditional Mexican spirituality in order to revive a faith they considered dormant because of neglect resulting from the anticlerical revolutions in Mexico. Many priests also clearly understood the necessity of responding to the communal longings of el pueblo, and to this end they employed processions, large gatherings, and ceremonies. They often complemented these techniques by invoking a type of Mexican nationalism.

Paradoxically, there existed a concomitant Americanization process. Besides simply providing education, Church schools usually began teaching in English, if not at first, shortly after their foundation. Father Ralliere, in Tomé, New Mexico, at the same time collected and preserved Spanish hymns and translated "America, the Beautiful," requiring it to be sung in his schools. The priests used traditional Mexican piety to revive the faith while insisting on the celebration of the holy days of the American Church calendar and the observance of the American Church discipline, such as abstinence from meat on Fridays. The French and American priests disregarded the architectural styles of the few existing church structures and erected European- and American-style buildings. Ideologically, the Church glorified the distant Spanish past, and except for fostering Mexican religious traditions that kept the faith alive, it generally attempted to ignore the Mexican social reality.

Nonetheless, as the historical record attests, Mexican Americans developed and retained their own spirituality. They did this in part on their own and in part with direction from the official Church, be it Spanish, Mexican, or American. The basic structure of that Mexicano spirituality can be summarized in the following

120

manner: A kind heavenly Father, together with a loving Mother, maintained the prescribed order of the community and watched over their children on earth. The trials and tribulations of life, including the exploitation that the people faced daily, were shared with the suffering Son, who through his death had made up for the failings of the children of God and had gained the Father's love and forgiveness for them. The day and week of Christ's suffering and death were, thus, the most holy of all celebrations. The *santos*, those revered holy men and women who had preceded the faithful and who took special interest in God's people, interceding for them, merited special commemoration as well.

This was especially true of the Blessed Mother, who appeared as the *Mexican* Nuestra Señora de Guadalupe. As such, she symbolized, and was of central importance to, the national faith community. She was also at the core of the family community and stood in for the Father, demonstrating his concern. A stanza in one of the most popular hymns to la Virgen reflects in a simple but powerful way the special and enduring personal tenderness of the relationship between the people and their Mother:

> Desde que niño nombrar te supe,
> Eres mi vida, eres mi vida,
> Mi solo amor.

> I knew your name [I could call upon you]
>   since the time I was little.
> You are my life, you are my life,
> My only love.

Like all belief structures, Mexican spirituality carried obligations and prohibitions. These centered mostly around communal responsibilities, particularly respect for and duties toward God and the saints and toward one's parents, padrinos, compadres, and neighbors. Blasphemies, lies, insults, and violence interfered with those relationships, particularly inner-group fellowship, and were therefore prohibited. Family relationships were close and lasting, and they carried obligations even beyond death, such as the commemorations on the Day of the Dead or on anniversaries. Beyond that, few things were of pressing importance, even official Church regulations. After all, the Church was a bureaucracy, with "made-up" rules that could be evaded or disregarded.

This is not to say the Church was irrelevant. It provided the basic rituals of entering into the community at birth (baptism, confirmation) and of leaving it at death. The Church played an important intercessory role with the Heavenly Father: it had blessings and prayers; it was the center of worship; it brought the community together. The churchmen and women who generously served the people were given respect and affection.

But the Church and the priests did not have a monopoly on those roles. There were rezadores and curanderos who invoked God's name and interceded with him. Like the priests, those individuals held power, and like the priests, they were also holy men and women, saints among God's people. As such, they commanded awe and respect, and their notoriety, along with their power, extended beyond their lives.

As Mexicans became more integrated into American society and culture after the 1930s, the relationship between them and the Church began to change. The first steps in the new relationship were taken in the 1930s, when the rising Mexican-American middle class and the Church joined hands to attempt to resolve some of the worst problems created by the Great Depression. Before this, in the 1920s, the middle class had been addressing discrimination in the schools and in the justice system. The Mexican-American generation that was the driving force of those reforms had evoked the Church's central role in colonial borderlands society and its continuing presence as a key contributing factor in the formulation of what it meant to be Mexican American. The middle class, then, shared the goal of Americanization with the Church and joined that institution in making the Mexicano more acceptable to the dominant society. At the moment of greatest crisis, during the Depression of the 1930s, the middle class assisted the Church in aiding the Mexicano community to survive hunger and disease and to stay within the political mainstream. Thus, the rising middle class and the Church worked together to prevent starvation and death among Mexican Americans as well as their cultural and social radicalization and alienation from American society.

World War II and postwar prosperity also contributed to the integration of Mexican Americans into American life. The commendable service of the new generation to the nation in wartime reaffirmed their sense of being American. The GIs then returned home after the war, demanding an equal place in society. They were helped with the veterans' programs for housing, health, and education that assisted all Americans in moving into the middle class. The migration to the cities during the thirties and forties was also critical for social mobility, since the urban economies, in contrast to the caste system in agricultural areas, were more complex and provided more employment "steps" that an individual could climb.

However, some Mexican Americans, particularly the more recent arrivals, remained trapped in poverty. This was especially true for those who had to migrate across the Southwest and to the Midwest in order to survive. For them, disease and death rates continued to be significantly higher than for the rest of the population. The middle class and the Church in the immediate postwar period, however, generally were oblivious to the plight of the migrants.

There was, however, one important Church advocate, Archbishop Robert E. Lucey. He committed the Church to social justice and involved it politically in that cause. He insisted that all the priests in his archdiocese be prepared to minister to Mexicanos in the barrio or in other parishes. He also worked to have the Church reach out energetically to instruct everyone, children and adults. His program for adult neighborhood discussions has an uncanny resemblance to the modern *Comunidades de Base*, small group communities. Very importantly, Lucey was instrumental in formation of the Bishops' Committee for the Spanish Speaking to lobby at the national level for structural changes that would combat poverty among Mexican Americans. Through that effort, he contributed significantly to meeting their economic and social needs and to their acquisition of a national group identity.

The formation of a national community for Mexican Americans did not preclude changes in the nature of the local community and of individual identity. At these levels the Mexican-American Church was being transformed by the Cursillo movement, a phenomenon that combined traditional Mexicano culture and spirituality with the post–World War II socialization processes Mexican Americans were undergoing. Urbanization and industrialization, accelerated in the forties and fifties by national and international developments, disrupted the familial bonds that held Mexicano communities together. Only a deep, radical personal renewal could restore the efficacy of those bonds. And to that end the Cursillo movement emerged, advocating the restoration of the role of males in the family and in community. The new role involved strength but not domination. Without challenging the authority of the clergy, the Cursillo movement also called for Mexican Americans to make the Church their own, reviving the unity of the faith community of colonial days. Not surprisingly, in this environment Mexicano vocations to the priesthood and the women's religious orders flourished.

Mexican-American women had, in fact, begun joining religious orders much earlier than men. This occurred in part because these groups were more open to Mexicans than the priestly ranks and because women religious played a number of roles, requiring different levels of education: teachers, catechists, social workers, and domestic helpers. The Missionary Catechists of Divine Providence, for example, recruited almost exclusively among Mexican Americans, and despite a very traditional training program, once in the field they responded to the cultural needs of Mexicanos.

The earlier inclusion of Mexican-American women in religious orders also reflects the longer and stronger participation of Mexicanas in the Church. Mexican women had always been the ones who, as mothers, *abuelitas* (grandmothers), and *tías* (aunts), passed on the faith to the next generation. They had kept alive the devotional fires in the community and had been the financial mainstay of the immigrant Church. To a large extent, it was their participation that kept the Church very "Mexican," while their very participation in the Church activities outside the home contributed to the assimilation of Mexicanos into the American world.

By the 1960s the Mexican-American community had been transformed. From the villages of Santa Fe and Taos and the Villa de San Fernando de Béxar in the sixteen and seventeen hundreds to the later migrant camps and barrios in the Southwest, the Mexicano community incorporated the traditions of centuries and adapted to new circumstances. El pueblo remained one even in its diversity and change, and the faith, with its various expressions, endured at its core.

As the Mexicano community survived wars and conquests, migrations and exile, exploitation, and social disintegration, it looked to the agonizing Christ and the Virgin who cried for the suffering of her children. El pueblo also called on Christ, the Blessed Mother, and the saints in its celebrations of unity and joy. The official Church was, of course, an important part of the Mexicano faith community. But at times the Church joined the conquerors and those who oppressed Mexicanos, just as at other times it led Mexican Americans in building community and finding security. National and internal changes in the 1960s and beyond would bring new challenges to which the Church and a subsequent Chicano generation would respond in different ways than Hispanics had responded in the past. Still, Mexican-American communities preserved a faith which was uniquely theirs and one that would perdure.

PART II

The Mexican Catholic Community in California

Jeffrey M. Burns

1

Establishing the Mexican Catholic
Community in California:
A Story of Neglect?

On Christmas Eve, 1969, Chicano activists clashed with Los Angeles police outside St. Basil's church as the cardinal archbishop of Los Angeles, James Francis McIntyre, celebrated midnight Mass within. The clash dramatically symbolized the growing tension between young Chicanos and the Catholic Church. One protester voiced a common perception among the protesters, "Any fool could see that the Catholic Church has done nothing for our people."[1] In the decade following the encounter, the protester's viewpoint became the standard historical interpretation of the relationship between the Catholic Church and the Mexican/Mexican-American community in California. Historian Manuel Servín wrote in 1970, "The Roman Catholic Church, aside from building churches and stationing refugee Mexican priests in Spanish speaking parishes, did little to aid materially or socially. Paradoxically it was certain Protestant Churches . . . that appeared to be most cognizant of the immigrant."[2] Two dissertations done at the University of California at Los Angeles in the late seventies agreed. One accused the Church of "failure . . . to involve itself in the situation of Los Angeles Mexicans,"[3] and the other stated that, "the Church's efforts to provide religious and social services to the newcomers failed miserably."[4] This perception also came to be accepted by Church representatives. In 1976, the Secretary of the Bishops' Committee for the Spanish Speaking, Paul Sedillo, observed:

> There is very little evidence that the structural Church was responding to the needs of the Spanish speaking, either spiritually or socially. . . . I need not elaborate because there was really very little done regarding spiritual and social needs. If anything, the Church practiced segregation between whites and Mexicans.[5]

By 1980, the fundamental perception was that the Church in California, and the United States, had failed its Mexican faithful.

129

These harsh judgments bewildered and angered two veterans of the "Mexican apostolate," Archbishop Joseph McGucken, and Rev. Augustine O'Dea, who viewed things quite differently. McGucken served as archbishop of San Francisco from 1962 to 1977 and had served as an auxiliary bishop in Los Angeles during the 1940s, where he had helped develop ministry to the Mexican community. O'Dea, a professor of pastoral theology at St. John's Seminary in Camarillo, the seminary for the archdiocese of Los Angeles, and longtime pastor of a small Mexican parish in North Hollywood, Our Lady of Zapopan, angrily denied the accusation that the Church had abandoned the Mexican. In a letter to McGucken in 1978, O'Dea attacked what he called "foolish misrepresentations and often d—— lies" being made by Sedillo and others. He urged McGucken to sponsor a course to "teach our young priests all that has been done—perhaps imperfectly—considering the great difficulties and poor resources, for the Mexicans."[6]

The difficulties to which O'Dea referred included the language barrier, the mobility of the Mexican migrant worker, deeply imbedded societal racism, the poverty of the Mexican worker, and a lack of Mexican or Spanish-speaking clergy. In 1942 O'Dea prepared a major study for the archbishop of Los Angeles, detailing the problems confronting ministry to the Mexican community and prescribing how those problems could be overcome. For the veterans of the Mexican apostolate, the Church had not failed the Mexican Catholic; given the magnitude of the demands created by nonstop immigration from Mexico, the Church had accomplished a great deal.

Regardless of one's attitude toward the Church's record vis-à-vis the Mexican/Mexican-American Catholic community, almost everyone has been concerned over the "loss" of the Mexican Catholic to Protestantism or other American faiths. The problem of "leakage," as it was called by previous immigrant groups, was ever present. In 1913 the newspaper for the archdiocese of San Francisco published an article entitled "A Sad Story of Neglect," which asked "will we American Catholics turn a cold shoulder to them [the Mexican Catholics] and drive them from Mother Church?"[7] Seventy-five years later the archdiocesan publication, the *San Francisco Catholic*, similarly cautioned: "A high percentage of the people in the Archdiocese cannot read this magazine. More than half the population here is Hispanic, many of them refugees or recent immigrants. Few priests can communicate with them, yet their numbers alone foreshadow or forewarn a future that could be lost."[8] As both quotes suggest, fear of losing the Mexican Catholic has been a key motivator in encouraging better ministry to the Mexican Catholic community.

Criteria for success in ministry to the Mexican-American community have fluctuated over the years, but one presupposition has remained constant and has been an enormous burden—the Mexican *is* Catholic and should always remain Catholic. The notion that a certain "loss" would occur with acculturation in America was inconceivable. Indeed within the Mexican-American community, the terms Catholic and Mexican were so intertwined in their identity that to convert to Protestantism was to deny one's family, country, and history. For all the worry, relatively little "leakage" occurred, though by the Church's own criteria any leakage was considered a tragedy and a source of guilt and regret.

Of greater concern is the underlying reason for leakage, what scholar Juan Hurtado has termed the "social distance" between the Mexican American and the Catholic Church in the United States. In his 1975 study of the problem, Hurtado suggested six basic reasons for the social distance: language, differing cultural value systems, power or the lack of it, lack of Chicano clergy, differences in ecclesial models, and the social status of the Mexican.[9] While all these factors contributed to what Church leaders referred to as "the Mexican problem," the overwhelming source of social distance between the Mexican and the Church, was the racism the Mexican American experienced in the American Church. The marginalized, segregated position Mexicans occupied in American society was simply reinforced by Church practice. Rather than experiencing the Church as refuge and mother, too often the Mexican experienced the same degradations and humiliations he or she had received at the hands of American society.

Like other immigrant groups, Mexicans were often disillusioned by the disparity between the promise of America and the reality. One immigrant expressed a typical reaction, "From Mexico we came to pick up gold in the streets, but we only pick beets in the field."[10] Similarly, immigrants coming from villages in which the rhythms of life were organized around the village Church and its seasonal devotions were disappointed, if not shocked, by the religious pluralism and secularism of the United States. One immigrant reflected, "this country is not like Mexico. One has no belief here. In Mexico we are *muy Católico*—very Catholic."[11] In addition, the Catholic Church they encountered in the United States was not the village Church they remembered from Mexico, but oftentimes a cold, bewildering institution. Again and again Mexican Catholics were made to feel unwanted or inferior. "Mexican only" signs attached to the last few pews of a church were common in southern California. The parish history of San Salvador parish near Riverside is typical: "In the 1920s, Mexicans were discriminated against in their own church. On Sundays, the priest would ask them to wait outside the Church until the Americans had entered. Then he would allow them to find places for themselves in the back."[12] Some priests were aware of the problem and tried to alert people to the damage it was doing. A speaker at the Priests' Conference on the Spanish Speaking for the Archdiocese of San Francisco reported in 1949:

> The people of San Jose's east side have largely been lost to the faith by reason of the lack of spiritual encouragement. They have been treated as unwanted and unwelcome intruders by Catholics who shrink away from them as poorly dressed and therefore unworthy to worship with them.[13]

The Mexican reaction was predictable. As one San Jose resident recalled, "Some of our people didn't feel they were very welcome [at the Church], so lots of times they just didn't go to church."[14] More than any other single factor, this treatment of the Mexican resulted in "social distance" between themselves and the American Catholic Church.

To acknowledge the Church's glaring failure in this area is not to disparage all the positive efforts of the Catholic Church on behalf of the Mexican/Mexican-American community as the many studies of the 1970s and 1980s have done. Church achievements have been neglected, in part, because few decent historical studies have been made of the relationship between the Mexican American and the Catholic Church in California. The majority of studies that have been done either lack a historical background or they are polemical. This study will attempt to correct this problem to some extent, by focusing on the Catholic Church in California and its relationship to the Mexican-American community during the period 1910 to 1965. Nineteen ten was chosen as the starting point of the study because in that year the Mexican Revolution began, and with it massive numbers of immigrants fled the turmoil it unleashed, entering California and the United States. The end date chosen was 1965 as in that year the Second Vatican Council came to a close. That year also marked the coming of age of the United Farm Workers. These two events inspired significant change within the Catholic Church, within the Mexican-American community, and in the relationship of that community with the Catholic Church in the United States. The greater part of the study will focus on southern California, since by 1930 over 75 percent of the state's Mexican population resided there.

THE NINETEENTH-CENTURY BACKGROUND

The discussion of leakage and social distance would have come as news to Bishop F. García Diego y Moreno, who in 1840 was appointed bishop of "Ambas Californias"—both Californias. García Diego and his able assistant González Rubio attempted to organize the remnants of the California mission system and establish regular church life in Alta and Baja California. In 1848 everything changed, as California was ceded to the United States in the Treaty of Guadalupe Hidalgo. The fate of the Mexican Californios (residents of California prior to its cession) in the last half of the nineteenth century was a bleak one.[15] They were stripped of their land, politically disenfranchised, and socially and economically marginalized. San Francisco's transformation into an "American city" occurred rapidly as the Gold Rush brought hordes of non-Mexican immigrants to the city in search of gold. In Los Angeles and Santa Barbara the transformation was more gradual, but by 1880 Anglo-American hegemony was a fact of life. The effect on the Californio population was devastating. In 1865, in an address to the California state legislature, Don Pablo de la Guerra, a native Californio, expressed their distress.

> It is the conquered who are humbled before the conqueror asking for his protection, while enjoying what little their misfortune has left them. It is those who have been sold like sheep—it is those who were abandoned by Mexico. They do not understand the prevalent language of their native soil. They are foreigners in their native land. I have seen seventy and sixty year olds cry like children because they have been humiliated and insulted. They have been refused the privilege of taking water from their own wells. They have been denied the privilege of cutting their own firewood.[16]

The depressed status of the Mexican community resulted in a steady decline in immigration from Mexico. After an initial burst of immigration from Mexico during the Gold Rush, immigration slowed to a trickle. By 1900 the foreign-born Mexican population in California numbered less than ten thousand.[17]

The status of the Mexican Catholic also changed. Out of respect for the large number of Spanish speaking in California, the first two bishops of California were Spaniards, Joseph Sadoc Alemany, O.P., and Thaddeus Amat, C.M. As the next century would show, the appointment of a Spaniard did not necessarily result in effective ministry to the Mexican community.

Despite their loss of power in San Francisco in the early 1850s, a significant group of Spanish-speaking Catholics continued to reside in the city. Alemany adopted a conciliatory attitude toward the recently displaced Spanish speaking and the newly arrived Mexican immigrants. Ministry was provided initially at St. Francis of Assisi parish in San Francisco, where a sermon in Spanish was provided at the 8:30 Mass on Sunday mornings. In addition, Franciscan Mexican priests, Prudencio Santillan and José María Suarez del Real, remained at Mission Dolores and Mission Santa Clara, respectively, in the early 1850s, ministering to the surrounding Mexican communities. In 1865 Father Gabriel Serrano was appointed by Alemany as *pastor hispaniorum* for the city of San Francisco.[18] Despite the ongoing ministry, by 1871 the Spanish-speaking community was in sad disarray. A group of Spanish leaders circulated a petition asking Alemany to establish a national parish for the Spanish speaking of San Francisco "to reestablish . . . the splendor, brilliance, and influence of our race." The petition reported that all other organizational efforts—political, philanthropic, and social—had failed to unite the Spanish speaking community, and that the Church alone was powerful enough to provide unity.[19] Alemany acceded to their request, and in 1875 he established Our Lady of Guadalupe parish *(Nuestra Señora de Guadalupe)* as a Spanish national parish, to provide better pastoral care for the Spanish-speaking residents of San Francisco, and to unite the Spanish-speaking community.

Alemany did not limit his attention to the Spanish-speaking community in San Francisco. Further south in the archdiocese large Mexican communities remained around Mission San Jose and Mission San Juan Bautista. In southern San Mateo County, another special parish for the Spanish speaking, Our Lady of the Pillar *(Nuestra Señora del Pilar)* was established in 1868. Alemany also provided a Spanish-speaking priest for the Mexican gold miners who lived in Sonora, California, in the 1850s. Furthermore, Alemany decreed, in the early 1850s, that the Mexican population could request a priest of their own nationality to perform their weddings, regardless of the parish they were in. As historian Michael Neri asserts, "Such a decree indicated Alemany's high regard for the Spanish-speaking Catholics in California."[20]

However, the institutional Church did not enjoy such amicable relations with the larger Mexican communities at Santa Barbara and Los Angeles. From the time of his appointment as bishop of Monterey and Los Angeles in 1853, Bishop Thaddeus Amat, C.M., demonstrated little sympathy for the Mexican Catholicism he found in his diocese. Amat set out to monitor the religious orthodoxy of his Mexican faithful and to bring them into closer conformity with the American Church. His efforts won him little popularity with his Mexican flock. In one of Amat's earliest pastorals he chastised the people for their careless attitude toward religious observances and the laxity of their moral behavior. As Neri points out, to many in the Mexican community, accustomed to the easy-going ministrations of the mission padres, the bishop's tone sounded judgmental and threatening rather than pastoral. Furthermore, Amat had little patience with Mexican popular piety. He prohibited many fiestas because he believed that their disorderly quality left the Church open to ridicule from Americans. Nonetheless, several fiestas were continued without official approbation. Other practices such as the rituals of the *curanderas*, or "folk-healers," were rigorously discouraged. In Santa Barbara in 1858 Amat suspended the Mexican Franciscans for (among other things) "fomenting superstition."[21] Their crime was that they tolerated Mexican folk customs, among which was the selling of burial shrouds. Amat contended that such practices amounted to attempts to "purchase heaven." The ancient practices were lost on him. Central to his objections was the fear that the "ceremonies, cults, and devotions of corrupt Catholicism" (a phrase used by one of Amat's priests in describing Mexican Catholicism)[22] would discredit the Church in the eyes of the increasingly predominant Anglo-American society. Amat's fears were not without substance. In 1855, a Protestant minister was aghast at the Sunday "observances" of Los Angeles Catholics. "What a spectacle. . . . Here in Sunday horse-racing is seen the fruits of Popery."[23] Similarly, a Protestant superintendent of the New Almaden mines described a Mexican religious festival celebrated at the mines as a "pagan riot."[24] To a Catholic churchman trying to show the compatibility of Catholicism and Americanism, the Mexican festivals may have seemed excessive.

At the center of the conflict, then, was the difficult switch from a Mexican to an American Catholic Church. The situation was aggravated by Amat's seeming lack of understanding of the social and historical context of post-Mexican California. His Spanish-speaking faithful "saw themselves as victims of American expansionism, who were being disenfranchised socially, culturally, politically, and economically under the new American regime."[25] Amat's policies and attempts to enforce strict discipline seemed like more of the same.

Despite the conflict with Amat, religion continued to permeate the daily life of the Mexican-American community throughout the nineteenth century. In the 1850s in Los Angeles, Mexican community life centered around the Plaza church located in downtown Los Angeles. Little distinction was made between religious and secular life. As one historian noted, the Plaza church "was the place where the community celebrated its traditional secular and religious fiestas, events which had a collective significance unifying the town and reaffirming traditional loyalties."[26] The numerous fiestas in Los Angeles were legend; central festivals focused on Holy Week, the feast of the Assumption, and numerous feasts in honor of Mary. One major fiesta, the feast of Corpus Christi, was celebrated several weeks after Easter, and was described by a contemporary in the following manner:

> On Corpus Christi Day, there was a procession around the Plaza. In front of their homes the wealthier families erected altars, many of which were decorated with satin, lace, and even costly jewelry. The procession started from the church after the four o'clock service and halted at each one of the altars in turn for formal worship, the procedure requiring not less than two hours, one feature being twelve men, who represented the apostles, carrying great candles.[27]

Most fiestas included bullfighting, dancing, and general feasting, all of which contributed to the general good spirits of the Mexican community. Despite the active fiestas and ceremonies, by the end of the nineteenth century formal religious participation was in serious decline among the Mexican community.

According to historian Albert Camarillo, the final two decades of the nineteenth century witnessed the first generation in southern California that had to face the reality of being "Mexican in an Anglo society."[28] During this period the Mexican-American community became socially and residentially isolated from the Anglo community and relegated to the bottom rung of the socioeconomic

ladder in California—a process Camarillo has termed "barrioization." This barrioization coincided with increasing neglect and isolation from the mainstream Catholic Church in California. By 1900
few Mexicans were attending the formal worship services of the
Church. As one historian concludes, "For most Mexican Americans,
the Church's symbolic and spiritual meanings were more important than its hierarchy" and formal services.[29] The most important
rites of passage—baptism, marriage, confirmation, and burial—
continued to be celebrated in the church, but more daily devotions
remained detached from parish life. In Los Angeles the growing
sense of religious isolation felt by the Mexican community from
the Anglo community was made complete with the opening of
St. Vibiana's Cathedral in 1876. The Hispanic community continued
celebrating at the Plaza Church in downtown Los Angeles, while
the Anglo community moved to the more fashionable cathedral
parish. In Santa Barbara "by the 1880s there was little other than
tradition that attracted the Chicanos to the Church. Importantly,
after 1883, a Spanish surnamed priest was seldom resident at the
parish or mission."[30] In San Jose no Mexican pastor was appointed
from 1852 to 1962, despite the large Mexican community in San
Jose.[31] In sum, by 1900 ministry to the Mexican/Mexican-American
community suffered from serious neglect.

THE TWENTIETH CENTURY

The twentieth century began a new era for Mexicans and the
Catholic Church in California. Developments in Mexico and California spurred increased immigration to California as Mexicans
left their homeland seeking more lucrative jobs or an escape from
political unrest. In the final years of the *Porfiriato* (the presidency of
Porfirio Díaz, 1876–1911), Díaz's policies of encouraging the expansion of the large haciendas at the expense of the small farmer and
of communal land holdings created a mobile, migrant labor force
which abandoned the rural areas for the cites. Many migrated to
northern Mexico, where growth in mining and industry promised
jobs with better pay than could be found in the central states.
The flight to the north was made easier by the completion of a
Mexican rail system to the northern states and contributed to the
transformation of the border towns of Tijuana and Mexicali into
major urban centers. For many, the border towns were merely a

way station on their way to the United States. Indeed, until 1917 the border was open, and Mexicans crossed the border freely and often.

Immigration was also inspired by the political unrest brought on by the Mexican Revolution of 1910. Many fled to the United States for refuge. For more than a decade Mexico was rent by violent insurrections as various revolutionary leaders—Pancho Villa, Emiliano Zapata, Venustiano Carranza, Alvaro Obregón , Francisco Madero, Victoriano Huerta, and others—battled for power. Their methods were crude and brutal. Historian Moisés Sandoval stated that the Mexican Revolution "was the bloodiest war in the Western Hemisphere, lasting ten years and causing far more casualties than the Anglo-American Civil War."[32]

	1910	1930	1940	1967
Tijuana	8,518	15,878	21,977	347,501
Mexicali	462	14,842	44,399	540,300

The Catholic Church in Mexico was also profoundly affected by the revolution. The Revolutionary Constitution of 1917 established a virtual persecution of the Church in Mexico. The Constitution mandated the expulsion of all foreign priests and women religious, proscribed religious education in the schools, forbade public displays of worship, nationalized church property, and required priests to register with state and local officials, besides giving the states the right of determining the number of priests for their state. Essentially, the Constitution placed the government in firm control of internal and external Church affairs. Until 1926 the anticlerical clauses of the Constitution were not enforced at a national level, though several states did use the Constitution to harass the local Church. In 1926 President Plutarco Calles attempted to enforce the anti-Church provisions. In response, the Mexican bishops ordered a cessation of all church services in Mexico, while the Catholic laity initiated an economic boycott. A more violent response was precipitated in central and western Mexico, where spontaneous insurrections coalesced into a virtual civil war. The revolt came to be known as the Cristero Rebellion, drawn from the battle cry of the insurrectionists, "¡Viva Cristo Rey!" ("Long Live Christ the King"). The rebellion produced three years of violent, though sporadic, fighting, with neither side respecting the niceties of civilized warfare. In 1929 a "modus vivendi" was reached between the Church and the Mexican state, ending the rebellion.

Relations between Church and state remained tense for another decade. In 1934 open hostilities were resumed when President Lázaro Cárdenas attempted to enforce the use of socialist pedagogy and propaganda in Mexico's schools. The Mexican bishops forbade their people from sending their children to such schools. Renewed persecution and conflict resulted. A lasting truce between Church and state was not reached until 1938.[33]

For nearly three decades the political unrest and religious turmoil propelled large numbers of Mexicans north of the border. One scholar estimates that between 1910 and 1932, about 10 percent of the entire population of Mexico migrated to the United States.[34]

Besides these "push" factors, a variety of "pull" factors emanated from California. The completion of the transcontinental railroad in 1869 initiated a period of enormous growth for southern California, as immigrants flocked to California from the Midwest. The rapid population growth, combined with improved systems of irrigation, resulted in a period of tremendous industrial and agricultural expansion. By 1930 California was the largest producer of fruits and vegetables in the United States, producing 40 percent of the entire U.S. output.[35] The economic boom created a pressing need for a cheap, reliable, mobile labor force to supply the needs of industry, railroads, and California's farms. The exclusion of the Chinese in 1882, the restriction of the Japanese in 1907, and of European immigrants in 1924 made Mexican immigrants the prime pool from which to satisfy the labor needs of southern California. They quickly became the largest single ethnic group in California agriculture. Demand was so great that factories and railways sent labor recruiters to border towns to contact arriving immigrants. Some even violated the law by sending agents into Mexico to encourage immigration.

The majority of Mexican immigrants were *mestizo* (of mixed ancestry, Indian and Spanish), and came from the central and northern states of Mexico: Michoacán, Jalisco, Zacatecas, Durango, Chihuahua, Sonora, and Guanajuato. Most of the immigrants entered through Texas, with most immigrants arriving in California only after having lived in Texas for five or more years.[36] The higher wages offered in California and the growing Mexican communities around Los Angeles pulled many immigrants to California. By 1929 Los Angeles was the second largest Mexican city in the world.

It is difficult to get an accurate figure for the number of immigrants who entered California and the United States. The numbers provided in Table 1 were derived from U.S. Census reports but do not accurately reflect the total picture. These figures are at best minimum figures. For the first two decades of the twentieth century the border was open, so Mexicans traveled back and forth freely. Many families in need sent one or more of their members to the United States to earn money, then return to Mexico. One scholar has suggested three types of immigrants came from Mexico—short-term, cyclical, and permanent.[37] Within these three categories they could be "documented" or "undocumented." The "undocumented" status was created between 1917 and 1924. Beginning in 1917 a head tax of eight dollars and a literacy test were required of immigrants from Mexico. The result was that many immigrants who would have been temporary or cyclical became permanent immigrants to avoid the rigors of the border crossings. Others devised means to avoid the tax and test, thus becoming "undocumented."

Table 1
Mexican Immigrants by Decade[38]

1900–09	31,200	1940–49	56,200
1910–19	185,000	1950–59	273,800
1920–29	498,000	1960–69	441,800
1930–39	32,700		

These restrictions were not very rigorously enforced as the onset of World War I increased the demand for cheap labor. Industry pushed hard to keep the free flow of workers from Mexico coming. In 1924 the national climate that led to the National Origins Quota Act also led to the creation of the Border Patrol. The task of the Border Patrol was to curtail "illegal" immigration. One historian summarizes the development, "In the first four decades of the twentieth century, crossing over from Mexico was transformed from a casual and easy task with perhaps a few questions asked by officials . . . to a tense, formal ritual full of suspicion."[39] Nonetheless, Mexicans continued to come. The massive immigration of the 1920s was sharply reduced with the onset of the Depression. As "pull" factors decreased, immigration lessened. More importantly, a hostile attitude toward immigrants and Mexican Americans made manifest in "repatriation" programs, discouraged immigration. State and local agencies offered to pay the train fare of Mexicans and Mexican Americans who desired to return to Mexico. As the Depression deepened, greater resentment was directed against Mexicans, who were accused of taking jobs away from "Americans" and draining the resources of welfare and relief agencies. Repatriation became less voluntary, as many Mexicans and Mexican Americans were rounded up and "returned" to Mexico against their will. Over one hundred thousand were repatrioted from California, either willingly or not, in the first years of the Depression.[40]

Immigration increased once more with the onset of the Second World War and exploded in the postwar years. Besides immigrants, a new type of "short-term" immigrant was brought to California through the *bracero* system. Through an arrangement between the government of Mexico and the United States, Mexican nationals were contracted to work in California for specific periods of time and then returned to Mexico; they were called *braceros*. Camps in which the braceros were to live were provided by employers and supervised by the government (in theory at least). In the 1950s, an average 336,000 braceros a year came to California.[41] The Bracero Program also had the side effect of increasing undocumented immigration. Estimates range from 500 thousand to 1 million undocumented immigrants entering California during the 1950s. The "illegals" or "wetbacks" as they were popularly called, were not entirely welcome. In 1954 "Operation Wetback" made a serious attempt to curtail illegal immigration by "repatriating" many Mexicans suspected of being illegal.

Despite the celebration of California's romantic Mexican past, the state's attitude toward Mexicans has always been ambivalent. While cheap labor was desired, the Mexican was not. This ambivalence is captured in José Villareal's novel *Pocho*.

> The ever increasing army of people swarmed across while the border remained open, fleeing from squalor and oppression. But they could not flee reality. . . . The bewildered people came on—insensitive to the fact that even though they were not stopped, they were not really wanted.[42]

Even when the border was closed, Mexicans continued to come and continued to encounter American ambivalence, if not downright hostility.

SETTLEMENT

Mexicans increasingly settled in California, primarily southern California. By 1930, 78 percent of all Mexicans in California lived in the southern counties. Though a high percentage of Mexicans were migrant workers, by 1930, 66 percent of the Mexican community was urban, a figure which jumped to 85.4 percent by 1960. Los Angeles was the largest Mexican city in the United States, but large Mexican communities developed in San Diego, Santa Barbara, San Bernardino, San Jose, San Francisco, and in a number of Los Angeles "satellite barrios" such as Watts. (See Table 2.) Again, the figures are not precise; the actual number of Mexicans is probably greater than the figures cited in the table. For much of the period 1910 to 1965, Mexicans and Mexican Americans were predominantly working class. As in the case of most blue-collar groups, they settled near their places of work in the industrial part of town. For Mexicans, this often meant near canneries, food processing plants, or railway yards. Carey McWilliams observed in 1948, "Wherever a railroad labor camp was established, a Mexican colonia exists today."[43] In Los Angeles, the Old Plaza in the downtown area, long the center of Mexican life in Los Angeles, remained the initial point of entry for most immigrants. Its affordable housing and the Mexican community that already existed there made it an attractive starting point. In the 1920s industrial expansion into the Plaza began pushing Mexicans east across the Los Angeles River. East Los Angeles—Boyle Heights, Belvedere, Maravilla Park—would soon be the largest Mexican center in California. The move to East Los Angeles was assisted by the development of an interurban rail system that enabled Mexicans to live further from their jobs. By 1930, the community of Belvedere had over 30,000 people. In most communities in California, Mexicans were segregated into specific areas of town, figuratively, and at times literally, forced to live on the "other side of the tracks." In the 1950s this changed somewhat as Mexicans, aided by the GI Bill, moved in significant numbers to the suburbs, but the majority remained in Mexican barrios.

Wherever they settled, the lot of many Mexicans was constant mobility. Even those considered "permanent" residents joined the

Table 2
Mexican Residents in California and Los Angeles[44]

	1900	1910	1920	1930	1950	1960
California	8,086	33,694	88,881	368,013	760,453	1,426,338
Los Angeles		5,000	33,644	97,116	272,000	260,000
Los Angeles County						576,000

mobile labor force on a seasonal basis, or when jobs were scarce in the city. For full-time migrants, the year-round growing schedule of California meant frequent travel. Figure 1 lists a typical cycle for some migrant workers.[45]

Figure 1

Months	Place	Crop
Jan.–Mar.	Salt River Valley, Ariz.	lettuce
Mar.–June	Imperial Valley, Calif.	carrots
June	Conejos, Calif.	apricots
July–Aug.	Tulare Co., Calif.	peaches
Sept.–Nov.	Fresno Co., Calif.	cotton
Nov.–Mar.	Salt River Valley, Ariz.	lettuce

José Villareal depicts a similar cycle. "The nomadic pace increased. Lettuce harvests in Salinas, melons in Brawley, grapes in Parlier, oranges in Ontario, cotton in Firebaugh, and finally Santa Clara, the prune country."[46] Labor was not limited to men, but included women and children as well. Men and boys picked the fruit, while women and girls processed and packed it. Many migrant families attempted to save money either to purchase a permanent home or to return to Mexico with a small stake. For much of the twentieth century this mobile labor force formed the "backbone" of California agriculture, making up close to 80 percent of the total farm labor force in the late 1920s.[47]

Despite the common perception that most Mexicans worked in agriculture, as of 1930 only 37 percent of the Mexican/Mexican-American work force was engaged in agriculture. Another 31 percent worked in manufacturing and 17 percent in transportation (i.e., for the railroads).[48] Whatever their occupation, Mexicans generally found themselves on the lower rungs of the socioeconomic ladder. In Los Angeles in 1917, 91.5 percent were classified as blue-collar workers, 68 percent unskilled.[49] Work beyond the home was not limited to men. Economic pressure also forced women and children into the work force. In Los Angeles in 1917, 40 percent of the women worked outside the home, largely in the garment industry. Most Mexicans experienced little upward social mobility as they were locked into the lower ranks by discrimination and other factors. One historian observes, "By the twentieth century, employment in California's large-scale agriculture had come to mean irregular work, constant movement, low wages, squalid working conditions, social isolation, emotional deprivation, and individual powerlessness so profound as to make occupational advancement a virtual impossibility."[50] As a result little upward mobility occurred even across generations. By the late 1930s, however, a small middle class had begun to develop, and it grew significantly after World War II. Although the constant influx of new laborers in the 1950s kept a large portion of the Mexican/Mexican-American community in working-class occupations, by the 1960s a significant number had moved from unskilled to skilled and semi-skilled occupations.[51]

As a primarily blue-collar population Mexicans tended to live in the poorer sections of town. Historian Albert Camarillo argues that Mexicans were forced by virtue of their race to accept the most menial jobs and forced to live in the less desirable parts of town. As noted before, Camarillo calls this forced segregation and marginalization "barriozation."[52] Barrios faced classic inner-city problems—poverty, lack of adequate municipal services and health care, the physical deterioration of the area, crime, disease, and other assorted urban problems. The name of Mexican barrio "Sal Si Puedes" (Get Out if You Can) in San Jose refers to the terrible roads that became impassible when it rained. Later the phrase was used by upwardly mobile Mexicans who looked for greener pastures beyond the barrio.

The barrio was not an entirely negative environment, nor was it entirely the result of discrimination. Many chose to live in the barrio or *colonia*. The barrio surrounded the immigrant with familiar sights, sounds, and tastes, and served as "a haven for Mexican and American born *Chicanos*. There they could adapt to American society while still retaining in their daily lives much of the flavor of Mexico."[53] Moreover, faced with frequent reminders of their outsider status in America, the barrio reinforced a positive sense of identity among the Mexican community, with the celebration of traditional fiestas and holidays, frequent family gatherings, and a vast array of Spanish-speaking entertainments, including theaters, newspapers, radio programs, and music. Anthony Rios-Bustamante and Pedro Castillo observe of the Los Angeles barrio, "Nurturing a tradition that valued family, nationality, and cultural continuity, Mexicans in Los Angeles operated as a social entity unto themselves . . . even as they struggled to deal with an aggressive Anglo mainstream."[54]

Three main institutions provided the cement to barrio life—family, the *mutualista* (mutual aid society), and the Church. Oftentimes the three institutions intersected. Particularly important was the intersection of Church and family in *compadrazgo* and *parentesco*. One of the most stabilizing elements in the barrio was the extended kinship network established and validated by the *compadrazgo* system. At each significant moment in a child's life—baptism, first holy communion, confirmation, and marriage—*compadres* (godparents) were chosen. The roles of the compadres were not mere formalities. The compadres became an integral part of the godfamily. They actively participated in family affairs and could be counted on in times of family crisis and distress. The compadrazgo system provided a sense of security and trust among parents, children, and godparents that contributed to the stability of the barrio.[55] The Church played an important role in validating this bond.

The importance of family and extended kinship ties during migration and settlement is ably demonstrated by Robert Alvarez, Jr., in his study *Familia: Migration and Adaptation in Baja and Alta California, 1800–1975*. Alvarez follows successive generations of immigrants through Baja California to California, documenting how they dealt with the physical and psychological dislocation caused by migration. He concludes, "This social history helps to illustrate how these and other families provided support to one another and created the culturally relevant relations that provided social equilibrium rather than social breakdowns throughout the process."[56] Immigrants not only immigrated to areas where previous kin had settled, they established extended kinship relationships at each new place of settlement. Another scholar summarizes the importance of the family in the barrio, "The role of family life in sustaining the cultural integrity which prevailed in the pre–World War II times in Los Angeles, was instrumental in the group's ability to survive the general and hostile anti-Mexicanism of the era."[57]

The Mexican immigrant family was patriarchal. The father enjoyed complete authority, in theory at least. The mother provided the emotional center of the family. A survey of Mexican immigrants in Los Angeles during the 1920s provides some insights into family life—27 percent agreed the wife's authority was equal to her husband's in the family; 27 percent disagreed. Seventy-seven percent agreed it was the wife's duty to obey her husband and care for her family at home. Fifteen percent said a man had the right to beat his wife, while 63 percent disagreed. And 96 percent agreed it was the duty of children to obey their parents all their lives.[58] Underlying the notion of male superiority was *"machismo."* One scholar points out, however, that the more negative aspects of *machismo*—wife beating and alcoholism—were the result of an unstable social environment.[59] These aspects created an ongoing problem for the Mexican community.

While the family provided stability, the family itself was not unchanging. Conflict often erupted between first- and second-generation Mexicans, who had differing notions of freedom and responsibility. In the United States, children were exposed to, and came to accept, the more egalitarian and less restrictive style of family life in America. When parents attempted to assert unquestioned authority and strict discipline, conflict resulted. The authority of immigrant parents was also undercut by their lack of standing in, and understanding of, American society, thus limiting their ability to assist their children in adjusting to the new environment. As the mother sorrowfully tells her son in José Villareal's autobiographical novel *Pocho*, "I am ashamed that we are going to fail in our great responsibility—we cannot guide you, we cannot select your reading for you, we cannot even talk to you in your own language."[60] The second generation provided an ongoing problem for the Mexican community, since the second generation child was neither fully Mexican, nor fully allowed to participate in American society. The problem of the second generation became especially troublesome after World War II. Despite these problems, the family remained the crucial institution in providing Mexican Americans with a sense of identity and self-worth.

The second important institution in the barrio was the mutualista, or mutual aid society. Mario Barrera claims that "it is no exaggeration to say that after the family, the mutualistas were the most important social organization among Chicanos from the late nineteenth century to the 1930s,"[61] and Albert Camarillo calls mutualistas the "life blood" of the barrio.[62] Most mutualistas provided the classic services of all mutual aid societies—sick and death benefits and unemployment insurance. In a community struggling against poverty these addressed very real needs. But mutualistas did far more: they celebrated patriotic holidays—especially the Sixteenth of September and Cinco de Mayo—provided a community forum, provided an avenue for indigenous leadership to develop within the Mexican community, and spoke out against discrimination and for civil rights. Many mutualistas took the names of Mexican heroes such as the Hidalgo Society in Brawley, or the Sociedad Benito Juárez in El Centro. Some were religious, such as the Sociedad Guadalupana, formed in Richmond in 1924. One of the most powerful mutualistas was La Alianza Hispano Americana, founded in Tucson in 1894. By 1920 multiple chapters of La Alianza had been opened in California, providing life insurance, financial services, and social activities.

Women played an important role in the societies, either in mixed groups or in mutualistas of their own. One important group of Mexican women which worked closely with the mutualistas was the Cruz Azul (Blue Cross), the equivalent of the American Red Cross. The Cruz Azul provided care for the sick and downtrodden in the barrio. Other groups of women worked hard in preparing social and civic celebrations and fiestas.

While the mutualista was important in and of itself, on several occasions mutualistas joined together in common cause. In 1926 in Los Angeles, groups came together to form La Liga Protectora Latina, a civil rights organization. Combinations of mutualistas also formed the bases of several Mexican labor unions, such as the Confederación de Uniónes Obreras Méxicanas (CUOM) in 1927, and La Unión de Trabajadores de Valle Imperial, which orchestrated the cantaloupe strike of 1928. The combination of mutualistas brought distant barrios into contact with one another and made Mexicans aware of life beyond their own barrios.

The third institution of major importance in the barrio, and the focus of the remainder of this study, was the Catholic Church. Particularly for first-generation immigrants, the Mexican identity was intimately intertwined with their Catholicism. One woman remembered the trauma of growing up Protestant in the barrio, "I got many tongue lashings and a few beatings for not being Catholic, because you just are not acceptable otherwise."[63] Another Mexican Protestant in San Jose observed, "Mrs. Padilla is such a strong Catholic that she makes us feel uncomfortable—she keeps shaking her head and telling us that our parents would be ashamed of us for turning our backs on our religion."[64] Catholic parishes, once established, played an integral role in barrio life, bringing different neighborhoods together and providing a meeting place for community groups. In her study of the San Jose Mexican community Margaret Clark asserted, "Churches are perhaps the single most important influence on informal community life. Many successful civic projects . . . have been strengthened by Church support, and without the endorsement of religious groups the effectiveness of such programs would be problematic."[65] Though the Church was not as intimate with the people as it had been in the Mexican village, it remained an important source of support for the Mexican community.

2

Catholic Ministry in the Era of the "Mexican Problem," 1910–1943

The rapid increase in Mexican immigration during the first three decades of the twentieth century presented the Church in California with an enormous problem: How best to care for its Mexican people? The Church response addressed two problems: first, how to provide for the practical and specific needs of the Mexican community, and second, how, and at what rate, to assist the assimilation of the Mexican into American society and into the American Catholic Church. We will consider the Church's response to the latter question first.

AMERICANIZATION AND ITS DISCONTENTS

One of the perennial problems which has confronted the Catholic Church in the United States is its relationship to mainstream American culture, a culture which has generally been hostile to Catholicism and suspicious of foreigners. As an immigrant, working-class church, the Catholic Church often found itself outside of, and in conflict with, that mainstream. Catholics were under constant pressure to prove the compatibility between their American citizenship and their Catholic faith. Despite the pressure, the reality of the immigrant church in nineteenth-century America allowed for a great tolerance of diversity. Germans, Polish, and others resisted rapid Americanization. Historian Colman Barry writes of the German immigrants, "adoption of the English language and conformity to the American Way of Life would have to be, to say the least, a slow process for the German immigrant."[1] By the twentieth century and increasingly as the campaign for immigrant restriction grew, the Catholic Church in America accepted as its responsibility the Americanization of the immigrant. It was during this latter period that the greatest numbers of Mexican immigrants began arriving. It is no surprise then, that in its ministry to Mexican immigrants, the Church took as one of its duties the responsibility

148

of ushering the Mexican into mainstream American life. Often this was done without a sufficiently critical attitude toward the American society of which they wanted the Mexican to become a part and without a sufficiently appreciative attitude toward the culture brought by the Mexican immigrant. As late as 1961 the Bishops' Committee for the Spanish Speaking could state, "The Church has a grave responsibility of expediting and directing the assimilation process . . . guiding them through periods of insecurity and anxiety and developing them for a full, complete participation in the American way of life and the Catholic Church."[2] The statement goes on to say that assimilation will occur with or without the Church's assistance. If it were to occur without the Church, "we may assume the change will be against us."[3] The quote reflects the conventional wisdom that the Mexican needed to be assimilated to both the American way of life and the American Catholic way of life.

In recent years scholars and activists have accused the Church of forcing Americanization on the Mexican people, stripping Mexicans of their culture and their roots. Typical of recent scholarship is a study of Mexican Los Angeles which rebukes the Church for being "obsessed with cultural assimilation."[4] As César Chávez noted, "Everywhere we went to school, to church, to the movies, there was this attack on our culture and our language, an attempt to make us conform to the 'American Way.' What a sin!"[5] The disgust with "Americanization" grew out of the social upheavals of the 1960s, in which the fundamental precepts of America were called into question. To some, America became a dirty word and Americanization an abomination. Any suggestion that Americanization was an acceptable model for Mexican ministry was held in contempt.

Prior to 1960 Americanization was not held in such disrepute, and after World War I the Church's policy of Americanization was rarely questioned. The Church joined the public school, the settlement houses, and civic institutions in attempting to Americanize the Mexican. Bishop John J. Cantwell of Los Angeles asserted that Americanization of the Mexican was "preeminently a Catholic responsibility."[6] In an era in which Americanism went unquestioned, the goal of Americanizing the Mexican was seen as a positive good. During World War I and the 1920s, the Church sponsored a variety of Americanization programs, including civics classes, courses in English, and home economics. Monsignor Thomas O'Dwyer of the Catholic Welfare Bureau of Los Angeles expressed a commonly held position. By seeking the restriction of

Mexican immigration, he said, "we could Americanize many of the adults and help stabilize their employment. We could educate the children and they would become absorbed in our national life."[7] Americanization, O'Dwyer argued, was beneficial to the Mexican.

The Church's program of Americanization also focused on making Mexican Catholics good American Catholics. A side effect would be that the Mexicans would be better citizens. The Report of the Associated Catholic Charities for the Diocese of Los Angeles for 1919 claimed, "We believe that in making better Catholics, we shall make them better citizens."[8] Again, assimilation was twofold, to the American way of life and to the American Catholic way of life. The two were intimately connected in the minds of many churchmen.

Forced Americanization was not a universal paradigm. Beginning in the late 1920s, several priests began working to modify the Americanization model of assimilation, preferring instead the more positive notion of the melting pot.[9] This new stance emanated from priests who had worked or who were working closely with the Mexican community. Irish-born priest Laurence Forristal, who had worked for thirteen years among Mexicans in San Diego, cautioned in 1939 against an overly narrow definition of Americanization, "if it means that every Mexican must be recast in a special American mold, the proposal is immense and impossible of accomplishment. . . . We cannot force them into the mold in which we were fashioned."[10] Forristal preferred the notion of the melting pot, in which each culture contributed something of value to a new American culture. In order for Mexicans to be able to make their contribution, Spanish-speaking ministers were needed. The older Mexicans, Forristal observed, would never speak English, and the younger generation preferred to pray and go to confession in Spanish. "For such families, Spanish will always be the language of prayer and religious practice; it is only through the medium of Spanish that we can reach their hearts."[11] Forristal also recognized the importance of Mexican nationalism and counseled sensitivity to it. "There is no more contemptible creature than the Mexican who is ashamed of his blood and race. Invariably he is also ashamed of his religion."[12]

Forristal was not alone in attempting to soften the Americanization model. In 1942 Father Augustine O'Dea, longtime pastor of a small Mexican parish in North Hollywood, developed a course to be taught at St. John's Seminary on the pastoral care of the Mexican community. O'Dea claimed, "the old ideal of Americanization is dead . . . [a] slow process is more desirable." He also noted that there was a "greater willingness to admire and preserve national traits than was the custom before."[13] O'Dea too stressed the need for Spanish-speaking priests.

Prior to this, even Archbishop John J. Cantwell had begun to question the Americanization model. In 1936, in a report to the apostolic delegate, he suggested rapid Americanization might not be the best policy as regards the Mexicans: "the children very readily accept American manners, frequently giving up their own finest traditions, and adopting the worst customs which they come into contact with here."[14] By 1940 he mandated that all his seminarians learn Spanish and obtain some knowledge of Mexican culture. Cantwell reflected in 1940 that assimilation would not occur as easily as previously thought. "Our proximity to the Mexican border, the demand of Mexican labor, the lack of immigration quotas, etc., makes it certain that there will always be great numbers of non-English-speaking Mexicans. The tenacity of these people in adhering to their national spirit, their unwillingness to be assimilated racially, and their isolation in *colonias*, will tend to make them retain their language."[15] Cantwell's analysis brought him to the conclusion that Spanish-speaking priests and priests sensitive to Mexican culture would be a necessity for some time to come. As O'Dea had observed, forced Americanization was dead.

Nonetheless, Americanization kept a firm hold on the imagination of many churchmen. Patrick McNamara, in Leo Grebler's study *The Mexican American People*, presents a memorandum written in 1947 by a Mexican priest working in southern California on "religious assistance to Mexicans in the United States." The memo, playing on a perennial fear, warns of the imminent loss of Mexican Catholics to Protestantism. He cites four major reasons for the coming loss: "psychological race differences," language, nationality, and most importantly, "the North Americans' desire to 'Americanize' the immigrant." The priest asserts that Americanization "is really equivalent to the loss of the Catholic faith."[16] To prevent this, Mexican and "native" Spanish-speaking priests are needed. Americans could never learn Spanish well enough to minister effectively to the Mexican community. McNamara, and other scholars, have taken the letter as an authentic and representative statement of the desires of the Mexican Catholic people. The bishops of California rejected the memo as being the opinion of one person. Bishop Charles Buddy of San Diego wrote a long response to the memo, rejecting all its main points. Buddy claimed that the priest failed to consider that a large number of Mexican youths no longer spoke Spanish. A priest who spoke only Spanish had little chance with Mexican-American youth. Buddy claimed further that many Mexican *colonias* preferred to be considered American. He proceeded to give a statistical account of the work being done in the Mexican community, suggesting there was no lack of attention or effort as regards the Mexican apostolate as the letter suggests. He concluded that Mexican Catholics were being lost no more frequently than American Catholics in American parishes were being lost.[17] In a similar response, Auxiliary Bishop Joseph T. McGucken of Los Angeles rejected the memo's main points. He acknowledged that though much more work needed to be done, much was already being done. He agreed with Buddy that Mexican priests were not the sole answer. "Our young American priests who speak Spanish are affectionately received by the Mexican people. The success of their work compares favorably with that of Spanish or Mexican priests."[18]

Though the argument over who was best suited to minister to the Mexican community, a Mexican, a Spaniard, or a Spanish-speaking American, was largely academic (there were never enough Spanish-speaking priests of any kind), it raged on through the 1950s. A Mexican priest in a parish in Los Nietos in 1957 claimed that Mexican youth chose to come to the "Mexican" parish because of "tradition and custom."[19] His letter was contradicted by a parish sister in his parish, who claimed that since his arrival the Mexican priest had destroyed the very successful youth work done by a young American priest, fluent in Spanish.[20] Beatrice Griffith, in her book *American Me*, reports a similar finding in a parish "not far from Los Angeles" in the 1940s. She dubs the Mexican priest a "reactionary *Mexicanista* priest," who killed the youth programs of a "progressive, young American priest."[21]

The problem as to who was best suited to minister to the Mexican community was a complex one due to the "ambivalent" attitude within the Mexican community itself regarding Americanization. The Mexican community, even within small barrios, was not a homogenous group. A wide variety of interests and backgrounds coexisted in the barrio, as did individuals at various stages of assimilation. As Albert Camarillo has suggested, there were only two common denominators in the barrio—poverty and segregation.[22] By the 1930s, most barrios had a significant number of second-generation immigrants, who tended to be more desirous of becoming American, even if Americans were not more desirous of accepting them. Older, first-generation immigrants tended to cling more tightly to the old traditions. Further complicating matters was the continual influx of new immigrants, as well as the large number of short-term and cyclical immigrants. The proximity of the Mexican border made frequent trips back to Mexico a possibility, a phenomenon that enabled Mexican immigrants to remain in closer contact with their home culture than immigrants who had migrated from great distances.

Despite the variety of interests and attitudes within the barrio, the vast majority of Mexican immigrants prior to World War II never became American citizens. Several reasons have been suggested as to why. First, many Mexicans regarded their stay in America as temporary, even though it frequently turned out to be permanent. As Manuel Gamio observed, "the uneducated Mexican may dwell in the United States physically for many years without ever coming to live there mentally."[23] Second, Mexicans maintained a strong attachment to their homeland. One immigrant expressed the intensity of that attachment, "I would rather cut my throat before changing my Mexican nationality."[24] The attitude of *"Mexicanismo"* was encouraged by the Mexican consuls in California in the 1920s and 1930s. Consuls were given the task of "Mexicanizing Mexicans outside the nation."[25] The consuls sponsored Spanish language classes, as well as courses in Mexican history. They established *Comisiones Honoríficas* in most cities. The "honorary commissions" operated as patriotic clubs which planned the celebrations for Mexican national holidays. While the Mexican consuls buoyed Mexicanismo, their efforts also suggest that Mexican customs were slipping as immigrants adjusted to California. Third, Mexicans associated becoming American with several quite negative qualities and practices—materialism, secularism, divorce, birth control, disrespect for one's parents and family. Carey McWilliams concludes, "where values are concerned they prefer to remain Mexican."[26] Finally, Mexicans resisted becoming American citizens because of the poor treatment they received from Americans. A young Mexican girl observed, "My father said that if you are a Mexican and take out your naturalization papers and pin them on your nose, an American would not see them because you are a Mexican."[27] And a priest in Los Angeles in the 1920s observed, as long as "Americans treated Mexicans as an inferior race, undervalued their work, paid low wages, and mistreated them in general, Mexicans will show little interest in becoming U.S. citizens."[28]

Nonetheless the longer Mexicans remained in California, the more they adjusted to the American way of life. As some strained to become American others fought to remain Mexican. Many customs began to fade. Albert Camarillo concludes, "The longer the Mexican immigrant remained in the United States the more they, and especially their native born children, put aside the language and folkways of Mexico."[29]

What historian George Sanchez has called "ambivalent Americanism"[30] aptly describes the Mexican-American community from 1910 to 1945. How best to minister to this "ambivalence" was a very complex problem. It was made all the more difficult by a lack of Spanish-speaking clergy. The experience of St. Frances of Rome in Azusa demonstrates the complexity of ministry to the Mexican/ Mexican-American community. In 1919 Bishop Cantwell sent a Mexican priest to the Mexican colonia in Irwindale, next to Azusa, to examine the plight of the Mexicans who were being preyed upon by Protestant proselytizers. As Irwindale was the responsibility of the parish of St. Frances, Cantwell sent a visiting Spanish-speaking priest for the Easter season, informing the pastor of St. Frances, "Mexicans in your parish are particularly anxious to have an opportunity of going to confession in the Spanish language." In 1922 Cantwell assigned a full-time Spanish-speaking assistant to attend the Mexican Catholics. In 1923 a separate mission for the Mexicans, under the care of St. Frances, was established. In 1925 a Mexican priest was sent as pastor. By 1932 an Anglo parishioner complained to the bishop that the pastor "can't speak English." The same year five Mexican societies requested that Cantwell send a priest who could speak both English and Spanish. By 1943 the parish was at least minimally bilingual. Several letters to parishioners were published in both English and Spanish, and special bulletins were printed in Spanish informing Spanish-speaking parishioners of sacramental programs, religion classes, and societies. In 1957 parishioners requested an "English-speaking priest who knows Spanish and understands the customs of the Mexicans." Such a priest is "usually very successful" with the Mexican-American community.[31] Bilingual priests who were also bicultural were in great demand as Mexican immigrant communities matured while at the same time new immigrants kept arriving.

The history of St. Frances suggests the complexity involved in ministering to a multifaceted Mexican-American community. The

Church's approach to the Mexican community remained an "Americanizing" one, but this process was more complex and nuanced than a simple condemnation of the process would suggest.

THE PRACTICAL RESPONSE

While the Americanizing impulse informed most Church programs, the Church also attempted to respond to the seemingly overwhelming pastoral needs generated by the large-scale immigration from Mexico. The 1923 report of the Associated Catholic Charities of the Archdiocese of Los Angeles captures the magnitude of the problem: "They come by the thousands, unheralded and unknown—They often have no address other than an indefinite district, living as they do in huts and shacks . . . or anything they can find in undeveloped districts."[32] The mobility of the Mexican population made normal parish life difficult and made follow-up charitable work nearly impossible. Especially pressing was the grinding poverty which beset the Mexican community. Various reports read, "The poverty of these people and the unsanitary living conditions form a serious problem."[33] And, "How can anyone live on this meager pittance, let alone support a large family?"[34]

Beyond the extreme poverty, several problems seemed to preoccupy those charged with ministry to the Mexicans. Many of the Mexicans who arrived did not attend Mass or the sacraments regularly, nor were they in the habit of financially supporting the Church and clergy, qualities essential in the American Church's definition of the good Catholic. Many immigrants came from sections of Mexico where clergy had been in scarce supply and where formal religious instruction and practice had been minimal. In addition, many marriages in Mexico had been contracted in civil services and had not been blessed by the Church. When these Mexicans arrived in America they were immediately set upon by Protestant proselytizers. Thus, the four main goals of the Church in regards to the Mexican immigrant were 1) to educate the Mexican in Catholic doctrine; 2) validate Mexican marriages; 3) provide charitable relief; and 4) protect the Mexican faithful from Protestant missionaries and other "false philosophies." To achieve these goals the Church relied on four strategies: 1) settlement houses, 2) charitable agencies, 3) the Confraternity of Christian Doctrine (CCD) and the parochial school, and 4) Mexican parishes and missions.

CHARITABLE ENDEAVORS

As the Church in California entered the twentieth century, care for the Mexican community had devolved upon several old parishes and several of the old California missions. In San Francisco, Our Lady of Guadalupe served as the center of the Mexican Catholic community in the Bay Area. In Los Angeles, Our Lady, Queen of the Angels in the downtown Plaza, affectionately known as "La Placita," remained the center of the Mexican community, while in Santa Barbara the Old Mission provided that function. With the rapid increase of Mexican immigrants, these churches were no longer sufficient to meet the needs of the people. In response to these growing needs, several settlement houses and community centers were established—in Los Angeles, Santa Barbara, and San Diego. Most of these centers were established and staffed by women, who bore the brunt of most Catholic charitable endeavors.

In 1897 a group of women in Los Angeles established the settlement house El Hogar Feliz (The Happy Home) to minister to the Mexican community. The home provided primary school lessons, classes in music, and most importantly, classes in Catholic doctrine. It also established a youth club and youth activities. The home moved three times before establishing itself next door to the Plaza Church, in the heart of Mexican Los Angeles. While the women directed the house, the pastor of La Placita, served as spiritual director.[35]

In 1901 another house, Brownson House, was established by Mary Julia Workman in Los Angeles. While Brownson House served a variety of immigrants, a large portion of its clientele was Mexican. Brownson House provided classic settlement-house services—catechism classes, courses in home economics and sewing for women, citizenship classes, athletic programs, home visitations, a clothing bureau, and a medical clinic. The house was also used as a meeting place for various neighborhood groups and at least one mutualista.[36] Founder Mary Julia Workman stated the problems which compelled her work: "Los Angeles has its problems of unemployment and poverty, as well as its problems of health, of education, of assimilation of the foreigner."[37] The settlement house tried to address these problems. While Americanization had long been a concern of settlement houses, it escalated with the onset of World War I, and with what historian Richard Romo has called the era of the "Brown Scare."[38] The Scare lasted from 1913 to 1918, as Mexican "subversives" (refugees from the Mexican Revolution) were rounded up and sent back to Mexico. In this environment the settlement houses tried to show their charges how to be good Americans. In 1927 Brownson House moved to East Los Angeles following the migration of the Mexican people to the east side of the city.

In 1920 another settlement house was opened, Santa Rita Settlement, under the auspices of the Catholic Welfare Bureau. In 1917 Bishop John J. Cantwell became bishop of Los Angeles and attempted to unify the disparate charitable efforts under a central administration. To achieve this he established the Associated Catholic Charities in 1919, later called the Catholic Welfare Bureau (CWB). In 1921 he appointed a young priest by the name of Robert Lucey to direct the Bureau. Lucey became an outspoken advocate for the poor and under-privileged, with a special concern for the Mexican people. He later became bishop of Amarillo, Texas, then archbishop of San Antonio, where he became a champion for the rights of his Mexican Americans. But in 1921 he attempted to pull together the various Catholic charities for the archdiocese of Los Angeles. Lucey immediately expanded the work and budget of the Bureau. By the time he left, in 1925, Lucey was overseeing the work of three settlement houses, three medical clinics, a maternity hospital, and a host of orphanages, nurseries, and boarding schools. Nine branch offices of the CWB were established in cites outside of Los Angeles.[39] His work was continued by Monsignor Thomas O'Dwyer.

While these charitable works were not directed exclusively to Mexicans, Mexicans were some of the chief beneficiaries of the Bureau. Historian Francis Weber argues that Cantwell did not believe in placing an ethnic label on charitable work. Thus, while there was work done in the Mexican community—over 50 percent of the charities' budget went to projects in Mexican areas—it was not labeled "Mexican" work.[40] Part of this was Cantwell's desire to encourage the notion that charitable burdens were to be borne by all, but part of it may have been a fear that anti-Mexican feeling might discourage contributions. In any case, in 1919 he established an Immigrant Welfare Division within the Associated Catholic Charities whose mandate was to assist Catholic immigrants. The department established its offices in the facilities of El Hogar Feliz. By 1929 the diocese was sponsoring five community centers in Mexican neighborhoods in Los Angeles, with additional centers established in Santa Barbara, San Diego, and Watts. By 1936 the archdiocese had added four more community centers. The centers were similar to settlement houses in that they provided recreational, educational, and social programs for women, children, and young adults. Santa Rita Settlement, responding to the high infant mortality rate within the Los Angeles Mexican community, established a medical clinic with special emphasis on prenatal and maternity care. By 1936 four free clinics were in operation in the archdiocese. After the diocese of San Diego was split off from Los Angeles in 1936, the newly appointed bishop of San Diego, Charles Buddy, placed a high priority on providing medical clinics for the Mexican colonias. Under the auspices of the Victory Noll Sisters clinics were opened in the 1940s in San Diego, San Bernardino, and Brawley.

While the centers and clinics provided much-needed services, the Catholic Welfare Bureau also provided direct relief and assistance to the Mexican community. In 1924 the Bureau became affiliated with the Community Chest of Los Angeles and was able to expand its programs with the additional funds. The Bureau became the largest single relief agency in the city, a fact somewhat consoling to the Mexican in need, who felt more comfortable seeking assistance from the Catholic Church. Governor C. C. Young's study of Mexicans in California in 1930 reveals that five major Catholic groups, as well as a number of smaller ones, were operating under the auspices of the Community Chest of Los Angeles: the Catholic Welfare Bureau, the Santa Rita Clinic, the Catholic Big Brothers, the Catholic Welfare Bureau of San Pedro, and the Convent of the Good Shepherd. In the years 1924 to 1928 the number of Mexican children assisted never slipped below 45 percent of the total number of children assisted in Los Angeles.[41] The number of Mexican families assisted was generally around 25 percent of the total assisted. Significantly, at the onset of the Depression the number of families assisted by the Catholic Welfare Bureau jumped from 4,637 in 1929–30 to 22,363 in 1930–31, accounting for 46.1 percent of the total care for the city of Los Angeles, a large percentage of which was Mexican. As one historian concludes, "The Mexican American looked to the Catholic Welfare Bureau for most of his assistance."[42] Catholic efforts were not limited to the CWB. The St. Vincent de Paul Society also assisted over 2,000 families the same year. Thus, the Catholic Church did provide rather substantial charitable assistance to the Mexican immigrant.

As was the case with other Church endeavors, the charitable and settlement ministries stressed Americanization. Catholic Charities' director Monsignor Thomas O'Dwyer expressed the need to assist public schools in their Americanizing efforts. In 1919 the CWB leased a large hall near the downtown Plaza to "be used for Americanization work."[43] As suggested earlier, Americanization did not have the decidedly negative connotations it has today. The Americanization of the CWB might be referred to as "benign Americanization." The intent was to assist the Mexican immigrant materially and socially. The Charities Report for 1934 reads, "Among southern California's Mexican Catholics, Welfare workers move everyday, interpreting American ideals, laws, customs and social facilities to the newcomers, seeking to better their material condition and endeavoring to protect them as much as possible from the ruthless exploitation of the unscrupulous type of industrialist and land owner. Most of the Mexicans are acutely poor. Many have exhibited great beauty of character in the face of adversity."[44]

EDUCATIONAL EFFORTS

Beyond providing for their material needs, the most glaring "problem" for those involved in the Mexican apostolate was that many Mexican immigrants lacked formal religious training and education. The director of the Confraternity of Christian Doctrine for the diocese of Los Angeles, Monsignor Leroy Callahan, described the situation in rather dire terms. "It is a missionary work, as truly missionary as evangelization of the heathen, with the sole difference that we are laboring amongst those who are Catholic by birth."[45] The most pressing need was to educate the newly arriving immigrants as to the fundamental tenets of the Catholic faith and its practices, albeit with an American twist. The need to educate seemed particularly acute in light of the vigorous proselytizing efforts of the Protestant churches among the Mexicans. Protestant missionaries, "who seek to tear out the heart of the foreigner"[46] had to be opposed. In addition, the Mexicans were confronted with an aggressively secular environment which, Bishop Cantwell charged, "bordered on the pagan."[47] It was imperative, then, that a wide-ranging program of religious education be developed.

Out of this need emerged the Confraternity of Christian Doctrine, founded in 1923 in Los Angeles. The CCD provided religious education for Catholic children who were attending public schools. In popular terms it was simply referred to as "catechism."

Historian Francis Weber calls the CCD "probably the single most effective of the many programs initiated for the Mexican American in southern California,"[48] during the 1920s and 1930s. Though the CCD was not limited to Mexicans, it originated from "the welfare work that was being done among the Mexican and Italian immigrants."[49] As had been the case with the settlement houses, a group of Catholic women were behind the creation of the CCD. In 1919 Miss Verona Spellmire with ten other women began providing catechism lessons for Mexican children in the little colonia of Simon's Brickyard in East Los Angeles.[50] Through her efforts, and those of Father Robert Lucey, the CCD was organized on a diocesan level. In the early days, the work was so closely identified with Mexicans that the CCD office had to advertise that the CCD was not just for Mexicans. By 1936 Los Angeles claimed a CCD program consisting of 211 centers, with 1,279 teachers, and 28,500 students, a large proportion of which were Mexican.[51] CCD remained a long-term solution to the "Mexican problem." Through the 1950s pastors in Mexican parishes were prodded by their bishops to establish effective CCD programs. In the 1950s Bishop Buddy of San Diego conducted a survey of public school children, then advised his pastors as to whether or not their CCD programs were extensive enough.

While CCD proved an effective program in the urban areas, it was less effective in the rural areas. In the outlying regions the lack of qualified teachers presented a constant problem. While most orders of women religious taught in Catholic schools, several orders chose as their purpose service to the CCD (i.e., children who did not attend Catholic schools). Two orders in particular stand out in their service to the Mexican community in California—the Sisters of the Holy Family, and the Our Lady of Victory Noll Sisters, also known as the Missionary Catechists. The Holy Family Sisters were founded in San Francisco with the express purpose of educating public school children. In the 1920s and 1930s they became quite active in teaching Mexican children in northern California and Los Angeles.

The preeminent group in Mexican work, however, was the missionary Sisters of Our Lady of Victory Noll from Indiana. The Missionary Catechists were founded in the 1920s by a Chicago priest, John Sigstein, and two young laywomen, Julia Doyle and Marie Benes, with the intent of doing missionary work among the Mexican community in New Mexico. An integral part of each Sister's training was instruction in the Spanish language. Interestingly, the main benefactor of the Sisters was an ex-Chicago policeman named Peter O'Donnell, who made a fortune in real estate in California. O'Donnell went to Bishop Cantwell with an offer of $25,000 to support a group of Sisters who had as their apostolate the instruction of Mexican children. Cantwell responded that he had no group in his diocese to do such work. O'Donnell eventually discovered Sigstein and gave his financial backing to the Victory Noll Sisters. In 1930 Cantwell invited the Sisters to work in his diocese.[52]

News spread rapidly of the good work the Sisters were doing among the Mexican Americans in New Mexico. In 1928 the Missionary Catechists were invited to establish their first center in California in the rural town of Dos Palos in the diocese of Monterey-Fresno. Over the next six years they established centers in other parts of California—Brawley, Santa Paula, Tulare County, Redlands, Carmel, Monterey, and San Pedro. By 1936 over sixty catechists were operating in California.

The plan of the Sisters was simple. They would establish a mission center, train lay catechists, then move on to another location. In the San Bernardino Valley alone they tended more than thirty mission centers.[53] As such, the Sisters were continually on the move, traveling from center to center. The Sisters also ministered to the migrant workers at migrant labor camps. At the camps the Sisters generally gathered the children for religious instruction between 11:30 A.M. and 1:30 P.M., the rest of the day the Sisters spent visiting the homes of the immigrants.

The catechists taught wherever they could find a place to gather the children. Over the years they taught in a vacant lot near Brawley, an abandoned gas station in Los Angeles, a seed mill in Imperial, an old hot dog stand in Azusa, and in a large bus in Dos Palos.[54] The bus turned out to be doubly practical as it was used for transportation as well.

Besides their catechetical work, the Sisters also staffed medical clinics in Brawley, San Bernardino, and San Diego which cared for the Mexican populace. As a result, many Sisters began course work to become public health nurses. One volunteer doctor praised the Sisters for providing "total care." "The Sisters are always interested in the social problems, and are anxious to get the home stabilized."[55] He noted, when the clinic was closed in 1961, that their "personal care" would be missed.

Other groups such as the Sisters of Social Service, the Maryknoll Sisters, and many others worked with the Mexican colonias in California, but none equaled the contributions of the Victory Noll Sisters to the Mexican community.

The importance of the CCD program from the diocesan viewpoint is reflected in the fact that in many cases the establishment of CCD mission centers preceded the establishment of the parish. Our Lady of Soledad, Our Lady of the Rosary of Talpa, and Our Lady of Victory in East Los Angeles, to name but a few, all began as catechetical centers. In San Bernardino, Redlands, and Santa Barbara, Mexican parochial schools were established several years prior to the founding of the parish. Again, education was the priority.

The establishment of Our Lady of Victory parish in East Los Angeles provides a typical example of the process. In 1942 the Missionary Catechists began teaching Mexican-American children in the outlying regions of Resurrection parish. As it was too far for the children to come to the parish facilities, the Sisters taught the children in the homes of two parishioners located near to where the children lived. As the ministry progressed, the number of children being taught grew to 150. The pastor of Resurrection parish then rented an abandoned garage, which served as the "new" classroom, with classes meeting twice daily. The following year the garage was renovated, and Sunday Mass was offered there, as Our Lady of Victory was established as a mission of Resurrection parish.[56] Eventually, Our Lady of Victory attained parish status. This pattern was repeated in numerous Mexican parishes throughout southern California.

FOUNDING MISSIONS AND PARISHES

At the heart of ministry to the Mexican community was the parish. In Linna Brissette's study for the National Catholic Welfare Council she observed, "most of the work for the Mexican people centered around individual parishes."[57] As stated earlier, in most cities as of 1910 in California, one parish served as the central Mexican parish for the entire community. The result was that Mexican parishes were often overcrowded. Brissette cites a parish that offered eight Sunday Masses, with each Mass having an average attendance of 2,500 to 3,000 people![58] In Los Angeles, people traveled from great distances to attend the Plaza church, Our Lady Queen of Angels—"La Placita." La Placita was considered the "unofficial cathedral for Hispanics."[59] Mexicans came from throughout the city to be married or have their children baptized there. By 1961 La Placita was performing the staggering number of 6,909 baptisms per year![60] A pastor of a small Mexican mission observed, "many people at San Conrado attend the Plaza as their national church, and are attached to it,"[61] while a popular magazine article observed in the same year, the Plaza Church "remains the heart and soul of our Latin community."[62]

Nevertheless, the rapid influx of immigrants in the 1920s resulted in the creation of new Mexican parishes and missions. In the city of Los Angeles alone, twelve Mexican parishes were established between 1923 and 1928: Our Lady Help of Christians, Santa Teresita, Our Lady of Guadalupe, Our Lady of Solitude (Soledad), Dolores Mission, San Miguel (Watts), Assumption, St. Turibius, San Antonio de Padua, Our Lady of the Rosary of Talpa, La Purísima, and Our Lady of Guadalupe (Rosehill). By 1936 the archdiocese reported forty-four Mexican parishes throughout southern California and more than seventy missions. By 1947 Bishop Joseph McGucken claimed there were sixty-four "Mexican parishes" in the archdiocese of Los Angeles alone.[63] This explosion of Mexican parishes was assisted by more than a hundred Mexican priests who were exiled during the Mexican Revolution and later during the Cristero Rebellion. These exiled priests were assigned to parishes throughout the southland. In one case a Mexican mission, La Sagrada Familia, in Westminster, had its inception at a community picnic in 1929, when several lay exiles from the Cristero Rebellion encountered an exiled priest. Together they formed the new mission.[64] In addition to exiled priests, seven exiled bishops and an archbishop found refuge in Los Angeles during the 1920s. Bishop Cantwell's open welcome to the exiles provided great benefits for his Mexican Catholics.

Even with the creation of so many new parishes, the need for Mexican parishes remained acute, particularly in the rural areas. In May, 1928, the archdiocesan newspaper, the *Tidings*, bore the headline, "Los Angeles Now Second Largest Mexican City: Mission Problem Acute."[65] The article publicized the upcoming collection for the "home missions." Parishioners were asked to be generous so that missions could be built for their Mexican brethren. The article warned that if this need were not met, "we will lose the next generation."[66] The specter of Protestant proselytizers was once again raised to encourage generosity.

The preferred strategy in ministry to the Mexican was to build a small mission chapel in the Mexican colonia. Four basic types of missions were established: 1) the rural mission which was attended from a central parish; 2) the urban mission that was within the boundaries of an "Anglo" parish; 3) the urban mission that was officially a mission but operated as a parish, with a resident pastor and little reference to the "parent" parish; and 4) the mission that eventually became a parish, resident pastor and all.

St. Boniface parish in Anaheim in Orange County provides a good example of the parish mission center. Father Patrick Browne, appointed pastor of St. Boniface in 1918, entered his pastorate aware of the need to provide better care for Mexican Catholics in California. Eleven years in Salinas (1907–1918), where he had learned Spanish, had made him sensitive to that need. During the 1920s, the Mexican population increased 348 percent in Orange County, with most Mexicans employed in the rapidly expanding agricultural industries. Browne established four missions in the colonias of Stanton, La Jolla, Manzanillo, and Independencia. Stanton and Manzanillo were established first as a result of Browne's initiative. Both chapels were dedicated to Our Lady of Guadalupe. Besides providing CCD, the missions offered Mass twice a month: Masses were offered at Stanton on the first and third Sundays and at Manzanillo on the second and fourth. The third chapel, also called Our Lady of Guadalupe, was established in 1925 in La Jolla, a colonia in East Anaheim. An outstanding layman, Emilio Vargas, asked Browne to establish a mission and then proceeded to raise funds for the new church through a series of community dances. The fourth mission, Sagrado Corazón in Independencia, was built in 1926. Browne had told a layman that if he could gather fifty signatures he would build a mission chapel. One hundred signatures were collected. In 1941 three of the missions were turned over to the care of Blessed Sacrament parish in Westminster.[67] The practice of a central mission parish which sent priests to minister periodically to the outlying missions was familiar.

The second type of mission, the Mexican mission within the boundaries of an Anglo parish, was the result of the inability of Mexicans and Anglos to coexist in the same parish. For example, in Riverside during the 1920s at St. Francis de Sales parish Mexicans were at best tolerated. Mexican parishioners were allowed to attend only the 8:00 A.M. Mass on Sundays and were allowed to sit in only the last four rows of the church. At the 10:00 A.M. Mass, the Irish pastor would walk down the aisles asking Mexicans to leave. The split came one Sunday when Mexican devotions to Our Lady of Guadalupe ran too long. Upset, the pastor allegedly told the Mexicans never to come back. Several of the Mexican families petitioned the bishop for a parish of their own. The bishop granted their request but did not allow them to call their mission Our Lady of Guadalupe and made them a mission of St. Francis de Sales. For several years the mission was known as St. Brigid's, and from 1940–1957 it was called St. Francis of Assisi. In 1958 the mission was allowed to change its name to Our Lady of Guadalupe Shrine. All the while it operated as a mission of St. Francis de Sales.[68] While conflicts were not always so blatant, the arrangement for a Mexican mission within an Anglo parish was not uncommon, particularly in suburban and well-to-do areas.

The third type of mission, the mission that operated like a parish, with a resident pastor, was somewhat rare. San Jose's Our Lady of Guadalupe Chapel operated in this fashion during the decade 1952 to 1962. Father Donald McDonnell was in residence and operated as pastor, with little reference to the church to which it was a mission. Officially, however, it was regarded as a mission, not a parish. Our Lady of Guadalupe parish in Delhi, Orange County, operated in the same manner.

Finally, many missions were what might be termed "transitory missions," as they were eventually raised to parish status. In this case, a small mission was established in a colonia until the congregation grew large enough to support a parish and a resident pastor. In East Los Angeles this was a familiar pattern. Within St. Mary's parish boundaries, five Mexican parishes were established. All five began as missions of St. Mary's, before they became parishes in their own right.[69]

Whatever the type, it was standard operating procedure to establish a Mexican mission to minister to the Mexican Catholic community. In so doing, Mexicans were given a place of their own where they could worship in their own language and celebrate their traditional feasts. The effects could be impressive. The *Los Angeles Tidings* reports of Our Lady of Solitude in the town of Coachella, "A few years ago a little chapel was built here and efforts were made to bring the Mexicans back to the Church from which they were drifting."[70] These efforts were enormously successful.

In sum, the mission strategy could be effective. Three basic reasons made the mission system expedient: first, the differences in customs between Mexican piety and American. In El Monte, the chapel of Our Lady of Guadalupe was established as a mission of Nativity parish, when Mexican participation at Ash Wednesday services was criticized as being excessive by Anglo parishioners.[71] In order to celebrate their feasts and devotions without disturbance and according to their traditions, Mexicans needed a place of their own. Second, due to their extreme poverty Mexicans were often unable to raise enough money to build a church or support a parish of their own. This financial problem was solved by placing the mission under the care of a wealthier parish, which provided financial assistance. For instance, according to Father Augustine O'Dea, in Los Angeles, Holy Cross parish built a Mexican mission church for the Watts colonia; Precious Blood parish bore most of the expense for the building of Our Lady of the Rosary of Talpa, and several parishes, Good Shepherd, St. Paul's, and Immaculate Heart, built a new chapel for the rural colonia at Roscoe.[72] The down side of this financial arrangement was that mission chapels were often small and at times ill-kept. In 1944 the Mexican mission in Santa Paula sent a "Committee of Five" to the chancery to protest the physical neglect of their church. On more than one occasion the Mexican mission was given the old church building when a parish built a bigger church. For instance, in San Jose, when St. Martin's parish built a new church, the old church was transported across town to become the new Our Lady of Guadalupe Chapel.

Mexicans/Mexican Americans have often been accused of failing to support their parishes. A number of explanations have been offered, with special emphasis being placed on the Mexicans' lack of familiarity with the voluntaristic style of Church support typical of the United States. Lack of support, however, was most directly a result of Mexican poverty. Bishop Charles Buddy of San Diego counseled a pastor in Redlands, "the Mexican people are constitutionally generous. If they have money, you will surely get a donation."[73] And a pastor in Coachella reported, "Since I came here the young Mexicans have been supporting me wonderfully."[74] Often Mexican support, or lack of it, was dependent on the approach of the pastor. A third reason for the mission system was racism within the Church. The example of Our Lady of Guadalupe Shrine in Riverside has already been cited. Unfortunately, its experience was not an isolated one. Thus, the establishment of a Mexican mission cut two ways: it provided Mexicans with a refuge where they could worship as they desired, but it also reminded them of their outsider status in the American Catholic Church. Many Mexican Americans can recall the pain of being told by Anglo pastors to "go to your own church."

THE NATIONAL PARISH

While the national parish and mission for Mexicans proved very effective, national parishes as a rule were not considered the best policy. The national parish had been the primary means used by the Church to assimilate and protect immigrants through the nineteenth century in the United States; it had provided a separate parish for each immigrant group, which had allowed them to adapt to American culture at their own pace, thereby enabling them to preserve the more positive aspects of their culture, especially the Catholic faith. By 1920 the national parish had fallen out of favor. In 1921 the chancellor for the diocese of Los Angeles noted "it is the wish of the Holy Father that national churches as far as possible be dispensed with in the United States."[75] The national parish, it was argued, detracted from the "universal" quality of the Catholic Church, establishing too many separate churches that placed ethnic pride and loyalty above attachment to the Catholic Church. Nonetheless, the presence of large communities of Spanish-speaking Catholics necessitated the maintenance of Mexican national parishes.[76] However, the growing success of the civil rights movement in the 1940s and 1950s inspired a renewed questioning of the national parish; the Mexican parish appeared to be a segregated Parish, the fruit of racism rather than of pastoral concern. Integrated parishes were now the preferred model. By the 1950s many of the national parishes had been assigned territorial boundaries, and requests for new national parishes were repeatedly denied. In 1950 a request for a national parish in San Jose was denied on the basis that Mexicans should be integrated into parish life rather than segregated. The previous year a priest working in the Mexican apostolate provided the rationale. "We are not working for a Mexican Nationalist Movement. We are American Catholics. The Church is one. We must certainly bring the Latin American Catholics to church by means of devotions in Spanish and by contact with priests in their own language, but our aim must ever be to assimilate and incorporate them into parish life."[77] Nonetheless, Mexican Catholics rejected this analysis and continued to petition for parishes of their own. The San Jose petitioners presented their petition with 1,278 signatures; it reiterated the basic reasons for establishing a national parish. They wanted

A church of their own, where they can worship God according to their devotions and customs . . . have easy access to confession in their own language at any time, understand the sermons at Sunday mass, receive the sacrament of matrimony from a priest of their own race, who understands their psychology and customs, and finally, where they can feel at ease in a Church of their own, without fear of humiliation due to racial discrimination which unfortunately still exists, even among Catholics.[78]

Again in 1955, a Jesuit priest working on the west side of San Jose asked that the old Italian national parish be transformed into a national parish for the Spanish speaking. "The people do come. They would come more if they are given a greater share in the life of the parish."[79] His petition was denied. Both sides of the question had the same goal—the greater participation of the Mexican in the life of the parish. They disagreed as to means. In 1960, when Our Lady of Guadalupe Chapel in San Jose petitioned for national parish status, they were given the standard reply, "The difficulties in administering a national parish are too complicated. The Church should be Catholic, that is, for everyone. The Mexican people want to be integrated with the Church as Catholics, not segregated."[80]

Allan Figueroa Deck has argued in his book *The Second Wave* that the lack of national parishes in the 1950s hurt Mexican Catholics. The rapid increase of Mexican immigration coincided with the decline in popularity of the national parish. Without the national parish, Mexicans were not allowed to develop their own organizations, or their own leadership as previous immigrant groups had done.[81] Scholar Robert Pulido agrees. By not having their own parishes, Mexicans were never able to move beyond "missionary status," and therefore became marginal in terms of the Church in the United States.[82] Antonio Soto asserts that integrated parishes always worked to the Mexicans' disadvantage. As long as Anglo members were dominant, Mexicans/Mexican Americans were expected to be docile followers. In such cases, further marginalization of the Mexican from parish life occurred.[83] Deck argues that a major reason for the lack of Mexican national parishes was the lack of Hispanic clergy to staff the parishes, "without their own priest, the people are at a great disadvantage in getting their portion of attention, cooperation and assistance within the institution."[84] As a result, Mexicans flocked to parishes offering services in Spanish "because they can't get what they need at the institutional parish."[85]

The observations of a young Anglo priest working in El Monte in 1949 concur with Deck. In 1949 the old mission chapel of Our

Lady of Guadalupe, the Mexican mission of Nativity parish in El Monte, was in need of repair. Rather than invest a substantial amount of money refurbishing the old church, a unification of the parish was suggested. John Coffield, a young priest ordained less than ten years, who was responsible for the mission, reflected that while the unification had several positive features—organizations would not have to be duplicated, fund-raising would be easier, the children were already attending CCD at Nativity anyway, and a 10:00 A.M. Sunday Mass with a Spanish sermon would satisfy the Mexicans—a number of significant negative factors had to be considered, primarily: "a feeling among some of the Mexicans that they are not wanted due in part to their shyness and in part to unfortunate situations in the distant past, and the present lack of understanding of Father Gerity [the pastor]. Some would feel the Church was not interested in them anymore."[86]

Coffield was going against the tide. National parishes still persisted, but increasingly prevalent were what Deck calls *de facto national parishes*,"[87] parishes in the middle of the barrio, and therefore composed almost entirely of Mexicans, but not officially designated as Mexican national parishes. These parishes operated as "unofficial" national parishes, drawing Mexicans from beyond their parish boundaries because they offered services in Spanish. The main drawback to the national parish was the second and third generations, who were bilingual and bicultural, or who spoke primarily English. In classic immigrant fashion, second and third generations were not as enthralled with the Mexican parish as their parents had been. In East Los Angeles the "problem" was "solved" by designating Our Lady of Lourdes as a parish where "American or English speaking" could go, rather than their own parish. In 1952, this practice ceased.[88]

The large number of new immigrants, plus the desire of older first-generation immigrants to maintain their traditions, kept many national parishes afloat in the 1950s. However, the problem remained. A parish Sister in Los Nietos highlighted the problem of the second generation and the national parish. In a letter to Bishop Timothy Manning she asked if the parish was to be a "national parish. Does that imply that anyone who does not speak Spanish is to go elsewhere? If so, how can we educate our youth to this . . . how can we get them to the sacraments?"[89] The best solution, she suggested, was a bilingual priest familiar with American and Mexican customs who could minister to young and old.

A Mexican Bishop in California? Conflict in San Diego

As Mexican Catholics struggled to obtain parishes of their own, some also sought to obtain a bishop of their own. Most ethnic groups, particularly the Germans and the Polish, have agitated to receive bishops of their own nationality. Little mention has been made of Mexican efforts to obtain a bishop of their own prior to the 1960s. In the late 1930s in San Diego conflict erupted between elements of the Mexican Catholic community and Bishop Charles Buddy of San Diego. (San Diego had become a separate diocese in 1936.) The encounter highlighted the conflict between Mexican Catholics and the American Catholic Church. Floating beneath the surface of the conflict was a move to obtain a bishop for the Mexican community in southern California.

Bishop Charles Buddy was appointed to the new missionary diocese of San Diego in 1936. He immediately took note of the complaints he was receiving against the Spanish Augustinian Recollects who were in charge of two major Mexican parishes—Our Lady of Guadalupe in San Diego and Our Lady of Guadalupe in San Bernardino. The complaints registered reflect the diversity of opinion within the Mexican Catholic community. Buddy received complaints against Father Augustine Cuartero in San Bernardino and Father Damian Gobeo in San Diego alleging that the dances each of them sponsored in their parish halls were "immoral" and "tempted" the young.[90] Several letters were directed to the apostolic delegate with similar complaints. One complained, "a venus danced a *rumba* to the beat of the music in which the thermometer of the youth rose with great rapidity."[91] Cuartero responded that the dances were held every two weeks in conjunction with parish *jamaicas* (fund-raising socials), and provided a healthy meeting place for Catholic youth. One of the protesters verbally attacked Cuartero at a Holy Name Society meeting, resulting in the protester's expulsion from the group. The protester led the protests against Cuartero in San Bernardino.

In San Diego complaints were brought against Gobeo for more than dances. He allegedly slighted the Mexican community. On one occasion he allegedly refused to provide shelter for a group of exiled Mexican nuns, and on other occasions he had prohibited the use of the church facilities to several Mexican groups. Another parishioner complained that he had not been allowed to place the flags of the United States and Mexico beneath the picture of Our Lady of Guadalupe.[92] One complaint concluded with a request for

Mexican priests, who "shall have sufficient patience to teach us the way of the faith through their example and teaching . . . in our own language and customs."[93] Buddy responded to the complaints by removing the Spanish Augustinians from San Bernardino. Buddy wanted the parish to be staffed by diocesan priests and used the complaints as a reason to intervene and remove the Augustinians. The removal was met by vigorous protests in support of the Augustinians. The Holy Name Society asked Buddy why he was removing Spanish-speaking priests from a diocese that was sorely in need of Spanish-speaking priests. If their requests were not met, they threatened to 1) petition the apostolic delegate; 2) get other Mexican parishes involved with the protests; and 3) picket the rectory, preventing the Augustinians from leaving, and preventing any other priests from entering.[94] Buddy was incensed. To him the protest was not simply a question of ethnic concerns; it was also a question of Church authority. He responded, "These misguided people must be taught their place."[95] Buddy sent a representative to San Bernardino to inform the Holy Name Society that they were all to resign. Suspecting the Augustinians were behind the discontent, Buddy removed them from San Diego as well.

The removal of the Augustinians from San Diego also resulted in community protests. The night before Father Gobeo was to leave, three hundred Mexicans gathered at the chancery to present a petition with 1,500 signatures in support of the Augustinians. Gobeo, the petition asserted, was "the founder of the Mexican colony," who had "Christianized our children."[96] Receiving no satisfaction from Buddy, the protesters sent their petition to Rome, signed by the heads of seven parish societies, asking the pope to intervene on behalf of the Mexican people in California. Similarly, protesters in San Bernardino sent a petition, signed by the heads of four parish societies, to the apostolic delegate, accusing Buddy of treating Mexicans poorly and claiming that he had removed Spanish-speaking priests and replaced them with Irish ones.[97] During the bishop's visit to San Bernardino to preside at the sacrament of confirmation at a neighboring parish, 300 protesters met with Buddy and were upset by his tone. Buddy's vicar general reported that the people felt that "the Bishop had treated the Mexicans badly at the meeting."[98]

Buddy again saw the problem as one of authority. He orchestrated an open letter in support of his actions to be signed by a "spontaneous committee." The letter was to disassociate the "faithful Mexicans," from the "small group of troublemakers."[99]

The letter was also to acknowledge "that there is such a thing as episcopal authority."[100] Buddy concluded, "We have no obligation to indulge the Mexicans."[101]

Buddy knew how to wield power. When a noted Mexican attorney, Guillermo Rosas of Los Angeles, sent Buddy a letter on behalf of the Mexican community, Buddy responded by having INS and FBI agents harass Rosas. When Rosas left the United States to visit Mexico, Buddy attempted to prevent his reentry to the United States. Buddy felt it was necessary "to teach this man a lesson not to interfere with the Church authorities in this country as pretentious Mexicans have done in Mexico."[102]

One final protest was sent to Pope Pius XII by Mrs. Paula Espinoza, the founder of the Congregation of Christian Mothers at Our Lady of Guadalupe in San Diego and president of the Society of Perpetual Adoration. Mrs. Espinoza wrote "on behalf of the members of her race." She reasserted the complaint that an "Irish" pastor had been assigned who did not know the language or the customs. Indeed, Buddy had appointed the Rev. Matthew Thompson. One of Thompson's earliest letters to Buddy suggests why the Mexican community may have been so upset. While Thompson promised to

> Preserve faithfully all the customs of our Holy Faith that are proper to the Mexican race, . . . the Church is Catholic before it is Mexican or American. . . . I said that it is not unreasonable to expect them to conform to the customs of the Church in America, and to avoid the trappings of Mexican customs which will bring the Church into disrepute in an American Country. I referred particularly to the Pagan custom of the Danizantes, who dressed themselves in weird costumes and painted their faces and disported themselves in ludicrous gyrations before the Blessed Sacrament carried in procession. This part of the custom was not permitted.[103]

Buddy's appointment in San Bernardino was better suited to the challenges that awaited him. Monsignor Joseph Núñez was appointed to replace the Augustinians. His presence resolved many of the controversies in San Bernardino, where he served for the next two and a half decades.

The problem was not so easily resolved in San Diego. While exact figures are difficult to obtain, Our Lady of Guadalupe allegedly suffered a decline in Mass attendance and parish support after the departure of the Augustinians. (Buddy denied this.) One woman remembers, "It is very strange going to Church there; that is why so many people left."[104] Allegedly, many people began crossing the border into Mexico to receive the important sacraments—baptism for their children, marriage, and confirmation. Prior to the conflict, many people had done this. Crossing the border was still rather free and easy, despite the presence of the Border Patrol. However, an increase in traffic across the border after the crisis is suggested by the fact that Buddy found it necessary to make a pronouncement forbidding members of his diocese from receiving the sacraments in Mexico.

The problem was further complicated by the intervention of Monsignor Felipe Torres Hurtado into the affair. Torres Hurtado was the vicar apostolic for lower California. He began circulating among the Mexican colonias in the San Diego area. He allegedly visited San Diego twice a week and invited the Mexicans to come to Tijuana. Hurtado then sent a letter to the apostolic delegate accusing Buddy of neglecting the Mexican Catholics in San Diego and of replacing Spanish-speaking priests with priests who did not speak Spanish.[105] Buddy was outraged by Hurtado's "meddling" and ordered him to stay out of his diocese. An investigation into the conflict revealed that Hurtado was agitating for the appointment of a Mexican bishop to take care of the Mexican colonias in southern California. His efforts never progressed to the stage of filing a formal petition with the apostolic delegate, but "clandestine" discussion explored the possibility.[106]

Buddy's response to the various protests provides a window to view his strategy regarding ministry to his Mexican and Mexican-American faithful. In letters to the apostolic delegate, Buddy asserted that a great amount of work was being done among the Mexicans, and he affirmed his love for them. They were not being neglected. The complaints of Torres Hurtado were the result of his listening to "a small group of troublemakers." Buddy's attitude toward his Mexican faithful at times slipped into condescension; referring to them as "poor, ignorant . . . easily misled," and observing that "bickering is characteristic of the majority of Mexican parishes."[107] Buddy's basic strategy was to assist the Mexicans in becoming good, "Mass and sacraments" American Catholics who would support their parish. Spanish and Mexican priests were not the answer. Spanish priests did not relate well to Mexicans, and Mexicans were the source of too many scandals. "We have had more than our share of serious trouble from the Spanish and Mexican priests."[108] Buddy's solution was to create a native San Diegan clergy who spoke Spanish and who could minister to the Mexicans. To encourage this he introduced Spanish classes at his seminary. The introduction of American priests had previously had positive results. The removal of the Augustinians had been necessary, according to Buddy. In a letter to the apostolic delegate he said: "The Augustinian Recollects were incompetent to direct the affairs of a Mexican parish. They let the Mexicans do just about as they pleased. We could not be satisfied with the results. Scarcely 15% of the Mexicans attended Mass on Sunday."[109] Few children attended CCD, according to Buddy, and support for the parish was minimal. This was not the result when American priests were appointed to Mexican parishes. Buddy argued that Mexicans did not care about the nationality of the priest; what they wanted was "GOOD PRIESTS."[110] Further he asserted, "There are thousands of other Mexicans scattered throughout the city, who are quite satisfied to attend English speaking parishes."[111]

Buddy also restated the basic strategy that had been used in Los Angeles: Mexican children had to be properly instructed in the faith. "The only hope of the Mexicans is to instruct them in the fundamentals of religion."[112] He advocated an aggressive program of education to be spearheaded by the Missionary Catechists. As had been the case in Los Angeles, education would include Americanization to protect the Mexican from the "communist threat." Buddy wrote, "The real danger to the Mexicans is not Protestantism, but communism."[113] To counter this danger, Mexicans had to be educated and Americanized. As for a bishop for the Mexicans in southern California, Buddy would be that bishop. Two bishops in Buddy's diocese would have been one bishop too many. Buddy remained bishop of San Diego until his death in 1966.[114]

CONCLUSION

Contrary to the accusation that the Catholic Church abandoned the Mexican immigrant, the Church, particularly in southern California, provided a variety of charitable, educational, and parochial services to the Mexican community. Statistical reports to Rome by Cantwell in 1936 and 1944, and by Buddy in 1947, though probably inflated, reveal an impressive commitment to the Mexican community. Historian Francis Weber's summary of the 1944 report claims eight child care centers, two boarding houses for girls, seven settlement houses, a maternity hospital and clinic, and over 200 CCD centers worked on behalf of the Mexican Catholic community.[115] In 1947 Buddy claimed the diocese of San Diego provided the Mexican community with thirty parishes and missions, three medical centers, and three recreational centers.[116] Cantwell's efforts on behalf of the Mexican refugees received a note of special gratitude from the Mexican hierarchy. In addition, he was given a special Mexican honor, the Golden Rose of Tepeyac, "One of Mexico's highest rewards."[117] Francis Weber has dubbed Cantwell, "The Irish born champion of the Mexican American,"[118] and his service to his Mexican faithful was impressive.

Not everyone agrees with this rosy assessment. Critics have charged that the Church was overly concerned with validating its own place in American society by aggressively Americanizing the Mexican. Others have accused the Church of a "patronizing" or "paternalistic" attitude toward the Mexican. A recent study of the city of Los Angeles makes a scathing assessment of Cantwell, "Yet his attitude toward his half million Mexican parishioners was characterized by unwavering condescension ('the simple people of God') and entrenched hostility to the community's progressive and nationalist current."[119] We have already cited the difficulties created by racism within the Catholic Church. Other critics charged that the Church was too preoccupied with Protestant proselytizers and sacramental validation at the expense of developing an "indigenous" Mexican leadership.[120] The result was that many leaders within the Mexican Catholic community were Anglo: Fathers John Coffield, Augustine O'Dea, Leroy Callahan, Donald McDonnell, and Thomas McCullough, to name but a few. Finally some critics have argued that the Church focused too much on the spiritual and not enough on social needs. In the mid-1960s a community group in East Los Angeles observed, "The Church has not been sufficiently aware of the socio-economic needs of the disadvantaged people of the community."[121]

All these criticisms involve larger questions as to what the proper role of the Church is. In the pre–Vatican II era, the prevailing model of Church in the United States insisted that the Church's primary goal was the preservation of the immigrant's faith and the salvation of souls, not the transformation of society. Provision of the Mass and the sacraments were understood to be the primary means of achieving both goals. Since the Second Vatican Council, greater emphasis has been placed on personal faith experience and on the transformation of society through the evangelical witness of Christians. The shift in models of the Church accounts for the harsh judgment of Cantwell and his contemporaries, but judged by their own model they did achieve some success.

3

Spirituality and Clergy

Most scholars of the Mexican American community have spoken of the clash between Mexican Catholic immigrants and the Catholic Church they discovered in America. The conflict in San Diego was just such a manifestation. Differences in piety, customs, leadership styles, and of course, language, provided the possibility of endless conflict. We have already discussed Amat's clash with Mexican customs in the nineteenth century. Many of the same conflicts recurred in the twentieth century. The continual immigration of Mexicans since 1910 has made these problems seem ever current.

Mexican/Mexican-American Spirituality

When Mexicans encountered the Catholic Church in America, it often seemed alien to the Church they had known in Mexico. In Mexican villages the church was usually located in the center of town, the plaza, and the rhythms of the community were closely associated with the rhythms of the liturgical seasons. Blessings, rituals, fiestas, and processions were an integral part of that experience. Carey McWilliams describes the Mexican society from which most immigrants to California came as what recent scholars call "pre-modern." He observes, "Superimposed on this folk society, the ceremonial aspect of the Catholic Church was emphasized somewhat to the detriment of its ethical teachings."[1] The Church the Mexican encountered in California seemed more severe, legalistic, and distant. One Mexican woman visiting a "gringo church" in Sacramento complained, "It doesn't feel like Church."[2] The number of churches and different religions also perplexed the Mexican immigrant. Another complained, "There are too many religions here."[3]

All Mexicans did not experience the idyllic, village church in Mexico. One historian notes, "A severe shortage of clerics [in Mexico] at the turn of the century, however, meant that parishioners were without their own village priests."[4] This was particularly true in the rapidly growing northern states. The result was that many

176

Mexicans became less dependent on a priest-centered religion and developed popular devotions which could be performed without a priest. Some scholars have suggested that this spirituality developed much earlier than this—the lack of priests merely reinforced devotions which had been established previously.

Mexican-American spirituality developed both private and public expressions. Private spirituality, which was practiced individually or within the family, stressed sacramentals and personal devotions, while the public religion stressed processions, fiestas, symbols, and symbolic action that displayed the beliefs of the Mexican Catholic to the rest of the community. Public actions also served to build up the community, bolstering community identity. Often the two worlds merged in paraliturgical devotions. For the most part, private devotions were the special province of women and children, while public events included both men and women. Underlying many of the practices, public and private, was a popular theology that stressed a deep awe and reverence for the supernatural, in which the natural and supernatural were not two distinct spheres but realities which intersected one another often. Mary, the saints, and Jesus took a personal interest in their children and friends, and were ready to respond to their appeals. They did not remain aloof from the struggles and trials of this world. The private and public expressions testified to the deep spirituality of the Mexican people. While the Irish-American clergy may have seen these practices as "magical" or "superstitious," a recent scholar suggests that they were in reality "expressive, colorful, and imaginative."[5]

The shortage of priests who spoke Spanish was a perennial problem in California, except for a brief period in the 1920s. Some migrant workers went months, even years, without seeing a priest. The shortage of clergy was compounded by the lack of hospitality exhibited by many American "Irish" parishes. As a result, the popular piety that had developed in Mexico apart from the clergy and the institutional Church had ample reason to continue its development in California. One Mexican immigrant woman in 1917 recalled, "We never saw a priest or a church since we were out in the desert. But I always had my devotions and the basic prayers. . . . One practice I always had was to make the sign of the cross at the spot where I was to place my first tortilla everyday, for it reminded me of the sacred host."[6]

The transmission of the faith in Mexican/Mexican-American households was left to the family, primarily to the mother and grandmother. Virgil Elizondo refers to the practice as "religión casera,"[7] while Gilbert Cadena has dubbed it "abuelita theology."[8] Another scholar describes the practice in the following fashion, "The greater part of one's faith life and devotional life is learned from mothers and grandmothers, who make use of novenas, prayers, and *imagenes* to communicate the religious sense and to foster a personal and family spirituality. This whole strain of religiosity has been developed without the need for the presence of priests and is generally unrelated to the official liturgical life of the Church."[9] The Mexican Catholic then, was not the average "Mass and sacraments" Catholic, but the faith remained an integral part of the Mexicans' life, nonetheless. The style of Catholicism that developed in the Mexican-American home stressed sacramentals—holy water, candles, rosaries, scapulars, medals, relics—and devotions—novenas and triduums. Many Mexican homes maintained family altars, or altarcitos. A study in 1920 in Los Angeles found 46 percent of the sample to have home altars, and a study of San José's Mexican community in the 1950s found more than 50 percent of the homes maintaining altarcitos.[10] Beatrice Griffith reports in 1948 of Los Angeles:

> In nearly all Catholic homes, of whatever economic class, you find the tiny shrine in a corner of the bedroom. There stands a statue of the Virgin (before a votive candle) adorned with fresh or paper flowers. Important letters, birth or marriage certificates, are frequently placed on the little shelf, together with the rosary, crucifix, special medals, novena prayers, and probably a small picture of the Virgin of Guadalupe.[11]

Not all homes had altars. Margaret Clark suggests the inroads of secularism into the Mexican community in the 1950s, as she observes that where one used to find an altar, one now found "a high fidelity record player."[12]

The veneration of saints was also integral to Mexican piety, and was expressed both publicly and privately. Saints were reputed to have special powers, and they were more approachable than God or Jesus. Medals and statues of the saints were common, and some were reputed to be the source of miracles. People prayed to their special saint for various favors—help in finding a job, recovery from sickness, protection from harm—in the form of *manda* or *promesa*. If the petition to the saint was granted, the person was obligated to make a pilgrimage to the saint's shrine or perform some other promised action. Some American priests worried that

Mexican veneration of the saints verged on superstition, or belief in magic, in which the medal or the statue was thought to have the power, rather than the saint. Many did use saint's medals to protect themselves from evil or misfortune. In the 1920 study, 36 percent of those polled believed that a saint's medal could protect one from an accident.[13] An immigrant from the 1920s recalls, "I never go to Church, nor do I pray. I have an amulet which my mother gave to me before dying. This amulet has the Virgin of Guadalupe on it, and it is she who protects me."[14] Blessings, novenas, and various sacramentals would also protect one from evils, such as ghosts and devils, and the havoc they might cause. Carey McWilliams refers to the "magical mentality"[15] that informed Mexican popular Catholicism, and Richard Rodríguez speaks of the "nightmare Catholicism of demons and angels."[16] Evil spirits were just as real in popular culture as were the saints. Two figures familiar to most Mexicans were the *bruja* (witch) and the *curandera* (healer). The curandera was able to provide herbal remedies and cures; the spiritual curandera was able to protect one from evil spirits. Some priests felt that the curandera, at times, usurped their roles.

The mixture of myth, magic, and genuine devotion worried some. In 1949 the Priests Conference for the Spanish Speaking for the Archdiocese of San Francisco reported, "Among the people there is widespread superstition, even the practice of witchcraft."[17] These had to be eradicated if the Mexican Catholic was to fit into the American Church.

Paraliturgical celebrations also flourished in the Mexican community, such as the celebrations of Ash Wednesday to begin Lent, the burning of Judas on Good Friday or Holy Saturday, Las Posadas and Los Pastores at Christmas. On Ash Wednesday virtually everyone in the barrio received ashes. As one Los Angeles pastor recalls, "All the 'bandidos' show up on Ash Wednesday."[18] Popular belief had it that if you received ashes you would live the rest of the year. If you did not, "you might die."[19] On Good Friday, the people would gather to burn a papier-mâché Judas, "the traitorous disciple." In San Salvador parish in Colton this attracted Spanish speaking from a wide area beyond Colton. On Christmas eve Mexican communities sponsored Las Posadas, in which two parishioners, dressed as Mary and Joseph, traveled from home to home in search of shelter. Their search usually ended with a fiesta at the parish center.

Most parishes sponsored a variety of ongoing devotional societies and devotions. A typical parish might offer devotions to Our

Lady of Perpetual Help each Tuesday, a holy hour on Thursday, a novena to Our Lady on Friday, a special Mass and rosary the twelfth of each month in honor of Our Lady of Guadalupe, and frequent exposition of the Blessed Sacrament. It might sponsor societies such as Las Hijas de María (Daughters of Mary), El Sagrado Corazón (the Sacred Heart), Le Vela Perpetua (Perpetual Adoration), or El Santo Nombre (Holy Name). In addition, each year or every other year a parish mission was held. The mission, much like a revival meeting, attempted to bring Mexican Catholics who were in danger of drifting from the Church, back to the faith, and to encourage them to greater devotion to and participation in the life of the parish.

The central figure in Mexican-American spirituality was the Mother of God. Like the saints, Mary acted as a mediator; in her humanity, she was more approachable than God, who at times seemed stern and distant. In addition, Mary's maternal love provided solace to the Mexican people, while affirming their dignity. Devotions to Mary in her various manifestations—Our Lady of San Juan de los Lagos, Our Lady of the Rosary of Talpa, de Remedios, de Zapopan—which flourished in various parts of Mexico, were transplanted by the immigrants in California. In so doing a vital part of village life and faith was brought to the new, and at times bewildering, environment, providing a sense of security and assurance.

The greatest Marian devotion, however, one that united the Mexican people, was devotion to Our Lady of Guadalupe, "La Morenita." In 1531, Mary appeared as a young Indian woman in native dress to an Indian named Juan Diego in the hills near Mexico City. She spoke to him in his native language, Nahuatl. Mary's appearance and message offered comfort to an oppressed and exploited native population. "I am thy merciful mother . . . I shall listen to your sorrows, and free you from all your misery, grief and anguish."[20] To the Indian and Mestizo population, Guadalupe instilled a sense of personal dignity in the face of the affronts of the Spanish colonizers. She was not only a religious figure but a national figure who gave birth to the Mexican faith and people. Richard Rodríguez captures the importance of the Guadalupe event.

> Above all mediators there was Mary, Santa María. . . . Whereas at school the primary mediator was Christ, at home that role was assumed by the Mexican Virgin, Nuestra Señora de Guadalupe, the

focus of devotion and pride for Mexican Catholics. The Mexican Mary "honored our people," my mother would say. "She could have appeared to anyone in the whole world, but she appeared to a Mexican." Someone like us. And she appeared, I could see from her picture, as a young maiden—dark just like me.[21]

To generation after generation the apparition of Our Lady of Guadalupe affirmed the Mexican people and provided solace to a people whose existence was often quite harsh, particularly in the United States.

Within every Mexican church (and in many Anglo churches) a picture of Our Lady of Guadalupe could be found. Mexicans often insisted that the picture of Guadalupe hang over the altar, a practice which at times brought them into conflict with Anglo priests, who failed to grasp the importance of Guadalupe to their Mexican parishioners. At Santa Clara parish in Oxnard conflict arose when an old picture of Our Lady of Guadalupe hanging above the altar was removed and a new statue of Our Lady of Guadalupe was installed, but at a side altar. A committee was formed to protest what was considered a demotion of Our Lady of Guadalupe. Attendance at devotions at the parish dropped until the picture was returned to its rightful place.[22]

The devotion to Our Lady of Guadalupe gave birth to the most common parochial organization for Mexican Americans, the Sociedad Guadalupana. Historian Moisés Sandoval calls the Guadalupanas the "main guardians of the culture and religious tradition of the Hispanic people."[23] The Sociedad's main task was to foster devotion to Our Lady of Guadalupe and to prepare for the annual celebration on the feast of Our Lady of Guadalupe, December 12. Each month, generally on the twelfth, the Sociedad attended a special Mass and rosary. The society was usually entirely female, but the importance of the devotion made the Sociedad, according to Allan F. Deck, one of the "centers of power in the parish."[24] The Sociedad also provided service to the parish, at times operating like an altar society. Participation in the Sociedad could increase one's attachment to the institutional church. In Santa Clara parish in Oxnard the pastor reported that since the creation of a Sociedad Guadalupana the reception of communion in the parish had increased noticeably.[25]

The devotion to Our Lady of Guadalupe provided an opportunity for another important aspect of Mexican-American spirituality and its most public profession, the procession. In 1927 a major procession in honor of Our Lady of Guadalupe was begun in East Los Angeles. The procession was held annually and attracted as many as 5,000 marchers, along with 30,000 spectators.[26] A recent historian of Los Angeles claims the procession "rivaled Cinco de Mayo in the community"[27] in terms of importance and popularity. It was quite elaborate, with floats, bands, and a statue of the Virgin impressively decorated. The procession began at the county line and proceeded through the streets to Our Lady of Guadalupe Church in Belvedere, East Los Angeles. Similar processions were held in Santa Barbara, San Bernardino, Santa Ana, and in most Mexican colonias. In Santa Ana in 1944 a procession was sponsored by the Holy Name Union and featured all the local parishes and missions, each providing either a float or a band for the occasion.[28] While not all cities were as elaborate in their processions, almost all featured a procession of some sort in honor of the Mexican Virgin.

The love of procession was not limited to the Guadalupan devotion. Two other major processions were held in East Los Angeles (and elsewhere)—the Good Friday procession and the Corpus Christi procession. While much has been made of the Mexican devotion to Mary, two other strains of piety are significant—devotion to the suffering Jesus, the Man of Sorrows, and to Jesus as present in the Eucharist. On Good Friday the crucifix was carried by candlelight procession through the streets of East Los Angeles. In May or June the Corpus Christi procession attracted numerous participants, and also celebrated the suffering Jesus. In the Corpus Christi procession a statue of Jesus, "persecuted and vilified,"[29] was carried through the streets. Other lesser, parish-centered processions were frequent events.

The devotion to the Eucharist was also manifested in the popular devotion "*Adoración Nocturna*." In 1927 regular all-night devotion was begun in Los Angeles. In the 1930s La Placita had the Blessed Sacrament exposed from 8 A.M. until 8 P.M. daily. In San Bernardino in 1928 the Confraternity of the Blessed Sacrament was established and sponsored all-day exposition. Allan Deck writes, "This devotion combines a sense of doing penance or making a sacrifice for God with a deep Eucharistic devotion."[30] This devotion was particularly attractive to men, and according to Deck, the devotion "balanced" some of the negative aspects of machismo.[31]

One final element of Mexican spirituality was the fiesta. At the conclusion of many processions, or on major feast days, a grand fiesta was celebrated, including dancing, music, traditional foods, beauty contests, etc. Like the procession, the fiesta was a public celebration of the community's faith, which not only expressed but reinforced the community's identity. The yearly liturgical cycle provided a variety of opportunities for this public expression. In Margaret Clark's study of the Mexican community of San Jose in the 1950s she draws an extensive portrait of the annual communal devotional life at Our Lady of Guadalupe Chapel. Many of the celebrations allowed for public and private devotions. Below is an abridged version of her portrait of possible celebrations.[32]

1. Día de los Santos Reyes, January 6 (Epiphany).
2. Día de San Antonio, January 17. Blessing of domestic animals.
3. La Candelaria, February 2 (Candlemas). Blessing of candles for use in the home.
4. Día de San Blas, February 3. Blessing of throats.
5. Lent (La Cuaresma): various devotions and sacrifices.
6. Ash Wednesday: beginning of Lent, reception of ashes on foreheads; preceded by "carnival" the night before.
7. Six Fridays of Lent: rosary and stations of the cross.
8. Palm Sunday: distribution of holy palms; some made small crosses with palms, tacked them over the doorways of their homes "to protect family members from illness or other harm."
9. Good Friday: Way of the Cross; procession with large crucifix.
10. Sábado de Gloria (Easter Saturday): end of Lent, burning of Judas.
11. Fiesta de la Vírgen de Guadalupe (December 12) Mañanitas (a morning serenading of the Virgin), mass and major fiesta.
12. Las Posadas (December 16–24).
13. Los Pastores (before Christmas).

While Our Lady of Guadalupe may have been extraordinary in its observance of all these feasts, it demonstrated the variety of devotions and celebrations that might be observed by the Mexican community. All these celebrations allowed the divine to break into people's ordinary lives. Richard Rodriguez suggests the power of these devotions and celebrations:

Of all the institutions in our lives, only the Catholic Church has seemed aware of the fact that my mother and father are thinkers— persons aware of their experience. . . . It has been the liturgical church that has excited my parents. In ceremonies of public worship, they have been moved, assured that their lives—all aspects of their lives from baking to eating, from birth until death—all moments possess great significance. Only the liturgy encouraged them to dwell on the meaning of their life. To think.[33]

This significant factor is oftentimes overlooked. For many Mexican immigrants, life consisted of often brutal, back-breaking work, made all the more burdensome by a stereotype that depicted the Mexican as dull or stupid. The Church broke through these stereotypes and hardships, allowing its people to see through their pain to redemption and meaning.

THE CRISTERO REBELLION AND MEXICAN SPIRITUALITY

The spirituality of Mexican Catholics in California in the twentieth century was profoundly affected by the Mexican Revolution. For more than two decades Catholics suffered severe persecution and discrimination at the hands of the Mexican government. The experience of persecution both reflected the depth of the Mexican Catholic faith and further deepened that faith. The intensity of Mexican attachment to the Church was most evident in a popular eruption against the persecution begun in 1926 that came to be known as the Cristero Rebellion.

Since the Constitution of 1917, the Catholic Church in Mexico had been increasingly restricted and harassed, but it was not until 1926 that President Plutarco Calles (1924–1934) attempted to enforce the anti-Church sections of the constitution; his actions were regarded by the Mexican hierarchy as the beginning of a persecution. They ordered a cessation of all formal church services in Mexico until the government relented its anticlerical policies. Calles was delighted. His light regard for the faith of the Mexican people is evident in his comment, "every week that passes without religious services will lose the Catholic religion about two percent of its faithful."[34] But Calles underestimated the devotion of the Mexican people. Spontaneous outbursts against the government were soon organized into a significant, armed opposition to the government. In the central and western Mexican states a "large guerilla force was organized to defend the clergy,"[35] the movement which was dubbed the Cristero Rebellion. From 1926 to 1929, a brutal civil war was conducted "without mercy,"[36] in which atrocities were committed by and against both sides. The violence of the Cristero War propelled many immigrants north. Prior to the rebellion, an estimated 150,000-plus exiles had arrived in Los Angeles. This number nearly doubled by 1929. Included among the exiles was over a hundred priests and seven bishops or archbishops. Bishop Cantwell of Los Angeles was outspoken in his opposition to the Mexican government and in support of the Mexican exiles. The revolt came to an end in 1929 with the signing of a *modus vivendi* which established peace between the Church and the government.

The Cristero movement had a major impact on the Mexican community in southern California, as the diocese of Los Angeles had been "a major support base for the Cristero revolt."[37] Large refugee communities, especially from deeply Catholic Jalisco, were formed in Los Angeles. Several parishes in southern California during the 1920s and 1930s were named Cristo Rey in honor of the movement. Exiled bishops presided over a variety of functions for the Mexican community. A film depicting the horrors of the persecution in Mexico entitled *Mexican Martyrs* was circulated through the Mexican parishes of southern California. In 1928 Mexicans from various southern California societies united to erect a shrine in honor of Our Lady of Guadalupe, celebrating "the freedom of religion they [now] enjoyed, that was lacking in Mexico."[38] In a similar vein, a religious procession in honor of Our Lady of Guadalupe was organized by the Hijas de María, which was also used as a means to protest the persecution of the Church in Mexico.

The intensity of the Cristero Revolt subsided after 1929 with an uneasy truce governing church-state relations; however, in 1934 the election of Lázaro Cárdenas precipitated another church-state conflict. Cárdenas attempted to amend the Constitution to require the teaching of socialist doctrine in all schools. His contempt for religion was well known; he had once observed, "every moment spent on one's knees is a moment stolen from humanity."[39] He chased the apostolic delegate from Mexico. In retaliation Mexican Catholic parents were forbidden to send their children to public schools. Exiles in America began to organize demonstrations to protest the policies of Cárdenas. Several years earlier, in 1929, a local radio personality and travel agent in Los Angeles, David Orozco, began organizing chapters of the Holy Name Society (Santo Nombre). By 1930 forty chapters existed in southern California. The Mexican Holy Name Society worked to promote "Mexican consciousness" and ethnic pride.[40] As the new persecution worsened in Mexico, Orozco called for a "prayer movement" by southern California Catholics on behalf of those suffering in Mexico. The Our Lady of Guadalupe procession begun by the Hijas de María in 1928 was transformed in 1934 to a major protest against the religious policies of the Mexican government. It was advertised as "a memorial service for those who had suffered persecution in Mexico."[41] Bishop Cantwell was to preside over the march and to preach at the rally.

The Mexican consulate in Los Angeles was quite upset by the growing public protest, fearful that such demonstrations might lead to American intervention in Mexico. The consulate began to urge all Mexicans "who are *real* Mexicans"[42] not to march or participate in any way. The consuls had previously hired detectives to follow exiled Mexican bishops to see if they were involved in gun-running to antigovernment forces, but they found no evidence. Despite the efforts of the consulate, in the second week of December, 1934, forty thousand people, including many non-Mexicans, marched in honor of Our Lady of Guadalupe to protest Mexican policies. Amidst floats depicting the apparition of Mary at Guadalupe were signs carried by protesters reading "atheism reigns in Mexico City and Moscow."[43] Speeches denouncing the Mexican government were hailed with cries of ¡*Viva Cristo Rey!* The demonstrations were described by the *Los Angeles Tidings* as one of the "most striking demonstrations ever held in southern California history."[44] The demonstration reflected not only solidarity with those Catholics being persecuted in Mexico, it also reflected an intense anticommunism that pervaded Catholicism in Los Angeles.

The following week Our Lady of Guadalupe parish in San Bernardino promoted a similar procession, allegedly to "celebrate the end of the Holy Year."[45] Suspecting the San Bernardino procession would turn into a protest similar to the one in Los Angeles, the Mexican vice consul in San Bernardino asked the sheriff's office to cancel the parade permit. The mayor of San Bernardino agreed to stop the march if there were any signs "slandering" the Mexican government as there had been in Los Angeles. Failing to get the permit canceled, the vice consul wrote a letter to the Mexican colonia, which was published in a local Mexican newspaper, calling for a boycott of the procession. The letter charged that "priests were traitors," and attacked the Spanish-born pastor of Our Lady of Guadalupe parish, Father Gabriel Pérez as "neither a Mexican nor a member of la raza . . . without any right to intervene in affairs purely Mexican."[46] The letter did not reach many in the colonia, as members of the Mexican Catholic youth group bought or stole as many copies of the papers as they could find and burned them. The message was reissued the following day and warned Mexicans that they might be participating in an "unlawful demonstration." Despite the fear tactics employed, over three thousand people marched in the procession and listened to a speech by Father Pérez denouncing the policies of the Mexican government.

The dispute did not end with the completion of the parade. Several days later, Pérez and the Holy Name Society sent a formal complaint to President Franklin D. Roosevelt accusing the Mexican consuls of attempting to deny them their constitutional right to freedom of religion and calling for the removal of the consuls. After a brief controversy, the consuls in San Bernardino and Los Angeles were reassigned. The historian of the consulate in Los Angeles concludes, "Religious fervor among *la raza* was much stronger than the patriotic ties linking the colonia to the consulate."[47]

This is an important point because there is a general perception among scholars that the Mexican commitment to the Catholic faith was minimal, a view often affirmed by American Church administrators. In Manuel Gamio's classic study of Mexican immigrants in the late 1920s many of those interviewed expressed statements such as, "I am Catholic, but I am not a fanatic," and "I am Catholic, but in Los Angeles, you will see it when you go there, there isn't the fanaticism that exists in Mexico."[48] Quotes like these have been used to suggest that Mexican Catholics in Los Angeles were not deeply committed to their Church; however, taken in the context of the Cristero Revolt, these statements simply show a desire by the Mexicans in Los Angeles to disassociate themselves from the extremism and terrorism of the revolt, not its aims.

The magnitude of the demonstrations does reflect the deep devotion of the Mexican community in southern California to the Church. Appropriately, the demonstrations were held in conjunction with the feast of Our Lady of Guadalupe. Again, the close connection between Mexican faith and nationality as symbolized in the Guadalupe event was demonstrated. Again, the image of Mary was invoked as solacing mother, consoling her people in time of persecution, while affirming their dignity and calling for justice.

The conflict also demonstrates the persistence of anticlericalism among certain segments of the Mexican community. On the day of the massive procession in Los Angeles, a government supporter broke into the Church of Our Lady of Soledad in East Los Angeles and desecrated the altar.[49] As Allan Deck asserts, "Anti-clericalism coexists in Mexican culture along with a strong, traditional Catholicism."[50] Such seemed to be the case in Los Angeles. To the Church in Los Angeles, anticlericalism was not only a problem because it attacked the Church; it was also feared because the Church believed that the most violent anticlericalism was preached by those thought to be most subversive to the Church—Communists and radicals. As such it had to be vigorously opposed.

The concern in Los Angeles with the persecutions in Mexico was continually fanned by the diocesan newspaper, the *Tidings*. Weekly headlines screamed the atrocities: "Priests Hunted and Jailed in Mexico," and "Nuns Driven from Mexico,"[51] and so on. In June of 1935 another massive march and demonstration was held in connection with the traditional Corpus Christi procession. Over thirty thousand marched. Highlighted in the march was opposition to the anticlerical policies of the Mexican government.[52]

While the crisis with the Mexican government eased after 1936, the impact of the Cristero movement on the Mexican community in southern California did not fade. At the 1938 Corpus Christi procession Mexican participants continued to shout, "*¡Viva Cristo Rey!*" The Cristero Revolt and the Mexican Revolution became an integral part of the identity of the Mexican immigrant community. Allan Deck writes of the Cristero Rebellion, "Its memory and harsh lessons live on in the minds of a whole generation of Mexican Catholics in California."[53] In 1941, when Archbishop Cantwell made a pilgrimage to the Mexican Shrine of Our Lady of Guadalupe, it was not only a political statement but an affirmation of the Mexican Catholic people of southern California and of their courage.

SPIRITUALITY, CLERGY, AND CONFLICT

While the Cristero Rebellion and its support in southern California demonstrate the deep faith of the Mexican Catholic community, the Church in California was confronted with much more mundane concerns in caring for the faith of the Mexican/Mexican-American community. The central problem the Church faced in this regard during the first half of the twentieth century was a lack of Spanish-speaking priests. This problem became acute in the 1930s, when many of the refugee priests who had been working in southern California returned to Mexico. The archives of most of the dioceses of California are filled with requests for Spanish-speaking priests who were sympathetic to the Mexican people and their customs. For instance, in 1935 the Mexican colonia at Calipatria sent a delegation to the chancery in Los Angeles to request a Spanish-speaking priest. In another instance in the 1920s, a group from Calexico wrote to Bishop Cantwell expressing disgust at the poor Spanish spoken by their pastor.[54] Most petitions wanted more than a priest who spoke Spanish well. The main source of conflict between pastor and parishioner was not language; it was the different understandings of Catholicism. In a survey of thirty-five priests working in the Mexican apostolate in 1965, thirty-three of them agreed that the basic definition of a good Catholic held by most American priests was that the good Catholic attended Sunday Mass, made his or her Easter duty, and supported the parish. Twenty-nine of the thirty-five agreed that the Mexican male held a different definition. All thirty-five agreed that American pastors lacked an adequate understanding of the Mexican male.[55]

The differences were not overcome simply by providing Spanish-speaking priests. Priests from Spain were often aloof and found it difficult to relate to their primarily working-class Mexicans. One Mexican priest in Los Angeles observed of Spanish priests, they have "difficulties . . . in understanding the psychology, manners, religious feelings and educational problems of the Mexicans."[56] And Antonio Soto observes, "sometimes Mexican Americans got along better with sympathetic and non-paternalistic Anglo priests than they did with Spanish surnamed priests from other countries, who were authoritarian."[57]

Various strategies evolved as to how best to serve the Mexican people. Religious orders such as the Claretians, Franciscans, Jesuits, Benedictines, Columbans, Augustinians, and Trinitarians all provided priests. Whether religious or diocesan, what was especially needed was good priests who were good men of whatever nationality. Though some scholars have accused Cantwell of being patronizing, his dealings with his Mexican faithful reveal a good deal of practical wisdom. In 1930, he advised a priest in El Monte "we have to handle the Mexicans in a very gentle way, as our experience is, that more is accomplished in this manner than in laying down the law."[58] Similarly, a canon lawyer for the archdiocese of San Francisco, Monsignor John M. Byrne, advised, "It looks worthwhile to stretch a few points in parochial discipline so as to hold them [Mexicans] to the Church."[59] Problems of proper documentation for weddings, first communions, and baptisms could create a bureaucratic nightmare. The confused condition of formal church life in Mexico as a result of the Constitution of 1917, combined with an inefficient means of communication between small Mexican villages and the United States, made proper sacramental documentation extremely difficult to obtain. What were major events to the Mexican Catholic—baptism, marriage, confirmation—became bogged down in the bureaucratic processes of the Catholic Church in the United States, which insisted on appropriate paperwork. The bewildering legalisms of the American Church were often lost on the Mexican faithful.

Not everyone agreed with Byrne and Cantwell. Chanceries often seemed to assert their authority over trivial issues. For instance, in the late 1940s a young priest working in a Mexican colonia requested approval of a small booklet he had written, "El Sacrificio de la Misa," as a guide to assist the Spanish-speaking at Mass. His request was denied. He was told that there were other sources already available which he could use.[60] That a priest working in the Mexican colonia might have a better idea of what his community needed than a textbook created elsewhere never seems to have occurred to his chancery judges. In another case, in 1958 a group of priests working with Mexican migrants had developed a book of communal songs and hymns used to encourage congregational singing. When sent to the chancery for approval, three of the songs were not acceptable. The directive read "I would suggest Father . . . substitute other melodies of a more musical nature. These are lacking in musical quality."[61] Folk hymns would have to wait until the 1960s. Most pastors who were successful with the Mexican community were priests who were open and able to grow in the job. Pastors, though not Mexican, who attempted to understand the Mexican culture and traditions often won the deep affection of their parishioners. One newly appointed pastor in Brawley wrote excitedly to Buddy, "I am learning the names of many foods, tacos, enchiladas, etc., but I will have to wait until the day of the fair to see what they are."[62] Other pastors were open to an interplay between themselves and their people. One woman recalls of her pastor in San Jose, "Father is better than he used to be about our traditions. The people have talked to him a lot about Mexican ways; he has helped us bring back some of our customs, but there are still a lot of things that people would like that he doesn't approve of."[63] The same pastor attempted to provide his people with a better understanding of the Mass by having a lay reader translate the Latin into Spanish during the Mass.[64]

Not all the priests developed a good relationship with their Mexican parishioners. Augustine O'Dea, in his study of Mexicans in Los Angeles, isolated five words Mexicans used to judge priests;

four of them were negative—*regañón*: scolder; *enojón*: grouchy; *dinerero*: money grubbing; *altanero*: proud. The one positive was *simpático* or kindly. O'Dea went on to offer a number of reasons why priests failed in working with the Mexican community: "language, dislike of race, too high expectations with subsequent discouragement, unjustifiable prejudice, harshness, impatience, maladjustment, lack of sympathy with their views, ignorance of the Mexican problem, no respect for Mexican psychology, money talks, refusal to accept the Mexican method of parochial work."[65]

As the O'Dea quote suggests, central to the clergy's difficulties was an inadequate understanding of the Mexican and an unwillingness to bend. Often the clash of the two cultures seemed too great to be overcome by goodwill alone. One aspect of Mexican Catholicism which disturbed Anglo clerics was its anticlericalism. For those of the revolutionary generation, the Church's alleged complicity with the corrupt Mexican government sullied the position of the clergyman. Too often the Church seemed to be on the side of the rich and powerful. Anticlericalism was particularly strong among, but was not limited to, men. One immigrant recalls the counsel of his grandmother, "My son, there are three things that pertain to our religion: the Lord, Our Lady of Guadalupe and the Church. You can trust in the first two, but not in the third."[66]

Equally disturbing was what Anglo pastors perceived as "superstitions": mandas, promesas, altarcitos, milagritos, and other forms of popular piety. Thirty-three of thirty-five priests polled in 1965 felt these things should *not* be stressed.[67] A rather revealing letter written by Bishop Buddy to the apostolic delegate reflects not only a disgust with superstitions but a fear of the Church appearing "ridiculous" in America. To some Mexican Americans Buddy must have seemed to be the reincarnation of Amat.

> A word about Mexican customs . . . [I] tolerate some, however I have definitely forbidden, for example, opening the Tabernacle during a baptism; dances in the church before a picture of Our Lady of Guadalupe, girls dancing before a procession of the Blessed Sacrament with the thought of driving away evil spirits; outdoor processions of the Blessed Sacrament through the public streets because there was not sufficient reverence or devotion to warrant it. After all, this is America, and we must protect the faith of our people. Many Mexicans have an exaggerated cult to certain saints. They do not say, for example, that the Blessed Sacrament is in the Church; but they say the Virgin is in the Church. This after

years of Spanish and Mexican administration. I beg to ask is it uplifting to the Mexican to join with them in their meaningless and senseless shouting re Our Lady of Guadalupe, and at the same time neglect the essentials of the Commandments, Easter duty, and valid marriages?[68]

Buddy's testimony articulates the "official" view of the clash of cultures and pieties.

In several other places, Mexican public processions and fiestas were discouraged. The public impression made by these events were considered scandalous by some and a "sacrilege"[69] by others. To preserve the faith of "Americans" these practices had to be prohibited. Nonetheless, with or without approval, they persisted, reflecting an authentic faith experience on the part of the Mexican/ Mexican-American people.

While the shortage of Spanish-speaking priests in general and, more specifically, the shortage of Mexican priests has always been a problem, there were instances of tremendous service on the part of Mexican priests to the Church in California. On several occasions, the persecution of the Church in Mexico resulted in an influx of refugee priests and bishops to California. While most refugees stayed only a brief while before returning to Mexico, a significant number remained to serve the Mexican community in California. In 1861 as a result of the harassment of Benito Juárez, several priests and seminarians, including the bishop of Sonora, found refuge in San Francisco, where Archbishop Alemany made use of their talents in serving the Spanish-speaking communities in the archdiocese. While most of these exiles returned by 1866,[70] one, Father Luciano Osuna, remained in the archdiocese until the 1880s, working with the Native Americans of northern California. Osuna became noted for his saintliness and piety, as well as for his unorthodox style of ministry. Osuna adopted the dress and lifestyle of the Indians he served. One contemporary observed, "A more dirty, ragged specimen of humanity is rarely seen." Osuna responded, "I have been with the Indians most of the time; they are sick and hungry, so I am hungry with them."[71] Osuna's close identification with the Indians caused the local Indian agent to accuse Osuna of insanity, and the agent tried to prevent him from going onto the reservation. Osuna was undeterred. While Osuna might be regarded as an aberration, his devotion and dedication suggest the Church in California was not totally bereft of heroic Mexican clergy. Had Osuna's example been followed by California clergy in their dealings with the Mexican-American community, much pain could have been avoided.

Another influx of refugee priests followed the Mexican Revolution in the 1910s and especially after the 1926 Cristero Revolt. Again, the majority returned to Mexico, but a number of them remained in California, where they enjoyed distinguished careers. While not attempting an exhaustive history of the Mexican clergy, I have chosen three significant priests—Fathers Jesús Ramírez, José Núñez, and José Origel—as examples of the efforts of the Mexican clergy on behalf of their compatriots in California. Father Jesús Ramírez of Durango, Mexico fled to Los Angeles in the years following the outbreak of the Mexican Revolution. According to one historian, he soon became Bishop John J. Cantwell's "de facto vicar for Hispanics for the entire diocese from San Diego to Los Angeles."[72] In 1919, Cantwell appointed Ramírez assistant director of Catholic Charities, with a special directive to care for the Mexican people. Over the course of the next two decades, Ramírez acted as Cantwell's point man on Mexican affairs, and as episcopal representative to the Mexican community. Ramírez visited, then advised Cantwell on the condition of Mexican communities throughout the diocese. He presided at church blessings and dedications. In 1935 he was sent as a special ambassador to the archbishop of San Francisco to ask his assistance in dealing with the many Mexican refugees and refugee priests who were flooding into Los Angeles. Ramírez was also busy at the local level; he established several catechetical centers in East Los Angeles that ultimately became parishes.[73] For nearly two decades Ramírez provided distinguished service to the diocese of Los Angeles.

Another Mexican clergyman, Monsignor José Núñez from Zacatecas, Mexico, came to the United States in 1926 at the outset of the Cristero Rebellion. Núñez established a missionary parish, Christ the King, in Rialto. In 1929 he returned to Tijuana, Mexico, where he served as apostolic vicar of lower California from 1929 to 1933. With the renewed persecution of the Church in Mexico in 1933, Núñez returned to California, where he served as pastor of several parishes until 1939. He was then appointed pastor of Our Lady of Guadalupe parish in San Bernardino, where he served until 1964. Núñez was brought into an extremely tense situation in San Bernardino; he was the first pastor after the removal of the popular Spanish Augustinians by Bishop Buddy. He succeeded in calming the community and set about rebuilding the parish. By 1964 he had the deep affection of the Mexican community in San Bernardino.

During his tenure, he assisted the Victory Noll Sisters in opening a free medical clinic, the parish school was reopened after having been closed for more than two decades, and he orchestrated the solemn coronation of Our Lady of Guadalupe.[74]

Our last example of Mexican clergy is Father José Origel. Origel fled the Cristero Rebellion in 1927. For several decades he would dominate parish life at the mission parish, Our Lady of Guadalupe in Delhi (Gloryetta), Orange County. The parish consisted primarily of Mexican workers who either picked or processed sugar beets. One historian describes Father Origel's leadership, he "cast a supervisorial eye over the community, reinforcing the traditions and customs brought from the small Mexican pueblos and haciendas. The Church calendar was superimposed on the seasonal rhythm's of agricultural production to organize time within the community."[75] Origel sought to reestablish the Mexican Catholic faith in the new environment. Though Origel was dominant, his control over the community was not absolute. In 1928, when the community decided to enact a pastorela, Origel typed out the script as dictated to him by a lay parishioner. Origel edited the "objectionable parts" out of the script; however, the actors put them back in during the actual performance. Despite the give and take, Origel was greatly admired and loved by his parishioners. His birthday became a major parish celebration. For several decades Origel faithfully served the Mexican community in the Delhi area of Orange County.

While these short biographies are in no way complete and are not an attempt to record a comprehensive history of Mexican clergy in California, they do suggest the dedicated service provided by many Mexican clergy to the Mexican people of California. Parishes that were fortunate enough to enjoy the services of such distinguished Mexican clergy flourished. Yet the problem remained— there simply were not enough Mexican priests to serve the massive numbers of immigrants who had come to California. In addition, Mexican clergy often had difficulty with the more Americanized members of their flock.

The spirituality manifested by the Mexican/Mexican-American community in California was a rich one, as evidenced by their devotions, processions, and other public acts of faith. As Bishop Joseph McGucken observed of Mexican/Mexican-American Catholics in 1947, "Where they have churches, priests, and sisters, there is vigorous and practical religious life, with frequently more evidence of piety and devotion than one finds in American parishes of similar size."[76] McGucken's assessment was not always shared by pastors and other church administrators, who found it difficult to accept the different style of Mexican spirituality. Yet successful pastors recognized and affirmed the validity of the Mexican faith experience in both its formal and popular manifestations. This latter approach would be affirmed in 1983 by the United States bishops in their pastoral letter *The Hispanic Presence: Challenge and Commitment*, which called for a greater openness to popular expressions of faith. Though official approbation did not come until 1983, the groundwork had been laid several decades previous to that.

For California, and for the rest of the United States, the post–World War II era was a time of great excitement. During this era, the Church began to pursue a number of new avenues. This was particularly true of its ministry to the Mexican/Mexican-American community, in which a new approach was developed.

4

A New Era: World War II and After

American Catholics emerged from World War II with greater confidence of their place in American society. For more than a century the Church in the United States had focused on the care of its immigrants and the preservation of their faith. This was done within the context of trying to demonstrate the compatibility between Catholicism and American ideals and institutions. This need faded as Catholics made it in America and were able to adopt a more aggressive stance toward American society. The postwar era saw the flowering of various Catholic apostolic movements as new avenues of ministry began to be explored. The Christian Family Movement, the Young Christian Workers, the Grail, and others, all flourished. New conceptions of Church were also in ascendance, particularly the notion of the Church as the Mystical Body of Christ, as defined by Pope Pius XII in his encyclical *Mediator Dei* in 1947. The responsibility of the Catholic laity was no longer simply "to pay, pray, and obey"; they were to take responsibility for the Church as being part of its Mystical Body. The new-found social status of Catholics in the United States plus new images for a revived laity ushered in a period of greater aggressiveness and activity on the part of the Church in the United States.

Similarly, World War II ushered in a new era for the Mexican-American community in Los Angeles and all of California. The large number of veterans returning from the war, combined with two well-publicized racial incidents, created a new aggressive attitude in regard to civil rights. In addition, for the first time in a century Mexican Americans were experiencing at least limited social mobility, as a small sector began to move into the ranks of the middle class. A large second generation, caught between the demands of the Mexican culture and the American society in which they lived, struggled to achieve an integrated identity. Even as this adjustment to American life occurred, immigration increased significantly once again in the 1950s, enlarging the number of first-generation immigrants present in California. Further complicating the question of identity was the introduction of the bracero system, that is, Mexican nationals who were contracted for seasonal labor in the United States and then returned to Mexico. All these developments led to fundamental questions as to how the Mexican identity was to be defined in the postwar world. The Church continued its efforts to serve the community, but concentrated on three main concerns: 1) juvenile delinquency and youth programs, 2) community organizing, and 3) care of the migrant worker.

CONCENTRATION ON YOUTH

Two widely publicized incidents focused the community's attention on Mexican youth. In Los Angeles in August 1942 a young Chicano, José Díaz, was found dead near a swimming hole popularly known as Sleepy Lagoon. The police, believing the death to be a result of gang activity, arrested twenty-two members of a local Chicano gang. All were indicted for murder; seventeen were convicted in "the largest mass trial for murder ever held in the country."[1] The accused were not allowed to change clothes, or get a shave or haircut during the trial. Outlandishly racist testimony was given by "expert" witnesses. Carey McWilliams provides this assessment of the Sleepy Lagoon case. "For years, Mexicans had been pushed around by the Los Angeles police and given a very rough time in the courts, but the Sleepy Lagoon prosecution capped the climax. It took place before a biased and prejudiced judge . . . it was conducted by a prosecutor who pointed to the clothes and styles of haircut of the defendants as evidence of guilt; and it was stated in an atmosphere of intense community-wide prejudice which had been whipped up and artfully sustained by the entire press of Los Angeles. . . . From the beginning the proceeding savored more of a ceremonial lynching than a trial in a court of justice."[2]

Less than two months later another dramatic encounter featured Chicano youth in what came to be known as the Zoot Suit Riots in June 1943. The zoot suit was a style with "billowing trousers" brought tight at the cuff and baggy coat. The suit became a badge of identity for certain Chicano youth, who came to be referred to as "*pachucos*." Pachucos also sported "high, pompadoured ducktail haircuts."[3] After the Sleepy Lagoon case, the Los Angeles press continually played up the dangers of "pachucoism," and the Los Angeles police engaged in a variety of harassing arrests and "unofficial" beatings of the pachucos. On June 3, 1943, rumors circulated of an alleged attack on a serviceman by a "zoot suiter."

With passions running high, ten days of riots began, as service-men began attacking Chicano youths throughout the city. Anyone found with a zoot suit on was stripped and beaten. "Riots" also broke out in San Diego and other communities. Police made no attempt to protect the Mexican community.

The uproar surrounding these two events caused Governor Earl Warren to appoint a citizen's committee to investigate. Warren appointed Auxiliary Bishop Joseph T. McGucken, later archbishop of San Francisco, as chairman of the committee. The committee concluded, "these riots were caused principally by racial prejudice, which was stimulated by police practices and by inflammatory news reporting."[4] Most Californians were not ready to accept the committee's judgment. Their findings were reasserted by noted community organizer and social critic Saul Alinsky when asked by the Los Angeles City Council to assess the reasons for the riots.

Rather than focus on the root problem of discrimination, most groups turned their attention to the problem of the second and third generation Mexican American. While a general "youth prob-lem" hovered over the United States during the 1940s and 1950s, the Sleepy Lagoon case and the Zoot Suit Riots intensified concern about the "Mexican youth problem." Most analyses focused on the tensions between first-generation Mexicans, who continued to cling to the old world ways, and the second and third generations, who were becoming Americanized. Mexican scholar Octavio Paz provided what became the standard analysis. "He [the pachuco] does not want to become Mexican again, at the same time he does not blend into the life of North America."[5] The result was that the pachuco experienced a double alienation, as he or she attempted to fashion a new identity in America. While the pachuco phenomenon never affected more than a small minority of Chicano youth (despite Anglo perceptions), the tensions involved in being bicultural did affect most second- and third-generation Chicanos.

Scholars have provided a variety of explanations for the pa-chuco phenomenon, which reflect on the problem of the second generation as well. Historian Douglas Monroy attributes their alien-ation to the "new, urban, industrial culture"[6] in which they now lived but to which they had no access. One result was the cre-ation of gangs. An earlier scholar of second-generation Chicanos wrote, "He yearned for the good things of life, school, clothes, amusements, yet he accepted the fact that they were not for him."[7] Many of the second generation were destined to remain outsiders from both cultures. To many, the second generation seemed a "lost generation."[8]

The outsider status also contributed to a sense of inferiority among some Chicano youth. A recent scholar observed, "For a minority of the adolescents, lowered self-esteem, distorted self-images, and generalized insecurity produced a major crisis of identity."[9] The sense of insecurity and confusion was reinforced by parental insecurity. Parents often felt incapable of providing direction for their children in the new society. A study done in 1949 suggested that the first generation's isolation from "the environment of their children" made it difficult for them to "help the children adjust."[10] The result was often intense generational conflict. While it is difficult to assess what proportion of Chicano youth were affected by the problem of pachucoism, the Anglo community perceived it to affect most Chicano youth. Juvenile delinquency statistics were manipulated, or conveniently ignored, to prove the depth of the problem. Besides the "secular" problems of pachucoism, the Catholic Church was particularly concerned about the apparent loss of faith among the second generation. An oft-cited quote from *American Me* suggests the lessening importance of the Church in the life of Mexican-American youth. One youth observed, "You start forgetting about it [the Church]. You don't come across it enough in your life, and after a while it just doesn't mean anything to you."[11]

While it is not unusual to find youth disaffected with the Church, it was particularly worrisome to parents, who still held the faith in high regard and to whom Catholicism still formed an integral part of their identity. As one scholar observed in 1933, "In homes where the children have become lax about religious duties, the parents grieve and are scandalized at the youthful independence about them."[12] The problem remained in the 1960s. A pastor of an urban parish observed, "the second and third generation are much less likely to be influenced by Roman Catholic values . . . many have lost contact with the official Church."[13]

The Church was faced with a major problem—how to become relevant to the lives of second- and third-generation Chicano youth. Some suggested a simple solution—appoint a Mexican priest. Others argued that the Mexican priest tried too hard to inculcate Mexican ways into a younger generation that had little use for them. A youth group at a Mexican mission in Riverside in 1948 wrote Bishop Buddy, "We, the younger generation, have been born and have grown up in this society, and are happy to have Father lead us and our spiritual and temporal activities in the American style. . . . We . . . wish to adopt and have our young children embrace American ways, without therefore denying we are Mexicans at heart."[14] A 1958 survey of Mexican parishes in Los Angeles suggests the complexity of the problems presented by the second-generation immigrant. Particularly pressing was the problem of Spanish-speaking parents/adults and English-speaking children. Many pastors suggested the need of "mixed parishes" rather than national parishes.

Various solutions to the youth problem were offered, but most agreed that the successful program depended on the priest. Whether Spanish, Mexican, or American, the priest had to be able to relate to the youth in terms of their world. At the same time, the priest had to relate to the parents' world as well, as he was often called to play the role of "mediator"[15] between the generations. One young man quoted by Beatrice Griffith reflects what Chicano youth expected of a priest: "The priest is a good man, but he doesn't know what we're up against. How can he? He doesn't even know English. He doesn't know that most cops are our enemies. . . . I go to church so I can pray for help, not that the priest will help me."[16] Another young man commented, "that priest is in another world. Why doesn't he get some clubs and things for us, you know, like that young priest did. They should know there's nothing to do but hang around the corner."[17]

Three groups provided the bulk of the ministry to Chicano youth: the Acción Católica Juventud Mexicano/Juventud Católica Feminina Mexicana (ACJM/JCFM), the Young Christian Workers/Young Christian Students (YCW/YCS), and the Catholic Youth Organization (CYO). The primary Mexican Catholic youth group in the 1930s was the ACJM/JCFM, described simply as "Mexican Catholic Action." The ACJM had enjoyed popularity in Mexico since the 1910s, where it had been the major proponent of the Mexican Bishops' Catholic Action program, and had led the opposition to the persecution of the Church in Mexico. Several ACJM members became leaders in the Cristero Rebellion, including the president of the ACJM, Capistran Garza, who was appointed first commander of the Cristero forces (though he proved ineffectual as a military leader). As a result, the ACJM that was transplanted into California was intensely devout and intensely nationalistic. The motto of the group was "Piety, Study, Action," and the clubs were designed to inculcate the Mexican Catholic religious heritage among Chicano youth in California. As one flyer announced, the groups were "to strengthen and preserve the Catholic religion in the Mexican family."[18] The groups operated as study groups, and meetings were conducted primarily in Spanish. They provided typical youth group activities, socials, dances, study clubs, parish service, and the production of dramatic plays. Over fifty such groups existed by 1941. These groups retained close ties to Catholic Action groups in Mexico. One scholar claims that the ACJM/JCFM "lived in symbiotic relationship with their counterparts in Mexico."[19] Significantly, every six months all of the groups would assemble for a grand *jornada*, in which young Mexican Catholics from throughout southern California gathered; some gatherings exceeded 500 people. In 1941, however, these jornadas were discouraged, and the ACJM was made "purely parochial."[20] The opposition to the ACJM may have been based on a feeling that the ACJM was "too Mexican." Following his dispute with Our Lady Of Guadalupe parish in San Bernardino in 1939, Bishop Buddy wrote the new pastor, "My thought is that it would be better to suppress the JCFM and have one organization, the CYO, established, at least in that parish," because Mexican Catholic Action had caused "so much trouble the past fifteen years."[21] The ACJM continued in the postwar era, but its influence was on the wane. One pastor criticized it for reducing Catholic Action "to nothing more than dances."[22] The ACJM may have lost some of its reason for existence as the church-state problems that had plagued Mexico were somewhat resolved by 1940.

Many priests began favoring the Young Christian Workers/ Young Christian Students (YCW/YCS) in their apostolate to Mexican-American youth. The YCW/YCS was based on the Cardinal Cardijn method of social action, employing the "observe-judge-act" formula for Catholic Action.[23] According to the formula, the youth observed their environment, judged what they had observed in accordance with Church teachings and the teachings of Jesus, then acted to lessen the distance between what they observed and the teachings of Jesus. YCW/YCS flourished in a number of Mexican parishes in the 1950s in northern and southern California. Many of the groups became interested in social justice particularly as it related to the migrant workers.

Groups dealt with seemingly general topics such as "parent-child relationships," "teenage crime," "being apostolic,"[24] but the genius of YCW/YCS was that the format allowed each group to deal with its own environment and situation. Thus, a discussion of the parent-child relationship would vary according to the family setting. Were parents and children both born in Mexico and recent immigrants? Were the children born in America of parents born in

Mexico? And so on. Each group would have a discussion unique to its locale, thus making the discussion immediately relevant.

Rev. John Coffield of El Monte enjoyed great success with both ACJM and YCW/YCS. In 1949 Coffield built a gymnasium and youth center all with volunteer labor. The key to good youth groups was providing activities which were directly relevant to the youth involved and which could show practical results. Coffield used the youth groups as a haven for Chicano youth who felt constrained by strict Mexican family customs. In strict families, no casual dating was allowed; all dates required chaperones. The youth groups provided a casual meeting place for Mexican-American young men and women. The YCW/YCS was not without its detractors. In the 1950s, the planned year's program for the YCS in Los Angeles, "Rebel With a Cause," was struck down by the chancery; the chancery felt that the topic was "too controversial."[25]

The primary agency for the youth apostolate in Los Angeles was the Catholic Youth Organization (CYO). The CYO is generally associated with athletics, and athletics were offered as a means of drawing Chicano youth back to the Church. Basketball, boxing, and baseball were all sponsored by the CYO; however, the CYO was more than athletic programs. The CYO participated in the Five Year Youth Project that was initiated by the City of Los Angeles in response to the Sleepy Lagoon case and Zoot Suit Riots. The CYO received $50,000 a year from the city, with which it hired twelve full-time social workers to work with Chicano youth. According to historian Robin Scott, by 1946 over 5,000 Mexican Americans were involved with the various CYO programs of sports, music, drama, art, and dances.[26]

The strength of the CYO was that it attempted to develop leaders from within the community. Unlike some other youth programs, the CYO did not base leadership on "academic standards,"[27] but recruited the "natural" leaders. Oftentimes this meant that they attempted to recruit gang leaders to be "youth directors." The "reformed" gang leader often became a very effective youth minister. And as a priest in northern California put it, "good leaders could clean up pachucoism."[28] The CYO also met the youth in their own environment; for instance, in 1954, the CYO sponsored two of the very popular "car clubs" in East Los Angeles, the Road Knights and the Starlighters. They did not question whether this was an appropriate undertaking for a church group; they simply responded to the fact that through car clubs they could reach many young people. Finally, the CYO was important because it projected a positive image of Chicano youth.[29] In a society in which negative images of Chicano youth were plentiful, the CYO attempted to provide a counterimage. At times, the CYO could be drawn into conflict. In the 1950s they worked with Councilman Edward Roybal in solving the problems of police brutality against Chicanos. Rodolfo Acuña summarizes the importance of the CYO to the Chicano community in the following manner: "Many young Chicanos were first exposed to organizational activity at meetings or discussion groups at the local Catholic church." The CYO helped develop a "group consciousness."[30]

James Francis McIntyre, appointed archbishop of Los Angeles in 1948, had a different priority. McIntyre's program for Chicano youth focused on providing more parochial schools in the Mexican parishes. In 1948, only 30 percent of the Mexican parishes had parochial schools, compared to 58 percent of the parishes in the rest of the archdiocese. By 1960 every parish in East Los Angeles had its own parochial school. McIntyre diverted funds which his predecessor had been saving for the construction of a new cathedral into a massive building program.[31] Several historians have suggested that McIntyre's goal was to "insulate the young Chicano from the secular values of the public schools,"[32] from Protestant proselytizers and from "secular liberalism" and "communism." Leo Grebler's study suggests two goals: first, "to preserve and defend the Catholic faith of the Mexican American and his offspring" from the foes mentioned above, and second, "to exhibit the Church to the larger society as an institution instilling American ideals into the laity of Mexican background."[33] In other words, the Church's own insecurity in American society propelled it into the role of Americanizer for Mexican Americans.

Regardless of the reasons, McIntyre provided Mexican Americans with parochial schools. The schools provided for a very real need and did magnificent work in the colonias. The desire to send their children to parochial schools was strong among Mexican parents,[34] and the appeal of Catholic schools was not limited to the United States. In fact, it was quite common for Mexican parents to send their children across the border to be instructed in American Catholic schools. In 1945, of the 363 students in Calexico, 157 were from Mexicali; by 1953, Mexicans made up 90 percent of the enrollment there.[35] Similarly, parents in Tijuana sent their children across the border to be educated. Part of their desire was for the children to learn English; part of their desire was for their children to receive proper religious education.

While most of the instruction in parochial schools was provided in English, of necessity some Spanish had to be used. While there are many horror stories about young Chicano students being forced to learn English quickly and of having their names Americanized, by 1961 three bilingual parochial schools did exist in Los Angeles.[36] The role of the Catholic school in the Mexican colonia is far more complex than just portraying it as an "Americanizing" institution.

COMMUNITY ORGANIZING

The whole concept of Americanization, as discussed earlier, was not necessarily seen as a negative by large numbers of the Chicano community after World War II. Veterans returning from the war made a conscious effort to become more involved in American politics and to enter the mainstream of American society. One veteran asked, "How long had we been missing out on benefits denied us as American citizens?"[37] A number of groups began demanding full civil rights. One major group was the American GI Forum, consisting of the Mexican-American veterans; it was founded in Texas but soon established chapters in California. In 1944 Unity Leagues began developing in Riverside and elsewhere in California. The groups stressed voter registration and education and demanded the integration of public schools and other public institutions.

The Chicano community celebrated a major victory in 1947 with the U.S. Circuit Court decision *Mendez* vs. *Westminster*, in which segregation in Orange County schools was declared unconstitutional. Other minor victories were occasionally won, such as integrating the public swimming pool in San Bernardino. Other community groups banded together to oppose police brutality. Whatever the endeavor, the Church continued "to be the meeting place for the Mexican American,"[38] in their efforts to better their communities.

The most important organization that developed in the postwar era was the Community Service Organization (CSO), founded by Fred Ross in California in 1947. Ross had been working with the Unity Leagues and experienced the need for greater organization within the Chicano community. "They had no one to speak for them; they weren't even registered to vote."[39] With an assist from Saul Alinsky's Industrial Areas Foundation, Ross began organizing the Mexican Americans at the grass-roots level. Ross believed

Mexican Americans would remain powerless until they became politically active. The CSO provided a two-pronged attack toward obtaining power: 1) voter registration and 2) citizenship classes. Mexicans had always been reluctant to become American citizens. As a result they lacked political power. Ross saw the need for Mexicans to become citizens so that they could develop a power base within the political order through which they could obtain their rights. Rodolfo Acuña wrote that the CSO was "a conscious attempt at further Americanization, i.e, assimilation."[40] Ross's initial attempts at organizing in Los Angeles were halting. He attempted to work with a group of Mexican veterans who were working to elect Chicano Edward Roybal to the city council. When Roybal lost, Ross approached the group with his plan. He was met with suspicion. The veterans suspected he was a Communist trying to infiltrate their group. To allay their fears Ross arranged an interview with Bishop Joseph T. McGucken. McGucken was so enthused by Ross's proposal that he wrote a letter endorsing Ross and urging all the pastors in East Los Angeles to be open to Ross. Soon, some 12,000 new voters were registered in East Los Angeles.

In 1952 Ross moved to the San Jose area to begin organizing rural Mexican Americans. Here he developed his standard operating technique, the house meeting. People were invited to a small party at a home in the neighborhood, where Ross would present his program. Ross received great support from two young Catholic priests, Donald McDonnell and Thomas McCullough. McDonnell introduced Ross to a young migrant worker named César Chávez, while McCullough discovered a Chicana named Dolores Huerta. Both became pivotal members in the development of the CSO throughout California. Chávez was intrigued by Ross's explanation of how poor people could obtain power. Chávez proved a master organizer and worked extremely hard. He became national director of the CSO but resigned in 1962 when the CSO refused to commit itself to organizing farm workers.

Church involvement in community affairs was not limited to support of the CSO. Several priests became involved in community action. A priest in San Bernardino was one of the plaintiffs in a suit against the City of San Bernardino over the integration of the city's swimming pools. In East Los Angeles, Father William Hutson, archdiocesan director of the CYO, and Joe Vargas, executive director of CYO, were key players in the attempt to incorporate East Los Angeles as a distinct community. Incorporation, many believed, would give East Los Angeles more control over its own destiny. Hutson had previously been instrumental in the incorporation of Pico Rivera.[41] Nonetheless, Church involvement in community organizing stemmed in part from defensive purposes. In the late 1950s Archbishop McIntyre expressed the need to become involved in the East Central Welfare Planning Council, a Community Chest organization. Motivating McIntyre was the fear that "radical" elements would take over the group.[42]

Within the Church in East Los Angeles there was an attempt to organize. An Eastside priests' council was formed in the 1950s to discuss common problems and to propose common solutions. Their initial report to McIntyre was met with little enthusiasm. McIntyre observed that their "suggestions were not very practical."[43] The organization soon disbanded, as the more "autocratic, conservative Mexican priests" found shared decision making too burdensome.[44]

Despite the new emphasis of the postwar era, certain old standards continued to be upheld. In a 1949 meeting of priests working in the Mexican apostolate, a Jesuit recently transferred from San Diego suggested the San Diego model as a paradigm for ministry to the Spanish speaking. He reported that Bishop Buddy "solved the problem of the Mexican people, 1) by constructing a shrine to Our Lady of Guadalupe in every highly populated Mexican colonia, and 2) by opening a free medical center including a medical clinic, dispensary, and pharmacy."[45] The onrush of immigrants and increased concern for the migrant workers and their plight made such solutions seem too simplistic.

NORTHERN AND SOUTHERN CALIFORNIA: DIFFERENT APPROACHES

As the two previous paragraphs suggest, there was some hesitancy in southern California about the new directions in ministry to the Mexican community. The innovations that transformed Mexican ministry were developed in northern California. Before discussing these developments, a brief review of the different approaches to ministry, north and south, might be helpful.

Northern California and southern California developed two distinctively different Catholic cultures. In San Francisco and the Bay Area, large numbers of Catholic immigrants and their descendants, especially of Irish and Italian stock, ensured that the Church in San Francisco would remain a definite presence in the area. In contrast, Los Angeles was primarily Protestant, and though the Church made its presence felt, it was never as comfortable or as secure in its position as the Church in San Francisco was in its position. This difference may have accounted for the differences in approach to the Californio/Mexican population by Archbishop Alemany of San Francisco and by Bishop Amat in Los Angeles. Alemany was more accommodating, while Amat stressed the need to bring the Californio/Mexican faithful into conformity with the American Church.

By the 1920s, the lead in ministry to Mexican Catholics had shifted to southern California. The massive numbers of immigrants who came to southern California from Mexico demanded attention. Bishop John J. Cantwell and his able lieutenants Fathers Robert Lucey and Leroy Callahan in the 1920s, and Fathers Augustine O'Dea and Joseph McGucken in the 1940s, developed a coherent strategy of ministry promoting primarily educational, charitable, and parochial endeavors. More importantly, Cantwell attempted to develop an American clergy fluent in Spanish; he mandated that all seminarians study Spanish, that the junior clergy be examined yearly on their proficiency in Spanish, and that courses in Mexican culture be taught at the seminary. Cantwell also proved most hospitable to clerical refugees from the Mexican Revolution, whom he put to work in Spanish-speaking parishes. Cantwell was known as a great friend to the Mexican people and greatly advanced the Mexican apostolate.

In contrast, ministry to Mexicans in northern California, where they were less visible, was limited to several national parishes, such as Our Lady of Guadalupe in San Francisco and Our Lady of Guadalupe in Sacramento. Indeed, Archbishop Edward J. Hanna acquired the reputation of being anti-Mexican. One historian labeled Hanna's attitude as "openly hostile" toward Mexicans.[46] The accusation stems from Hanna's call in 1926 for the restriction of immigration from Mexico, claiming that immigrants from Mexico placed an undue burden on social and civic institutions.[47] While it is difficult to explain away several of the stereotypes Hanna invoked to support his argument, his culpability is somewhat mitigated by the fact that he was speaking on behalf of, and as president of, the California State Commission on Immigration and Housing, not as archbishop, and also by the fact that he was simply reiterating the standard position of organized labor regarding Mexican immigrants. San Francisco was a strong union town, and the Church's support of labor in San Francisco was legendary, thanks to the efforts of Rev. Peter C. Yorke at the beginning of the twentieth century. It was this strong association with labor that led to Archbishop Edward Hanna's unfortunate statement on Mexican immigration. To describe Hanna's attitude as "openly hostile" is too simplistic and historically inaccurate. Hanna's work on behalf of Mexican migrant workers with the California State Commission on Immigration and Housing, which monitored and sought to improve the lot of the Mexican migrant, in addition to the hospitality Hanna provided to refugees from the Mexican Revolution (though his hospitality did not equal that of Los Angeles) and his outspoken condemnation of the persecution of the Church in Mexico as president of the National Catholic Welfare Conference indicate a deep respect for the Mexican Catholic. More precisely, Hanna's attitude toward the Mexican was not one of hostility; rather it was one of neglect.

During the post–World War II era, the initiative in Mexican ministry once again swung to northern California. With the arrival of Archbishop James Francis McIntyre in Los Angeles in 1948 and the continued leadership of Bishop Buddy in San Diego, ministry to the Mexican community continued along familiar lines in southern California. Efforts at community organizing and social action began to develop, but such efforts were regarded with suspicion in an ecclesial and cultural environment that was obsessed with the threat of communism. In conjunction with this was an episcopal authoritarianism which showed little inclination toward innovation.

In contrast, Archbishop John J. Mitty of San Francisco, a man conservative by nature, allowed a series of innovations that helped transform Mexican ministry. Mitty was popularly perceived as being rigidly authoritarian, but the image was deceptive. Mitty demanded above all else respect for the office of the archbishop, but in his role as archbishop he consistently placed what he considered to be best for the Church and its faithful above his own personal predilections. Mitty had tremendous respect for his priests, and when he gave them a position of authority, he supported them unequivocally. When the activities of the priests Mitty had assigned to the Mexican apostolate drew criticism from Los Angeles, San Diego, and from within his own archdiocese, Mitty stood behind his priests. His policies, and his faith in his priests, created a period of extremely high morale in the archdiocese of San Francisco and an environment which encouraged innovation, as well as a deeper devotion to the Church. Within this context, ministry to the Mexican community began to explore several new avenues. The most important innovations took place in the Church's ministry to migrant workers, the subject of the next chapter.

5

Migrants and Braceros

While urban ministry to Mexican Americans developed, ministry to migrant Mexican farm workers was practically nonexistent. Few, if any, priests went out to the migrant worker. Migrants were expected to find their way to a locale that had a church. A study of migrants in the Imperial Valley in 1926 concluded, "the Catholic Church is not ministering adequately to the Mexican problem there. . . . Mexicans in the labor camps reported the priests never visited them."[1] By 1945 things were not much better. Another report reads, "In the lower Coachella Valley it is very difficult to give proper attention to the scattered Mexican families."[2] A report on northern California in 1950 reports similar problems, "[the migrants] are completely out of contact with the Church. . . . For the most part the last time they went to communion was in Mexico."[3]

The Church found it difficult to minister to a people who were always on the move. The Church's traditional parochial and diocesan structures were ill-suited to minister to the migrants. Parishes that were established near labor camps suffered when the migrants moved to their next job. The pastor of one such parish in Calexico reported, "Everything is fine in Calexico, but now most of my people are beginning to leave for the northern part of the state, which will leave our income slender for the next four months."[4] The migrant lifestyle also made it difficult to establish a stable organizational life in migrant parishes. One pastor observed, "the majority of the people are moving from one place of work to another. They have no opportunity to become organized."[5] The pastor's observation reflected that of activist Ernesto Galarza, who observed that "institution building requires a rooting process."[6] The absence of organizations and institutions that were able to travel with the migrant made them rely more intensely on their families and extended kinship networks.

Most ministry to migrant workers was left to mission churches, which often lacked a Spanish-speaking priest. Most missions were visited only occasionally by priests, who had to travel long distances to attend to their scattered flock. Even when missions were available, it was difficult for the migrants to get to them.

209

The problem of migrant ministry was compounded with the introduction of the bracero system in 1942. During World War II, the heightened demand for agricultural laborers brought the Bracero Program into existence. In theory, the governments of the United States and Mexico oversaw the program. With the end of World War II the program was continued and was formalized in 1951 under Public Law 78. During the 1950s more than 300 thousand braceros were imported each year. In 1964 the system was eliminated. During the period 1942–1964 more than 4.8 million braceros came to work in the United States. A side effect of the bracero movement was a marked increase in the number of undocumented immigrants to the U.S. During the period 1942–1964 an estimated 5 million undocumented immigrants entered the U.S., though exact figures are hard to come by. The undocumented presented an especially difficult challenge for the Church. As Allan Deck noted, "they have become a kind of sub-class living in fear and unable to plan ahead with any degree of confidence."[7] Incorporating these people into parish life was difficult, if not impossible.

The braceros faced many problems, not the least of which was a feeling of resentment toward them from the Mexican-American community. Braceros were the outsiders of an outsider group. They were resented because they allegedly depressed wages, increased unemployment, prevented unionization, and increased the foreignness of the Mexican-American community.

Care for the bracero was erratic in California. Responsibility for the bracero was generally delegated to the parish nearest the bracero camp. For instance, in 1946 St. Frances parish in Azusa was instructed to take care of the Mexican nationals in its area. Through the 1940s and 1950s this was the standard procedure in bracero ministry. More energetic parishes provided transportation from the labor camp to the church, either in busses or trucks. For instance, Holy Family parish in San Jose developed a "truck brigade" which brought over a thousand braceros to Mass each Sunday.[8] Many braceros stayed away from American parishes, because "the braceros do not feel at home in a congregation of American people."[9] Ministry to the bracero had received a boost in 1944 when the archbishop of Mexico City requested that the apostolic delegate investigate whether the bracero was receiving adequate care in the United States.

Eventually specific priests were assigned to care for the braceros and migrants. In San Francisco the Spanish Mission Band, a

group of young priests who were given a special apostolic assignment to care for the Mexican migrants and braceros, was created
in 1950. In 1955 in Los Angeles, Father Augustín Alvarez was appointed to take care of the bracero camps from his base at St. John's
Seminary in Camarillo. In San Diego in 1958, Rev. Maximiliano
Gómez was appointed bracero division coordinator. He oversaw
the work of eleven priests ministering to twenty-six bracero camps.
Beyond these diocesan attempts, several priests from Mexico came
to serve the bracero, then returned to Mexico when the bracero
returned.

Initially, service to the migrants and braceros was primarily
spiritual; priests were warned about becoming politically involved.
The priest visited the camp whenever it was possible, though Sunday Mass was not offered at camp too frequently. A typical camp
visit went as follows: the priest arrived at the camp in the evening,
and announced that Mass was to be offered the following day,
before work, usually at four in the morning. The night before, the
priest heard confessions, prayed the rosary, and gave a short talk
on doctrine. Some sort of entertainment might be provided such as
a movie, boxing match, or the like. During the 1950s many bracero
priests requested the privilege of saying an evening Mass, so as
to make Mass available to more workers. Others requested the
privilege of saying three Masses in one day in order to cover more
camps. Before leaving the camp the priest handed out medals, holy
cards, scapulars, rosaries, and devotional pamphlets. Occasionally
a "mission" was preached for the workers. As camps might go for
long periods between clerical visits, popular devotions flourished
in the camps.

Though priests were warned to stay out of politics, they did
criticize the Bracero Program on two grounds: it led to the breakup
of the family, and it exposed the bracero (and migrant) to numerous vices—gambling, drinking, prostitution, etc. One bracero priest
observed, "The average bracero finds it rather difficult to stay out
of sin, when he has not the grace of the sacraments, and is under
the constant pressure of temptation."[10] A growing awareness of
these evils and other inequities increasingly moved bracero priests
toward the political realm.

At most camps popular devotions, particularly devotion to
Our Lady of Guadalupe flourished. One priest observed, "I never
visited a camp that did not have its shrine, small or large, to Our
Lady of Guadalupe."[11] Braceros looked to Mary to intervene on

their behalf and to protect them. Ernesto Galarza reports that at a prayer meeting he attended in Soleded, twenty braceros gathered in front of a shrine to Our Lady of Guadalupe and prayed to Mary, asking that she provide them with more work, that the harsh foreman be removed, and that their contract be renewed. When Galarza asked why they did not have a committee to intercede on their behalf, they replied that previous committees had gone but had never returned. The simple dictum *"a trabajo o a México"* (to work or to Mexico) seemed to apply. In their powerlessness the braceros turned to Mary, their traditional source of support.[12]

A number of priests received acclaim for their work among the braceros and migrants. What is striking in the examples I have chosen is the ethnic backgrounds of the bracero priests: Irish, Mexican, German, French, and Italian.

Father James Gray began an active ministry to the migrants/braceros in Riverside and Redlands. He supported the development of popular devotions in the camps, particularly novenas and *tridua*. A Jesuit priest, José Peña, began visiting migrants and braceros in 1943 from Holy Family parish in San Jose. Peña was alarmed to find that many of the workers had "abandoned entirely their Catholic religion." He was equally struck by the extraordinary poverty of the workers.[13] In 1946, Peña was transferred to El Centro in southern California, where he continued his ministry to the migrant workers. By the mid-1950s he had returned to San Jose, working until he suffered a heart attack in 1965. The annalist for Our Lady of Guadalupe parish in San Jose reported that up to the time of his heart attack he was "doing the work of legions. He alone averages one hundred marriages a year and baptisms innumerable."[14]

One of the most impressive migrant/bracero priests was Franciscan Arthur Liebrantz. Liebrantz began giving missions in the Los Angeles area in the early 1940s. He purchased a trailer, converted it into a traveling chapel, and for nine years traveled up and down the San Joaquin Valley offering missions, Masses, baptisms, and marriages. Like Gray and Peña, Liebrantz "confined himself to spiritual and sacramental matters, and thus the ranch managers rarely opposed his entrance into the camps."[15]

Father Charles Philipps of Oakland and Father Victor Salandini of San Diego also served the migrants, but they chose not to concentrate solely on the spiritual realm. (See below.) One great service Salandini provided in the late 1950s was a system that he developed to ensure that the money the workers sent back to Mexico actually got to the people for whom it was intended. Migrants gave him the money they intended to send, the address of the person to whom they wanted it sent, and Salandini sent the money via registered mail. He kept careful journals to make sure the money got to where it was supposed to go. Through Salandini's efforts migrant workers were protected from swindlers who attempted to defraud the workers of their money.[16]

TOWARD SOCIAL ACTION

While priests were urged to remain purely spiritual in their approach to the migrant workers, their experience in the bracero and migrant camps made it increasingly difficult to do so. In 1943 Father Peña wrote of the migrants, "I was deeply touched when visiting them. I saw the extremely poor conditions in which many of them live; and I wondered how any father, earning modest wages, could properly support his wife and numerous offspring. . . ."[17] Another priest reporting on the migrants near Stockton in 1948 observed, "As an overall picture, however, the plight of most agrarian Mexican workers here in the valley is deplorable and heart rending."[18] Confronted with such misery, it is not surprising that priests became involved in social justice efforts that sought to ameliorate the material needs of the migrant worker. Nonetheless, the move into the social action arena was not without its tensions, as it involved a fundamental shift in the notion of priesthood. A resolution passed by the first annual bracero priests' conference held in Sacramento in 1957 captured the tension. It read:

> The priest is the man of Christ. He is not a policeman, not a social worker, not an investigator for some government agency. He is the agent of God, and his mission is to men's souls. Yet his very care for souls will sometimes lead him among men whose physical, moral and economic conditions have become not only highly conducive to vice, but also offensive to Christian customs and religious practice. Such unusual situations demand from the man of God unusual zeal and unusual missionary technique.[19]

The most innovative group in regard to social action was the Spanish Mission Band of the archdiocese of San Francisco, who definitely exhibited unusual zeal and unusual missionary technique. The Spanish Mission Band came into existence in 1950 and was composed of four recently ordained priests—Fathers Thomas McCullough, Donald McDonnell, John García, and Ralph Duggan. In 1956 Duggan was replaced by Ronald Burke. The ground had been prepared for the Band by Rev. Charles "Pop" Philipps, considered to be the "Godfather" of the Band.[20] Philipps was a French immigrant, ordained for the archdiocese of San Francisco in 1911. In 1929 he was named special minister to Basque shepherds. In 1930 he was appointed to Sebastopol, where, during the Depression, he interceded with local banks to prevent the foreclosure on a number of apple orchards. In the 1930s he was appointed the archdiocesan director of the National Catholic Rural Life Conference (NCRLC). The principles he evolved as director of the NCRLC were later used by the Spanish Mission Band in their ministry to the migrant worker: the promotion of credit unions and cooperatives, and the advocacy of family farms. Philipps and the archdiocesan NCRLC went on record against the growing "agribusiness" and "farm factories" that were coming to dominate California agriculture and displacing the family farmer in the process. He testified before state congressional committees, a task that would become familiar to Band members. Philipps argued for a 160-acre limit to the size of farms, thereby insuring the survival of the family farm. He argued that the migrant problem could be solved by providing each migrant worker two to five acres on which to farm. The migrant would then be stable and self-sufficient.

In 1936 Philipps was appointed pastor of St. Mary's parish in West Oakland, which included responsibility for the outlying farm areas. Here he encountered the Mexican migrant. By 1942 he was calling Archbishop John Mitty's attention to the "Mexican problem." Philipps's initial programs reflected the traditional approach to Mexican ministry: he supported a local laywoman of Mexican descent, a Mrs. Erickson, the archdiocesan director of the Pan American Division of the National Council of Catholic Women, in her effort to establish a CCD program for Mexican children in Oakland. She also sought to keep the Mexican Catholic community informed by publishing a small Catholic newspaper in Spanish entitled *El Mesentero*. She and Philipps suggested to Mitty that ministry to Mexicans should be organized on a district rather than parochial basis, utilizing designated district centers. This suggestion was later adopted by the Spanish Mission Band.

Before the Band was organized, the young priests went to Philipps for his advice. Among the many things Philipps told them, he stressed that they must root themselves in the locale in which they found themselves; they should know the local problems and concerns, and they should be known by local groups. As the Spanish Mission Band developed, members of the Band often called on Philipps for advice. Duggan and Burke lived with Philipps at St. Mary's on different occasions. Interestingly, the young priests also wrote Father Liebrantz to obtain his advice before starting the Band.

The idea of the Mission Band was first conceived in 1948, after McDonnell and Duggan had attended the Fifth Regional Conference on Ministry to the Spanish Speaking, a conference sponsored by the Bishops' Committee for the Spanish Speaking.[21] (The BCSS was established in 1943 to encourage better ministry to Mexican Americans.) Duggan and McDonnell returned from the conference committed to the idea that something positive had to be done for the Spanish speaking in the archdiocese.

In 1949, they began sponsoring a series of conferences for priests of the archdiocese of San Francisco to explore the current state of Hispanic ministry in the archdiocese, particularly in the rural areas. The reports were grim. More priests were needed. John García wrote, "By and large the country people are being lost . . . the loss of faith is appalling."[22] He later reflected on his early ministry, "When I arrived, there was very little in the way of providing anything in Spanish for these people [in the Brentwood area]."[23] Many migrants told García that they rarely saw a priest. The early meetings stressed the usual worries over the need "to educate" the Mexican, and the fear of losing the Mexican to Protestant proselytizers. However, Band members also stressed that what was particularly needed was "personal contact" with the Mexican migrant. This could not be accomplished through the traditional parochial system, where the burden of locating a church or mission was placed on the migrant. The Band called for "missionary techniques,"[24] where the priest went out to the people where they were—in the fields. As Duggan recalls, our approach was "direct contact with the people: the poor and needy who had little or no association with the regular parish."[25] John García was particularly adept at home visitations; he used to arrive at a home, his car filled with beans, rice, and flour, and immediately establish contact.

The Band was officially formed in 1950, and operated out of St. Patrick's Seminary in Menlo Park. The group was given no parochial duties; they had a mandate to minister directly to the poor, migrant workers. Their activities initially were primarily spiritual and reflected the regular work of bracero/migrant priests. They performed missions, said Masses in the outlying camps, heard confessions, prayed the rosary, taught catechism, and encouraged various devotions and organizations. Shortly after they were founded, they divided the various areas of the archdiocese according to county: García took Contra Costa County; McCullough, San Joaquin; McDonnell, Santa Clara; and Duggan, Alameda. They established centers in various locations: Tracy, San Jose, Russell City, Santa Clara, and Stockton. These were to be centers for education, liturgy, social and cultural events. Due to the scarcity of priests, the Band placed a high priority on developing effective lay leaders. The variety of programs the Band initiated required active lay involvement and support.

The Band began a number of creative programs: credit unions, cooperative housing, and job referrals (the State Department of Employment advertised jobs through McDonnell). McDonnell was particularly creative. In 1952 he replaced Philipps as archdiocesan director of the NCRLC. Philipps wrote, "He is an excellent choice. He is a mystic, and therefore a realist."[26] And a scholar later observed of McDonnell, "He became known for his unorthodox manner of ministering to the people and of his identification with them. He said masses in migrant camps and in homes at a time when this was considered a radical thing to do."[27] McDonnell provided extremely practical services. To avoid the high cost of funeral parlors and undertakers, McDonnell learned that in California an undertaker was not needed if the person was buried the same day he or she died. Many funeral parlors were amazed to see McDonnell arrive and claim the body, thereby saving his parishioners a considerable sum of money. McDonnell's untiring efforts gained him the deep affection of the Mexican Catholic community. The annalist for Our Lady of Guadalupe parish in San Jose noted of McDonnell, "To say the people 'like' him is an understatement. . . . Fr. McDonnell gave himself to the people here . . . he was completely at their service . . . he loved his people and they knew it."[28]

As the Mission Band worked among the migrants and braceros they began to realize that providing spiritual care alone was not enough. Father Thomas McCullough remembers, "During the first few years, our main concern was that [the migrants] were being lost to the Church: our concern with poverty was . . . that through poverty they were becoming morally disorganized . . . hurting themselves and losing the Faith."[29] The Band soon turned to "larger, structural problems." While working in Tracy, the Band was exposed to Ernesto Galarza's attempt to unionize the tomato pickers. While preparing for Mass one evening, McCullough heard a commotion as several workers began shouting, *"Huelga!* (Strike!)." The following day, McDonnell wrote to auxiliary Bishop Hugh Donohoe on behalf of the Band, asking for permission to attend union meetings to explain to the workers the Church's social teachings as presented in the great papal social encyclicals. Donohoe granted permission "in order to explain the teachings of the Church on management–labor cooperation."[30]

As the Band became interested in social justice issues, McDonnell and McCullough became frequent witnesses at congressional and legislative hearings on farm labor. They spoke as official representatives of the Church, speaking through the NCRLC. They became outspoken in their opposition to the bracero program. The bracero program was not only destructive to the bracero, destroying his faith and undermining his morals; it also was unnecessary—more than enough American workers were available to do the work. On one occasion, McCullough organized a "reverse strike."[31] While a huge contingent of braceros was arriving, unemployed Mexican Americans worked for free on a garden surrounding McCullough's mission center. The object was to show that workers were available and willing to work. Theoretically, braceros were allowed only where they did not take jobs away from Americans. In reality the bracero program increased unemployment, depressed wages, and hindered the unionization of the farm workers.

McDonnell and McCullough reiterated the basic premises of the NCRLC as previously articulated by Father Charles Philipps. In a statement in 1956 McDonnell asserted, "What the NCRLC has long hoped for is an adequate wage or piece work rate for farm workers, so as to stabilize families in communities and enable the frugal to eventually own small farms."[32] In their work of publicizing the plight of the farm worker, McDonnell and McCullough did not use scare tactics or rely on overstatement. Instead, they attempted to present hard, cold facts that they felt would appeal to people's common sense of justice. McDonnell's personal files were filled with farm reports, labor reports, and crop statistics. In 1956, he conducted a statewide study of the production of fruits and vegetables in the state of California. McDonnell and McCullough strove to make their testimony before congressional committees reflect both the teachings of the Church and an accurate description of California farm life. The Band also sought to dispel commonly held stereotypes of farm workers and farm life. Again and again they heard the lament that braceros were necessary because they were the only ones who would do "stoop labor." The Spanish Mission Band undercut the positive propaganda for the bracero program in a wonderful parody entitled, "The Legend of Pancho Sanchez, or the Boys of 78, or All This, and Money Too." Accompanying each line of the legend was a comical cartoon that depicted the "real" situation.

The Legend of Pancho Sánchez

Because the American people just won't do stoop labor and because of the shortage of skilled agricultural workers who are qualified to harvest our essential crops . . . (indeed, a mysterious labor shortage in an industry where, it is said, one man working by himself can earn up to forty dollars a day, and take the family on a vacation at the same time) . . . and in order that the imported workers may be lifted up to the American Level, those fine rugged individualists, unspoiled by vicious labor racketeers, make a free contract by a kind of collective bargaining entitling them to everything that the American worker gets and guaranteeing prompt investigation of all complaints, which, however, are generally found to be groundless. They are willing to be alone, away from their wife and children to come here just to make a little extra so they can look forward to something in their old age and so they can get a little land of their own. They are welcome to share in the hospitality of the U.S.A. and the hard working American farmer. With plenty of good fresh air and a touch of healthful outdoor living, in the thrilling adventure of coming to an exciting new land, it is a life that seems to satisfy their search for something better. Some don't ever want to leave. But really they don't stay here for very long. Then they all go right back to Mexico and go back home to work in their own little corn patch.[33]

As suggested by the publication and distribution of the legend, the Band did not shy away from controversy. Equally as controversial, the Band led the singing of union songs and protest songs at gatherings of workers. One telling song that they led, having passed out mimeographed copies of the words, was Henry Anderson's "Ballad of Christ the Bracero." Written in the form of a Mexican corrido, the ballad expressed the sentiments of the Mission Band.

Ballad of Christ the Bracero (an excerpt)

I see you O Christ in the face of the Bracero,/You come Christ Our King disguised as Ricardo/But you won't have a name when you work in our country,/For only "Bracero" shall be your name. . . . /Is this the best way we can grow our big orchards,/By using poor men who are desperate and hungry,/By using poor men such a long way from home? . . . [34]

After more than a decade of agitation against the Bracero Program by the Spanish Mission Band and other groups such as the Bishops' Committee for the Spanish Speaking, and organized labor, the bracero system was brought to an end in 1964.

The Spanish Mission Band also worked with and encouraged "secular" groups. McDonnell worked with the American GI Forum in San Jose, helping them develop a Boys Club on the east side. The major group they assisted, however, was the Community Service Organization. After having established the CSO in Los Angeles, Fred Ross arrived in San Jose in 1952. In McDonnell and McCullough he found willing allies. McDonnell assisted Ross in developing citizenship classes, English classes, and voter registration. As stated earlier, it was McDonnell who introduced Ross to a young migrant worker by the name of César Chávez, and it was McCullough who introduced Ross to a young Chicana from his parish in Stockton, Dolores Huerta.

ORGANIZING FARM WORKERS

McDonnell and McCullough increasingly came to realize that unionization of the farm worker was the only way to ensure justice for the workers. Though they had originally intended only to explain the Church's teachings as regards labor, they now found themselves becoming involved with the actual organizing. They began by appealing to established labor unions, including the national AFL-CIO, in an attempt to get them involved in unionizing the farm workers. None of the established labor unions seemed interested or willing to make a commitment to the farm workers. The Spanish Mission Band tried to taunt the unions into action by publishing a "WHERE IS OLLIE?" (organized labor) symbol on all their publications. Discouraged, McCullough and the Band decided to organize the farm workers themselves. In 1958 McCullough began the Agricultural Workers Association—AWA: *agua* means water in Spanish. The AWA was formed on the model of a mutual aid society and was designed to improve the lot of the farm worker.[35] McDonnell and McCullough, assisted by Dolores Huerta, wrote the constitution for the AWA. The following year, 1959, the AFL-CIO sent Norman Smith to California to organize the farm workers. He established the Agricultural Workers Organizing Committee (AWOC) in 1959. The same year the AWA voted to become a part of AWOC. McDonnell and McCullough continued to support AWOC, even after Smith had moved his headquarters to southern California.

The Spanish Mission Band was not without its critics. Some pastors disliked what they perceived as "loose cannons" operating in their parishes. Many farmers were less congenial. Typical complaints read, "Father McCullough has been antagonizing the good will of Catholic farmers in the county,"[36] and "As a Catholic farmer, I am disturbed by the fact that the Catholic Church is developing a statewide reputation as being anti-farmer."[37] Despite the complaints against the Spanish Mission Band, Archbishop John Mitty stood behind his priests. Father Ronald Burke reports that Mitty was "delighted" by the reports of the Band and "admired" the work they were doing.[38] Historian Moisés Sandoval writes, "the growers, realizing they could not intimidate Mitty, started to pressure other bishops in California."[39]

In 1961 the growers got their chance in what came to be known as the El Centro incident. McDonnell and McCullough were invited to provide an invocation at a workers' meeting during the AWOC-led lettuce strike in El Centro. Before going to the meeting they visited Bishop Buddy in San Diego to inform him of their actions. At the meeting they provided the invocation and led the workers in several songs, a couple Spanish hymns and "Glory, Halleluia, the Union Makes Us Strong." The following day a local newspaper reported that two priests representing Bishop Buddy were stirring up trouble among the braceros. Buddy vigorously denied the reports that they were representing him. Buddy reasserted his belief that priests should limit their activities strictly to the spiritual care of the workers. As justification he cited the complaints of farmers who wrote, "Keep Catholic priests out of the camps. They are agitators and trouble makers."[40] Buddy sent a forceful letter to McDonnell and McCullough asking them to explain their actions. When the whole matter was clarified, a cloud still hung over McDonnell and McCullough.

Though the incident was seen as the death blow to the Spanish Mission Band, it was only one of many reasons for the Band's demise. In 1962 three dioceses were split off from the archdiocese of San Francisco, thereby dividing the various areas in which the Mission Band was working. In addition, the main focus of the Hispanic apostolate was transferred from the Mission Band to the newly created Archdiocesan Catholic Council for the Spanish Speaking, which was fashioned after the Chicago Council. Since 1945 the Bishops' Committee for the Spanish Speaking had promoted regional offices to oversee the apostolate to the Spanish speaking at the local level. One of the most successful regional offices was the Cardinal's Committee for the Spanish Speaking in Chicago, under the direction of Father Leo Mahon. San Francisco adopted the Chicago model. The council was to coordinate all aspects of Hispanic ministry in the archdiocese, rural and urban. Finally, the great defender of the Spanish Mission Band, Archbishop John J. Mitty, died in 1961 after an extended illness. Mitty's chancellor, Leo Maher, was less enthused about the work of the Band and presided over its dismemberment and demise following Mitty's death.

Nonetheless, the Spanish Mission Band had made a significant contribution to the service of migrant workers and to the Mexican-American community. They truly pointed the way to the 1960s.

6

The Mexican-American Catholic Community Comes of Age, 1960–1965

The 1960s ushered in an important new era for Mexican-American Catholics. ¡Viva Kennedy! clubs sprang up in support of John F. Kennedy, reaping the benefits of the voter registration drives of the 1950s. Mexican-American leaders expected greater influence as a result of their support of Kennedy's successful presidential bid. In 1964 the Bracero Program was ended. Within the Catholic Church itself new models of church were being introduced with the Second Vatican Council. Most of the changes in the Mexican-American Catholic community, however, had less to do with Vatican II than with currents which had been developing since 1945.

During the period 1960 to 1965 the Mexican-American Catholic community experienced two important thrusts—one inward and the other outward. The inward thrust transcended the attempt to create Mass and sacraments Catholics and went beyond the notion of the traditional devotional Catholic; this new thrust, as represented by the Cursillo movement and by the programs of Leo Mahon, attempted to create a more authentic, personal Christianity. The inward thrust was balanced by a thrust outward into the community. Groups such as the Latin American Mission Program (LAMP), the Mexican American Neighborhood Organization (MANO), and finally the United Farm Workers (UFW), reflected a coming of age for, and a new confidence in, the Mexican-American community.

The movement that had the greatest impact on the Mexican-American community was the Cursillo de Cristianidad (a short course in Christianity). The Cursillo was an intense, three-day retreat which provided an "in depth discussion of the fundamentals of the Christian message and their relationship to the modern world."[1] The Cursillo was particularly attractive to Mexicans/Mexican Americans because of its use of Spanish and its sensitivity to Mexican customs. The weekend sought a "conversion experience," in which the *cursillista* made a deeper, more personal commitment to Christ and his Church. The cursillistas were "moved to be more open to further opportunities to serve in the Church and in the broader civic community."[2]

Integral to the Cursillo was leadership training. Antonio Soto, director of Cursillos in San Francisco in the early 1960s saw this as the Cursillo's real significance. It was the "first movement to stress the leadership potential of the Chicano and to dramatically change his role within the Church throughout the United States."[3] The effect on participants was often dramatic. One skeptical Chicano newspaperman sent to cover the movement came away converted. "I rediscovered my own people, or perhaps they redeemed me."[4] The conversion experience was sustained by follow-up meetings called *ultreyas*, which perpetuated an extended family network among cursillistas.

The Cursillo originated in Mallorca, Spain in the late 1940s. In 1957 two American airmen experienced a conversion through Cursillo there and brought the Cursillo back to America. The first Cursillo in the United States was offered at Waco, Texas. In September 1960, McDonnell and Duggan of the Spanish Mission Band made Cursillos in Austin, Texas, while their colleagues Burke and Garcia made Cursillos in Phoenix, Arizona.[5] The Band soon linked up with Franciscan priests in Stockton who were interested in the movement. Franciscan father Reynaldo Flores made his Cursillo in October. The Franciscans were operating St. Mary's parish in Stockton, which was largely Mexican. Father Alan McCoy, O.F.M., had been using St. Mary's as a training ground for young friars working in the Mexican apostolate. The Franciscans joined with the Spanish Mission Band in offering the first Cursillo in California, February 9–12, 1961, at St. Mary's in Stockton. The movement spread quickly to San Francisco, Fresno, Sacramento, San Diego, and Los Angeles by 1964. The effectiveness of the Cursillos was generally acknowledged. The chairman of the Catholic Council for the Spanish Speaking in San Francisco wrote in 1962, "The *Cursillos de Cristianidad* would seem to be the best instrument so far as the training of apostolic Latin Americans."[6] And Antonio Soto claimed, "As a movement of self-assertion by the Mexican American within the Church, the *Cursillo* probably has no equal."[7] One of the most celebrated cursillistas, César Chávez, obtained many of his first recruits for the UFW from his fellow cursillistas.[8] The bulk of workers and leaders for other apostolic movements, such as the California Migrant Mission Program, were also cursillistas.

Beyond developing leadership, the Cursillo was important because it appealed to men. Traditional stereotypes relegated religious concerns to the sphere of women. Machismo and anticlericalism were supposedly rife among Mexican-American males. The Cursillo broke through these stereotypes and succeeded in getting the Mexican-American male involved in the life of the Church. The Grebler study reports, "It has made active participation in Church life respectable for Mexican American men, and laid the basis for a social apostolate contrasting with the individualistic piety in much of Latin religious worship."[9] Franciscan Father Oliver Lynch, pastor of Mexican parishes in Los Angeles and Oakland, argued that the Cursillo was attractive to men because it provided them with a challenge. It called for a "lifestyle that demands what only a virile man can give. . . . To be a Christian is not possible for a moral or spiritual weakling."[10]

Another manifestation of the inward thrust was the *Familia de Dios* (Family of God) program developed by Father Leo Mahon, director of the Cardinal's Committee for the Spanish Speaking in Chicago, which was utilized by a number of parishes in California. Mahon developed his program to provide for a more effective evangelization of Latin American Catholics, whose main problems he identified as distance from the institutional Church, a lack of formal knowledge of the faith, and a lack of leadership. These observations were not original with Mahon. Mahon believed, however, that it was not enough to teach Latin Americans to be "practical Catholics." A problem that had hindered ministry to the Latin American Catholic was that the means, i.e., the sacraments, were confused as ends in themselves rather than as means to the real end, i.e., building "the Kingdom of love and justice."[11] What was important was the quality of one's faith witness.

In 1965 St. Peter's parish in San Francisco developed a program of "little parishes" based on Mahon's Familia de Dios program. Assistant pastor John Petroni, with the assistance of eight seminarians, established eight little parishes, consisting of eight to fourteen people each. The little parishes, using Mahon's guidelines, operated as study clubs which reflected on Scripture in "practical terms,"[12] and attempted to apply the Scripture directly to their lives. The groups met in the homes of different parishioners, and at the end of ten weeks a mass was held in each of the little parish centers. In 1965 six of the little parishes were conducted in English and two in Spanish. The following year six groups were offered in Spanish and six in English. The little parish program was not an overwhelming success in terms of the parish, but it did have a positive effect on many of the participants, who became more active in the parish and the community.

Less enthused about the philosophical implications of the program was Archbishop Joseph McGucken, now of San Francisco, who had more practical concerns. When granting permission for Mass in Spanish, or for home Masses at St. Peter's, McGucken clearly delineated his criteria for successful Hispanic ministry. In 1964 McGucken approved of Mass in Spanish, writing, "It might be a way of bringing a number of people to Confession and counteracting the intense amount of proselytizing activity that is going on in the Mission District."[13] The following year, while he approved the home Masses for the little parishes, he requested that the pastor inform him as to "whether or not they [home Masses] have the effect of bringing more negligent Catholics to the parish church."[14] The following year, in requesting the home Masses, the pastor assured McGucken that the little parishes had increased Mass attendance and increased CCD enrollment.[15] Not so easily appeased, McGucken warned, "Our reports on dispensations requested in similarly situated parishes indicate that there are many more validations in the parishes where priests spend less time holding meetings, and more time maintaining apostolic contacts."[16] The thrust of the little parishes seemed lost on McGucken. The little parish philosophy highlighted the conflict between the old notion of the church in which success was judged by the number of sacraments received and the post–Vatican II notion that success was to be judged by the quality of one's faith. The latter criterion was more nebulous and conducive to greater anxiety to those accustomed to quantifiable judgments. The old criteria for successful ministry obtained in other dioceses as well. In 1963 Bishop Buddy rebuked the pastor of Our Lady of Guadalupe parish in San Bernardino for neglecting the education of Mexican-American children attending public schools. The pastor responded by noting that his parish sponsored twenty-three catechetical centers to provide the needed education.[17] While new techniques evolved, the old criteria of the previous four decades remained important.

Significant innovations were being made in catechetical instruction, and one of the main pioneers in the field was Mexican immigrant Sister María de la Cruz Aymes of the Society of Helpers. From 1938, when she entered the order, until 1955, she worked in Mexico. In that year she came to America to work in the Religious Education Office of the archdiocese of San Francisco. Disgusted by the quality of the materials available to teachers, she began developing her own materials. Ultimately she was one of the main creators of the innovative *On Our Way* series, first published in 1962. While these materials were intended for all Catholics, she would later develop materials specifically designed for use in the instruction of Hispanic children and Hispanic adults.[18]

The old debate over the efficacy of the national parish also continued into the 1960s. The civil rights movement of the 1950s and 1960s had driven the final nail in the notion of a separate Mexican parish. A separate parish would be perceived as a segregated parish. In addition the old arguments that the Church was "one" and therefore should not be divided, and the argument that Mexicans did not really want separate parishes, were invoked. An Anglo pastor in San Jose asserted that Mexicans "are very well assimilated," and they "want to be part of American parishes."[19] While his statement was no doubt true in certain cases, his observations were undercut by continued requests from churches in Chicano areas to be designated national parishes. In 1962 Our Lady of Guadalupe Chapel in San Jose requested national parish status, but its request was denied. Archbishop McGucken did permit Our Lady of Guadalupe to provide the sacraments for all the Spanish speaking in the area, regardless of their parish, but he refused to grant it national parish status.[20] Also contradicting the conventional wisdom regarding national parishes was the fact that parishes that had Spanish-speaking priests and which provided services in Spanish became "unofficial" centers of Mexican church life.[21] *La Placita* in Los Angeles continued to enjoy enormous popularity in the Mexican community; Spanish speaking from throughout Los Angeles County came to be married and have their children baptized there. In San Jose, besides Our Lady of Guadalupe, the parish of Holy Family, staffed once again by Father José Peña, performed more than a thousand baptisms per year.[22] In San Francisco, where Our Lady of Guadalupe parish had long been the national parish for the Spanish speaking, Hispanics started attending parishes closer to their homes in the Mission District, where Spanish services were now being offered. Despite not being officially recognized, Mexicans created their own *de facto* national parishes.[23]

The official model remained the integrated, "melting pot" parish, in which Mexicans, Chicanos, Anglos, and other groups melded together to form one united parish. The pastor of a parish in El Monte captures the essence of the integrated parish, "If such a church could be the religious center for all, regardless of race, there might soon cease to be any racial question in the community."[24] The reality, however, was that rather than becoming integrated, more times than not the Chicano community formed a separate community within the parish, or what the pastor of St. Mary's in Gilroy called "a parish within a parish."[25] What occurred in many "integrated parishes" was that a certain Mass became the Spanish Mass; separate Spanish-speaking groups and organizations were established, and separate feasts, such as Our Lady of Guadalupe, were celebrated. Parallel parishes were the result; tensions and friction between the groups were a fact of mixed parish life. In transitional neighborhoods, older residents often resented their newer Mexican co-parishioners.[26]

The history of Our Lady of Lourdes parish in Los Angeles reflects the tensions involved in mixed parishes, but it also reflects the creation of a truly integrated parish. In 1934 Mexicans experienced little acceptance at Our Lady of Lourdes. They were told, "Attend your own 'low' churches. You are too lazy to get up early." By 1943 resentments were present in both communities. Anglos complained that the pastor "preferred Mexicans to whites," while Mexicans complained that they had not felt welcome to attend the parish mission, because of a rumor that only "those with Irish or German names" were wanted. Several years later a young Benedictine priest by the name of Louis Sittere pushed the parish toward integration. When he was transferred, the chancery was besieged by Anglos and Chicanos trying to prevent the departure of Father Louis. As one parishioner reported, Father had "organized various church groups for the sole purpose of bringing about better understanding among all the nationalities of people who make up the parish." Integration was also assisted at Our Lady of Lourdes by a large number of second- and third-generation Chicanos in the parish.[27]

While integrated parishes remained rare in the early 1960s, progress was being made in getting Chicanos more involved in parish life. In 1965 Antonio Soto reported to Archbishop McGucken, "there has been a definite effort on the part of a number of parishes to attract their Spanish speaking and with a good measure of success."[28] Cursillos played a crucial role in increasing Mexican/Mexican-American involvement; Cursillos also played an important role in bridging the gap between Anglo and Chicano communities in mixed parishes.

The Mexican-American Catholic community also began to look beyond the parish in the 1960s. Groups such as YCW and the CSO had already pushed the community beyond traditional parish concerns in the 1950s. In 1962 the YCW Cardijn Center in San Diego, under the direction of Father Victor Salandini, gave birth to MANO, the Mexican American Neighborhood Organization. MANO was not a CSO-style organization but a missionary outreach group designed to assist the poor in Mexico. MANO opened and supplied medical clinics in the border towns of Mexicali and Tijuana.[29] MANO was inspired by a more ambitious organization which preceded it in northern California, the Latin American Mission Program (LAMP), a spinoff of the Spanish Mission Band. LAMP had a threefold strategy, according to former Mission Band member Father Ronald Burke, one of the founders of LAMP. First, LAMP was to develop missionary workers among the Mexicans in California, especially lay missionaries. An offshoot of LAMP was CAMMP, the California Migrant Mission Program founded in 1962. CAMMP consisted of over fifty laypersons who ministered to the migrant workers in the labor camps. Second, LAMP, like MANO, sponsored mission outreach programs to the border areas of Mexico, and finally, LAMP was to provide missionaries to Latin American countries. In 1966 Burke was allowed to go to Mexicali as a missionary, and in 1969 he went to Guatemala, where he served until 1980.[30]

Before Burke was released to become a LAMP missionary, he became embroiled in a major controversy in the rural community of Gilroy. In 1962 Burke was sent as an assistant pastor to St. Mary's in Gilroy. While there, he established a parish LAMP group, a Mexican-American YCW that began investigating the migrant labor situation, and the Interfaith Migrant Committee (IMC), which became the source of great controversy. The IMC was an ecumenical group that began hosting conferences on problems relating to the migrant workers—health, education, religious services. Conflict arose when the IMC began to investigate the housing conditions at the migrant camps. The conditions they observed were scandalous. Burke began showing slides of the terrible conditions which existed in the camps. (The IMC would later sponsor self-help cooperative housing ventures.) During one of Burke's slide shows, a farmer whose camps were shown as an example of the terrible conditions that existed was outraged. Several farmers registered complaints with Archbishop McGucken, labeling Burke a Communist. Burke forged ahead and encouraged the IMC to investigate other controversial issues associated with farm labor—wages, working conditions, and unionization. One farmer's wife wrote, "We who are Catholic farmers have been put in a very embarrassing position by the activities of Father Ronald Burke."[31] McGucken supported Burke, but pastor John Dwyer was put into a difficult situation as the farmers began placing financial pressure on St. Mary's. Sunday collections dropped noticeably. Dwyer had a problem: the more Burke alienated the farmers, the more he was loved by the Mexican parishioners. Dwyer observed simply of Burke's relationship to the Mexicans, "He has a knack—he understands them."[32] In all of Burke's programs he built solid, grass-roots support and emphasized lay leadership and involvement. In 1965 Dwyer saw a way out: grant Burke's request to become a LAMP missionary; his supporters would have no basis to complain, and the farmers would be pleased by Burke's removal. Thus, Burke went to Mexicali as a LAMP missionary. Prior to his departure, there was a great outpouring of love for Burke, particularly from the Spanish speaking of the parish.

Crucial to the Mexican-American Catholic community's turn outward was the success of the Cursillo movement, which supplied the manpower for the various apostolic movements. Crucial to the success of the Cursillo were the Franciscans, who became prime movers in Mexican ministry in the 1960s. St. Mary's parish in Stockton, under the direction of the Franciscans, became the center of the Cursillo movement, hosting twenty-three Cursillos by 1963, and initiating many others in locations throughout California.

Franciscan influence extended beyond the Cursillo. In the late 1950s, Alan McCoy, O.F.M., began a program in which newly ordained Franciscans spent an apostolic "fifth year," working at St. Mary's parish in Stockton, primarily in ministry to Mexicans/Mexican Americans. In 1962 more than a hundred bracero camps were being visited by the fifth-year Franciscans, with Our Lady of the Field Center at St. Mary's serving as their base. One contemporary called St. Mary's "an apostolic power plant."[33] In addition to St. Mary's, the Franciscans took care of other crucial Mexican parishes throughout California, including Our Lady of Guadalupe in San Jose, St. Anthony's in San Francisco, St. Elizabeth's in Oakland, and St. Joseph's in Los Angeles. All these parishes promoted Cursillo, YCS/YCW, LAMP, community organizing, and self-help projects. It is somehow appropriate that the religious men who first evangelized California were integral in building the new Mexican-American community of the 1960s. Significantly, many of the

Franciscans working in this regard were Mexican/Mexican American themselves, most notably Father Ernesto Sánchez, at St. Anthony's, San Francisco; Father Antonio Soto at Our Lady of Guadalupe, San Jose; and Father Reynaldo Flores at St. Mary's, Stockton. The Franciscans assisted the Mexican-American Catholic community in its turn outward.

The most important movement among Mexican Americans that transcended parochial and local concerns was that of César Chávez and the United Farm Workers. Chávez organized migrant farm workers using techniques he had learned from Fred Ross and the CSO. He also utilized the Church's teachings on social justice, which he had learned from Spanish Mission Band priest Donald McDonnell. Chávez referred to his relationship to McDonnell as that of "student" to "teacher." Chávez recalled,

> [Father McDonnell] sat with me past midnight telling me about social justice and the Church's stand on farm labor, and reading from the encyclicals of Pope Leo XIII in which he upheld labor unions. I would do anything to get the Father to tell me more about labor history. I began going to the bracero camps with him to help with mass, to the city jail with him to talk with the prisoners—anything to be with him.[34]

McDonnell pushed Chávez, impressing on him the need to organize his people. Chávez later reflected that it was easier to move away from poverty than to stay in its midst and attempt to change it. Chávez remembered.

> He [Father McDonnell] had a picture of a worker's shanty and a picture of a grower's mansion; a picture of a labor camp and a picture of a high priced building in San Francisco owned by the same grower. When things were pointed out to me, I began to see but I didn't learn everything the first time.[35]

McDonnell urged Chávez to attend a home meeting organized by the CSO's Fred Ross. The result: by 1960, Chávez was national director of CSO. In 1962, when CSO refused to commit itself to the organization of the farm workers, Chávez resigned and began the National Farm Workers Association (NFWA), with the help of Dolores Huerta.

The emergence of the NFWA was extremely important for the Mexican-American community. Chávez consciously merged Catholic and Mexican symbols, making prominent use of the Virgin of Guadalupe and the Aztec eagle in a popular movement that also promoted the civil rights of Mexican Americans. The positive, progressive posture established a new identity for the Mexican American and Mexican-American Catholic that influenced a whole cadre of young Chicano activists. The Church had not always played such a positive role in support of the migrant workers' attempts to organize. Often in the past the Church had discouraged agricultural unions from fear that they were Communist controlled. In fact, in the 1930s Communists were the most significant organizers in the fields, as organized labor had abandoned the farm worker to his own devices. Historian Cletus Daniel claims that in the 1933 strikes which rocked the Imperial Valley, "growers and their supporters contacted Catholic priests in predominantly Mexican parishes and persuaded them to warn their parishioners of the potential dangers facing citrus workers who participated in communist efforts to disrupt the harvest."[36] In 1961 the Church seemed to oppose the lettuce strike in El Centro as it became embroiled in the controversy over the "unauthorized visit" of McDonnell and McCullough. A study of the 1961 strike claims that the strike failed, in part, because of "the Church's long time failure (in this area) to teach and lead people in social justice . . . at the time of the strike there was an open bias to the position of the grower."[37] Church leaders in San Diego maintained that Church intervention in the strike would not be prudent.

More disturbing to Chávez was that while he was being actively supported by the Rev. Chris Hartmire and the Protestant California Migrant Ministry, his own church was unsupportive. Chávez asked, "Why do the Protestants come out here and help the people . . . while our own priests stay in their churches, where only a few people come and usually feel uncomfortable. . . . we could not get any help at all from the priests in Delano."[38] And the West Coast representative of the BCSS lamented, "It made me sad indeed that the representatives of the Catholic Church were not in the forefront of the battle along with their Protestant brethren."[39] Nonetheless, Chávez continued to look to the Catholic Church for support.

Chávez realized that a successful movement had to recognize the strong ties between the Mexican migrant worker and the Church. When Chávez had begun organizing, he had often been called a Communist. To counter these charges, the priests of the Spanish Mission Band put out a statement denying the charge. Chávez recalled, "In those days, if a priest said something to the Mexicans, they would say fine."[40]

This had a negative side as well. Although the vote to join the Filipino-led AWOC (AFL-CIO) strike in September 1965 was taken in a Catholic church, Chávez and his movement received little support from the local church and priests. In fact, at Our Lady of Guadalupe parish in Delano the pastor spoke out against the movement and urged the strikers to return to work. Chávez observed that his biggest worry during the first six months of the strike was that the workers would picket the bishop and the local churches during Mass. Many strikers, he contended, stopped going to Mass altogether in response to the Church's reluctance to side with the workers. It was priests from outside the diocese of Fresno who first supported Chávez unequivocally. In 1966 Chávez's famous march from Delano to Sacramento gathered Church support throughout the state. By the late 1960s UFW-sponsored boycotts were being supported in parishes everywhere in California.

The militancy of the UFW and its conscious merging of Catholic and Mexican symbols gave birth to a new generation of Mexican-American Catholics who were much more aggressive in their relationship to the Catholic Church. Groups such as Catolicos por La Raza, the Chicano Priests Organization, PADRES, and HERMANAS emerged, insisting that Mexican Americans have an authentic voice within the official decision-making processes of the Church. Their goal was partially achieved with the appointment of several Mexican-American and Latino bishops for California in the 1970s and 1980s. In addition, Mexican Americans played a more active role within the Church at every level: in chanceries, on parish councils, within religious orders, and in other Catholic institutions.

CONCLUSION

A new era had arrived but not without a struggle. The Mexican Catholic community had weathered the nineteenth century in California, where they had become all but invisible to Church leaders. Ministry to Mexican Catholics in California was aptly described as "a sad story of neglect." During the first decades of the twentieth century, the flood of new immigrants fleeing the political, religious, and economic turmoil of the Mexican Revolution demanded some response from the Church. The Church did respond with a variety of educational, charitable, and parochial endeavors. However, the Mexican Catholic community was regarded as a community in need of evangelization, that is, as a docile rather than dynamic community, despite many manifestations of a vibrant spiritual life. The Church in California accepted as its main responsibility the adaptation of the Mexican to the American way of life and to the American Catholic Church.

New attitudes and approaches to Mexican ministry and to the Mexican/Mexican-American Catholic community began to develop in the post–World War II era. Community organizing, apostolic movements, missionary apostolates, Cursillo, the UFW, and other developments all contributed to the growth of an indigenous Mexican-American leadership. The Mexican-American Catholic community could no longer be regarded as a community simply to be acted upon; it was now dynamic, playing an integral role in the development of the Church in California and beyond. A new community, proud of its Mexican heritage but intent on participating in American society in a meaningful way, had emerged. In 1983 the National Conference of Catholic Bishops proclaimed, "At this moment of grace, we recognize the Hispanic community among us as a blessing from God."[41] After a long struggle the Church had come to recognize the Mexican presence as a gift and a blessing rather than a problem. The Mexican-American Catholic community had truly come of age.

PART III

The Catholic Church and the Making of Mexican-American Parish Communities in the Midwest

David A. Badillo

1

Midwestern Catholicism and the
Early Mexican Parishes, 1910–1930

Despite their traditional identification with Catholicism, Mexican Americans have been neglected by Catholic historians and immigration scholars alike. Most Mexican immigrants settled in the Southwest; however, those coming to the Midwest represented an important component of the Mexican-American experience. There, as elsewhere, the Church played a major role in the formation of communities. This study analyzes the Church as an evolving institution and seeks to illuminate the workings of Catholicism among Mexican Americans in midwestern parish communities during the formative period 1910–1965. Mexican immigrants represented a new feature in race relations as a distinct ethnic and racial group, not fully accepted or understood, yet not totally rejected.

The Midwest since the early twentieth century has served as an important area for the settlement of Mexican immigrants, although it lies outside the border states that once comprised the northern frontier of Spain and Mexico. Railroad connections existing since the mid-1880s from northern Mexico to the Midwest allowed individuals early access to temporary work, but no historic communities formed in major cities until after the turn of the century. The two decades following the outbreak of the Mexican Revolution in 1910 witnessed economic, political, and religious struggles both within Mexico and among immigrant settlements in the Midwest. Immigrants and exiles arrived in large numbers during the 1920s as transportation linkages solidified connections with Mexico.

Industry's need for cheap labor pulled Mexicans to many areas of the Midwest, ranging from the Central Plains of Kansas to the Great Lakes industrial belt running from Milwaukee to Toledo. Moreover, an increasing number of cities, towns, and rural areas drew upon the agricultural migrant stream in the states of Ohio, Michigan, Illinois, Indiana, and as far north as Minnesota.

Three separate movements of Mexican immigrants fed the region throughout the period under examination. One consisted of Mexicans recruited from the interior of Mexico to come to work for the railroads, in the steel industry, the auto factories, and other factories located in big cities. A pattern of continuous and spontaneous movement emerged along rail lines running through the state of Kansas into the Kansas City region, on to Chicago and the Calumet region in adjacent northwest Indiana, and then to Detroit and points in Michigan. Mexican Americans from Texas, originally agricultural workers, comprised the second thread. They tended to settle in the small towns, such as Saginaw, Michigan, and eventually in the large cities. The third stream of entry consisted of migrant agricultural workers from the United States and Mexico who followed the crops north and returned home after the harvest, including a wave of Mexican nationals contracted under the Bracero Program from 1942 to 1964.

Work occupied most of the time and energy of Mexicans, dictating settlement patterns and length of stay in the region. Large midwestern corporations involved in the growing and processing of beet sugar first recruited Mexicans around 1915 to replace European immigrants. These seasonal workers, called *betabeleros*, constituted a continual source of labor, channeling discontented or unemployed workers increasingly into urban industrial locations. The plight of betabeleros was particularly difficult since employers prevented their permanent settlement in the region when they were not actually tending beets, resulting in almost continual geographic mobility. During World War I many companies recruited Mexicans to work on railroads, in manufacturing plants and stockyards, as well as in the beet fields. Many such workers remained after their contracts expired. Other recruits served, often unwittingly, as strikebreakers.[1]

The Midwest offered distinct variations in the development of barrio communities, depending on labor needs and responses. Mexican labor shifted between the Chicago-Gary and Detroit regions. Few Mexicans rose to the ranks of the skilled at this time, primarily filling up the least desirable positions previously abandoned by European immigrants. Sometimes they also pushed them out. With the arrival of Mexican immigrants, native-born Americans and previously established European immigrants moved into positions of greater skill and security. In the 1920s midwestern employers, seeking a heterogeneous work force as one means to control wages and contain labor activism, recruited Mexican labor on both sides of the border region. A ready supply allowed companies to dispense with Mexican labor when no longer needed. Immigrants coming directly from Mexico tended to gravitate toward large cities, such as Kansas City, Detroit, and Chicago, which served as relatively safe havens, despite periodic outbursts of racial intolerance. In isolated midwestern communities local townspeople often shunned Mexicans in schools and factories.[2]

Midwestern neighborhoods where Mexicans settled became known as *colonias* or *barrios*, the sites of immigrant residences, Mexican businesses, and other institutions. Mexicans arriving in midwestern cities could generally escape notice at first due to their dispersal in relatively heterogeneous immigrant neighborhoods. Colonias developed therein, centering social activities on boardinghouses and pool halls. Unlike their counterparts in Texas or California, they generally consisted of persons of Mexican origin distributed among a vast array of others. Urban Mexicans typically lived near their places of employment, among Poles, Italians, and others from previous waves of immigration. Steel companies, automobile assembly plants, and packing plants, along with railroads and sugar beet companies recruited Mexican workers from the Southwest and across the border in large numbers. Sometimes they supported themselves in railroad work and agriculture along the way. Often arriving decades after European immigrants, they also traveled a different path and brought unique cultural baggage.[3]

Ethnic strife affected many aspects of daily life. Mexicans could not patronize certain restaurants, barbershops, movie houses, and other businesses outside barrio settlements. Interethnic violence peaked during the mid to late 1920s, a time of unprecedented Mexican immigration to the Midwest. Many colonia residents cited repeated examples of collaboration between police and European ethnics. Several theaters in the steel belt restricted Mexicans to balconies. Although physical proximity forced the sharing of residences and workplaces, religious practices developed along separate lines on the basis of language and ethnicity. In midwestern industrial cities, the boundaries of national parishes traditionally served to define the neighborhoods of Catholic ethnic groups. Parishes arose in these neighborhoods and strengthened their importance for cultural solidarity.[4]

Although not as numerous as Mexican immigrants, Texas Mexicans, or *Tejanos*, sought employment in the Midwest as economic and social conditions along the border worsened. Most were born in Mexico, having moved north early in the Great Migration of

1910 to 1930. Especially during the 1920s, many Tejanos arrived in the Midwest after residing in cities such as San Antonio and El Paso. Those with families tended to be *norteño* in origin, from Mexico's northern border states, where proximity and ease of entry facilitated access to better-paying jobs in the north. The Texas experience, involving castelike Anglo-Mexican social relations and *de facto* segregated institutions, provided a harsh introduction to life in the United States which those immigrants who bypassed the area entirely were spared. Moreover the strength of the Protestant churches and the weakness of the Catholic Church along the border presented a religious landscape considerably different from the midwestern immigrant parish, an urban phenomenon. In the 1930s Tejano families began a "settling out" process from the arduous sugar beet fields and other agricultural work into more permanent jobs offering residence and increased economic stability in nearby cities. There they first became involved in midwestern parish organizations. No parishes emerged in the tentative and unstable environment of the beet fields; thus cities became the mainstay of institutional Catholicism for Mexicans in the Midwest.[5]

The Catholic Church used a nineteenth-century model for receiving immigrants. It failed to adapt to Italians and found Mexicans even more confusing. The establishment of parishes required active support from bishops and the advocacy of pastors, as well as the presence of a core group of Mexican residents willing to support the church. The hierarchy had gained considerable experience with earlier waves of Europeans, particularly Italians, whose high rates of return as "birds of passage" made them similarly "quasi-immigrants." The inroads of Protestant material aid and evangelization also slowed the assimilation of the newcomers into midwestern Catholic institutions.

Protestants, long aware of the Mexican presence in the Midwest, offered evangelization, social services, and charity to Mexicans. Their administrative structure, while extensive, provided no overall plan for permanent integration of the Mexican immigrant. However, the use of segregated congregations bridged the language gap somewhat. Their missionaries spoke Spanish and sometimes counseled practicing Catholics as well. Missions generally began with interdenominational Sunday schools for Mexican children. Charitable offerings of food, clothing, and entertainment, sometimes including free transportation, induced attendance at chapels and schools among the curious or the needy.[6]

The 1920s marked the beginning of the phasing out of national parishes, which since the mid-1800s had been the church's way of absorbing non-English-speaking newcomers. The Church served as an agent of assimilation, but had not developed methods that worked well among Mexicans. Second-generation European immigrants, increasingly became assimilated into both the church and the local community. The midwestern Church adopted policies designed principally to keep Mexican Americans within the fold, while it attempted to cope with demographic changes. Whereas in the nineteenth century most bishops and pastors viewed the parish as the guardian of the immigrant's culture and religion, this commitment began to wane by the 1920s as Catholicism became more accepted within the religious pluralism of the United States.[7]

Mexicans revised their concepts and practices of Catholicism north of the border, remaining loyal to their homeland but taking on characteristics unique to the United States. Mutual aid societies, or *mutualistas*, important as labor and economic institutions in Mexico, became crucial institutions in midwestern barrios for reinforcing ties with Mexican Catholicism and for keeping alive Mexican culture. Often they helped raise money for church building. The most educated persons of the community organized the mutualistas, which were usually tied to the parish. These organizations also assumed secular functions, producing leaders who, in turn, founded other social and fraternal groups.[8]

The local parish was the place where tensions between traditional Mexican Catholicism and the more detached church-state apparatus in the United States were played out. However, it became more than a unit of religious administration and introduction to United States culture by bringing homeland customs and beliefs into the migration and settlement process. The parish focused on a collective identity, offering a place to feel at home and to be Mexican. In the Midwest a vast network of urban parishes offered Mexicans a site for introduction and adaptation to the new environment. However, parish boundaries often did not coincide with industrial ones, as in the Calumet steel belt along the Illinois-Indiana border. The South Chicago steel mill parish was in the Chicago archdiocese, while nearby mills in Northwest Indiana fell within the Fort Wayne diocese. The scattered dispersement of the work and workers made it difficult for the institutional Church to serve them efficiently.[9]

The comparative analysis that follows looks at some dominant cities and how their parishes served as the representative units of institutional Catholicism in the years before 1965. Thereafter, the implementation of the reforms of the Second Vatican Council and the assumption by the federal government of many of the social service functions of parishes permanently changed United States Catholicism. A wide range of sources, including parish and chancery archives, community histories, government documents, and anthropological case studies record a wealth of diverse individual and collective experiences during this period. Rural Mexican and Mexican-American migrants also commanded the attention of Church leaders, especially after 1945, and the records of bishops' conferences and of national Catholic organizations reveal official institutional policies.

THE MEXICAN REVOLUTION,
ANTICLERICALISM, AND IMMIGRATION

Mexicans coming to the United States left a country where Catholicism dominated religious and cultural life. The Catholic Church remained one of the pillars of the regime of Mexican President Porfirio Díaz, which lasted from 1876 through 1910. Under the *Porfiriato* the Mexican hierarchy and clergy continued to have a monopoly on education, marriage, and religion. But Catholicism also performed a validating social function, linking Mexicans with their pre-Hispanic past in a manner that was independent of priests and institutional structures. To the dismay of the hierarchy a strong native clergy never developed in Mexico, where historically the peasant viewed both the institutional Church and the state as outsiders.[10] Internal Mexican problems constituted "push" factors for emigrants destined for the North.

From 1910 to 1930 revolutionary violence and economic dislocation precipitated the destruction of the hacienda system. A massive northward movement consisted predominantly of displaced small farmers *(campesinos)*, as well as some skilled artisans and merchants. Patterns of chain migration sometimes attracted newcomers to the Midwest from the same small ranchos or villages. These networks did not, however, facilitate the transfer of Catholicism or the development of stable Catholic institutions. Railroads directed passage throughout the state of Kansas and from there northeast to the factories and farms of the Great Lakes states. Many people "leapfrogged" past the Mexican and U.S. border states from the densely populated and ardently Catholic states of the *mesa central*, or central plateau, predominantly Michoacán, Jalisco, and Guanajuato. This area accounted for over three-quarters of the immigrants during the 1920s; other Mexicans came from northeastern Mexico. Poor education, with literacy rates in the mesa central ranging from 10 to 30 percent, discouraged the dissemination of religious publications and restricted any sense of identification with United States society.[11]

The persecution of the Mexican Church and expelling of many religious began a chain of events that greatly enhanced the development of barrio parishes north of the border. The outrage concerning expulsion, confiscation of church property, and violence unleashed in the revolutionary turmoil fueled concern among the United States hierarchy over the Mexican situation. Prominent Catholics in the United States such as Father Francis C. Kelley, editor of *Extension* magazine, wrote and spoke of the persecution and injustice of successive regimes. Kelley charged in 1915 that President Venustiano Carranza and "the Constitutionalists in Mexico have attempted to destroy, and practically have destroyed, three-fourths, if not more, of the Catholic Church in their country. They did it deliberately, and as a result of a prearranged plan."[12] Kelley cited a nun's statement that "the revolutionists have closed the temples and prohibited the sacraments to the degree that any priest daring to hear confession or offer the Holy Sacrifice is shot. Confessionals and some of the statues of the saints have been burned in the public squares."[13]

In a 1917 testimonial, the Mexican Catholic bishops vehemently and publicly opposed the provisions of the new constitution that enabled the confiscation of church property, specifically the provision that "Episcopal residences, rectories, seminaries, orphan asylums, and . . . collegiate establishments of religious associations, convents, or any other buildings built or designed for the administration, propaganda, or teaching of the tenets of any religious creed, shall . . . be used exclusively for the public services of the Federation or of the State within their respective jurisdictions."[14] The bishops argued, "there can be no religious freedom where the church buildings are left in the hands of those not belonging to the clergy and faith, or where they are not the property of religious organizations."[15] They further criticized the provision that only a Mexican by birth may be a minister of any religious creed in Mexico, as it not only ended clerical privilege but specifically excluded the numerous Spanish priests who served in Mexico.

By 1919 the position of the Catholic Church in Mexico had improved somewhat. The most blatantly anticlercial provisions of the 1917 Constitution had lapsed, and many Mexican bishops, priests, and nuns returned from their exile in the United States, where they had developed some contact with Mexican communities. President Alvaro Obregón expelled Spanish clergy and religious in the early 1920s and many remained in the United States through the decade. Others arrived from Mexico according to the dictates of changing local circumstances.

Since 1905 the Extension Society had provided funds for church buildings and missionaries that local communities could not afford on their own, particularly in areas with few Roman Catholics. In 1918 the Society, based in Chicago, financed a seminary for Mexicans at Castroville, Texas. It also helped priests and nuns escape from Mexico, offering them training for the establishment of schools and other Catholic institutions. In a visit to San Antonio, Kelley met with a dozen or so Mexican bishops who claimed to have arrived disguised to conceal their identities along the border. They reported hundreds of Mexican priests scattered over Texas. Kelley also requested that Mexican clergy be sent to Chicago to prepare a small history of Mexico for the benefit of United States clergy.[16]

Protestants, with the backing of U.S. groups, had established missions in Mexico after 1870 and had made some inroads in the ensuing years. However, by 1910 Protestants accounted for only 1 percent of the total Mexican population, with some 30,000 faithful and perhaps 100,000 sympathizers. At that time, there were approximately 4,500 priests, as against fewer than 300 Protestant ministers. Proselytizers generally avoided the mesa central area and focused on the north. Most immigrants from the interior therefore had little contact with organized non-Catholic religious institutions in their homeland.[17]

Anticlerical policies precipitated the violence of the Cristero Revolt of 1926–1929, and the armed conflict spread throughout the mesa central. Church-state issues were volatile for many years thereafter. From 1926 to 1929 the Mexican bishops ordered all churches in the republic closed in an effort to force President Plutarco Elías Calles to rescind the regime's anticlerical legislation. During much of this time, government officials prohibited priests from saying Mass and closed many churches. Calles executed about ninety priests during this rebellion, which claimed the lives of 60,000 *Federales*, along with 40,000 Cristeros. Violence persisted even after the Cristeros laid down their arms in 1929, as did mistrust of the government, and in 1930 many churches, convents, and schools remained empty.[18]

Catholic leaders saw Protestant failures to denounce this religious persecution in Mexico as a sign of moral weakness. Not until the mid-1930s did President Lázaro Cárdenas considerably ease anticlerical measures, cementing the modern conciliatory relationship between church and state in Mexico. The era of anticlericalism, in Kelley's words, served to "introduce the church in Mexico to the church in the United States."[19] Given the antagonisms between federalist soldiers and rural campesinos in the Cristero Revolt, many immigrants brought with them ambivalent attitudes toward formal affiliation with the Church. However, anticlericalism rarely surfaced in midwestern communities and never became part of the midwestern "Mexican situation."

The religious dimension of the overthrow of the regime of Porfirio Díaz had important ramifications for Mexicans in the United States. In 1922 Father Kelley noted that although growing numbers of Mexicans lived as far north as Chicago, they remained concentrated in the Southwest. "Whole villages of them," he wrote, "are without schools, and there are still many settlements without churches." He observed that "the worst of their situation is that the largest number of Mexicans go to the poorest of our dioceses, those least equipped to bear additional burdens." Kelley mistakenly believed that the Mexican Revolution and its accompanying anticlericalism would preclude the migration north of a helpful cadre of surplus priests. Kelley's plan to found missions and develop them into parishes focused mainly on the Southwest; he also saw a great need for establishing schools and training teachers for the new immigrant populations. "If we can save the children now they will supply both priests and teachers later on," he suggested.[20]

Catholic officials struggled to identify the dispersed settlement patterns of Mexican immigrants. The focus on the point of entry ignored the growing midwestern urban and rural settlements. The National Catholic Welfare Council's Bureau of Immigration assisted Mexican immigrants on the border beginning in 1924 at the El Paso Immigration Station. A 1928 report pointed to the need to "safeguard the Faith of the Catholic immigrant[s] and also to assist them in becoming desirable residents of this country by helping them to a knowledge of its language, its laws and its ideals, and to aid them in many difficulties which they may encounter."[21]

A 1927 meeting of the Bishops of the West, however, revealed concerns about emerging Mexican settlements. One Nebraska bishop sought financial assistance for his parishes, noting that "the Mexicans are great movers, here today and gone tomorrow" and "it looks as far as any proposition of this kind can be judged, that this will be permanent." He observed, "I have Mexican people in the city of Lincoln, especially in the southwestern part of the city, where they seem to have centralized. I am using a [Knights of Columbus] building for Mass, marriages, and administration of the other Sacraments. I have been contemplating buying an abandoned church for a school. This will help solve the problem." Another bishop concurred on the gravity of the Mexican immigration problem, observing, "They are constantly moving about from place to place and do not stay long anywhere. In Wichita . . . the Americans do not appear to want them. The Protestant denominational churches for awhile worked [among them] but after awhile they discovered that it was very unprofitable and so they combined and have worked together with considerable success."[22] Essentially the Church took the loyalty of Mexicans for granted, although it was slow to learn their traditions and expressions of religiosity.

The accepted tenet on both sides of the border that all Mexicans were rightfully and fundamentally Catholic conditioned Anglo-Mexican relations in the Midwest. European immigrants observing the influx into their neighborhoods conveniently believed that Mexicans were better off in their own national parishes, although they did little to encourage their development. Exiled clergy and religious necessarily functioned under the authority of United States bishops. Their presence, though limited, helped to surmount linguistic barriers, although numerous cultural and social problems within the parish structure developed. Mexican priests remained scarce in the Midwest, and the earliest ones became roving missionaries without permanent parochial attachments.

Various factors affected community and parish building. Exiled priests helped establish midwestern parishes and worked with Sisters in ministering to the growing immigrant population. Religious exiles, due to their knowledge of the language and culture of Mexico, greatly facilitated the establishment of numerous missions and over a half dozen "pioneer parishes" in the Midwest before 1930, thereby channeling the energies of immigrants toward community building. The bishop and local parishioners generally supported these efforts in relation to the larger needs of developing community structures in an alien society. The local Anglo clergy oversaw the construction of buildings where men, women, and children could come together for recreational and educational as well as religious activities.

RAILROAD TOWNS AND PARISH
COMMUNITIES IN KANSAS AND MISSOURI

Among the early Mexican parish communities in the Midwest were those constituted of rail workers. Prior to 1905 the Santa Fe Railway employed Mexican laborers principally in New Mexico and Texas from May to October, at which time they usually returned to Mexico. In 1907 it actively recruited them to work in Kansas City, Kansas, on the repair and maintenance of lines, opening up further settlement in the Midwest. After their contracts expired, some workers remained, and some companies permitted their workers to live in boxcar settlements in rail yards. Packinghouses nearby subsequently attracted Mexican labor. By 1914 some six to seven hundred Mexicans lived in six distinct barrios in the greater Kansas City area, straddling both sides of the river separating the Kansas and Missouri barrios. Streetcars integrated the settlements and made churches accessible.

These particular circumstances of geography, work, and residence facilitated cooperation on the part of Mexican immigrants which was crucial in the subsequent formation of Mexican parishes. Meanwhile, the number of Mexicans throughout Kansas jumped from over 8,000 in 1910 to some 14,000 in 1920, and increased to 19,000 in 1930. Thousands more passed through the Kansas City area on their way north and east to the Great Lakes states.[23]

Track work constituted the initial source of Mexican employment, keeping Mexican immigrants on the move and slowing down permanent settlement. The first Mexican immigrants in Kansas City were generally *solos* or unaccompanied men, who often lived alone for a few years before sending for their families. Migratory workers also spread throughout the state of Kansas along railroad stops, settling in Emporia, Wichita, and eastward. Beginning around 1910, Westside, in Kansas City, Missouri, grew to be the largest barrio in the area, as Mexicans replaced northern European immigrants, predominantly German, Swedish, and Irish employees of the rails and packing houses. Greater Kansas City served as the gateway to the Mexican Midwest and the site of early parish communities in the central plains.[24]

The first exiled clergy from Mexico, as well as other religious refugees, also followed this route. Father José Muñoz, a Spaniard first brought to Mexico by the bishop of Morelia to staff his diocese, helped establish the pioneer parish in Westside. Muñoz fled to Matamoros in 1913 and then left by train for Brownsville, Texas, remaining there until early 1914, when he arrived in Kansas City. Here, along with another exiled priest, he offered Mass at Sacred Heart Church for some twenty Mexican families. Soon he moved to a vacant house with a storefront.[25]

Within a year a temporary chapel was constructed in the heart of the barrio on Twenty-fourth Street and several hundred Mexicans from throughout the city attended Mass there. Father Muñoz, although an Iberian from Salamanca, became known far and wide as the "Mexican priest." He visited ill or dying section hands and other laborers for miles around, serving in the area until 1917, at which point he embarked on missionary ventures throughout the Midwest. By this time the Church of Our Lady of Guadalupe, named, typically, for the patroness of Mexico, had become solidly established. Muñoz returned to the parish for another brief stay a decade later, before moving on to further endeavors in midwestern locales.[26]

In Ottawa, in northeast Kansas, a Mexican colonia had resided since 1907 in houses constructed from railroad ties on the property of the Santa Fe Railroad. During the winter of 1915–1916, when most of the Mexicans had returned to winter in El Paso, the local Anglo pastor, whose service to Mexicans since their arrival included administering last sacraments to laborers in the town hospital, consulted the twenty-five families staying through the year. Fund-raising among Mexicans faltered because of their continual changes of location as they were dispatched "here and there to different points, as the Santa Fe sees fit, to keep up the track in proper condition."[27] The clergyman managed to secure pledges from the laborers to pay regular dues to construct a mission church. The Extension Society donated $250 and the bishop of Leavenworth gave $500 to the new mission. Other contributions included the altar, pews, and statues. The cornerstone for the new Ottawa Catholic church was laid in 1916 with several exiled priests as well as Mexican families from nearby towns attending.[28]

The dedication several months later featured a Spanish sermon. The bishop later congratulated the parishioners for having the first Mexican church in the diocese (a Mexican missionary still served the diocese at large). The pastor of Sacred Heart Church said weekly mass at the new parish, and an exile priest made monthly visits from Topeka until his return to Mexico shortly thereafter. In the summer months the parish served some 250 Mexicans in the camp. Bishop Ward of Leavenworth, observing that the worshipers now enjoyed freedom of conscience, asserted that they therefore owed a debt of gratitude to the U.S. government for granting them entrance.[29]

Observers in Ottawa noted that banners of devotional societies from Emporia and Topeka adorned the chapel. The early involvement of Guadalupe societies gives evidence of the rapid transplantation of Mexican religious practices to the Midwest. The use of interior decorations in red, white, and green, the colors of Mexico's flag, indicated some acceptance of symbols of religious and national identity and the subtle yet continuing shift away from the "simplicity" of nineteenth-century Irish Catholicism toward new standards of religiosity and ceremonialism. Similarly, German priests in 1886 in the Abbelen Memorial demanded "beauty, pomp, and splendor" for their immigrants, urging also that Americanization proceed slowly and naturally. Mexican religious customs in the Midwest increasingly reflected the ancestral culture. Unlike Germans, however, and more akin to the Irish model of parish administration, Mexicans depended heavily on priestly initiative rather than on lay governance for leadership in community affairs.[30]

Throughout rural western Kansas, Catholic churches practiced the segregation of Mexicans in the back pews when they tried to attend local Masses. Many Mexican Catholics therefore chose not to return to church and worshiped and received baptisms for their children and other sacraments at home, administered by whatever pastor would oblige. The first Mexican churches, usually one-room wooden structures, slowly expanded, adding rectories, recreational halls, and, much less frequently, parochial schools on adjacent properties. In Kansas City, Missouri, supporters purchased a Lutheran church for use as the Mexican parish.[31]

Protestant religious work among Mexicans was begun in Wichita around 1910 by a Presbyterian, who decided to teach English on the Mexican south side of town. In the winter of 1912–1913, a group of women from the Disciples of Christ opened a soup kitchen in Kansas City's Westside for unemployed track workers. Within a few years they had established the Mexican Christian Institute, run by a Spanish-speaking Anglo minister who had served as a missionary in Mexico. A Sunday school soon followed. The Institute developed departments for religious and social work as well as a clinic for administering vaccinations to children. Many other Protestant missions and churches arose specifically for Mexicans in the region, most often in the heart of the colonia, sometimes adjacent to Catholic mission churches. Religious conversion sometimes facilitated the fulfillment of material as well as spiritual needs, through the procurement of assistance in acclimating to new communities.[32]

Other Protestant churches later arose as persistent but generally unsuccessful competitors to the Catholic religion. The Santa Fe Railway Company donated two railway cars for classes in religious instruction for fifty Mexican Catholic families living in Argentine, Kansas early in 1919. The measure unintentionally offset the efforts of the Methodist minister, even though the shortage of Mexican priests prevented the offering of Mass in the coaches. In Kansas throughout the 1920s, Sunday schools for Mexicans focused on literacy in Spanish, English, or both. They generally preceded the establishment of missions or churches. Tenuous and fitful connections existed between Mexicans and Protestants in the Midwest, with a blurring of the relationship between charitable contributions and thinly disguised attempts at proselytizing.[33]

Parish environments provided cultural as well as religious centers. In 1926 the Amber Club's Guadalupe Center opened for Mexican community activities in Kansas City's Westside. Health clinics and other activities arose to counteract Protestant proselytizing among Mexican and Italian immigrants. Parishes fostered unity but also insulated their members and sometimes placed them under restrictive leadership. The Spanish-language newspaper, *El Cosmopolita* which was published in Kansas City from 1914 until 1919, informed immigrants of events back home and provided a voice for the group of former businessmen and landowners known as *ricos*. These "elites" of Mexico represented an emerging middle class in the United States.[34]

During the recession following World War I more than 100,000 Mexican workers in the United States lost their jobs and returned home. It also tested the fledgling Mexican settlements in Kansas. Unemployment underscored the economic factors involved in parish building. Several Catholic missions and parishes became depopulated. Agricultural workers suffered most severely the effects of unemployment, but many packinghouses, steel mills, and other enterprises employing Mexicans in and around Chicago closed. Protestant charities came into prominence. A Methodist mission in Argentine, Kansas, where no Catholic parish existed at the time, helped the Mexican consul at Kansas City, Missouri, to organize a trainload of some 800 destitute workers from the Westside barrio for their journey back to Mexico. Not many of the Mexican families attended the prayer meetings at the mission, according to the women teaching the religion classes, despite high attendance at the various clubs and social meetings held there. Some Mexican mothers living in the district sent their children to the mission, believing that it offered better care than Catholic institutions.[35]

Father Muñoz with the assistance of the Augustinian Fathers had participated in the formation of the nearby Armourdale, Kansas, parish, which arose as the number of Mexican families increased within the congregation of St. Thomas parish during World War I. These families felt they were discouraged from participating in other local Anglo-Catholic churches. In 1923 about eighty-five Mexican families in the area formed a separate unit, the parish of Our Lady of Mt. Carmel, though it still used the Church of St. Thomas for religious services. In 1924 a fund-raising drive was held to erect a permanent Mexican church building for a national parish in Armourdale, with the aid of a group of Anglo women known as the Guadalupe Guild. Moreover, the husband of one of the Guild members, a devout Catholic who supervised the track forces in Argentine, encouraged all Mexicans employed by the Santa Fe to donate one dollar from each paycheck to the building fund. Dedicated in 1925, Our Lady of Mt. Carmel Church served Mexicans through the late 1930s, and then the bishop organized another Mexican national parish in Argentine.[36]

Father Muñoz tried to insulate his parishioners and competed with the rival forms of Mexican community organizations that, in many cases, represented attempts at cultural continuity as much as Americanization. In the late 1920s the Unión Cultural Mexicana (Mexican Cultural Union) successfully organized some of its members into a thirty-five piece band, but several members encountered difficulties with the pastor. Father Muñoz reportedly feared that the attraction of the band would cause the church to lose hold of the people. He also alleged freemasonry and godlessness among some parishioners, regarding all secular voluntary associations in Westside as undesirable. In 1927 the pastor resigned to conduct mission work among Mexicans in Kansas, Illinois, Pennsylvania, and Michigan. He died in July 1941 at Newton, Kansas. The Franciscan brotherhood eventually took charge of his Kansas City ministry.[37]

MEXICAN PARISH COMMUNITIES IN CHICAGO

Permanent Mexican settlement in Chicago began as early as 1916; in 1918 the archbishop of Guadalajara took notice of this growing community in a visit to the city. By 1920 over 1,000 Mexicans lived in Chicago, but their wide dispersion tended to hide them from further official attention at the time. The Presbyterian Church first opened a mission for Mexicans in Chicago in 1913. In 1923 Father Kelley of the Extension Society wrote to Archbishop George Mundelein expressing his surprise upon learning that "there were so many Mexicans here." He noted, "There are Mexicans all along the Railroads from Chicago to Texas, and Kansas City already has a makeshift church and Sunday-school for them. . . . You may remember that our Board favored the idea of securing two Mexican priests to look after these scattered Mexican laborers. The proper place for these priests to live would be Chicago. . . . Several have already promised to assist."[38] Though no concrete plans emerged at that point, within a short time the Chicago archdiocese became more involved with Mexican Catholicism.

Industries in the Chicago area, including steel, meat-packing, and railroad lines, recruited in the city's expansive midwestern hinterland using a variety of techniques. By 1930 Chicago had become the fourth largest Mexican-American city in the United States and the largest in the Midwest, with some 20,000 Mexicans. During the 1920s it had three well-defined and relatively large Mexican settlements: the Near West Side, near downtown; South Chicago, in the midst of the steel mills; and Packingtown in the Back of the Yards section.

The Near West Side colonia began earliest, around 1919. One pastor who had operated a mission in South Chicago, began Protestant work there beginning in 1924. By the mid-1920s Congregationalists and Presbyterians had united in their Mexican missionary work at Firman House. They also served the isolated boxcar camps housing some 10 percent of Chicago's Mexicans. The staff consisted of a full-time, Spanish-speaking American pastor, a Cuban ministerial student helper, a full-time children's worker and home visitor, and a part-time medical worker.[39]

In 1922 Mexicans first registered with the Immigrants Protective League in Chicago's Near West Side; in the mid-1920s genuine communities of families formed. Their increased visibility throughout the decade sometimes made Mexicans a target for lawmakers seeking their inclusion in the quotas proposed in the National Origins Plan aimed at restricting immigrants from southern and eastern Europe. One Congressman stated, "They are filling the streets of Chicago. You see them everywhere, fighting, brawling, quarreling, not fitting into American life at all."[40] Some business leaders, such as Robert Wood, president of Sears, Roebuck and Company, also supported restriction. Most public officials in Chicago, however, sided with Texas employers who believed that Mexican immigration remained entirely a southwestern question. More importantly, they may have believed that Mexicans would not permanently settle outside the Southwest.[41]

Few Mexicans sought United States citizenship due to nationalism and ethnic pride, their relative proximity to the border, and uncertainty concerning family reunification. Those who became naturalized generally kept it to themselves to help remain "Mexican" in spirit.[42] Others found themselves rejected in their bid for assimilation. An Illinois Mexican newspaper attacked as "renegades" two Mexican steelworkers from Joliet who attempted to pass themselves off as Spaniards. One individual, according to the editor, "has forgotten the little and bad Spanish which he learned in his country. He regards everything Mexican as bad, and antiquated. He chews tobacco, and, worse [sic] of all, he denies his nationality, no matter how dark-skinned he is."[43]

Settlement houses still thrived in the late 1920s in immigrant neighborhoods and many developed Mexican programs. These institutions reinforced prevailing attitudes concerning the need for assimilation, as well as social reform and moral improvement among immigrants. Chicago settlement houses catering to Mexicans with Protestant affiliation claimed that they did not proselytize, but many of them included religious services among their Americanization activities. Mexicans became integrated into the programs of the settlements, although often they were only grudgingly accepted. On one occasion a group of Italians came to Hull House, Chicago's famous settlement, threatening to stop renting Bowen Hall for weddings and other festivities if they had to share it with Mexicans. Despite this episode, settlement house activities generally reinforced the integration of Mexicans into changing neighborhoods, while favoring the containment of African Americans. Thus Mexicans, at least temporarily, fell on the white side of the color line. This perception gave way in the mid-1920s to stronger anti-Mexican sentiments with racial overtones. Moreover, some Catholic pastors criticized Jane Addams for permitting such anticlerical groups as the Giordano Bruno Society to meet at Hull House.[44]

Leadership among the Mexicans in the Chicago area developed slowly. Noted one Mexican observer, "There is really no Mexican in charge who is regarded as a leader, or with particular prestige.

The consul . . . is looked up to by the less educated but the more sophisticated regard him lightly."[45] The consul worked through the settlement houses or churches to solicit help in specific crises, but he often sought to discourage rather than facilitate immigration from Mexico. A meeting in 1924 between the Mexican consul general and representatives of Chicago's various Mexican societies failed to federate the disparate groups, although it did attract passing interest.[46]

Into this leadership vacuum stepped Cardinal Mundelein, who sought to "Americanize" Catholics of diverse backgrounds in neighborhood parishes. Between 1916 and 1929 Mundelein commissioned the foundation of forty-two parishes, only nine of which were national; two of these national parishes served Mexicans. He also centralized numerous archdiocesan organizations and societies that controlled parish activities. In an effort to save Italian churches from fiscal disaster, the cardinal turned them over to Italian religious orders such as the Scalabrini and Servite Fathers. By the time of his death in 1939, Cardinal Mundelein had put ten of the twelve Italian national parishes in Chicago under the care of religious orders.[47]

St. Francis of Assisi Church in Chicago's Near West Side, first a German and later an Italian parish, as late as 1923 had only eleven Spanish names on its register. However, a Mexican parish soon flourished under the Spanish-born Father James Tort in a new pattern of parish succession. In 1927 St. Francis officially completed the transition from an Italian national parish to a Mexican one. Nearly a thousand worshipers attended the Latin Mass, and a shrine at one side of the church exhibited the Virgin of Guadalupe. A benefactor of the parish furnished funds for the transportation of four Cordi-Marian Sisters from Mexico to form the nucleus of the first faculty of the parish school, soon attended by forty-two Mexican children, with more than a thousand children in catechism classes.[48]

Mundelein's policy concerning Mexicans represented a pragmatic variation of Americanization. He recognized that the restriction on European immigration marked a turning point for national parishes. However, since this pattern did not apply to Mexicans, whose greatest influx took place after the onset of immigration restriction, he reverted to an old model, the national parish. Mundelein's elevation to cardinal in 1924 signified the growing importance of the Midwest and was a step to counter anti-Catholicism. That same year Mundelein convened the first International Eucharistic Congress in Chicago, attended by bishops from almost two dozen countries, which succeeded in raising the profile of midwestern Catholicism.[49]

Protestant groups, especially Methodists, Baptists, and Presbyterians, worked actively among Italian immigrants in midwestern cities. Few American Protestants spoke Italian and most American Protestant churches had little contact with Italian immigrants. In addition to establishing churches and missions, Protestant denominations sought to aid the adjustment of Italians and their children by establishing social settlements in ethnic areas. Their work alerted the Catholic hierarchy to the Italian presence and to the need to utilize Italian-born clergy to keep the immigrants within the fold. The strategies of the failed Protestant effort to proselytize Italians were later transferred, equally unsuccessfully, to Mexicans.[50]

Protestant church leaders seemed more determined to undermine Italian Catholic parochial and cultural traditions than they did those of the Mexicans and felt less urgency due to the smaller numbers, lesser visibility, and shorter period of residence of the latter. Mexicans, moreover, were less contemptuous of the clergy and did not manifest the aversion to parochial life observed among Italian immigrants. The Catholic Church in Italy was strong, but weak in Mexico. In Mexico, nationalism and Catholicism opposed each other for different reasons. Religion represented the people, *la raza*, with a shared experience of *mestizaje*, blending Spanish and Indian cultures in a process clearly distinct from anything Anglo-European. Moreover, regional differences among the new immigrants focused on core versus periphery, that is, central plateau versus northern frontier, rather than on town identity. No conflicts arose because of devotion to local Mexican saints and "national heroes," as had been the case among transplanted northern and southern Italians.[51]

Unlike Mexicans, neighborhood traditional feasts among Italians expressed their independence from the Church hierarchy and their primary allegiance to the village church in the old country. Although a tolerance for folk practices necessarily existed due to the lack of a strong commitment to institutional Catholicism, some so-called pagan rites affronted the clergy. Other clergy feared "socialist anticlericalism." The Mexican Catholic church, in contrast, was much weaker and remained so during the years of immigration. Many Mexican officials believed religion to be merely an activity for pious women and the lower classes, particularly those from Mexico's mesa central, the perennial Catholic stronghold. By the time the Mexicans had settled in the Midwest, fear of socialism and labor violence had replaced Americanization as the greatest concern of the Catholic hierarchy.[52]

Mexicans, isolated without a native clergy, often needed surrogates to build parishes. Religious orders offered an economical solution for the Church's "Mexican problem." Members of the Claretian Missionary Fathers, a Spanish religious order founded in the mid-nineteenth century and committed to service, organized and maintained the Mexican work in the emerging barrios. Sisters from Mexico also served the Mexican population during the 1920s as teachers in parish schools and for social work within the Mexican community. Priests visited storefront chapels in nearby railroad camps, where Mexican track laborers and their families lived under uncomfortable and overcrowded conditions. In the Chicago suburb of Waukegan, a Claretian mission served 800 Mexicans in 1925. Elsewhere, traveling priests filled in where necessary. As Spaniards, however, these priests offered little reinforcement of Mexican culture.[53]

Mundelein broke with his established policy of discouraging national parishes by sanctioning the construction of Our Lady of Guadalupe in Chicago's steel mill colonia. Mexicans in South Chicago, unofficially restricted from renting or buying homes and almost uniformly charged higher rents than their neighbors, faced discrimination in existing Catholic ethnic parishes. Mundelein acknowledged that European ethnics of South Chicago were unlikely to incorporate the Mexicans into their churches. He knew he had to compete with the proselytizing efforts of Protestant churches, and he hoped to provide a more satisfactory ambiance for the immigrants than the poolrooms, barbershops, restaurants, and other traditional gathering sites. In 1924 Mundelein helped raise funds from James Farrell, president of U.S. Steel, the company employing most of the Mexican workers. Farrell contributed $12,000 for the construction of Our Lady of Guadalupe Church. The exiled Claretian Fathers took charge of the parish from a Jesuit who had helped organize the congregation the previous year. Naturalization and citizenship classes were held in the parish hall.[54]

As the Mexican colony in South Chicago grew in the late 1920s Father Tort directed plans for a larger complex. An expansive church of the same name seating over a thousand persons replaced the original wooden chapel in 1928. Father Tort vocally advocated Americanization and assimilation. Irish groups and other ethnics as well as Holy Name Societies marched beside Mexicans at the dedication. In 1929 the National Shrine of St. Jude was established at Our Lady of Guadalupe Church. By 1930 the pastor claimed that three-fourths of the more than four thousand Mexicans in South Chicago belonged to the parish, with some five hundred attending weekly mass, offered with a Spanish sermon.[55]

Mexicans entered the South Side packing plants in the Back of the Yards gradually before 1921. In that year, however, a strike made many more jobs available with the largest industrial employer in the city. A protracted battle against the major packers lasted from the union organization drives in 1917 until their defeats in early 1922. By 1930 some 2,500 Mexicans lived in and around Packingtown, an area characterized by overcrowded housing. Mexicans did not attend the national parishes of other groups because of the language barrier as well as the widespread distrust of outsiders on the part of older parishioners. Mundelein did not encourage the casual and unsupervised mingling of Mexicans in European national parishes either, and this forced the local clergy to assume an active role in the church affairs of Mexicans. St. Francis parish maintained a social program integrated with other ethnic settlements on the West Side. Priests from St. Francis commuted to the Back of the Yards for about ten years, but until the establishment of a mission there in the 1940s, Catholic ministry to Mexicans failed to compete with Protestant groups, despite the presence of over a dozen Catholic churches.[56]

MEXICAN CATHOLICISM IN NORTHWEST INDIANA

Midwestern colonias expanded in the 1920s, helped by employment recruitment within and outside the region. The experiences of Mexicans in northwest Indiana, part of the steel belt stretching from South Chicago to Gary, began around 1917. Some Mexicans already worked at the factories when strikes erupted following the First World War. In Gary, Mexicans walked out with the other strikers. In most other cases, including Indiana Harbor, the immigrant district within the town of East Chicago, Indiana, steel companies recruited Mexican strikebreakers. After the collapse of the strike many Mexicans stayed on, and more entered the mills thereafter.[57]

A recruiter during and after the strike noted that his company "sent me to get more Mexicans to work for them. I got some at Chicago, others at Omaha, Kansas City, a few at St. Louis. I even went down to El Paso and some cities in Texas. They were coming up here for over a year."[58] Mexicans in East Chicago first lived in boxcars and "bunk shacks" on company property adjacent to the mills. By 1926 some 2,500 Mexicans worked for Inland Steel in Indiana Harbor, as well as in several other plants. They soon comprised over 10 percent of the work force in the steel towns of northwest Indiana. The colonia developed in the immediate vicinity of the mills, where Mexicans rented homes alongside a vast array of European-origin workers, including the Slavs, Poles, and Italians who had occupied the immigrant neighborhoods since before the turn of the century.[59]

One Mexican, a former track worker, recalled that before coming to Inland Steel from Kansas City in the 1920s he had never heard of steel mill work. Nonetheless, out of a youthful sense of adventure, he went north by train along with a friend as part of a larger group of about fifty or sixty recruits. Subsequently, he observed trains arriving in East Chicago several times weekly, bringing men from distant points.[60] During the early years of the 1920s the Mexicans had tried attending Mass at various parishes in Gary and Indiana Harbor. The attitude of local Catholics and their priests varied, ranging from hostility to neglect. One Mexican steelworker, after coming to Gary, first attended the nearest Catholic church, whereupon he was directed to another that was "better for Mexicans." There he found to his dismay that he was expected to contribute regardless of his circumstances. In Mexico, he said, "We just went to church and it didn't cost anything if we didn't have money. Here it cost twenty-five cents at the door and twenty-five cents in the plate."[61] Another Mexican steelworker's complaint that the local priest refused to baptize children of parents who did not attend church reflected antipathy toward the demands of parish finance.

In East Chicago a petition by Italian immigrants to Bishop Herman Alerding of the Fort Wayne diocese requested a national church and promised financial support for its pastor should he remain. In response, an Italian priest, Ottavio Zavatta, became attached to the Sacred Heart Mission in a storefront building. Father Zavatta, recently expelled from Mexico, spoke Spanish and took an interest in local community affairs in Indiana Harbor. He arranged special transportation for Mexicans who wanted to go to church on Sundays and rented space in a church to conduct regular services for them. Father Zavatta also invited Father José Muñoz, founding pastor of Our Lady of Guadalupe in Kansas City, to speak to his congregation and help them form a parish.[62]

The ranks of Mexican unskilled laborers in East Chicago included some professionals and intellectuals, many of whom were political and religious refugees. In an effort to preserve their cultural identity and in hopes of regaining their former status, they created and sponsored theatrical productions through parish and mutual aid societies. The most active of three or four groups sponsoring plays in East Chicago during the twenties was the Círculo de Obreros Católicos "San José," a mutualista founded in 1925. Its projects included raising funds for the construction of a church and a library, and providing "wholesome forms of recreation" for all members. By 1926 they had raised over $1,500 and acquired building materials from Inland Steel, Youngstown Sheet and Tube, and the Universe Atlas Cement Company. Círculo members and other prospective parishioners in the Harbor worked after their shifts in the mills to construct the new church. In accordance with these broader goals, the Cuadro Dramático was created, with professionals as well as amateurs performing dramas based on scripts brought from Mexico. St. Francis of Assisi Church in Chicago also had a cuadro, though it was not nearly as elaborate.[63]

The educated elite that formed Los Obreros established a drama group and promoted other cultural activities for the *fiestas patrias*, including Mexican Independence Day. Los Obreros rejected the methods, if not objectives, of the Mexican Revolution because of its anarchy, violence, and particularly anticlericalism. They maintained a commitment to nationalism over assimilation, as their fund-raising and advocacy of the Church in the Mexican conflict demonstrated. Their weekly newspaper, *El Amigo del Hogar* (the friend of the home), circulated free of charge to over fifteen hundred households in Indiana Harbor between 1925 and 1930. It provided much information for and about the Mexican community. One editorial warned the Mexican people to conserve their faith and be aware of Protestant proselytizers, revealing a strong nationalist bent:

> The ambitious North Americans, not content with monopolizing our gold, our industries, and our oil, have taken steps to monopolize our ideas of the supernatural. Behind a mask of physical culture, Protestantism intrudes itself, disorganizing our people. Protestant propaganda is today intensely active, seeking to exploit the differences between the Mexican government and Mexican Catholics. Its hope is to supplant Catholicism with Protestantism, a cold religion that can find no roots in the warm hearts of those

who carry Spanish and Indian blood in their veins. . . . We neither wish, nor are able to be, Protestant.[64]

Father Apolinar Santacruz, who replaced Father Zavatta in 1927, had served as parish priest of San Martín Hidalgo in Jalisco, Mexico, from 1920 to 1922. During this time two small Protestant congregations existed within his parish limits. In response to frequent visits from their missionaries he observed in 1922, "Protestant propagandists have bothered us a great deal."[65] To retain the allegiance of the parish he built chapels in areas of Protestant influence. Protestantism in Mexico, although not substantial, represented a further weakening of parish clergy in a beleaguered country and brought condemnation from exiled clergy. Revolutionary movements in many areas of the mesa central introduced social cleavages that helped bring about the Cristero movement. The parish clergy effectively organized peasants in the countryside and to a lesser extent those in urban areas.

Father Santacruz, concerned about the small numbers attending services, soon clashed with members of Los Obreros Católicos. He denied parishioners the opportunity to hold dances and games of chance in the building they had built and refused donations from these activities. Santacruz founded his own group, La Sociedad Mexicana de Indiana Harbor, open to both men and women, to offset the influence of Los Obreros and attracted many former members of the latter group. The right of the San José society to call itself Catholic came under attack after accusations that they "talked against the priests." As an exile priest in East Chicago, Santacruz conducted affairs as if he were in a Cristero municipio, and in his new role he failed to provide an effective organizational framework for the parish. His imposition of traditional views of Mexican Catholicism seemed out of place in the industrialized, multi-ethnic urban setting. Another exile priest who had previously been pastor of a parish in Gary, replaced Father Santacruz, who returned to Mexico in 1929. By then El Círculo had splintered and many of its members had returned home.[66]

The Mexican community in Indiana Harbor was larger and more autonomous than that in Gary. In both cities Mexican parishes depended upon outside leadership to mediate with the larger society. The south side "hunkietown" housed immigrants, including by 1930 over 3,000 Mexican-born out of the city's total population of some 100,000. Local boosters presented Gary not as a Chicago suburb but as a "city that has everything."[67]

Industrialist Elbert H. Gary had donated $10,000 each to five ethnic Catholic parishes in 1913 for European national parishes in the steel city he helped create. Assistance to national parishes helped keep workers contented and apart. To help assimilate immigrant Catholics, Bishop Herman Alerding of the Fort Wayne diocese appointed Austrian-born John De Ville, who was fluent in Italian, to serve in Gary in 1911. Father De Ville, a naturalized citizen, first emigrated to Pennsylvania in 1893 at the age of nineteen. He traveled to Belgium in August 1915 and helped orphans and refugees relocate to the United States during World War I. After returning to the United States in 1919 he worked for the Americanization of immigrants, particularly Italians and Mexicans. Father De Ville appealed to corporations for financial support. U.S. Steel sent Alerding $100,000 for Gary parishes and donated $130,000 to De Ville for his special projects. De Ville, according to Bishop Alerding, also effectively countered "radical agitation" in Gary "without creating a financial burden for the diocese."[68]

Gary's International Institute first functioned as a surrogate to help ease urban adjustment, housing the Mexican mutual aid society, La Sociedad Protectora Mexicana. Despite the cooperation of De Ville, Elbert Gary, and Bishop Alerding, Mexicans lacked a parish of their own until 1924, when the Gary-Alerding Settlement established the parish of Our Lady of Guadalupe. The forty-room Gary-Alerding Settlement House, a nonsectarian yet Catholic-sponsored institution, opened in 1922, complete with a gymnasium, a clinic, an employment bureau, and game and craft rooms. Inside the settlement, St. Anthony's chapel offered Mass for many of the city's 3,000 Mexicans, 3,000 Italians, and 2,000 Spaniards. Americanization classes were also held there.[69]

In a speech to the Gary Rotary Club in 1928, two years before his final return to Europe, De Ville chastised Mexicans for being "uncivilized and unable to be Americanized as the man from southeastern and southern Europe." Further, he added, "I stood with the Administration in its policy of protecting American interests in Mexico, but I have no sympathy with the so-called religious conflict in that country."[70] The reaction of Mexican-American members of that community included a letter to the editor from immigrant José Gallardo, who, referring to events in the homeland, wrote that "the sons should not be blamed for the father's failures."[71] That same year De Ville wrote wearily, "my life has been very miserable indeed trying to keep up the work on very slender means. We are ministering to working people who have no wealth in Gary, or for that matter, in the whole diocese of Fort Wayne. Though on the fringe of Chicago, we have no more help from or claim to it than we have upon Detroit and New York. We are, truly, orphans."[72]

In February 1927, Bishop John F. Noll, Alerding's successor, asked the missionary catechists from Gary, who had worked among Mexicans in other parts of the United States, to teach Mexican children in Indiana Harbor. They traveled several times a week to the Harbor to hold religious instruction classes in Our Lady of Guadalupe Church. In 1929 a convent near the church opened and eight sisters of Our Lady of Victory taught and served there. In the following decade their presence proved valuable in assisting unemployed and displaced Mexican parishioners.[73]

THE ESTABLISHMENT OF OUR LADY OF GUADALUPE PARISH IN DETROIT

In Detroit the demobilization of the defense industry compounded the postwar recession. Recently arrived Mexicans were hit particularly hard, as they depended upon the high wages of the Ford Motor Company and other manufacturers to send remittances back home to help their families, as well as for their own survival. In December 1920 the Detroit colonia had swelled with betabeleros flocking to the city in search of jobs. Estimates ran as high as 8,000 members. Within two months, however, economic decline saw the colonia dwindle to about 2,500.

The St. Vincent de Paul Society had previously provided social service to European immigrants in various dioceses, specifically the Italian poor, to counter the Protestant charities. Early in 1921 the Detroit branch became aware of "the pitiable conditions both spiritual and material prevailing in the Mexican colony [and] undertook to defray the expense of any worthy Mexican who tried to return to his own country."[74] This charitable effort, drawing over $11,000 from appeals to a broad sector of the Catholic community, helped finance transportation of over 500 Mexicans to the border. Mexican bishops contributed another $12,000, while the Mexican government assured the immigrants of passage to their homes. The depression ended in 1921, however, and company recruiters turned again to Mexican labor as a readily available and easily exploited resource. Immigration climbed steadily, boosting the barrio's population to approximately 5,000 in 1926 and at least twice that number two years later. The colonia included immigrants with increasingly diverse occupational backgrounds, including some skilled tradesmen among its residents.[75]

The first Mexican national parish in the Great Lakes region began in Detroit, then the nation's fourth largest city, in 1920, preceding by three years the construction of a separate church. Bishop Michael Gallagher brought in Father Juan Alanís, a Spanish priest from Monterrey, Mexico, to minister to the Mexican automobile workers scattered around the Detroit plants. Sunday services were first held in St. Mary's parochial school, part of an old German downtown parish with a Spanish morning Mass. Social activities in the afternoon for men and women included political discussions and the singing of *corridos*. Children attended English and Spanish language courses. When the pastor of St. Mary's abruptly and inexplicably ended the rental arrangement in 1923, Father Alanís appealed to the bishop for support for a new church, stating "the uncertainty of our actual situation has diminished the number of my parishioners to such an extent that in the event of meeting further difficulties, I would find it necessary to return to my country without having obtained that for which I have labored incessantly for years." He warned also of "the unknown religious handicaps encountered by me and the three or four thousand Mexicans, mostly illiterate, whose souls would be perishing for want of light and priests."[76]

Father Alanís noted in his annual report the helpful participation of "the greater part of Spanish-speaking residents of this city" who "generally came to the help of the church, and in a relatively short time, a piece of property was bought. They drew up plans, they built, and they furnished the new Church of Our Lady of Guadalupe."[77] Some 150 Detroit Mexican families belonging to the parish without a church in 1922 contributed over $6,000 for the construction of the new church building that opened the following year. Father Alanís offered a daily Mass and three on Sunday, the latter "filled to overflowing."[78] Assistance promised from Spanish-speaking Jesuit priests from the University of Detroit never materialized. Although Mexicans composed the vast majority of the congregation, many Anglos also attended, since the church stood far outside the Mexican barrio (as a result of an attempt to take advantage of cheaper land costs in the outlying neighborhood). Alanís subsequently lobbied the bishop for many concessions, such as in 1924 when he sought to expand the church to provide a meeting place for several societies and a Sunday school, in order that they not interfere with church business.[79]

The founding of Our Lady of Guadalupe occurred during a period of extensive urban growth and the accompanying expansion of a network of churches. Bishop Gallagher approved the use of foreign languages in thirty-two of the ninety-eight parishes established in his domain from 1918 to 1929. The building of Our Lady of Guadalupe in Detroit offered no permanent solution for Mexican Catholics. A major concern that soon proved intractable dealt with the poor location of the church. This not only discouraged the formation of a strong community nearby, but necessarily involved the weakening of the Mexican character of the parish, since it also had to accommodate Anglo Catholics who lived in the neighborhood.[80]

Venezuelan-born Father Luis Castillo succeeded Father Alanís late in 1926, when Alanís moved to Pennsylvania after having been removed as pastor, over the objection of parishioners, reportedly for indiscretions involving a local woman. Castillo quickly discovered the problems of organizing a parochial school there. Even though he proposed no tuition, with free books and transportation and Spanish included as a subject and claimed to have scheduled several hundred children for the opening, only fifteen appeared, the others apparently dissuaded because of the distance involved in the commute from Mexican residences. One concerned Anglo parishioner urged that the proposed school for Mexicans be built elsewhere, noting the low attendance at Our Lady of Guadalupe parish. He pointed out that most Mexicans lived several miles from the "so-called Mexican church," with children having to be brought to communion there by car.[81] He further observed that "the poor Mexican has not a ghost of a chance to appreciate his religion here" as streetcars and other facilities were not available and urged that the diocese "locate the priest within reasonable distance from his people. Give him an opportunity to come into contact with his people, otherwise the future will be a continuation of the past— Failure!" The letter concluded with the warning, "Let us learn a lesson from the Protestants! They are after the Mexicans [and] wisely locate in their midst. At present we are spectators to our own loss."[82]

Mexicans remained spatially concentrated near other Roman Catholic churches closer to the barrio along Michigan Avenue. Some Mexicans patronized Holy Trinity; but as the colonia moved westward, membership declined. Other national parishes sometimes received Mexicans who had moved to their neighborhoods, but barriers of language and culture precluded permanent solutions to their predicament. Although they sought unity in ritual Catholicism, Mexicans in these churches found the European parishes impenetrable. The problems of location, lack of attendance, and factionalism at Our Lady of Guadalupe Church hindered development of a sense of community. Church-associated fiestas and celebrations that normally would have served to expand religious influence had not yet been organized. Religious disputes in Mexico brought many Cristeros to Detroit around 1926, temporarily boosting attendance at Our Lady of Guadalupe.[83]

OTHER MIDWESTERN MEXICAN COMMUNITIES

Many transitional barrios without a strong economic base or a strong sense of community among its residents never developed parishes. St. Louis, for example, had served as a temporary way station for agricultural workers since the first decade of the twentieth century. Some residents formed a mutualista, but no parishes catering specifically to Mexicans developed there. In Omaha, similarly, no religious organizations or churches served Mexican immigrants during the 1920s, although they had come in considerable numbers during World War I to work in the stockyards and railroads near the city. By the mid-1920s the Spanish Augustinian Recollect Fathers from Kansas City, Kansas, had begun limited care for Mexicans, competing with the Baptist Mission Society. However, these short-lived missions never developed into parishes. No real community took hold, and by 1935 the Mexican population remained one of "floaters," with many single men moving from one place to another in search of employment.[84]

The first Mexicans came to Flint, Michigan, around 1923, after having been recruited in San Antonio by beet company agents, and many subsequently worked in industrial jobs. Flint, with its expanding auto factories and diverse immigrant population, was fast becoming a General Motors company town. No Mexican parish developed until the 1950s, however. Non-Catholic institutions designed for European immigrants, such as the local International Institute, served Mexicans and others, providing language and citizenship classes, recreation, and job referrals. Mexicans' mutual aid societies also sponsored fiestas for the annual commemoration of Our Lady of Guadalupe and Las Posadas.[85]

The first Mexicans came to Milwaukee in the early 1920s to work as strikebreakers at the Pfister and Vogel tannery and were housed in a dormitory set up in one of the company's factories. In an effort to squelch union organization, some Milwaukee companies recruited in Texas and Mexico. In time, their families joined them and they filtered out into nearby housing. Mexicans expanded southward to form a colonia as Poles and others moved out. Mexicans had contact with old immigrant clergy that assisted in the foundation of a Mexican parish as the immigrant population increased rapidly in the mid-1920s. Holy Trinity Church, originally constructed for German immigrants on the South Side in 1850, served for the occasional baptism of Mexican children. An energetic core of Mexican tannery workers with the support of a German pastor from Holy Trinity established the Church of Our Lady of Guadalupe in a converted store in late 1926. Father Tort, the Spanish Claretian, traveled from Chicago to preside at the dedication.[86]

THE LEGACY OF THE PIONEER PARISHES

Mexican identity became transformed in the 1920s. Mexican immigrants arrived at a time when attempts to "Americanize" and otherwise assimilate previous waves of sometimes recalcitrant European immigrants and their descendants dominated institutional Catholicism. Americanization ultimately fell short of remaking Mexicans. Competition from the Protestants led Catholic leaders to establish and multiply social welfare agencies and charitable institutions under Catholic auspices. The process of religious assimilation, difficult to measure but pervasive throughout the region, constituted an important feature of the historical development of Mexican-American communities. The newcomers and the Church influenced one another greatly, and their relationship with the United States hierarchy and clergy reached deep into the secular life of developing communities, exerting a stabilizing influence in the formation of early midwestern Mexican communities.

Educated Mexicans were loyal members of the pioneer parishes, and in several instances they provided crucial financial and moral support. However, they often objected to what they considered the arbitrary and autocratic policies of exile priests, generally of Spanish birth. Spanish and Anglo clergy only reluctantly acknowledged the importance of Mexican culture, and this sometimes introduced factionalism within parishes. Nonetheless, parishioners themselves contributed greatly to the anchoring of communities under difficult and generally unfavorable circumstances. The virtual absence of financial support from the homeland that characterized Mexican-American Catholicism during the 1920s impeded the development of Church institutions. The financial crisis of the 1930s delayed programs for training Mexican seminarians and compounded existing problems in the pioneer parishes.

2

Depression, Survival, and
Fragmented Religiosity, 1930–1945

The harsh economic realities of the Depression shut off the influx of immigrants and sent many unemployed workers back to Mexico. Massive layoffs beginning in 1929 triggered hard times for thousands of Mexican nationals who had been in the United States for a relatively short time, fragmenting communities and highlighting the tenuous quality of Mexican settlement in the Midwest. Parishes faced a demographic crisis precipitated by economic disaster and compounded by anti-Mexican sentiments, culminating in policies of involuntary repatriation in many cities. The Depression froze residence patterns, reduced mobility, and disrupted the social functions of the pioneer parishes. Families that remained in the Midwest found in the fledgling institutions a surprisingly resilient refuge.

Mexican parishes, regardless of their specific structures or origins, became focal points for involvement in the larger society. Linguistic, cultural, and religious bonds reinforced one another. Alternative modes of leadership soon developed as many of the exiles, including priests and organizers of the mutualistas, returned to Mexico. The laity, meanwhile, became increasingly active in shaping parish affairs and in organizing religious programs during a time of depleted resources. Some institutional development occurred and several new parishes formed.[1]

LAY ACTIVISM IN KANSAS CITY

President Herbert Hoover's 1930 "Hire American" policy endangered the Mexican labor on the region's railroads. The greater Kansas City area lost over half of its Mexican-origin population during the 1930s, prompted especially by unemployment in the meat-packing industry. Mexicans and Mexican Americans dispersed throughout the Midwest and many returned to Mexico. The

Santa Fe Railroad actually deflected repatriation pressures directed against Mexican labor by claiming that most of the company's Spanish-surnamed employees were U.S. citizens from New Mexico, even though Mexican nationals worked for the railroads. This ploy helped shelter local Mexican enclaves. Nevertheless, voluntary return depleted the population of Mexicans in the state of Kansas from 19,000 to 5,000 between 1930 and 1940 while that of the Kansas City metropolitan area dropped from 6,000 to 2,500. Those remaining were generally citizens.[2]

In Kansas City, Kansas, contention between Protestants and Catholics vying for the faith of Mexican Americans remained high. The Methodist Mexican missionaries served to mediate between health and welfare agencies and the barrio population. Beginning in 1933, the Works Progress Administration provided recreational and educational activities for the mission. In 1935 the mission was organized into a church; this exacerbated long-standing competition between Methodists and Catholics. Within two years the Catholic bishop designated the Argentine barrio as the site of St. John the Divine. This second Mexican national parish in Argentine helped unify the dispersed Kansas City area barrios in the face of declining population and overcame the Protestant challenge to community building.[3]

The history of our Lady of Guadalupe Parish in Kansas City's Westside illustrates an impetus for organization coming from concerned non-Mexican Catholics involved in charitable work. In 1922, at the behest of the bishop, the Amber Club, a group of Anglo women devoted to social work and community service, sponsored the Guadalupe Center. It served for many years as a Catholic settlement house in the rectory of Our Lady of Guadalupe Church. Throughout the Depression years it held religious classes for youngsters during school break. Sisters from a nearby orphanage conducted parochial school instruction during the year. The Amber Club tried to foster mutual understanding and respect while overcoming racism.[4]

In 1936 the Guadalupe Center moved to a new building donated by the family of Amber Club director Dorothy Gallagher. During the mid-1940s Guadalupe Center served as a social settlement under the direction of the Catholic Charities for the Mexican community in Kansas City. In 1945 the Sisters of Social Service came to Kansas City at the invitation of the archbishop to direct and organize activities at Guadalupe Center. Both Mexicans and Americans volunteered. The church, the center, and the Mexican

Cultural Union building remained the nucleus of the Mexican-American community. [5]

During the Depression parishes and other community organizations promoted cultural entertainment, once the exclusive preserve of the mutualistas. Professional and amateur performers traveled from Mexico to celebrate patriotic and religious holidays, organizing theater, dances, and civic and literary meetings. From 1933 to 1935, in particular, parish groups performed plays for Mexicans at several midwestern sites, including the Mexican parishes of Kansas City. Other sites included St. Paul's Neighborhood House, the Lithuanian Hall in Detroit, and several Mexican parishes in the Chicago area.[6]

RESPONSES OF WOMEN AND WORKERS IN THE STEEL BELT

Although economic factors among many European immigrants historically accelerated the return to their homeland, notably among Italians, Mexican repatriation in the Great Lakes region took on a coercive and strongly nativist dimension during the Great Depression. This cast a shadow over the entire Mexican-American experience of the 1930s, creating a sense of injustice previously absent in the region. For the most part, native-born local politicians in East Chicago, Gary, Detroit, and St. Paul, among other locations, conducted organized campaigns of deportation of Mexicans. This involuntary repatriation, along with return migration forced under the economic duress, multiplied the ill effects on midwestern parishes struggling for stable membership and financial viability by unfairly targeting recent immigrants. The Catholic Church offered no official condemnation of this process, although in its aftermath laity and women religious helped consolidate the communities in crisis.[7]

The closing down of the steel mills in northwest Indiana in 1929 brought hard times for Mexican workers. East Chicago's Inland Steel, which had become the largest single employer of Mexicans in the United States, discharged many of its most recently hired workers as factory employers began restricting employment to United States citizens and gave preference to its senior workers. Recently arrived and undocumented immigrants often returned to Mexico on their own; but many stayed on, hopeful of being rehired. Industries with little need for a labor reserve and financially strapped local governments concocted numerous schemes to avoid caring for unemployed Mexicans. Lacking cash to pay the railroads for transportation, officials in Lake County, Indiana , arranged with steel companies within its jurisdiction to accept scrip in return for tax credit and thereby finance the return of trainloads of Mexicans to the border. Religious and other groups remained mute; only the International Institute opposed these measures. Approximately 3,000 Mexicans left from East Chicago and Gary during 1932, including some U.S. citizens. Repatriation began on a voluntary basis, supposedly for "humanitarian" reasons, but soon developed into a tool for expelling unwanted workers. Whereas the 1930 census counted 4,300 Mexicans in East Chicago, by 1940 the number stood at about 1,400, while the city's population remained steady at about 55,000. The process in Gary similarly devastated its barrio.[8]

Indiana Harbor's Our Lady of Guadalupe, the once-thriving pioneer parish, served as a staging ground for assistance to Mexicans during the Depression. During 1931 the Missionary Sisters and lay volunteers cooperated in providing shoes, clothes, and groceries, as well as moral support for those families lucky enough to have breadwinners still working at the steel mills. They distributed the materials first from the convent and, when larger quarters became necessary, from the church basement. Unfamiliar with social agencies and reluctant to seek relief, Mexicans turned to the Missionary Sisters of the parish for assistance in social service as well as religious matters. The Sisters learned of cases of desperate need through home visitations and often acted as interpreters at relief agencies. The major work of the Sisters focused on the Mexicans who remained in Our Lady of Guadalupe. However, they also assisted those facing repatriation by making referrals to local relief agencies and helping to secure return tickets to Mexico. Some 400 families depended almost entirely on what they received there, until supplies became exhausted in early 1932. The wives of working Mexican laborers also volunteered their services. After a 1939 fire destroyed Our Lady of Guadalupe Church, Bishop Noll assisted in establishing a new one in a more central location for the mobile Mexican population. It opened the following year, with the help of many parishioners and donations from several manufacturers and businesses.[9]

Other Catholic groups in Indiana Harbor also endured strains in parish life. While Mexican Catholics in the Harbor succeeded in forming a national parish in the 1920s, Italians had only a promise from the bishop. Not until 1935, after the Depression's worst effects had passed, did Italian clergy, with the help of unemployed workers, manage to construct Immaculate Conception, the national parish served by an Italian pastor. The Polish St. John Cantius Church had deeper roots in the city. Nonetheless, skyrocketing indebtedness of $278,000 prompted parish leaders to organize bazaars, carnivals, picnics, and other "wholesome entertainment" in an attempt to raise funds. Such established communities more easily pooled resources to cushion the impact of unemployment.[10]

In the 1930s, workplace issues, grievance procedures, and seniority became more important than ever for steel mill workers. Mexican families remained in sufficient number to enjoy these benefits. By 1937 the mills had recovered, and for the first time significant numbers of East Chicago Mexicans had become naturalized citizens, boosting thereby their prospects for employment and unionization. Their organization into labor unions improved working conditions considerably and propelled them into activism in the strikes of 1937. On May 26, 1937, John L. Lewis's Steelworkers Organizing Committee called a strike at the Youngstown and Inland "Little Steel" plants of Indiana Harbor. In the "Memorial Day Massacre" of May 30, in which police fired into a large group of demonstrators picketing the Republic Plant in South Chicago, six Mexicans were injured. The participation of Mexicans in the unions helped bring about smoother relations with their neighbors. By 1941 employment had increased significantly, Mexicans had begun serving as shop stewards, and contracts provided for grievance procedures and for promotions based on seniority, giving workers and their families a more secure economic foothold.[11]

U.S. Steel in Gary operated at only 10 percent of capacity during 1932 and seldom much above 50 percent in the following years. The chapel in St. Anthony's Church remained as the parish church for Gary's Italians and Mexicans, with each having priests speaking their native tongue. Father José Muñoz for a while made monthly visits in a makeshift ministry there. In 1936 a Mexican bishop confirmed almost 500 children, including many from other locales. That same year the Mission St. John Bosco Convent in the Gary-Alerding Settlement House opened and continued the religious instruction of Catholic children in the public schools.[12]

Lay activism in Gary emerged from unlikely quarters in the person of "Sister" Felicitas, a woman who came from Mexico in the 1920s to join her cousins. She remained permanently, acting as a go-between for priests and Sisters of St. Anthony's parish, conducting visitations and assisting individuals throughout the region in their religious duties. During World War II she reportedly fulfilled a vow to the Virgin of Guadalupe of taking up alms from the Mexican people to purchase a jeweled crown and place it upon the head of the statue in the church if all the boys from St. Anthony's returned safely from the front.[13]

REPATRIATION AND PARISH CONFLICT IN DETROIT

Ford Motor Company's Mexican employees in Detroit were caught in a chain reaction of devastating layoffs in the early years of the Depression, forcing many to leave the area entirely. Those who remained faced a continual struggle for survival. Their experience offers an interesting perspective on the shortcomings of repatriation and its failure as a policy in which the two countries cooperated. After Mexican Consul General Ignacio Batiza unsuccessfully attempted to gain aid for his charges, the Mexican government endorsed a repatriation program in late 1931. The sustained emigration of workers had alarmed partisans of Mexican industrialization. Moreover, the return of able workers would facilitate government attempts to establish new communities along the northern border. By the end of 1932, the U.S. government in combination with local agencies had repatriated some 1,500 Mexicans from Michigan. Many of them passed through Detroit. In the remaining weakened Mexican-American communities, the quest for work and survival took precedence over that of preserving religious and cultural identity.[14]

The Great Depression reduced the size of the Mexican national parish in Detroit, while decimating mutualistas and other voluntary organizations. Neighboring parishes fared somewhat better. Repatriation occurred under the auspices of the Detroit Department of Public Welfare. In theory it resulted in desired savings in the face of a failing economy. The federal government provided transportation for those who had been in Detroit prior to 1929; the Public Welfare Department financed the return for the more recent immigrants. Disregarding established procedures, caseworkers implementing repatriation often resorted to coercion or otherwise violated the due process rights of the immigrants. Moreover, they urged even the family members of some naturalized citizens to repatriate. Those who stayed faced family breakups and uncertain prospects for work.[15]

Our Lady of Guadalupe's continued disintegration in the late 1930s was reflected in the decline of lay leadership and loss of

membership as Detroit's Mexican population dwindled to approximately 1,200 in 1936, less than 10 percent of the pre-Depression
figure. Mexican parishioners demonstrated their concern over the
decline and an interest in directing events, including the ouster of
unpopular pastors. In 1933, Simón Muñoz and other prominent
leaders in Detroit's Our Lady of Guadalupe parish petitioned the
bishop to remove the Venezuelan-born Father Castillo, noting:

> the majority of our colony used to be good Catholics until a few
> months ago when a disastrous propaganda against our Faith
> started; first, by a strong propaganda to make Mexicans embrace
> the Baptist Church, and they have succeeded in a good measure
> especially by a recent revival. . . . Secondly, by a society of Mexican
> workmen which meets every Saturday and carry out [sic] every
> doctrine against our Holy Mother the Church, inducing Mexicans
> to become Communists. One of the leaders is that great Mexican
> painter, Diego Rivera, of whom you have perhaps read in the
> papers. He talks against the existence of God.

Muñoz believed that other private societies worked against the
spiritual and financial well-being of the Catholic Church and concluded, "We feel abandoned and without any leader in this serious
matter."[16]

The conflict lasted for several years, and the anti-Castillo fac-
tion called for an episcopal investigation into the community's
"loss of faith." In May 1936 leaders of several Catholic societies
petitioned Bishop Gallagher to remove the pastor "or else have a
committee appointed to take care of and handle the financial affairs
of our parish. . . . We parishioners and workers of this church are
fed up with the negligence, lack of interest and general ineffeciency
[sic] of said Pastor."[17]

Factionalism in the national parishes of several other ethnic
groups in the Detroit archdiocese during the 1920s and 1930s
concerned either animosities imported from the homeland or questions of control over finance and administration. Among Mexicans,
parish turbulence centered more on personality conflicts and strategies for leadership. Disagreements easily escalated into lasting ri-
valries pitting the pastor against outspoken parishioners.[18]

Although Detroit's Mexican parish disintegrated due to poor
location and a dispersed membership, lack of leadership also
played a part. While virtually all ten candidates submitted for Our
Lady of Guadalupe's Church Committee (a lay board of advisors)
were Mexican for the years 1923 through 1926 under Father Alanís,

and again from 1927 through 1930 under Father Castillo, the number of non-Spanish-surnamed persons increased with changes in parish demographics, from three in 1931 to four the following year, five in 1934, and to seven in 1935. At the same time Mexican priests exercised little clout within the archdiocese; without viable Mexican candidates for appointment to barrio parishes, let alone major positions such as auxiliary bishop, appeals to the local hierarchy for appointments based on nationalism or ethnicity lacked leverage.[19]

In 1939 Father Castillo relinquished his position at Our Lady of Guadalupe under some pressure from above. The Mexican national parish, the first and only one in Detroit, closed permanently. Archbishop Edward Mooney brought in a Mexican priest to conduct services at Holy Trinity Church, closer to the downtown Mexican settlement. During his brief tenure, Father López attempted to organize several societies previously supervised by Our Lady of Guadalupe Church and held frequent dances in an effort to attract younger members, in addition to his efforts to exert more control over the laity in a dispersed area of settlement. However, the newly arrived Archbishop Edward Mooney, discouraging the persistence of Mexicans in national parishes, reportedly ordered the societies, including Padres de Familia and Damas Católicas, disbanded.[20]

The lack of Spanish-speaking priests in Ste. Anne's and other parishes serving Mexicans typified the problems of this transitional period. Failed attempts at assimilation in parochial schools added to the difficulties. The St. Vincent de Paul Society provided scholarships for Mexican children in 1938 but stopped the following year. In 1939 only three Mexican children attended Holy Trinity's parish school. Parochial education offered no reinforcement for Mexican religiosity, and the reversal of Mexican immigration patterns during the Depression obscured any genuine indifference to Catholic schools that may have existed among the immigrants.[21]

There remained a sustained threat from Protestants offering Spanish services in Detroit. In July 1935, a Puerto Rican Baptist minister from Wichita came to Detroit to assume the role of pastor to about thirty Mexican families. Despite such efforts, ministers generally claimed that they made no efforts to convert active Catholics because those joining only as a protest against their church rarely remained active in the congregation. Nevertheless, lacking personnel and seeking to retain the loyalty of Mexicans, Cardinal Mooney in 1941 recruited Father James Barrett, a Redemptorist from Texas, to serve as the Detroit "Mexican priest." For the next five years his ministry revolved around the parishes of

Holy Trinity, Ste. Anne, St. Vincent, and St. Boniface. The chapel behind Ste. Anne's Church became the "Spanish parish church" where Father Barrett held Sunday Mass. He also set up a religious library, sent out a monthly bulletin, "La Voz Católica Mexicana," and organized a drama troupe, the Mexican Catholic Players, to perform in Holy Redeemer auditorium as well as in small theaters throughout the city.[22]

During the Depression and throughout the recovery period folk Catholicism persisted in cities where Mexicans settled. One individual who helped establish the Comité Guadalupana in Detroit in the early 1930s later noted the importance of Guadalupe rituals: "The Feast of the Virgin of Guadalupe is always the greatest feast and it is observed in all the churches in all the cities, but especially in the capital city of each state. Processions are held—although there was a time they were not permitted" in Mexico. She remembered one occasion in Detroit: "We made a float; it carried several youngsters dressed like the Virgin of Guadalupe and Juan Diego. . . . We enjoyed it when the apparitions of the Virgin of Guadalupe were dramatized." Other Mexican traditions came north as well, including Day of the Dead, celebrated in early November with the traditional placement of flowers on tombs and other commemorative activities.[23]

PARISH DEVELOPMENTS IN THE CHICAGO ARCHDIOCESE

Chicago's diverse economy, unlike that of the company towns, helped offset organized repatriation pressures. Nonetheless many Mexicans, facing high unemployment and often having exhausted their savings, turned to relief programs as their only means of survival, sometimes with the assistance of Sisters or concerned parishioners. Neither politicians nor relief executives organized repatriation campaigns or otherwise expressed hostility toward the newcomers. Donations from both public and private groups throughout the Chicago area silently counteracted repatriation pressures. The two parishes, St. Francis and Our Lady of Guadalupe, anchored barrio life. Between 1930 and 1940 a halt in Mexican immigration, coupled with return migration, reduced Chicago's Mexican-origin population from 20,000 to 16,000, a modest decline compared with other locations. The westward advance from the Near West Side indicated assimilation beyond the limited sphere of parish life. However, as Mexican families moved into areas outside the older districts they left behind the settlement houses and churches.[24]

Church leaders failed to recognize the Mexican presence in national organizations such as the National Catholic Welfare Conference, and the Chicago political machine virtually ignored Mexicans in the distribution of its patronage. However, New Deal programs offered opportunities for church action, even though they supplanted much of the charity work previously performed by ethnic and religious organizations. In 1933 Cardinal Mundelein named the Catholic Charities Bureau and Society of St. Vincent de Paul as a unit of the Illinois Emergency Relief Commission, the state's distributor of funds from the Federal Emergency Relief Administration. Although religious violence in Mexico had diminished in the decade after the Cristero Rebellion, Cardinal Mundelein in 1935 formally urged President Roosevelt to speak out against recurring instances of religious persecution there. The Catholic Church in the Midwest, meanwhile, had grown more secure in its national position.[25]

Cordi-Marian Sisters from Mexico in 1936 occupied the former St. Joseph Home for Working Girls on Chicago's Near West Side. The new Cordi-Marian Center offered English classes, instruction in art, music, and crafts, and a social center for boys and girls. The Immigrants Protective League, headquartered at nearby Hull House, stepped up its traditional efforts to naturalize alien immigrants, including Mexicans, during the Depression. When federal guidelines restricted employment by the Works Projects Administration to U.S. citizens in 1938, a large number of Mexicans sought naturalization. Not long afterward, the war defense boom brought more skilled jobs, and employers came to insist upon first naturalization papers.[26]

During the Depression years Chicago's Mexican immigrants achieved greater solidarity with the United States working class in the Back of the Yards neighborhood. Mexicans participated in the Packing House Workers Union of the Congress of Industrial Organizations in the mid-1930s. Their activities helped erase the image of strikebreakers formed during the 1921 packinghouse strike and validated their presence in the community. Social changes followed, and eventually many Polish-Mexican intermarriages took place there. Among Mexicans the shortage of native clergy hampered the growth of parish communities, while the workplace remained isolated from religious issues. Limited financial assistance and some encouragement came from the Back of the Yards Council and the pastors of neighboring churches, but ethnic separatism delayed efforts of parishioners and church leaders to expand institutional Catholicism among Mexican Americans in the stockyards.[27]

Although other ethnic groups had national parishes in this immigrant neighborhood, until 1945 none existed for the Mexicans. Mexicans could attend St. Francis of Assisi, but the lack of time and transportation inhibited most from active participation in religious activities in distant areas. During the 1930s the University of Chicago Settlement took on unforeseen functions. It served as headquarters for some Mexican societies and acted for a while as a surrogate parish community. Almost immediately after their arrival the Mexicans gravitated toward the Settlement. It officially opened a Mexican department in 1929. Mexican enrollment rose to about 200, making them the fourth largest ethnic group in that settlement house in 1930, after Poles, Lithuanians, and Bohemians. The Settlement also offered the Mexicans athletic activities and dances, as well as a hall to hold meetings, citizenship classes and movies. Most Mexican groups, moreover, used its meeting rooms. By the late 1930s they were the largest group using its facilities. Director Mary McDowell raised over $1,000 earmarked solely for the purpose of Mexican work, much of it from the packers.[28]

Before 1945, weddings of Mexican-American residents of the Back of the Yards took place at St. Francis Church, several miles north. Mexicans in South Chicago enjoyed closer ties to their church. During the late 1930s Claretian priests from St. Francis traveled to the Back of the Yards and held Sunday Masses in storefront chapels. Door to door collections helped pay for religious services, including carfare for the priest and a group of Cordi-Marian Sisters; catechists taught preparation for communion lessons once a week at different locations throughout the neighborhood. These activities helped sustain ethnic identity. Both Protestant and Catholic organizations neglected the Mexicans in the stockyards region. In 1931 a group of Mexican women there formed the Our Lady of Guadalupe Society, a fund-raising and church-service organization. Lay interest in parish formation proved helpful. In 1939 a Mexican volunteer at the Settlement began a small Catholic mission on South Ashland Avenue, reportedly using an icebox for an altar. Nuns from Our Lady of Guadalupe in South Chicago helped carry on the program.[29]

Archdiocesan initiative in Back of the Yards supplemented lay activism. In a formal recognition of parish function involving finance and investment, Father James Tort lobbied for support from Archbishop Samuel Stritch, Cardinal Mundelein's successor, while encouraging parishioners to hold bazaars and carnivals. In the early 1940s an assistant at St. Francis who was serving the growing Mexican community in the new mission helped collect funds. By 1944, along with Father Tort and other supporters, he bought four storefronts in Back of the Yards and oversaw the construction of a modest church. The Archbishop encouraged Father Tort and his building committee to make the chapel and social center larger "even if it costs an additional $20,000." The Claretian Order opened Immaculate Heart of Mary Vicariate in the fall of 1947. The mission was placed under the jurisdiction of St. Francis parish.[30]

Mexicans in the Midwest rarely developed strong attachments to radicalism or joined leftist organizations during the Depression, although clashes in political ideologies sometimes entered into local affairs. In 1936 a Chicago chapter of El Frente Popular Mexicano, housed at the University of Chicago Settlement House, sponsored a series of meetings, discussions, and lectures regularly attended by more than 200 people from all three Mexican neighborhoods. *El Ideal Católico Mexicano*, a local newspaper for Mexican Catholic workers, warned parishioners not to attend any of the lectures, particularly those given by "so-called" Catholic priests. On one occasion audience members shouted down a pro-Franco Spanish priest from St. Francis of Assisi speaking in support of the insurgents' cause. Despite a common language, political and cultural differences separated the Spanish Claretians from their Mexican parishioners.[31]

Religious orders remained active during the Depression, opening a few new parishes while maintaining existing ones. In 1936 the Carmelites took over Joliet's St. Mary's Church and encouraged the establishment of the chapel of Nuestra Señora del Carmen as a place of worship for Mexicans. In 1944 Mexican parishioners expanded the chapel and added a community center that later became a branch of the Catholic Youth Organization.[32]

TEJANO MIGRANTS AND POPULAR RELIGIOSITY

The midwestern Mexican presence remained both an urban and a rural phenomenon through the Depression and the war years.

Employment in the cities or the beet fields of the Midwest enabled some workers to survive the difficult times. In the mid-1930s there was a new wave of migration from Texas, composed of Tejanos who were largely United States citizens. The Winter Garden area in Texas and the town of Crystal City, in particular, became an important source of agricultural workers for many midwestern areas. The *troquero* system of the 1930s involving Tejano middlemen acting as recruiters and interpreters developed for distributing workers and their families to the beet fields on trucks. Migrants sought to find work or fulfill contracts. The midwestern beet fields offered them at least the possibility of permanent employment with enhanced wages and better education for their children. This ultimately led to a decrease in agricultural unemployment.[33]

Few Mexicans or Tejanos in the Midwest became farmers. Rural landlords often refused to rent long-term housing to the Mexicans, forcing them into cities after they completed their annual cycle of field work. For Tejanos, a bond of survival formed among families, relatives, and friends on the seasonal journey to the Great Lakes region. By the early 1940s many Tejanos also supplemented sugar beet work with the burgeoning fruit industry. During the 1930s neither federal nor local governments provided assistance to jobless agricultural migrants. The earliest flow of Tejanos began in 1935 and expanded steadily until 1942, when movement from Mexico was relatively light. During the years 1938–1942 the first Saturday night *bailes*, or dances, began among migrant farm workers. Many musical groups, or *conjuntos*, passed through the Midwest, attracting hundreds of families to their performances.[34]

These migrants emerged from the border region where Catholic churches sparsely dotted the border counties. The ranchos had no churches, but Mexican Americans still observed many religious celebrations. Religion on the rancho centered on home and the family. At Christmas time, a group of devoted women performed a variation of ceremonies of the Mexican rural villages and faithfully recited the rosary. Whenever possible, they taught children the catechism. Rituals played an important part in the life cycle celebrations of birth, baptism, marriage, and death. In various midwestern locales the singing of *La Virgen Ranchera* during the Mass represented an attempt to retain the folklore of the rural setting, the land, and ranch life, symbolizing a bond with the past.[35]

Institutional Catholicism shaped concepts of religiosity within its reach. Elsewhere, continuity with the past survived informally in the disrupted lives of transitional rural migrants. Several months following the various crops through Illinois, Indiana, Michigan, and as far north as North Dakota and Minnesota, threw families from diverse Texas communities together. While the immigrant parish ameliorated differences in the local ethnic mix, homogenization and assimilation varied according to several factors, including relationship to ethnic neighbors, workplaces, and diocesan politics. With time, changing social attitudes as well as economic advances reshaped inter-ethnic religious relations, expanding the sphere of folk Catholicism in the absence of national Mexican parishes.[36]

In 1931 the parish of Our Lady of Guadalupe was established for the betabeleros on St. Paul's West Side, served by a succession of Anglo pastors after the completion of a church complex the following year. From the start the parish tackled social problems and all during the Depression years operated a substantial relief program, with funds from the Guild of Catholic Women. During these years the church served to anchor St. Paul's Mexican colony. Beet workers tried to wait out the Depression in the fields if possible, although dramatic declines in wages eroded hopes of material gains and propelled them to St. Paul. By 1936, about 1,200 out of an estimated total of 1,500 Mexican Americans in St. Paul were on relief; to their neighbors they represented unwelcome urban competition. An organized repatriation campaign emerged in the city virtually unchallenged in the late 1930s. In 1938 local authorities deported over three hundred Mexican families, including some U.S.-born children. Typically, it hindered community and parish formation; yet by the mid-1940s Our Lady of Guadalupe parish again served the region's Mexican Americans, attracting migrants from throughout the area for weddings and other celebrations.[37]

The organization of work and daily life in the countryside made contacts beyond the family more difficult and offered little potential for parish support. Moreover, during this period of massive economic dislocation and crisis the fields attracted neither exiled Spanish-speaking priests, Americanizing bishops, nor sympathetic European-origin coreligionists. The seasonal nature of the agricultural work interrupted the arduous process of securing grounds and financing and constructing buildings. Rural Mexicans and Tejanos had little opportunity to build parishes like those of European immigrant groups due to their later arrival and the changed circumstances of their urban reception. Unlike European Catholics previously immigrating to the region—Czechs in the 1880s, for example—Mexicans could not rely on grants of land contributed by parishioners for church and school sites.[38]

Priests and Mexican Culture in Toledo

Ever-present Protestant missionaries succeeded in introducing a wedge between immigrants and homeland until Catholics responded. Tejano and Mexican newcomers gravitated toward national parishes but joined whatever local Christian church existed. Toledo, some ninety miles south of Detroit, was a major junction point on the eastern rim of the midwestern migrant stream. Toledo Mexicans, or *Toledanos*, settled near the business district and fanned out in low-density clusters nearby, especially on the South Side, sharing communities with Germans, Irish, Poles, and Hungarians. Weekly services had first been conducted in Sts. Peter and Paul Chapel. The establishment of a Catholic mission in 1929 attracted approximately a hundred Mexican-American families with over five hundred parishioners, causing the virtual collapse of the Mexican Baptist congregation.[39]

A priest from Mexico organized the Toledo colonia into a Spanish-language mission, Our Lady of Guadalupe, without fixed territorial boundaries. In 1931 an Ohio-born priest of German descent, Raymond Gorman, who had become fluent in Spanish after having studied in Colombia, succeeded the Mexican pastor and consolidated the fledgling mission, serving from 1931 to 1951 and bringing together Tejanos with Mexican immigrants. He viewed himself as having saved the colonia from Protestantism. In an attempt to purify folk Catholicism in Toledo, Father Gorman "Romanized" religious practices. He tried to eliminate several aspects of Mexican folk culture which he interpreted as lingering superstition, particularly those pertaining to such phenomena as *mal de ojo* and *susto*. At baptismal ceremonies he urged godparents, or *compadres*, to develop a stronger allegiance to Catholicism. However, he did not understand folk Catholicism. Even individuals who neglected Sunday Mass and some of the sacraments considered themselves loyal to their church.[40]

Guadalupe societies, largely parish-based, sprang up during the Depression years in the Midwest, channeling the expression of Mexican culture. The Church reluctantly adapted, with some ambivalence about the spread of folk Catholicism. Local clergy often attempted to exert control over the *Guadalupanas*, Mexican devotional societies, without understanding the symbolic importance of La Virgen de Guadalupe. Increasingly the women organized these groups within specific parishes, generally under the supervision of the pastor. Many men also saw these societies' activities, particularly the annual feast on December 12, as a validation of nationality. Devotions to the Virgin of Guadalupe transcended parish structures and typically required no priestly participation.[41]

EXTERNAL INFLUENCES ON PARISH COMMUNITIES

In the absence of activity by national Catholic organizations in the Midwest, local initiative determined actions taken concerning Mexicans. Beginning in the mid-1930s the Home Missions Council of North America, a consortium of Protestant churches conducting missionary work throughout the nation, effectively reached out to migrants. The HMC first entered the Midwest in 1931 at the invitation of the Methodist Church of Mt. Pleasant, Michigan, conducting religious services for recently settled Mexican beet workers. In 1936 the council opened a summer school and offered a church program there. It kept separate schools for Mexican Americans, Anglos, and Blacks. One Tejano Methodist minister, who reportedly always carried Catholic and Protestant Bibles, opened a nondenominational church in Shepherd, Michigan, and held religious services for Mexicans in surrounding towns.[42]

With Mexican immigration to the Midwest largely closed during the 1930s to priests as well as lay people, Anglo-American and European-origin Catholic clergy often took it upon themselves to protect Mexicans from perceived spiritual decline. One pastor, monitoring the situation in 1939 from the newly created Saginaw diocese, confirmed the threat of competition: "The various Protestant societies maintain thirty missionaries in this state for the sole purpose of converting the Mexicans to their own particular belief. The Baptists are the most active. All of the Protestant missionaries are well supplied with religious tracts and Bibles that are printed in Spanish."[43] Yet he noted very little progress for all their trouble. In 1940 the Home Mission Council formed the Michigan State Migrant Committee to help provide food and shelter for migrants. From charitable assistance flowed an informal ministry that although reportedly aimed solely at winning over non-believers also doted on non-practicing Mexican and Mexican-American Catholics.

In 1942 the U.S. and Mexico negotiated contract labor agreements under the Bracero Program (repeatedly extended until 1964). This allowed for the seasonal use of imported Mexican labor in various sectors of the economy to avoid worker shortages at key growing and harvest times. The Bracero Program provided transportation, a minimum wage, and adequate housing, primarily for male laborers. In 1943 the War Manpower Commission began the recruitment of railroad hands directly from Mexico to keep national transportation systems functioning. In the Midwest these braceros were sometimes housed in boxcars on railroad property. Between 1943 and 1945 more than 15,000 Mexican railroad workers came to Chicago as braceros, and seven railroad camps were established there during the 1940s.[44]

In the 1940s Mexicans became more integrated into the industrial labor force. Those in agriculture lived in temporary, makeshift accommodations in camps far removed from institutions of organized religion. Tejano migration to the Midwest declined in 1943, precisely when workers from Mexico were entering the country in great numbers and some cities encouraged them to settle out from the migrant stream to jobs in war production. Not until World War II did many Mexican-American males enter the ranks of skilled labor. Then even some women joined the urban labor force in large numbers, including temporary stints in the midwestern defense industry.[45]

As part of the war effort, the United States Office of Inter-American Affairs in 1943 provided a grant to organize the Mexican Civic Committee to help develop community leaders, primarily among Mexican Americans on Chicago's Near West Side. This organization served as a liaison between barrio settlements and the larger Chicago community. Its director, Frank Paz, in a report on local institutions, criticized barrio churches for their lack of leadership in local issues. Mexican Americans in other midwestern cities with second generation populations, such as Saginaw, Michigan, also organized effectively during the early 1940s.[46]

In summary, immigration and urbanization during the 1930s boosted the development of parish communities in midwestern Mexican communities and offset some of the damage of repatriation. Economic gains toward the end of the Depression decade allowed for demographic recuperation. However, by 1945 the surviving pioneer parishes remained in a fragile stage of institutional development. Still, they played a key role in reshaping the identity of the emerging second generation. The distinct regional origins and experiences of parishioners coming from Mexico, the Southwest, and other points in the Midwest foreshadowed the increasing diversity of the post–World War II years.

3

Parish Growth and
Barrio Diversity, 1945–1965

The exploding population of Mexico, along with declining mortality rates, fed emigration northward during the two immediate post–World War II decades, a period when few other immigrant groups arrived in the United States. Local geography and residence patterns, as well as their relationship to the labor supply, remained important factors in the development of Mexican-American Catholicism. Immigrants entering the urban Midwest after 1945 generally chose the oldest neighborhoods for settlement. Federally funded housing, urban renewal programs, and the construction of new highway systems in the 1950s and 1960s displaced the older barrio residents as well as many newcomers. Diocesan officials and local clergy responded to the growing presence of Mexican Americans and Mexican immigrants by offering Spanish-language sermons and by sanctioning the symbols and practice of Mexican folk Catholicism. Thus previously Anglo "territorial" parishes often came to function as Mexican national ones in areas receiving new immigration.

Meanwhile, the threat of Protestantism took on renewed force. In the 1940s the Protestant Home Missions Council oriented its activities toward mission work for migrants more aggressively than did Catholics, while soft-pedaling urban ministry. The HMC served migrant workers in varying capacities before the Catholic Church systematically addressed their needs. The National Council of Churches, HMC's successor, formalized this attention with its migrant ministry program beginning in 1950. Later in the decade it turned toward evangelism. Protestants depended more heavily than Catholics on local support for their charitable activities. Competition and misunderstanding often characterized Protestant-Catholic relations in the period leading up to Vatican II.

One Catholic observer thought that Protestants lavished more attention on Mexican nationals than on Tejanos, claiming, "Our priests have been highly successful in routing the evangelists. Here and there the Protestants sponsor nursery schools for the Texas

285

children. The damage done is negligible—as far as the children are concerned; however we try to crowd the Protestants out lest the parents be contaminated."[1] Tejanos dominated the migrant labor force in the upper Midwest. Their travels between Texas and the Midwest during the summer often created difficult family situations. Many appealed to the church for help when they became stranded along the way, much to the chagrin of pastors who believed they should have better planned their affairs in advance.[2]

NATIVE-BORN GENERATIONS AND
MEXICAN-AMERICAN PARISHES IN GREATER KANSAS CITY

Kansas City's Westside underwent several changes in its parish structure that were typical of midwestern parishes and that affected the delivery of religious services. A flood in 1951 closed Our Lady of Mt. Carmel parish in the packinghouse district of Armourdale, forcing many Mexican-American families to take refuge, at least temporarily, in Westside, across the river in Missouri. Guadalupe Center, operated by the Kansas City diocese, became a distribution center for food, clothing, and medicine. Urban renewal projects and highway construction in the 1950s and 1960s transformed the neighborhood, forcing the relocation of more than a thousand people. The Mexican-American population dropped from 13,000 in 1940 to less than 7,000 in 1970. Many people left for California, Chicago, and elsewhere. With the easing of residential restrictions many higher-income families moved out of the barrio to newly developed areas in the suburbs. Intermarriage with non-Mexican Americans steadily increased.[3]

The integrated parish model sought to avoid the reproduction of national parishes in the suburbs. It allowed greater flexibility for a mobile metropolitan population, and made it easy to drop services in any particular area when they were no longer needed. However, sustained Mexican immigration complicated this process, adding an inexhaustible source of newcomers that delayed outward residential mobility. Until 1962 the Mexican-American Catholics who had moved out of Westside kept their membership at Our Lady of Guadalupe Church, attending services regularly. Thereafter Bishop Cody adopted a strict policy of territorial parishes within the Kansas City diocese, insisting that Mexican-American families attend the church nearest their residence, as did Catholics of other ethnic backgrounds. Observers estimated that non-practicing Catholics comprised one-third of the Mexican Americans of Kansas City's Westside. Moreover, priests of Our Lady of Guadalupe parish visited few homes, and the parishioners failed to take the initiative in going to the church.[4]

Since the majority of people, particularly among the younger generation in Kansas City, chose close friends to sponsor their children at baptism, non-practicing Catholics frequently became godparents. Protestants, although representing a very small minority, sometimes could not serve as godparents for the offspring of friends and relatives. The institution of *compadrazgo* accentuated extended family ties and sanctioned identity apart from regular parish affairs. It also helped ease the stress of urbanization and, for the older generation, tempered the alien environment with the introduction of Mexican traditions.[5]

The Protestant threat varied among dioceses. In Wichita, women from thirty-nine churches supported the Mexican Protestant church's interdenominational program. One Mexican Baptist who managed a nursery attended by many Catholic children observed, "We treat them nice so they know now what the priests said about us is not true."[6] In 1960 over a dozen national parishes survived throughout the small Kansas towns of Dodge City, Emporia, and Garden City as well as Kansas City, Wichita, and Topeka.[7]

The intervention of federal, state, and local government that took place in the midwestern metropolis and cultural differences among parishioners increasingly reshaped parishes. Intermarriage between ethnic groups increased among those who moved out of the city. Second- and third-generation Mexican Americans increasingly assimilated and in some areas spoke English exclusively. One Mexican who spent twenty-four years as a pastor in Kansas observed, "We may say that English has definitely supplanted Spanish in nearly all Mexican families, and Spanish is now only a secondary language."[8] The Kansas experience differed from elsewhere in the Midwest, given its lesser immigration after the end of the railroad era. The Great Lakes states, by contrast, attracted more newcomers to industry and agriculture, and therefore more native Spanish-speakers. Many Mexican immigrants came to work in the region's booming steel mills during the 1950s, pushing the older Mexican-American population outward into established parish communities of first- and second-generation European-origin immigrants. Suburban trends in the United States metropolis also changed the composition of barrio parishes.[9]

RESHAPING MEXICAN-AMERICAN CATHOLICISM IN CHICAGO

The transformation of the Chicago metropolis and its Catholic institutions reflected the movement of Mexicans and Mexican Americans. Midwestern parishes, reinforced by sustained migration from Mexico in the early 1940s, remained the focus of assimilation in the face of social and economic change. Railroad work and meat-packing no longer constituted the economic base for the Mexican barrios of the Near West Side and Back of the Yards. During and after World War II these dwindling industries left behind barrio residents who now had to seek employment outside their historic neighborhoods. Our Lady of Guadalupe retained its following in the postwar decades and its parishioners, constituting about one quarter of the total population of the neighborhood by 1970, dispersed among groups of European ethnics and African Americans. Throughout the period 1945 to 1965 the rhythm of steel production continued defining barrio activities. South Chicago began its decline much later with the closing of steel plants. However, this working-class community soon became overshadowed as the locus of Mexican settlement.[10]

The Cordi-Marian sisters from Mexico had established a settlement on the West Side in 1936, continuing the area's tradition of separate ethnic institutions. The Cordi-Marian Center offered English classes as well as instruction in art, music, and crafts. It also assisted working mothers during World War II and became an agency of Catholic Charities in Chicago, serving children of many different ethnic and religious backgrounds. One Mexican-American doctor who practiced twenty years among the Mexican poor in Chicago found the sisters and the Claretian fathers a source of unity and strength in the barrios. The Cordi-Marian Center served as a settlement house providing day-care and other services to the Mexican community. Priests noted that few social agencies worked with Mexican Americans in the 1950s "and so these women turned to their churchmen and their doctors for help."[11]

In 1970 Chicago's Mexican-American population was fourth in the nation, behind only Los Angeles, San Antonio, and Houston. Its largest barrio, the Pilsen-Little Village area, surpassed in size all others in the Midwest. Its growth had begun in the late 1920s, accelerated in the 1940s, and boomed in the early 1960s as urban renewal and highway construction projects in the Near West Side neighborhood just to the north forced the dispersion of many Mexicans and Mexican Americans westward. Pilsen, an

old Bohemian-American territory, soon became a primary settlement area, housing over 40 percent of the city's 106,000 Mexican-
Americans by 1970. It also became home to an increasing array
of Mexican businesses. Westward movement into adjoining neighborhoods and suburbs reshaped Catholic institutions beginning in
the late 1950s and early 1960s as many parishes "turned" Mexican;
others did so increasingly thereafter.[12]

Since European-origin residents in the Pilsen had neither the
resources nor the inclination to accommodate incoming Spanish-
speakers in their congregations, Mexican Catholics traveled to the
older churches to attend Mass. By 1961 weekly attendance at St.
Francis reportedly reached 5,000, that of our Lady of Guadalupe
2,000, and Immaculate Heart of Mary Vicariate, 700. Four other
West and South Side parishes attracted at least 1,000. About sixty
other area parishes had at least some Spanish-speaking parishioners, including Mexican congregations in suburban Palatine,
Waukegan, and Chicago Heights. About one-fifth of the Spanish-
speaking population in the Chicago archdiocese attended Sunday
Mass, a percentage somewhat higher than the national average for
Spanish-speaking Catholics.[13]

The missionary function of the Claretians declined with the
stabilization of the parishes under their direction. They retained
important roles in both archdiocesan and community networks
even though the Mexican-American community had become dispersed over a wide area, well beyond the borders of the three
national parishes. Only a handful of Mexican or Mexican-American
priests served Chicago's barrio parishes and they were temporary
missionaries, not long-term residents.

Few suburbs developed stable Mexican parishes under the care
of religious orders. St. Casimir in Chicago Heights, once a Lithuanian church, in 1948 began a Mass with a Spanish sermon as
part of its Sunday schedule. However not until the late 1950s did
archdiocesan personnel implement more systematic measures for
outreach and assimilation. During the summer of 1956, St. James
parish began hosting classes for the Spanish-speaking children of
migrant workers from Texas and Mexico who were harvesting
crops on truck farms near Arlington Heights. By 1958 a community center and a clinic there served Mexican Americans. Nuns
and seminarians taught catechism, first in the summer and later
year-round. In 1961, St. Theresa Church in Palatine became Santa
Teresita Vicariate, with a Spanish-speaking priest appointed vicar.[14]

Advances in farm technology and mechanization resulted in the conversion of many small farms into large residential subdivisions and thus brought on population growth in rural areas. Mexican itinerants on Chicago's southern and northwestern periphery, although less migratory than elsewhere in midwestern agriculture, presented challenges to the ordinary pattern of parish formation and assimilation. Many Tejano migrants in rural fringe areas avoided settling in urban barrios entirely. They then stayed on to worked in factories or at other year-round employment.

PUERTO RICANS IN BARRIO PARISHES

Puerto Ricans constituted an important and distinguishable component of Spanish-speaking communities in midwestern cities after World War II. They supplemented the work of Tejanos and Mexicans in several labor markets, concentrating in Chicago, Milwaukee, and Detroit, but extending also along the migrant stream. Puerto Ricans did not seek work in Kansas or elsewhere in the Central Plains. In those areas where they became parish neighbors they prompted the church to create new strategies for their care. Like braceros, they first came to the Midwest in large numbers as contract workers but their United States citizenship gave them more mobility. Several midwestern companies advertised in Puerto Rico's newspapers and over the radio; word of mouth from friends and relatives already on the mainland attracted others.[15]

In 1940 Samuel Stritch, former bishop of Milwaukee, became Chicago's archbishop; in 1946 he was named cardinal. His approval of the formation of seventy new parishes, twenty-four in the city of Chicago and forty-six in the suburbs, reflected an awareness of ethnic and spatial changes. Stritch oversaw the Catholic Interracial Council's efforts to improve relations with African Americans, and he also attempted to bridge cultural differences among Spanish-speaking Catholics. His initial interest in working with Puerto Ricans came out of concern for their lack of community organizations and their proclivity to join Pentecostal churches. They had no parishes of their own.[16]

The Cardinal's Committee for the Spanish-speaking, organized in 1955 under Cardinal Stritch and restructured in 1962 under his successor, Albert Cardinal Meyer, sought to assimilate the Spanish-speaking community through developing and sustaining voluntary organizations. By 1958 the largest society of Spanish-speaking persons in the Midwest was the church-based Caballeros de San Juan, composed mostly of Puerto Ricans. Its counterpart, Hermanas en la Familia de Dios, sponsored social and religious activities for women. The Puerto Rican population grew precipitously, from 8,000 for the entire Midwest in 1950 to 32,000 for Chicago alone in 1960 and 78,000 in 1970. Puerto Ricans settled apart from Mexican Americans, primarily on the North Side.[17]

Community groups often cooperated with Church goals and policies, complementing their efforts. The Illinois Federation of Mexican Americans brought together some twenty-five religious, political, and social clubs associated with the Cardinal's Committee. In conjunction with St. Francis Church, the Federation assisted the residents of the Near West Side in relocating. However, limited personnel, according to a 1961 report, impeded social and political work "as a necessary concomitant of truly effective work on the religious plan . . . first recognized some 4 or 5 years ago."[18] In 1962 twenty-one parishes in the Chicago area offered Spanish sermons, although they were often delivered by Anglo priests with limited foreign language skills. The potential audience encompassed the Mexican American population of 90,000 as well as Puerto Ricans and other Spanish-speaking Catholics in the archdiocese.

Puerto Ricans both followed and joined Mexican Americans residentially and mixed within other barrio parishes of northwestern Indiana. By the mid-1960s about 6,500 persons of Mexican origin and 3,000 Puerto Ricans resided in East Chicago. Mexican Americans expanded into neighboring Catholic parishes in Indiana Harbor as well as neighboring Gary and Hammond. Spanish-speaking parishioners comprised almost one-third of St. Patrick's congregation, which had been predominantly Irish and Italian, and about one-fifth of St. Joseph's, originally a Polish parish. Our Lady of Guadalupe, a pioneer parish, maintained a congregation of several thousand, including a broad range of newcomers. Competition over housing exacerbated tensions in the community.[19]

Milwaukee, despite the relatively small numbers of either Mexican Americans or Puerto Ricans, experienced tensions between the two groups. Mexicans historically dominated formal organizations of Spanish-speaking residents, including the revived mutualistas and branches of veterans' groups. In 1944 an Anglo priest helped revive the Mexican national parish until the Franciscans, whose members had little training in the Spanish language, took charge. During the 1950s and 1960s a Puerto Rican neighborhood developed on the East Side. Urban renewal soon forced many of the migrants into a settlement on the South Side. Mexican Americans and Puerto Ricans, although living next to one another, early on came to patronize different bars, grocery stores, and restaurants. There was minimal interaction between the two groups except in rare cases of intermarriage.[20]

Puerto Rican Catholicism differed in several respects, including devotions, saints, and folk religion, from that practiced by Mexican Americans. In 1966 the Milwaukee archbishop merged Our Lady of Guadalupe, financially solvent and expanding, into Holy Trinity, with a declining Anglo population. The former church building gave way to other uses for the diocese, including the housing of preschool programs. The new parish remained predominantly Mexican, while St. Patrick's, only eight blocks away and primarily Anglo, retained most of the area's Puerto Ricans. The distinctiveness of each national group in the midwestern landscape often escaped notice by all but the most discerning of the clergy, as well as by the general population. Moreover, the lack of a combined parish represented a lost opportunity to create a new model for the integration of Mexican Americans and Puerto Ricans under a single linguistic rubric with multi-ethnic components.[21]

Anglo Clergy and Barrio Parishes in Detroit

Southwest Detroit's distinctive cluster of barrio parishes included Holy Trinity in the "Corktown" district and Ste. Anne's and Holy Redeemer on the Southwest Side. All came to house a mixed Spanish-speaking population. Parish leadership proved decisive in assimilating Mexican families, especially in light of the effort waged to implement territorial parishes. Cardinal Mooney wished that "no racial or nationality distinction be made toward the Mexican" and prohibited any priest from encouraging special Mexican organizations, "religious or otherwise."[22] Mooney spent several years as a missionary in India and Japan early in his career, but by the start of his twenty-year tenure in Detroit in 1937 his missionary impulses had become transformed into policies of forced assimilation for Mexican Americans.[23]

Basilian priests who had learned Spanish in Texas and Mexico served Mexicans in Ste. Anne's Church in the Detroit barrio after 1940. In 1946, a separate chapel offered a Sunday Mass with a Spanish sermon, designed ostensibly for the older residents who knew no English. Mexican-American children attended Mass in the main church with the English speakers. The Caballeros Católicos, made up mostly of American-born sons of Mexican immigrants, became active in Ste. Anne's in the 1950s. That organization requested permanent Spanish-speaking priests and also urged that the Virgin of Guadalupe be legitimized in the church. By the 1960s the increase in Mexican congregants dictated that Spanish be used in the main chapel, making it function more like a national parish for the many Mexicans, Tejanos, and braceros entering at various junctures in the migration process. Puerto Ricans also attended, developing strong affiliations with some of Ste. Anne's religious clubs, despite Cardinal Mooney's earlier warnings.[24]

In the late forties and fifties the construction of a new expressway pushed many Mexicans beyond the fringes of the Detroit barrio. Thereafter the massive Holy Redeemer Church received more Mexican-American parishioners than any other in the state. Yet it relegated the Spanish services, typically, to an annex chapel in the church basement. The fact that a Guadalupe Society met regularly in the parish shows how contradictory the territorial parish policy proved to be. Yet by 1961 some 200 Mexican-American children out of a total of 1,200 students had entered Holy Redeemer's elementary school, and many went on to the parish high school. This reflected a growing commitment to Catholic education as well as a willingness to accept assimilation on the part of the parents.[25]

The arrival of Puerto Ricans in Detroit, as elsewhere, sparked confusion and prompted concern among the clergy. In 1950 agents of Saginaw Valley Sugar Beet companies traveled to Puerto Rico and recruited some 5,000 laborers for their fields. However, the migrants encountered poor living and working conditions that violated the provisions of their contracts. They soon left and went to Detroit in search of work, catching the attention of Father Clement Kern, pastor of Holy Trinity, who eased their settlement in the barrio. Kern later remembered, "We worked very hard winning friends."[26] About one hundred of the migrants remained in Detroit and brought their families over. Although less versed in formal Catholicism than Mexicans, Puerto Ricans, according to Kern, "all seem to feel friendly toward it [although we] have not influenced very many at all." He concluded that "they should not be judged by the standards of American Catholic parishes yet."[27]

Father Kern's good will applied equally to Mexican Americans. After having studied in Mexico he came to Holy Trinity Church in 1943, filling a leadership vacuum and catering to the needs of

Detroit's barrio residents. A flexible and universally popular pastor, Father Kern initiated evening English and citizenship classes for Mexicans, helped organize Casa María, a social work agency designed especially for the needs of women, and made regular trips to Mexico. He also began the practice in 1949 of having seminarians and Mexican clergy offer church services. During the 1950s, under his aegis, the city's St. Patrick's Day parade became a unifying event whereby Irish-American parishioners from throughout the city joined Mexican-Americans at Holy Trinity.[28]

Kern encouraged the formation of Guadalupe societies everywhere, recognizing that the devotions helped unify the Mexican community, reinforcing ties with Mexico in the process. In 1947 he wrote to inquire about affiliating his Confraternity of Our Lady of Guadalupe with the Universal Archconfraternity, noting "it is quite important to the Mexican Colony; we have the devotions once a month on the 12th and have followed quite closely without knowing it the rules of the Universal Confraternity. It is truly a wonderful devotion and the effects are marvelous."[29] For La Fiesta de Guadalupe in 1953 a priest from Saltillo delivered the sermon at Detroit's St. Boniface Church, with confessions held the Friday before at Ste. Anne's. Father Kern believed in pooling human and material resources among the different parishes. By 1955 four Confraternities of Our Lady of Guadalupe operated in the archdiocese: Most Holy Trinity, the center for the devotion, St. Joseph's parish and St. Mary's parish in Adrian, Michigan, and Sacred Heart parish in Imlay City. A local travel bureau held well-publicized pilgrimages each year to the Virgin's shrine in Mexico City.[30]

In Mexico, Guadalupe societies often consisted of women whose principal duty was to prepare for the Mass on the twelfth day of each month in the local chapel and decorate the altars with flowers. Processions began ten days before the feast, offering a break from the daily routine and relaxation with family and friends in church-sponsored recreation. Financial contributions were expected at regular intervals throughout the year, with collections taken at each Mass and special assessments made at the time of fiestas. Masses for the dead also required fees and work had to be donated for the repair and maintenance of Church properties. Mexican traditions took on new forms in the Midwest. According to a longtime Detroit resident, the first *posada* began in 1948 at the initiative of one of her neighbors. Detroit's Father James Barrett reportedly encouraged the incorporation of celebrations from private homes into the church's pre-Christmas schedule. *(Las posadas,* beginning nine days prior to Christmas, reenacts Mary and Joseph's search for a room on the first Christmas Eve, culminating in the placing of the infant Jesus in a nativity scene; a celebration follows.) Immigrant families celebrated the posadas in Detroit in much the same way as they did in Mexico.[31]

According to a leader in the National Council of Catholic Women, Kern demonstrated farsightedness in using the laity effectively. A Mexican-American woman long active in church affairs recalled, "Father Kern said we should branch out and go to different parishes each year where there were Spanish-speaking people, so we did. We all worked very hard."[32] Kern sought to encourage priests and lay groups in midwestern dioceses to work with migrants. He suggested that the dedication of the laity was "the great hope" of the midwestern Church in caring for migrants.[33] He also looked toward the prospect of institutional reform within the Catholic Church, lamenting the prohibition of lay people from saying Mass or hearing confession.

Kern believed that Catholics could make greater gains in charity and justice and lose some of their "inferiority complexes" with greater cooperation with other religious groups "in the areas of housing, health, living conditions and wages." He also noted, "Where the Church is taking care of the Catholics there was not much proselytizing."[34] Kern considered the migrant a "forgotten man" long before it became fashionable to do so. He incorporated the struggle for social justice and the rights of workers into his religious work. In the 1960s he opposed the extension of the Bracero Program and supported César Chávez very early in the farm workers' movement. He also succeeded in building coalitions between the church and the government for community development. Kern trained associates for work with migrants, one of whom, Father José Valdés, helped establish a Mexican Center in the small town of Port Huron to house a mission for migrants.[35]

During the mid-1950s the number of organized camps grew. Braceros, as Mexican nationals, presented both sticky jurisdictional problems as well as potential political bonuses for Catholic leadership in the Midwest. Even though their contracts did not require them to work on weekends, few braceros refused work in order to attend services. Some of those who did found themselves locked out when they returned to the compound. Employers sometimes prohibited church vehicles from entering their fields. When braceros felt discrimination over contract violations, they sometimes voiced their complaints to priests rather than to the local Mexican consul. In 1946 one group left the fields near Millington, Michigan, and walked about eighty miles to the heart of the Mexican colonia in Detroit.[36]

DIOCESAN STRUCTURES AND THE MIGRANTS

In the face of desperate conditions and a shortage of priests for migrants several midwestern dioceses early on developed special programs and strategies for the spiritual care of Mexican migrants. The Saginaw Mexican Apostolate was organized in 1947 with several missionary centers. Each furnished an automobile to visit migrants in the area in the hope of reducing Protestant influence in that city. The Guadalupe Center played a particularly important role, conducting censuses to determine religious and other needs and holding weekly Mass. Superiors released several Spanish-speaking priests and diocesan seminarians for the summer to assist beet workers, whose numbers approached 10,000 annually in the early 1950s. Around mid-July these migrants moved to Grand Rapids for the cherry crop before returning to Saginaw for the October sugar beet harvest. Very few of the priests along the migrant route knew Spanish. Moreover, the scattered farms impeded the organization of parishes and resulted in neglect of a large number of Catholics. Tejano agricultural workers throughout the Saginaw area attended St. Joseph parish, located in a neighborhood where Mexican Americans had lived since the early 1920s, but not within the rural focus of the Mexican Apostolate.[37]

In the 1940s and 1950s the Social Mission Sisters of the Holy Ghost came from the Southwest and other regions to operate a maternity house along with a health clinic as part of the Guadalupe Center for migrants and local residents. In the diocese of Grand Rapids, Michigan, some fifty parishes assisted the fifteen to twenty thousand braceros and Texas Mexicans in the diocese. In the summer of 1956 a priest in Erie, Michigan, petitioned the Detroit archdiocese for a Spanish-speaking priest, noting that a Guadalupe Society had already been established. The Council of Catholic Women carried out a lay apostolate among the migrants in Detroit, Saginaw, Toledo, and Madison. Most of their work entailed teaching catechism, as well as collecting and distributing clothes, religious articles, and surplus food.[38]

Individual associations within communities cared for the migrant in the farm regions of Indiana. Catholic groups included the Legion of Mary, particularly strong in caring for migrants and braceros in South Bend, Indiana. The St. Vincent de Paul Society, the Christian Family Movement, and Protestant organizations such as the Migratory Committee for the Indiana Council of Churches during the 1950s and 1960s planned a variety of educational, religious, recreational, and general welfare programs for migrants, sometimes in conjunction with representatives of the state's Farm Placement Office. Some smaller growers helped communities by providing recreational and religious facilities for migrants. Tejana women increasingly came north to work with their migrant husbands, settling out in cities in the late 1950s.[39]

THE BISHOPS' COMMITTEE FOR THE SPANISH SPEAKING AND THE BRACEROS

From 1942 to 1964 the bracero arrangement channeled migrants on six-month visas to understaffed parishes; the situation both discouraged stable community settlement and multiplied priestly responsibilities. These workers embarked on solo journeys from those Mexican states classified as "distress areas." The Mexican government decided who received permits according to the overall needs of United States agriculture in any given year. Braceros, not knowing if they would be granted permits, rarely set aside enough money for the following year's trip, and their lack of resources often forced them to ask friends and relatives to help them meet the costs of transportation to processing centers. The care and education of children generally placed a great burden on spouses and other family members left behind. Other concerns included the disruption and possible breakup of family life, the undermining of labor unionization, and the promotion of vice and gambling.[40]

Catholic bishops noticed rapid increases in the number of Spanish-speaking migrants throughout the Midwest in the late 1940s and the 1950s. In 1952 the bishop of Grand Island, Nebraska, wrote, "Our great need in the diocese is a couple of priests who can speak the Mexican language. Just now, we are so short of priests that I cannot send any away to study, and it appears that some years will pass before I shall be able to remedy the situation."[41] He voiced particular concern for Texas Mexican migrants.

In the summer of 1952 Mexican bishops wrote directly to San Antonio Archbishop Robert E. Lucey, a crusader for social justice for Texas migrants and founding member and director of the Bishops' Committee for the Spanish Speaking. They expressed concern that the Church in the United States did not provide adequate pastoral care for Mexican migrant workers, warning Vatican officials of the successes of "Protestant propaganda" among braceros. They also noted that returning workers constituted "a serious problem in Mexican cities and towns since they teach Protestantism and hatred of religion or indifferentism" to their fellow campesinos. Although Protestants never comprised more than a small percentage of the Mexican population, the bishops feared the growth of Protestant influence in the suburbs of the large Mexican metropolitan centers. They renewed their earlier (1945) offer to supply Spanish-speaking priests as well as some "Catholic Action laymen to help the Mexicans in the U.S."[42]

Lucey responded that fall by sending out a letter to all the bishops, requesting estimates on any Mexican migrants within their dioceses. He received much important data that revealed the extent of the migrant stream and the surprisingly large numbers and wide dispersal of Spanish-speaking in the region's dioceses. Lucey's concern for social justice took precedence over assimilation as practiced in the cities during the immigrant generation. Moreover, his strategy diverted attention from the needs of urban Mexican Americans scattered throughout much of the Midwest without a native clergy. The Bishops' Committee for the Spanish Speaking (BCSS) sought to borrow priests from Mexico, especially from the diocese of Guadalajara, to care for the foreign nationals. At least in principle domestic migrants working in targeted dioceses would also receive attention. Local clergy cooperated with the visiting priests while diocesan seminarians served as chauffeurs and interpreters. Dioceses generally paid the missionaries $25 weekly plus expenses.[43]

Rev. James Hickey, director of the Saginaw Mexican Apostolate, noted, "The Bishop has taken steps to care for the resident Spanish-speaking, the assistance of the Bishops' Committee made it possible for him to expand to meet the rural migrant needs as well." He observed many Mexican priests: "In Saginaw, four of the eight are Mexican. The four Spaniards are useful, but do not obtain the same results as the Mexicans. It would be too much to hope that all future missionaries brought be Mexicans, yet the more the better!" Despite the general shortage of Mexican clergy in the Midwest, three Michigan dioceses, Grand Rapids, Lansing, and Saginaw, used Spanish-speaking priests. Saginaw obtained South Americans and Spaniards on leave from their dioceses or members of religious orders. Hickey wrote, "A few of the Spanish-speaking priests and seminarians take a religious census of a given area for Mexicans or Texans, then establish Mass centers with Spanish sermons."[44] Bracero priests could not reproduce the patterns of village life in Mexico with which religion had been so closely associated, yet they offered solace to many.

Braceros, along with Texas Mexicans, took an interest in attending services, sometimes traveling miles for Mass. Concerning the bracero priests' performance of their duties, Hickey noted, "Undoubtedly many of the priests have far easier tasks in Mexico, yet they carry out their work here with real determination and zeal. We have found them willing to work for all. There is a tendency, of course, to favor the nationals, the work among them is far more consoling even from our own diocesan clergy. The Mexicans greet the priests with real warmth, much hand-kissing and with remembrances of home. The Texans are indifferent, cold and often icy."[45] In 1958 Father Joseph Crosthwait, field representative of the Bishops' Committee, wrote that, "Texas Mexicans, God bless them, have the faith and are dear to these priests but they have not been trained and are not at all able to support the Church through Sunday collections."[46]

Not all dioceses received Mexican priests, creating a pressing situation for the care of Tejanos and nationals alike. Crosthwait argued that ministry to migrant workers was an obligation incumbent upon all pastors rather than a matter of personal choice for the zealous. He noted the "lack of sufficient religious instruction" among migrants originating in the northern Mexican states of Sonora, Chihuahua, and Coahuila, whose geographical and historical isolation, plus a sparse and widely scattered population, "have retarded the missionary work of the Church." Within the United States, however, he found the Protestants well organized: "There was no city, no remote camp, there was no farm in which the Protestant was not active. This is their Number One program throughout the country—to help the migrants [although] one wonders about their sincerity."[47] The widespread perception of Church activists that Mexican Americans were rightfully Catholics caused continual resentment of Protestant ministers and their staffs. One Minnesota pastor lamented, "It is unfortunate that the Protestants have been able to secure a minister from Cuba who spends the entire summer going from camp to camp and holding therein religious services. We do want something similar for the Catholics."[48]

In preparation for a conference of the Bishops' Committee, an organizer in 1956 urged bishops around the country to utilize Catholic Action apostles to help migrants. Lucey offered a reexamination of Protestantism in a 1958 address designed to encourage the activities of Catholic laity, urging visits to labor camps to inform braceros of the location of the nearest church and other services. He expected bishops to organize councils of itinerant priests who could provide the migrants with religious articles and protect them against proselytizing.[49] Crosthwait also called for the organization of lay apostles "by the thousands" to help reduce the burden for busy parish priests. He believed that Protestantism bred religious indifference among Mexican Americans as well as defection from the Catholic Church, claiming that "within two years one-half of her converts defect from Protestantism and end up belonging to no church whatsoever. This is the tragedy of their activities."[50]

A study by Crosthwait on the religious care of migrants discovered that while the Mexican missionaries made significant contributions to Catholicism in the United States Church the local clergy only reluctantly interacted in the process of religious care. Rumblings of dissatisfaction with Operation Migratory Labor began in the late 1950s, reflecting a skepticism about "whether a diocese is not in many instances putting off its own obligation of taking care of their Spanish-speaking migrants and residents."[51] Only a few major seminaries in the Southwest even offered a course in Spanish and resident pastors generally resisted migrant ministry.

The hierarchy and even the urban clergy continued to focus on migrants. This BCSS policy, however well-intentioned, ignored new metropolitan configurations in the Midwest as well as prevailing ethnic patterns. The national church believed a native clergy more important for temporary Mexican immigrant workers than for resident Mexican Americans. The Mexican hierarchy's concern with its nationals overlooked the religious needs of Mexican Americans. Nonetheless, several Mexican priests worked on their own initiative in several dioceses in Michigan and elsewhere in the Midwest. The termination of the Bracero Program in 1964 also marked the end of Operation Migratory Labor. At its meeting that year in Rome the American hierarchy authorized the Bishops' Committee to coordinate the apostolate to the Spanish speaking in the United States. Lucey had laid the groundwork for many subsequent church organizations for Mexican Americans, both locally and nationwide.[52]

EDUCATION AND CATHOLICISM

Apart from Operation Migratory Labor, other Catholic programs focused attention on rural education, usually beginning with summer schools. One of the most ambitious projects funded a boarding school for the Crookston diocese in the Red River Valley along the border of Minnesota and North Dakota. The Sisters of St. Benedict staffed the local parochial school and became concerned about the children of the Mexican migrants too young to accompany their parents to the fields. In 1952 a pastor noted, "We are using two school buses, two panel suburban cars, and two passenger cars to transport the children from their rural homes to the barrio schools where they remain from Sunday afternoon until Friday afternoon. Food and all supplies are furnished by the Diocese in the Spanish Education Program conducted from June 15 to July 31st."[53] It emphasized religious education in Spanish, with other subjects taught in English. Priests, seminarians, and nuns served as teachers and conducted educational programs reaching hundreds of children.

Education did not involve assimilation as much as social service work. In May 1954 officials of the Sacred Heart Church in Imlay City appealed to their chancellor to buy a school bus for the transportation of the children to their religious instruction. The great distances in rural Michigan presented problems, as did "parental discontent." The pastor added, "There are many Mexican children whom I cannot get unless I furnish transportation for them. They simply have no way of coming in to their classes. For [them] I hope to have a lady of Spanish origin as teacher, should I get the bus."[54] One local pastor turned his home over to seven teachers and also established a parish social center for migrant families, distributing food and other supplies. In rare cases Mexican priests actually followed migrants in their travels and ministered to them. All area pastors offered their parish facilities as instructional centers, yet the cost of schooling put many parishes out of the business of education.[55]

Father Daniel Kennedy in 1947 persuaded the pastor of St. John Cantius in Indiana Harbor to rent one floor of his large school building to Guadalupe parish and then another priest drove a school bus route each morning during the school year through the parish to bring the children of Guadalupe parish to the building. Tireless missionary Sisters during the 1950–51 school year gave supplemental religious training to more than five hundred Mexican children attending the public schools in that city.[56]

In the early 1960s the bishop ordered the parochial school of the Mexican-American parish and the Polish school at St. John Cantius to consolidate their resources by sharing the same building. Both groups ignored the order; the Poles apparently disliked Mexican Americans and the latter felt slighted. The merger eventually occurred, but only on condition that all personnel and facilities, including classrooms, restrooms, instructors, and the teaching orders of nuns remained separate for the two groups. In 1964 the Mexican-American school was discontinued. In 1965 in East Chicago only about 15 percent of the parochial school enrollment was of Mexican or Puerto Rican descent, with almost 69 percent concentrated in two Indiana Harbor schools, St. Patrick's and St. John Cantius.[57]

The education of midwestern migrants involved a multipronged effort involving social welfare, health care, and literacy activities. In the mid-fifties the migrant worker community in northwest Ohio numbered about five thousand. Some Catholic women from Norwalk, members of the Daughters of Isabella, conducted a religious education program for children and adults at the migrant workers' camps. Catholic nurses checked the health of migrants and the committees distributed toys and used clothing. Norwalk's non-Mexican parishes helped in the project. In other parts of the diocese, nuns, priests, and lay people established summer camps and catechism programs for the migrant workers. The United Church Women of Ohio helped carry out migrant ministries beginning in the summer of 1954 in five Northwest Ohio communities.[58]

THE CHANGING METROPOLITAN LANDSCAPE AND PARISH RESPONSES

In 1952 a priest in St. Paul observed that "the efforts of Protestant missionaries in Minnesota dioceses seem to be directed chiefly towards winning migratory workers from our southern states. The nationals, I am told, are not much affected by this work."[59] On St. Paul's West Side, the largest of the city's Mexican-American settlements, Our Lady of Guadalupe Church hosted a fund-raising society composed of about eighty Mexican women. In the late 1960s the parish, which had been forced to move to a new location as a result of a devastating flood in 1952, helped to define the community and give it a Mexican tone. It welcomed Anglos moving into the community as well as Mexican Americans living outside the barrio. The church served a key role as a community center, having a fairly active membership in organizations such as the Holy Name Society. The Guadalupe Area Project included a Catholic welfare society and a neighborhood house headed by a Sister attached to the local church. It remained associated with the Church at a time when community agencies took over many of the traditional functions of parishes.[60]

South Toledo's Our Lady of Guadalupe parish came to serve Mexican Americans in all of northwest Ohio. Since it had no fixed boundaries, migrant workers occasionally ventured in from southern Michigan and northern Indiana. The building itself was a converted and renovated Southern Baptist church seating 220. An almost entirely Mexican congregation attended regularly with almost equal numbers of men and women. Mexican Americans not living in the South Side attended the Catholic church nearest them but always referred to Guadalupe as "our Church" and often returned for Mass on special occasions, sometimes traveling long distances. Our Lady of Guadalupe served as a language mission to which, according to Church policy, Anglos and the non-Spanish-speaking generally could not belong. Each Sunday the American priest, Father James Southard, said the high Mass and the sermon was delivered, reportedly with some difficulty, in Spanish, followed by a low Mass with English sermon for the younger parishioners.[61]

Father Southard discouraged devotionalism among Mexican Americans. After his 1962 transfer out of Our Lady of Guadalupe Chapel, parishioners immediately organized a procession, the first since his arrival ten years earlier, to celebrate the Virgin of Guadalupe. The devotion thereafter unified the city's Mexicans and Mexican Americans. However, urban renewal in Toledo's South End dispersed parish members from the historic barrio throughout the city. In 1963 the parish of Our Lady of Guadalupe merged with the nearby church of Sts. Peter and Paul, the German national parish that had lent support to the founding of the Mexican mission almost forty years earlier. Now, for the first time, a Mexican-born priest from Michoacán became minister for the combined congregations at Sts. Peter and Paul, first as an assistant and then as pastor. A bilingual pastor of Polish extraction followed him. During the early 1960s many Toledo Mexican Americans continued to receive cultural support and social welfare services from the Guadalupe Center in the old church building. Significantly, most of Toledo's prominent Mexican-American leaders had either received training under diocesan organizations or remained affiliated with the local church.[62]

The Cristo Rey Church in Lansing began in 1961, along with a community center of the same name, and performed a wide range of services for farm workers and recent settlers in central Michigan. A series of non-Mexican priests who spoke Spanish proved highly popular with Mexican-American parishioners. They became involved in celebrations, social work, outreach for the church, and pastoral programs. In 1965, as displacement by highway renewal loomed for the Mexican church, an Anglo pastor suggested the replacement of the parish with a social service center to serve a multi-ethnic population. It was assumed that the migrant population would cease growing with the end of the Bracero Program. The bishop moved the colonia to North Lansing, resulting in the destruction of the Mexican parish. The new community center catered to several different ethnic groups in its administration of social programs, including federal antipoverty and educational funds. It utilized professional community workers and introduced a bureaucratic apparatus that initiated an era of increased external funding for secular functions once performed by the church. In the mid-1960s the Michigan Migrant Agency developed as an interfaith outreach program to minister to migrants. In 1965 the agency obtained a sizable grant from several antipoverty programs. It conducted outreach to braceros near Lansing and became a center for the national Cursillo movement.[63]

Mexican-American Lay Activism

The Cursillo movement helped overcome the tendency of Mexican-American men toward non-participation in religious affairs. Unlike the devotions, which almost exclusively involved women, Cursillistas believed that the core of the Christianity lay not in rosaries or novenas but in "a life of conscious and growing grace." Frequent reception of the sacraments and active engagement in the Church's apostolic work of evangelization constituted a large part of this movement. Generally cursillistas became well integrated into parish life, and most parishes came to appreciate their enthusiasm. The Cursillo, a weekend course in Christianity with continued weekly meetings, successfully maintained participation in the Church by integrating the personal experiences of parishioners. More Christ-centered than traditional Mexican Catholicism, it also attracted many Anglo-American Catholics in many midwestern parishes. The Cursillo movement anticipated many of the reforms and renewals of Vatican II, seeking to involve the laity in the life of the Church; but it still restricted them to auxiliary roles.[64]

The Church played a constructive role in helping the farm workers' movement in the Midwest. Some Michigan growers regularly violated minimum wage, housing, and social security laws and for many years prevented members of the Lansing Catholic Diocese from conducting a migrant program in their camps. Groups within the Catholic Church, among them the Centro Cristiano de la Comunidad in South Bend, formed in 1964 and remained with migrants. Farm workers in the Midwest began to organize independent unions. By 1967 Obreros Unidos and the Farm Labor Organizing Committee (FLOC) in Wisconsin and Ohio, respectively, had become involved in civil rights and labor activities. In both midwestern unions urbanized Mexican Americans assisted as well. Besides the Church, many other organizations developed among Mexican Americans. The League of United Latin American Citizens (LULAC) and the GI Forum expanded from their Texas base and entered the Midwest in the 1960s, helping to establish political leadership across class lines.[65]

In 1961 an office of the Committee for Migrant Workers opened in Chicago, but within three years it had become a branch office of the Bishops' Committee, whose headquarters remained in San Antonio. In 1965 the Chicago office of the Bishops' Committee was under the supervision of Archbishop John Cody and his staff. It devoted much of its time and attention to the grape pickers' strike in California. The plight of the Mexican-American migrants in California and Texas attracted national attention. Midwestern migrants, meanwhile, remained largely invisible for much of the 1960s, despite their activism within and outside the Catholic Church.[66]

VARIANTS OF MIDWESTERN MEXICAN POPULAR CATHOLICISM

Remnants of rural life-styles and rhythms often became obsolete within the secularized urban environment. Mexican village families had both religious and civil sanctions for marriages, normally involving separation of the bride and groom before the marriage ceremony. In the new environment these practices faded. Mexican-American women retained elements of folk medicine. They sometimes treated "conditions" or illnesses with herbs.

Throughout the Southwest the widespread system of *curanderismo* embodied health systems that included healing techniques for natural and "magical" illnesses, all having a religious component. Mexican folk culture took root in the Midwest; it was extra-parochial and generally met with the disapproval of the Church.[67]

Traditional folkways existed in one small Indiana town, the subject of an anthropological investigation, where a family of curanderas claimed to have received their calling from the Virgin of Guadalupe and El Niño Fidencio, a Mexican folk saint. The mother received the "gift" during her youth in Mexico while the daughter had her healing vision in the Midwest. Lengthy healing sessions took place in a curing temple every weekend from May through October for up to 200 clients, mostly migrants and their families. Familiar Catholic hymns accompanied them. The elder curandera achieved a reputation throughout the area and exerted her influence among some former migrants in the Chicago area who offered devotions to El Niño at home altars. She revived the figure of Fidencio, who achieved popularity in Nuevo León in northern Mexico in the 1920s as a symbol of both Jesus and Guadalupe.[68]

Catholic healers regarded their practice as part of their religion and ignored the Church's criticism of their devotion to folk saints and healing rituals. Guadalupe devotions and folk medicine comprised an important part of the Mexican-American comprehension of Catholicism in the Midwest. The Southwest for Tejanos served as a bridge to Mexican culture, but knowledge of folk medicine common among many first-generation women in the Southwest faded in the Midwest. Guadalupe appealed to the immigrant generation of Mexicans in the Midwest. Lighting candles fulfilled a personal obligation not necessarily involving or affecting the community at large. As in Mexico, the parish priest presided over devotions. This aspect of Catholicism had less to do with seeking to buffer the urbanization process or integrating a former religious identity within a new context than with cultural maintenance.[69]

Although many midwestern priests failed to understand the Virgin's deep symbolism and her uniquely Mexican meaning, Crosthwait of the Bishops' Committee observed that Guadalupe devotions served to retain the loyalty of Mexican Americans "in Texas and throughout the entire Southwest [who] are forgetting their previous heritage. It is our duty to explain to the children and the teenagers of high school age what Our Lady of Guadalupe means to Mexico, its history and its culture, and more important, what she means to them."[70] Father Crosthwait reported favorably on the few Guadalupe Societies founded specifically for the spiritual care of migrants in rural Indiana and Wisconsin. Mexican Americans in the Midwest brought with them a folk Catholicism that blended Spanish Catholicism with pre-Columbian survivals and they retained it tenaciously.[71]

Rural Mexican religion never took root in the United States. Considerable diversity existed among urban Tejanos, braceros, and Mexicans in the Midwest, especially after 1945. Urbanization in the midwestern metropolis portended a radical departure from the cultural rhythms of the homeland. Unlike the Southwest, where parishes were few and far apart and the liturgy was not available, Mexicans in the Midwest had opportunities to attend Mass and generally to assimilate, despite racial hostility. They made permanent contributions to the parish structure in midwestern cities and towns. In rural areas transportation difficulties hampered the establishment of Mexican-American Catholic parishes. Women found new ways to become involved in the Church beyond their already active role teaching catechism and prayers at home and otherwise transmitting religious values.

CONCLUSION

Throughout the period 1910 to 1965, Mexican parishioners demonstrated considerable resourcefulness. The Mexican Revolution had weakened the bond between the Church and Mexican Catholics. Exiled clergy and religious, such as Kansas City's Father Muñoz, as well as women religious in the Chicago region, came north as a result of political and religious crises in Mexico. Mexicans could not, because of turmoil and instability in Mexico, petition the clergy in the old country to send them Spanish-speaking priests. Religious order clergy frequently served parishioners, linking them with the hierarchy.

The Catholic Church assimilated Mexican immigrants in midwestern parish communities. The process of parish building occurred largely on the terms of the Church but not without the contributions of Mexican-Americans. Midwestern Catholicism in the early twentieth century was totally unprepared for the Mexicans, but the utilization of national parishes proved effective in providing cultural stability and a structure for gradual assimilation. They served as a focus for social and cultural activities and eventually adopted a service orientation.

Mexican Americans established and sustained their parishes largely through voluntary associations, including mutual aid societies. These groups, although "facing southward" to the homeland, assumed leadership functions during the 1920s. Some dissent and disunity surfaced among lay leaders and between these leaders and pastors. Beginning in the 1930s the concern of the hierarchy had changed from managing immigration to confronting political and demographic changes. The Depression left local clergy to manage their problems with scarce resources. Priests increasingly challenged the episcopal dominance characteristic of earlier periods through their own initiative. Lay leadership emerged as the parish ceased to be the exclusive domain of the priest.

Chicago's Cardinal Mundelein purposely chose not to integrate barrio parishes although he early on established territorial parishes elsewhere in the archdiocese. By comparison, Detroit's Cardinal Mooney did not regard Mexicans as a special case in the 1940s and 1950s when he implemented the integrated parish model and he adopted no special policy for them. Detroit's Father Kern successfully negotiated relationships outside the parish in a progressive Catholicism. Like Lucey, he worked to realize a commitment to social justice. Many others worked to fill gaps in resources as well as leadership.[72]

Midwestern bishops failed to remake barrio parishes function as effectively as did European national parishes in earlier eras. The bishops did, however, help develop a stable institutional structure, incorporating lay initiative while facilitating limited access to the larger society. Operation Migratory Labor, the attempt during the 1950s to provide priests for Mexican nationals, represented a stopgap measure with no long-term design. Archbishop Stritch of Chicago, chair of the American Board of Catholic Missions, examined the social and religious conditions of urban Mexican Americans, but his efforts had limited impact.

Mexican Catholicism in the Midwest emerged quietly, without the symbolic artifacts of Spanish missions or a legacy of colonial Catholicism. It matured within the changing context of United States urban and social history as a distinctive regional component of the Mexican-American experience. However, it remained tangled in an antiquated framework of European immigration. The concept of a larger unit of identity based on common linguistic and cultural bonds among Spanish-speaking Catholics had not fully evolved in the Midwest, but its roots had taken hold in the relationship of Mexican Americans to institutional Catholicism.[73]

NOTES

Prologue

The author wishes to thank his colleagues at the University of Texas at San Antonio, Antonio Calabria, Robert M. Hill, David R. Johnson, and Linda K. Pritchard for reading the manuscript and offering critiques. For helpful advice thanks are due to Sister Yolanda Tarango, Father Robert E. Wright, Father Rosendo Urrabazo, Father Virgilio Elizondo, Father Baltazar Janecek, Leonard Anguiano, and Robert J. Torrez, as well as the advisory board of the project on Hispanics in the Catholic Church organized by the Cushwa Center at the University of Notre Dame. And thanks also to Gladys Novak, Archivist at the Oblate Archives, for her help in locating documents. Finally, the author wishes to dedicate this work to his immigrant parents and relatives.

1. *San Antonio Express News*, 14, 15 June 1992. Sermon delivered at St. Matthew's Catholic Church, San Antonio, Texas, Sunday, 21 June 1992.

2. For a lengthy discussion on the role of popular religiosity in Latin America, see Robert E. Wright, "Popular and Official Religiosity: A Theoretical Analysis and a Case Study of Laredo–Nuevo Laredo, 1755–1857" (Ph.D. diss., Graduate Theological Union, Berkeley, 1992). The "Summary" of chapter 4, pp. 168–75, encapsules the theoretical analysis.

1. Antecedents to the Twentieth Century

1. For an analysis of the New Mexican Indian community see, Ramón A. Gutiérrez, "*When Jesus Came, the Corn Mothers Went Away*": *Marriage, Sexuality, and Power in Colonial New Mexico, 1500–1846* (Stanford: Stanford University Press, 1991), pp. 8–11, 24–25.

2. William W. Newcomb, Jr., *The Indians of Texas: From Prehistoric to Modern Times* (Austin: University of Texas Press, 1961), 44–45, 53–57. T. N. Campbell and T. J. Campbell, "Cabeza de Vaca among the Indians of Southern Texas," in T. N. Campbell, ed., *The Indians of Southern Texas and Northeastern Mexico: Selected Writings of Thomas Nolan Campbell* (Austin: Texas Archeological Research Laboratory, University of Texas at Austin, 1988), pp. 22–23. Jean Louis Berlandier, *The Indians of Texas in 1830*, John C. Evers, ed. (Washington, D.C.: Smithsonian Institute Press, 1969), pp. 59, 64–65. Martín Salinas, *Indians of the Rio Grande Delta: Their Role in the History of Southern Texas and Northeastern Mexico* (Austin: University of Texas Press, 1990), pp. 132–35.

3. There is a considerable literature on evangelization and its links with the socioeconomic development of the colony. Among the best-known works are Robert Ricard, *The Spiritual Conquest of Mexico*, trans. Lesley B. Simpson (Berkeley and Los Angeles: University of California Press, 1966) and Charles Gibson, *The Aztecs under Spanish Rule: A History of the Indians in the Valley of Mexico* (Stanford: Stanford University Press, 1964). Recently, Louise M. Burkhart, *The Slippery Earth: Nahua-Christian Moral Dialogue in Sixteenth-Century Mexico* (Tucson: University of Arizona Press, 1988) de-emphasizes the fusion of Spanish Catholicism and Indian religion. Examples of studies on the colonization process in specific areas include Oakah L. Jones, Jr., *Nueva Vizcaya: Heartland of the Spanish Frontier* (Albuquerque: University of New Mexico Press, 1988); Philip Wayne Powell, *Soldiers, Indians, and Silver: North America's First Frontier War* (Berkeley and Los Angeles: University of California Press, 1952); Edward H. Spicer, *Cycles of Conquest: The Impact of Spain, Mexico, and the United States on the Indians of the Southwest, 1533–1960* (Tucson: University of Arizona Press, 1962); and Cecilia Barba, "The Role of the Church in the Colonization of Michoacán," (M.A. thesis, University of Texas at San Antonio, 1983). Overviews of the process in what is now the United States include John Francis Bannon, *The Spanish Borderlands Frontier, 1521–1821* (Albuquerque: University of New Mexico Press, 1974); Donald E. Chipman, *Spanish Texas, 1519–1821* (Austin: University of Texas Press, 1992); Thomas D. Hall, *Social Change in the Southwest, 1350–1880* (Lawrence, Kans.: University Press of Kansas, 1989); Oakah L. Jones, *Los Paisanos: Spanish Settlers on the Northern Frontier of New Spain* (Norman: University of Oklahoma Press, 1979); and David J. Weber, *The Spanish Frontier in North America* (New Haven and London: Yale University Press, 1992).

4. A large historiography treats the conflicts between the religious orders that ministered to the Indians and the civilian authorities in New Mexico. For a more general treatment of the work of the Church

and the religious traditions in the far northern frontier see Gutiérrez, *"When Jesus Came, the Corn Mothers Went Away"* and Fray Angélico Chávez, *My Penitente Land: Reflections on Spanish New Mexico* (Albuquerque: University of New Mexico Press, 1974. John L. Kessell, *Kiva, Cross, and Crown: The Pecos Indians and New Mexico, 1540–1840* (Washington, D.C.: National Park Service, United States Department of Interior, 1979) and "Spaniards and Pueblos: From Crusading Intolerance to Pragmatic Accommodation," in David Hurst Thomas, ed., *Columbian Consequences*, Vol. 1: *Archaeological and Historical Perspectives on the Spanish Borderlands West* (Washington, D.C.: Smithsonian Institution Press, 1989), pp. 127–38; and Robert E. Wright, "Local Church Emergence and Mission Decline: The Historiography of the Catholic Church in the Southwest During the Spanish and Mexican Periods," *U.S. Catholic Historian* 9, nos. 1–2 (Winter/Spring, 1990): 27–48. For a treatment of the blending of culture and religion in the post-Independence period see Francis Leon Swadesh, *Los Primeros Pobladores: Hispanic Americans of the Ute Frontier* (Notre Dame, Ind., University of Notre Dame Press, 1974).

5. Gilberto M. Hinojosa, "The Religious–Indian Communities: The Goals of the Friars" and Gerald E. Poyo and Hinojosa, "Conclusion: The Emergence of a Tejano Community" in Poyo and Hinojosa, eds., *Tejano Origins in Eighteenth-Century San Antonio* (Austin: University of Texas Press, 1991), pp. 61–83, 137–42; See also Hinojosa, "The Enduring Faith Communities: Spanish and Texas Church Historiography," *Journal of Texas Catholic History and Culture* (March 1990) 1:20–27; and "Friars and Indians: Towards a Perspective of Cultural Interaction in the San Antonio Missions," *U.S. Catholic Historian* 9, nos. 1–2 (Winter/Spring, 1990): 7–26. Wright, "Local Church Emergence," and "Hispanic Church Communities Outside the Missions during the Colonial and Mexican Periods," paper presented at Second Annual Quincentenary Symposium, National Park Service, San Antonio, Texas, Nov. 8, 1991. An excellent summary of the entire missionization process can be found in Weber, *Spanish Frontier*, pp. 92–121.

6. Wright, "Popular and Official Religiosity," pp. 374–467. Hinojosa, *A Borderlands Town in Transition: Laredo, 1755–1870* (College Station: Texas A & M Press, 1983), pp. 11, 17–22, 99.

7. See Henry F. Dobyns, *Spanish Colonial Tucson, A Demographic History* (Tucson: University of Arizona Press, 1976); James E. Officer, *Hispanic Arizona, 1536–1856* (Tucson: University of Arizona Press, 1987); and Douglas Monroy, *Thrown among Strangers: The Making of Mexican Culture in Frontier California* (Berkeley: University of California Press, 1990).

8. Hinojosa, *A Borderlands Town in Transition*, pp. 98–102, and "Class and Race in Borderlands Society: An Interpretative Essay," in Tricia Takacas, ed., *Natives and Newcomers: Challenges of the Encounter* (San Diego: Cabrillo Historical Society, forthcoming); and Gerald E. Poyo, "Canary Islanders, Mexicans, and Indians: The Sociedad de Castas on the Spanish Texas Frontier" (unpublished paper).

9. Hinojosa and Ann A. Fox, "Indians and Their Culture in San Fernando de Béxar," in Poyo and Hinojosa, *Tejano Origins*, pp. 108–10. Weber, *Spanish Frontier*, pp. 304–8, 326–33. See also Jesús F. de la Teja, "Land and Society in 18th Century San Antonio de Béxar: A Community on New Spain's Northern Frontier" (Ph.D. diss., University of Texas at Austin, 1988) and Jack Jackson, *Los Mesteños: Spanish Ranching in Texas, 1721–1821* (College Station: Texas A & M Press, 1986). Wright, "Popular and Official Religiosity," pp. 374–467.

10. David J. Weber, *The Mexican Frontier, 1821–1846: The American Southwest under Mexico* (Albuquerque: University of New Mexico Press, 1982), pp. 69–82.

11. See Wright, "Local Church Emergence," pp. 47–48, and "Popular and Official Religiosity," pp. 496–534.

12. Angélico Chávez, *The Old Faith and Old Glory: The Story of the Church in New Mexico since the American Occupation, 1846–1946* (Santa Fe: privately printed, 1946), p. 11. Michael Romero Taylor, ed., "Introduction," in Henry Granjon, *Along the Rio Grande: A Pastoral Visit to Southwest New Mexico in 1909*, trans. Mary W. de López (Albuquerque: University of New Mexico Press, 1986), p. 6. Moisés Sandoval, *On the Move: A History of the Hispanic Church in the United States* (Maryknoll, N.Y.: Orbis Books, 1990), pp. 25–40. See also Angélico Chávez, *My Penitente Land* (Albuquerque: University of New Mexico Press, 1974); Juan Romero, *Reluctant Dawn, Historia del Padre A. J. Martínez, Cura de Taos* (San Antonio: Mexican American Cultural Center, 1976); and Thomas J. Steele, *Penitente Self-Government: Brotherhoods and Councils, 1797–1947*. W. J. Howlett, *Life of the Right Reverend Joseph P. Machebeuf, D.D.* (Pueblo, Colo.: Franklin Press, 1908); reprint: Thomas J. Steele, S.J. and Ronald S. Brockway, eds. (Denver: Regis College, 1987). A very readable summary of Bishop Machebeuf's life is found in Thomas J. Noel, *Colorado Catholicism and the Archdiocese of Denver, 1857–1989* (Denver: University of Colorado Press, 1989), pp. 7–46. J. B. Salpointe, *Soldiers of the Cross: Notes on the Ecclesiastical History of New Mexico, Arizona, and Colorado* (Banning, Calif.: St. Boniface's Industrial School, 1898; reprint, Salisbury, N.C.: Documentary Publications, 1977).

13. For a critical view of the work of the Church in Texas, see José Roberto Juárez, "La Iglesia Católica y el Chicano en Sud Texas, 1836–

1911," *Aztlán* 4, no. 2 (Fall 1973): 217–55. Carlos Eduardo Castañeda, *Our Catholic Heritage in Texas, 1519–1936* (Austin: Von Boeckman-Jones, 1958) 7: 23–28, 45–50, and Patrick Foley, "Jean-Marie Odin, C.M., Missionary Bishop Extraordinaire of Texas" in *Journal of Texas Catholic History and. Culture* (March 1990) 1: 42–60, stress the dedication of the clergy and the religious men and women to the goals of administering the sacraments and providing religious education. Foley is preparing a book-length manuscript on Odin and his work with the mostly European and American "immigrant" Church. Noel, *Colorado Catholicism*, pp. 36–39, addresses a similar problem in that state.

14. For the importance of Galveston, see Kenneth W. Wheeler, *To Wear a City's Crown: The Beginnings of Urban Growth in Texas, 1836–1865* (Cambridge, Mass.: Harvard University Press, 1968).

15. Juárez, "La Iglesia Católica," *Aztlán* 4: 229, 235–43.

16. Hinojosa, "Enduring Hispanic Faith Communities," *Journal of Texas Catholic History and Culture* 1: 27–36. James Talmadge Moore, *Through Fire and Flood: The Catholic Church in Frontier Texas, 1836–1900* (College Station: Texas A & M University Press, 1992), p. 183.

17. Henry Granjon, *Along the Rio Grande: A Pastoral Visit to Southwest New Mexico*, p. 61.

18. Swadesh, *Los Primeros Pobladores*, pp. 88–95. Robert J. Rosenbaum, *Mexicano Resistance in the Southwest: The Sacred Right of Self-Preservation* (Austin: University of Texas Press, 1981), pp. 53–67, 111–24, 153–57. Suzanne Forrest, *The Preservation of the Village: New Mexico's Hispanics in the New Deal* (Albuquerque: University of New Mexico Press, 1989), pp. 17–31.

19. Arnoldo de León, *The Tejano Community, 1836–1900* (Albuquerque: University of New Mexico Press, 1982), pp. 202–10.

20. Timothy Matovina, "Our Lady of Guadalupe Celebrations in San Antonio, Texas, 1840–1841" (paper delivered at the Texas State Historical Association annual meeting, 28 February 1992).

21. Nancie L. González, *The Spanish-Americans of New Mexico: Heritage of Price* (revised, Albuquerque: University of New Mexico Press, 1969), pp. x, 25–28, 54–55, 78–83. George E. Sánchez, *Forgotten People: A Study of New Mexicans* (Albuquerque: University of New Mexico Press, 1940), pp. 15–26. For the Nuevo Mexicano experience of prejudice in the military, see Jacqueline Dorgan Meketa, ed., *Legacy of Honor: The Life of Rafael Chacón, a Nineteenth Century New Mexican* (Albuquerque: University of New Mexico Press, 1968), pp. 241–47, 273–75.

22. De León, *Tejano Community, 1836–1900*, pp. 50–112. See also Lawrence A. Cardoso, *Mexican Emigration to the United States, 1897–1931* (Tucson: University of Arizona Press, 1980), pp. 1–37; and David

Montejano, *Anglos and Mexicans in the Making of Texas* (Austin: University of Texas Press, 1987), pp. 24–99.

23. *Brownsville Daily Herald,* 29 January 1897, p. 3.

24. Montejano, *Anglos and Mexicans,* pp. 75–99. Also see Mario Barrera, *Race and Class in the Southwest: A Theory of Racial Inequality* (Notre Dame: University of Notre Dame Press, 1979), pp. 34–57.

25. Granjon, *Along the Rio Grande,* pp. 58–59.

26. Rev. William Demouy, bishop of Denver, cited in Robert J. Torrez, *El Primer Siglo: A Centennial History of San José Parish, Los Ojos, New Mexico, 1883–1983* (Los Ojos: Parish Council, 1983), p. 11.

27. Summary Tables, insert, *The Official Catholic Directory* (New York: P. J. Kenedy, 1870, 1890, 1910).

28. Mosqueda, "Twentieth Century Arizona, Hispanics and the Catholic Church," *U.S. Catholic Historian* 9 (Spring 1990): 96, describes the challenge presented by geography. For one of many descriptions of the rancho circuit see Jean Bapiste Odin to Lyons Council, 4 May 1857. Cited in Robert Wright, "Popular and Official Religiosity," pp. 642–43.

29. Doyon, *Cavalry of Christ on the Rio Grande, 1849–1883* (Milwaukee: Bruce Publishing Co., 1956), pp. 142–52.

30. Moore, *Through Fire and Flood,* 170–74. See also, Martha Ann Kirk, C.C.V.I., "Lead Them with Love: The Spirit of Evangelization Found in Mother St. Pierre Cinquin," presentation at the Texas State Historical Association annual meeting, 1991. Maria Luisa Valdez, C.C.V.I., "The Pilgrimage of Hispanics in the Sisters of Charity of the Incarnate Word," *U.S. Catholic Historian* 9 (Spring/Winter 1990): 182–86.

31. Robert Wright, "Popular and Official Religiosity," pp. 634–48. Moore, *Through Fire and Flood,* pp. 198–99.

32. Florence Hawley Ellis, "Tomé and Father John B. Ralliere," *New Mexico Historical Review* 30 (April–July, 1955): 89–114, 195–220. For a brief but insightful analysis of the alabados, see Yvonne Guillon Barrett, "Alabados of the San Luis Valley," in José de Oñís, ed., *The Hispanic Contribution to the State of Colorado* (Boulder: Westview Press for University of Colorado Centennial Commission, 1976), pp. 141–51.

33. *Diary of the Jesuit Residence of Our Lady of Guadalupe Parish, Conejos, Colorado: December 1871–December 1875,* edited and annotated by Marianne L. Stoller and Thomas J. Steele, S.J., with José B. Fernández, trans., *The Colorado College Studies,* no. 18, Timothy Fuller, ed. (Colorado Springs: The Colorado College, 1982), pp. 1–26.

34. Chávez, *Old Faith and Old Glory,* pp. 8, 11, lists the native-born New Mexican clergymen and religious women.

35. Hawley, "Tomé," *New Mexico Historical Review* 30: 211, n. 35, provides Father Ralliere's Spanish rendition of "America the Beautiful."

2. The Immigrant Church, 1910–1940

1. Mario T. García, *Desert Immigrants: The Mexicans of El Paso, 1880–1920* (New Haven and London: Yale University Press, 1981), pp. 33–45, 48–63. David Montejano, *Anglos and Mexicans in the Making of Texas, 1836–1986* (Austin: University of Texas Press, 1987), pp. 103–10. Oscar J. Martínez, *Troublesome Border* (Tucson: University of Arizona Press, 1988), pp. 46–52.

2. Lawrence A. Cardoso, *Mexican Emigration to the United States, 1897–1931: Socio-Economic Patterns* (Tucson: University of Arizona Press, 1980), p. 54.

3. Gary D. Nash, *The American West in the Twentieth Century: A Short History of an Urban Oasis* (Albuquerque: University of New Mexico Press, 1977), pp. 63–133.

4. Cardoso, *Mexican Emigration*, pp. 52–53, 91–95.

5. Sister Frances Jerome Woods, *Mexican Ethnic Leadership in San Antonio, Texas* (Washington, D.C.: Catholic University of America Press, 1949; reprinted New York: Arno Press, 1976), pp. 18–20.

6. Cardoso, *Mexican Emigration*, pp. 38–95. See also, Garcia, *Desert Immigrants*, pp. 134–35.

7. García, *Desert Immigrants*, pp. 223–32. Emilio Zamora, *The World of the Mexican Worker in Texas* (College Station: Texas A & M University Press, 1993), pp. 86–109. Rodolfo Acuña, *Occupied America: A History of Chicanos*, 3rd ed. (New York: Harper & Row, 1988), pp. 169–72.

8. Douglas E. Foley with Clarice Mota, Donald E. Post, and Ignacio Lozano, *From Peones to Politicos: Class and Ethnicity in a South Texas Town, 1900–1987*, revised and enlarged ed. (Austin: University of Texas Press, 1988), pp. 29, 40–44. García, *Desert Immigrants*, pp. 157–71.

9. Arthur J. Rubel, *Across the Tracks: Mexican Americans in a Texas City* (Austin: University of Texas Press, 1966), pp. 1–10, 23–24, 39–49. Garcia, *Desert Immigrants*, pp. 139–46, 151–52.

10. Guadalupe San Miguel, *"Let Them Take Heed": Mexican Americans and the Campaign for Educational Equality in Texas, 1910–1981* (Austin: University of Texas Press, 1987), pp. 18–25. For population figures in various Texas counties, 1920–1950, see Lyle Saunders, *The Spanish-Speaking Population of Texas* (Austin: Occasion Studies, University of Texas Press, 1950) reprinted in Carlos E. Cortez, ed., *The Mexican Experience in Texas* (New York: Arno Press, 1976).

11. San Miguel, *"Let Them Take Heed,"* pp. 32–58. Gilbert G. Gonzá-lez, *Chicano Education in the Era of Segregation* (London and Toronto: Associated University Presses, 1990), pp. 62–76.

12. Foley et al., *From Peones to Politicos*, pp. 6–12. David Monte-jano, *Anglos and Mexicans in the Making of Texas*, pp. 162–254. Acuña, *Occupied America*, pp. 141–90. See also Mark Reiler, *By the Sweat of Their Brow: Mexican Immigrant Labor in the United States, 1900–1940* (Westport, Conn.: Greenwood Press, 1976).

13. Sarah Deutsch, *No Separate Refuge: Culture, Class, and Gender on an Anglo-Hispanic Frontier in the American Southwest, 1880–1940* (New York and Oxford: Oxford University Press, 1987), pp. 134–61. See also Foley et al., *From Peones to Politicos*, pp. 13–17.

14. Anonymous, "An Economic and Industrial Survey of San Anto-nio, Texas," mimeographed bulletin (San Antonio: Public Service Co., 1942), cited in Woods, *Mexican Ethnic Leadership*, p. 21.

15. Woods, *Mexican Ethnic Leadership*, pp. 28–36. Rubel, *Across the Tracks*, pp. 46–51.

16. Summary tables, insert, *The Official Catholic Directory* (New York: P. J. Kenedy, 1910, 1920, 1930).

17. Carlos E. Castañeda, *The Church in Texas since Independence, 1836–1950*, vol. 7 of *Our Catholic Heritage* (Austin: Von Boeckmann-Jones, 1958), pp. 133–64. Chapters 6 and 7 of this work discuss the expansion of the diocesan and regular clergy (pp. 206–84) and chapters 7 and 8 outline the expansion of the educational and health and social services, in which women religious have a very important role (pp. 285–321).

18. For information on outside funding, see Castañeda, *The Church in Texas since Independence*, pp. 165–205.

19. Edwin E. Sylvest, Jr., "Hispanic American Protestantism in the United States," in Sandoval, *On the Move*, pp. 115–30.

20. Lawrence J. Mosqueda, *Chicanos, Catholicism, and Political Ideology* (Lanham, Md.: University Press of America, 1986), pp. 58–59.

21. Gabino Rendón, *"Hand on My Shoulder" As Told to Edith Agnew* (New York: Board of National Missions, Presbyterian Church in the U.S.A., 1963), pp. 52–57, cited in Randi Jones Walker, *Protestantism in the Sangre de Cristos, 1850–1920* (Albuquerque: University of New Mexico Press, 1991), p. 94.

22. Mosqueda, *Chicanos, Catholicism, and Political Ideology*, p. 59.

23. Walker, *Protestantism*, pp. 49–87, 100–105, 110–15.

24. Chávez, *Old Faith and Old Glory*, pp. 11–13.

25. Castañeda, *The Church in Texas since Independence*, pp. 178–205.

26. Sandoval, *On the Move*. Linne E. Bresette, *Mexicans in the United States* (Washington, D.C.: National Catholic Welfare Conference, 1929), p. 42, cited in Mosqueda, *Chicanos*, p. 83.

27. Stephen A. Privett, S.J., *The U.S. Catholic Church and Its Hispanic Members: The Pastoral Vision of Archbishop Robert E. Lucey* (San Antonio: Trinity University Press, 1988), p. 13. See also, Mosqueda, *Chicanos*, pp. 60–61, 67–69.

28. For a discussion on popular religiosity/Catholicism, see Allan Figueroa Deck, S.J., *The Second Wave: Hispanic Ministry and the Evangelization of Cultures* (Mahwah, N.J.: Paulist Press, 1989), pp. 113–19.

29. Patrick H. McNamara, "Bishops, Priests, and Prophecy" (Ph.D. diss., University of California, Los Angeles, 1968), p. 76 and "The Business of the Church," *The Tidings*, 22 October 1937, p. 8. Both cited in Mosqueda, *Chicanos*, pp. 59–60.

30. Ruth Dodson, "Don Pedrito Jaramillo: The Curandero of Los Olmos" in Wilson M. Hudson, *The Healer of Los Olmos and Other Mexican Lore* (Dallas: Southern Methodist University Press, 1951), pp. 9–70.

31. Interview quoted in Foley et al., *From Peones to Politicos*, p. 33.

32. Thomas Steele, S.J., "Peasant Religion: Retablos and Penitentes" in José de Oñís, ed., *The Hispanic Contribution to the State of Colorado* (Boulder: Westview Press, 1976), pp. 124, 137. See also Allan Figueroa Deck, S.J., "The Spirituality of United States Hispanics, An Introductory Essay," *U.S. Catholic Historian* 9 (Spring 1990): 144–45.

33. Zamora, *The World of the Mexican Worker*, describes the organization of various workers. See also Juan Gómez-Quiñones, *Sembradores, Ricardo Flores Magón y El Partido Liberal Mexicano: A Eulogy and Critique* (Los Angeles: Chicano Studies Publications UCLA, 1977), pp. 27–32, cited in Emilio Zamora, "Sara Estela Ramírez: Una Rosa Roja en el Movimiento," in Magdalena Mora and Adelaida R. Del Castillo, *Mexican Women in the United States: Struggles Past and Present* (Los Angeles: Chicano Studies Research Center Publications UCLA, 1980), pp. 163–65.

34. José E. Limón, "El Primer Congreso Mexicanista de 1911: A Precursor to Contemporary Chicanismo," *Aztlán* 5, nos. 1–2 (1974): 85–115. Cynthia E. Orozco, "The Origins of the League of United Latin American Citizens (LULAC) and the Mexican American Civil Rights Movement in Texas with an Analysis of Women's Political Participation in a Gendered Context, 1910–1929" (Ph.D. diss., University of California, Los Angeles, 1992), pp. 175–200.

35. Interview with Juan González, the owner of "La Reynera Bakery," Laredo, Texas. Cardoso, *Mexican Emigration*, pp. 144–51. See also Acuña, *Occupied America*, pp. 198–244. Abraham Hoffman, *Unwanted Mexican Americans in the Great Depression* (Tucson: University of Arizona Press, 1974).

36. Julia Kirk Blackwelder, *Women of the Depression: Caste and Culture in San Antonio, 1929–1939* (College Station: Texas A & M Press, 1984).

37. George Sessions Perry, "Rumpled Angel of the Slums," *The Saturday Evening Post*, 21 August 1948, p. 32, cited in Juan Gilberto Quezada, "Father Carmelo Antonio Tranchese, S.J., A Pioneer Social Worker in San Antonio, Texas, 1932–1953" (M.A. thesis, St. Mary's University, 1972), p. 24.

38. Bernard J. Tonnar, S.J., "He Had a Date with a Dream," *The Savior's Call*, April 1946, pp. 98–99, cited in Quezada, p. 25.

39. Blackwelder, *Women of the Depression*, pp. 94–108, 130–51.

40. San Benito Codex Historicus, vol. 1 (henceforth cited as SBCH), 2 June 1925, p. 60. Oblate Archives.

41. "Report of the Mission preached at Bastrop Co., Texas, with the Motor-Chapel St. Peter, by the Rev. Fathers J. Massaro and E. de Anta, O.M.I., June (4–18) 1916," and "Report of the Mission at the Belto Mines Given by Fathers E. de Anta and J. Massaro, O.M.I." (1916?), both found in "Chapel Car," Vertical Files, Oblate Archives.

42. For pattern of town plans, see Rubel, *Across the Tracks*, pp. 3–12 and Foley et al., *From Peones to Politicos*.

43. SBCH, 10 April 1910, p. 3; 2 and 22 May 1910, pp. 4–5; n.d., 1910, p. 9; 25 December 1910, p. 11; January 1911, p. 12; and 25 December 1929, p. 77.

44. SBCH, n.d., 1916, p. 16; n.d., 1929, p. 49, and n.d. June 1931, p. 88.

45. SBCH, 10 April 1910, p. 3 and May 1939, insert.

46. SBCH, n.d. March 1912, p. 12; 12 April, p. 15; and n.d. (1940?), p. 77.

47. SBCH, 2 June 1925, p. 64. For a discussion on the lack of tradition on the frontier regarding the sacrament of marriage, see Weber, *The Spanish Frontier*, pp. 329–32.

48. SBCH, 2 June 1925, pp. 60–61.

49. SBCH, 2 June 1925, pp. 61–62.

50. SBCH, 16 March 1914. Steele, "Peasant Religion," pp. 131–37. Orlando O. Espín, "Tradition and Popular Religion: An Understanding of 'Sensus Fidelium,'" in Allan Figueroa Deck, *Frontiers of Hispanic Theology in the United States* (Maryknoll, N.Y.: Orbis Books, 1992), pp. 70–71.

51. SBCH, 2 June 1925, p. 63.

52. SBCH, 2 June 1925, p. 64.

53. Interview with José H. Hinojosa.

54. On the Civil Register see Richard N. Sinkin, *The Mexican Reform, 1855–1876* (Austin: University of Texas Press, 1979), pp. 133–46.

55. Espín, "Tradition and Popular Religion," pp. 62–87. Robert E. Wright, "Popular and Official Religiosity: A Theoretical Analysis and a Case Study of Laredo–Nuevo Laredo, 1755–1857" (Ph.D. diss., Berkeley: Graduate Theological Union, 1992), pp. 168–75.

56. Joan Moore, *Mexican Americans* (Englewood Cliffs, N.J.: Prentice-Hall, 1970), p. 86, cited in Lawrence J. Mosqueda, *Chicanos, Catholicism and Political Ideology* (Lanham, Md.: University Press of America, 1986), p. 57.

57. Comment made by a priest to the author.

58. See also Mosqueda, *Chicanos, Catholicism and Political Ideology,* p. 79, n. 73. See also Luis Medina Ascencio, S.J., *Historia del Seminario de Montezuma: Sus precedentes, fundación y consolidación, 1910–1953* (Mexico: Editorial Jus, 1962).

59. SBCH, 31 July 1929, p. 81.

60. SBCH, 2 June 1925, p. 63.

61. SBCH, 12 April 1912, p. 15.

62. SBCH, 1 July 1912, p. 16; 7 February 1914, pp. 17, 19; and *San Benito News,* 2 January 1962, clipping in Oblate Archives.

63. SBCH, 14 December 1930, p. 86.

64. SBCH, 1 October 1931, p. 89.

65. SBCH, 25 December 1930, p. 79.

66. SBCH, 7 February 1914, p. 18.

67. SBCH, 12 December 1931, p. 90.

68. SBCH, 7 February 1914, p. 19, and n.d. September 1931, p. 90. Interview with Concepción González de Hinojosa and Adela González. See also San Miguel, *"Let Them Take Heed,"* pp. 32–58.

69. Interview with Adela and Delfina González.

70. SBCH, 2 February 1912, p. 12; 7 February 1925, p. 55; and 12 December 1931, p. 90.

71. Montejano, *Anglos and Mexicans in the Making of Texas,* pp. 125–28. Acuña, *Occupied America,* pp. 162–63. Walter Prescott Webb, *The Texas Rangers,* 2nd ed. (Austin: University of Texas Press, 1965), pp. 474–78.

72. SBCH, 3 January 1916, p. 32.

73. SBCH, 25 December 1911, p. 10.

74. SBCH, 25 December 1916, p. 16.

75. SBCH, 15 May 1957, v. 2, p. 26; 30 March 1959, v. 2, p. 39; and 21 May 1963, v. 2, pp. 44–45.

76. Arnoldo de León, *Ethnicity in the Sunbelt: A History of Mexican Americans in Houston* (Houston: Mexican American Studies Program University of Houston, 1989), pp. 9–14.

77. Our Lady of Guadalupe Parish Codex Historicus (henceforth OLGCH), n.d., 1911, p. 1, Oblate Archives.

78. OLGCH, 12 December 1911, pp. 2–3.

79. OLGCH, broadside, February 1912, insert, pp. 2–3.

80. Year end entries for 1919, 1921, 1922, and 1923, OLGCH, pp. 11, 15, 17, 19.

81. 13 May 1923, OLGCH, p. 21.

82. 2 September and 25 December 1923, OLGCH, pp. 23–25.

83. Sister Mary Paul Valdez, *Missionary Catechists of Divine Providence* (privately printed, 1978), pp. 2–29. Also see, de León, *Ethnicity in the Sunbelt*, pp. 29–30.

84. Report of the Mission Preached at Bastrop Co., Texas, with Motor-Chapel St. Peter, with the Rev. Fathers J. Massaro, O.M.I., and E. de Anta, O.M.I., June (4–18), 1916, typescript; and Report of the Mission at the Belto's Mine Given by Fathers E. de Anta and J. Massaro, O.M.I., with the Motor Chapel St. Peter, n.d., typescript of letter, E. de Anta to Ledvina, Oblate Archives.

85. Reports of Missions at Bastrop and Belto.

86. Report of Missions at Bastrop and Belto.

87. Reports of Missions at Bastrop and Belto.

88. Reports of Missions at Bastrop and Belto.

89. Owens, *Carlos M. Pinto*, pp. 90–92.

90. Memoirs of Sister Mary John Berchman García, cited in Owens, *Carlos M. Pinto*, pp. 82–83, 98–100, 109–28.

91. Owens, *Carlos M. Pinto*, pp. 144–45.

92. Granjon, *Along the Rio Grande*, pp. 36–37.

93. Ibid., pp. 58–59.

94. Ibid., p. 61.

95. Ibid., pp. 39–40.

96. Ibid., p. 42.

97. Ibid., pp. 45, 88–89.

98. Ibid., p. 60.

99. Ibid., p. 39.

100. RoseMary Buchanan, *The First 100 Years: St. Genevieve's Parish, 1859–1959* (privately printed), pp. 19–36.

101. Robert J. Tórrez, *El Primer Siglo: A Centennial History of San José Parish, Los Ojos, New Mexico, 1883–1983* (privately published, 1983), p. 11.

102. Ibid., p. 11.

103. Ibid., pp. 1–33.

104. Sister Mary Paul Valdez, C.D.P., *Hispanic Catholics in the Diocese of Dallas, 1890–1990* (privately published, n.d.), pp. 5–16.

105. Sister M. Nellie Rooney, O.S.F., *History of the Diocese of Amarillo* (privately printed, 1950), pp. 11–37.

106. Rev. Mark J. Woodruff, *A History of Sacred Heart Parish in Abilene, Texas, with an Account of the Beginning of St. Francis of Assisi Parish, Abilene and a Review of the Career of Father Henry Knufer* (privately published, 1991). (Pages not numbered.)

107. Rev. Larry J. Droll, ed., *Sacred Heart Cathedral Parish, Centennial History Project* (privately printed, 1984), pp. 10–12.

108. Magdalena Gallegos, "Hispanic Life in Auraria, Colorado: The Twentieth Century," *U.S. Catholic Historian* 9 (Spring 1990): 206.

109. José Antonio Navarro, "History of the School and the Church of Our Lady of Guadalupe" (unpublished manuscript, St. Mary's University Special Collections), p. 10, cited in Juan Gilberto Quezada, "Father Carmelo Antonio Tranchese, S.J., A Pioneer Social Worker in San Antonio, Texas, 1932–1953" (M.A. thesis, St. Mary's University, 1972), p. 9.

110. Inscription on the cornerstone, Our Lady of Guadalupe Church, San Antonio, Texas.

111. Richard A. García, *Rise of Mexican American Middle Class: San Antonio, 1929–1941* (College Station: Texas A & M University Press, 1991), pp. 151–52.

112. Ibid., pp. 155–56.

113. Ibid., pp. 156–59.

114. Ibid., pp. 158–59, 167–74.

115. Ibid., pp. 154, 163–66.

116. Ibid., pp. 173–74.

3. The Mexican-American Church, 1930–1965

1. Cynthia E. Orozco, "The Origins of the League of United Latin American Citizens (LULAC) and the Mexican American Civil Rights Movement in Texas with an Analysis of Women's Political Participation in a Gendered Context, 1910–1929" (Ph.D. diss., University of California, Los Angeles, 1992), pp. 178–88, 200–206, 222–48.

2. Richard A. García, *Rise of the Mexican American Middle Class: San Antonio, 1929–1941* (College Station: Texas A & M University Press, 1991), pp. 259–68.

3. Ibid., pp. 283–99. Guadalupe San Miguel, *"Let Them All Take Heed": Mexican Americans and the Campaign of Educational Equality in Texas, 1919–1981* (Austin: University of Texas Press, 1987), pp. 140–47.

4. García, *Rise of the Mexican American Middle Class*, pp. 191–92, 300–322. See also Edward D. Garza, *LULAC: League of United Latin American Citizens* (San Francisco: R and E Research Associates, 1972).

5. Mario T. García, *Mexican Americans: Leadership, Ideology, and Identity, 1930–1960* (New Haven: Yale University Press, 1989), pp. 175–86, 197–98, 204–8, 215–18, 221–27.

6. W. Elliot Brownlee, *Dynamics of Ascent: A History of the American Economy* (New York: Alfred A. Knopf, 1974), pp. 312–20, 351–57. Jonathan Hughes, *American Economic History* (Glenview, Ill.: Scott, Foresman/Little, Brown Higher Education, 1990), pp. 493–505, 519–34.

7. See Raúl Morín, *Among the Valiant* (Alhambra, Calif.: Borden, 1966).

8. Carl Allsup, *The American GI Forum: Origins and Evolution* (Austin: Mexican American Studies Center, University of Texas at Austin, 1982), pp. 33–40. Arnoldo de León, *San Angeleños, Mexican Americans in San Angelo, Texas* (San Angelo: Fort Concho Museum Press, 1985), pp. 67–83.

9. Rodolfo Acuña, *Occupied America: A History of Chicanos*, 3rd ed. (New York: Harper & Row, 1988), pp. 251–78.

10. The trip North is vividly described in the novel by Tomás Rivera, who grew up in a migrant family, in . . . *Y No Se Lo Tragó La Tierra — And the Earth Did Not Part* (Berkeley: Editorial Justa Publications, 1971).

11. Pauline R. Kibbe, *Latin Americans in Texas* (Albuquerque: University of New Mexico Press, 1946), pp. 129–34, 167–208.

12. García, *Mexican Americans*, pp. 297–98. Arnoldo de León, *Ethnicity in the Sunbelt: A History of Mexican Americans in Houston* (Houston: Mexican American Studies Program, University of Houston, 1989), pp. 132–33. Ozzie G. Simmons, *Anglo Americans and Mexican Americans in South Texas: A Study in Dominant-Subordinate Group Relations* (New York: Arno Press, 1974), pp. 358–97.

13. García, *Mexican Americans*, pp. 231–44. For the context of Castañeda's work, see Gilberto M. Hinojosa, "The Enduring Hispanic Faith Communities: Spanish and Texas Church Historiography," in *Journal of Texas Catholic History and Culture* 1 (March 1990): 23–26, 31–33.

14. García, *Rise of the Mexican American Middle Class*, pp. 310–22.

15. See Pearl Couser Wright, "Religious *Fiestas* in San Antonio" (M.A. thesis, St. Mary's University, 1946).

16. Simmons, *Anglo Americans and Mexican Americans*, p. 94.

17. Wright, "Religious *Fiestas*." Simmons, *Anglo Americans and Mexican Americans*, pp. 90–94.

18. Arthur J. Rubel, *Across the Tracks: Mexican Americans in a Texas City* (Austin: University of Texas Press, 1966), pp. 155–200.

19. R. Douglas Brackenridge and Francisco O. García-Treto, *Iglesia Presbiteriana, A History of Presbyterians and Mexican Americans in the Southwest* (San Antonio: Trinity University Press, 1974), pp. 106–12.

20. Simmons, *Anglo Americans and Mexican Americans*, pp. 91–92.

21. Brackenridge and García-Treto, *Iglesia Presbiteriana*, pp. 106–12.

22. Mark J. Woodruff, *Sacred Heart Parish of Abilene* (privately published, 1991).

23. Simmons, *Anglo Americans and Mexican Americans*, p. 92.

24. Brackenridge and García-Treto, *Iglesia Presbiteriana*, pp. 116–18.

25. Simmons, *Anglo Americans and Mexican Americans*, p. 91.

26. Comment made to the author by a priest friend who had worked with Mexican Americans for a long period.

27. Summary Table, insert, *The Official Catholic Directory* (New York: P. J. Kenedy, 1930, 1940, 1950, 1960).

28. Ibid.

29. Rev. Msgr. Alexander C. Wangler, ed., *Archdiocese of San Antonio, 1874–1974* (privately published, 1974), pp. 286–300. Fray Angélico Chávez, *The Old Faith and Old Glory: Story of the Church in New Mexico Since the American Occupation, 1846–1946* (Santa Fe: privately printed, 1946), p. 20.

30. Castañeda, *Our Catholic Heritage*, pp. 202–4.

31. Celebrations of 1936, 1948, Vertical Files, Oblate Archives.

32. *San Benito News*, 15 January 1962, insert in San Benito Codex Historicus (henceforth, SBCH), v. 2, pp. 35–36, Oblate Archives.

33. *Fiftieth Anniversary, 1912–1962* (privately published).

34. SBCH, vol. 2, 11 November 1962, p. 39, and 24 August 1964, pp. 56–69.

35. Simmons, *Anglo Americans and Mexican Americans*, pp. 87–88.

36. Minutes of District Meetings for the District of Mercedes, 14 March 1950, Codex Historicus, Our Lady of Mercy Parish, Mercedes, Texas, p. 131. Oblate Archives.

37. Edward Kennedy, O.M.I., *A Parish Remembers: Fifty Years of Oblate Endeavor in the Valley of the Rio Grande, 1909–1959* (Our Lady of Mercy Parish, Mercedes, Texas) (privately published, 1959), p. 62.

38. September 6 and 30, 1943, Sacred Heart Parish Codex Historicus, McAllen, Texas (henceforth SHPCH), pp. 2–3. Oblate Archives.

39. SHPCH, 25 January 1945, p. 12.

40. SHPCH, 14 June 1945, pp. 15–16.

41. SHPCH, September 1955, p. 23.

42. SHPCH, September 1968, p. 53.

43. SHPCH, 6 and 24 February 1956, pp. 27–28; December 1958, p. 55; March 1959, p. 58; June 1960, p. 69; 7 May 1961, p. 77; and 11 May 1966, p. 111.

44. SHPCH, December 1958, p. 55, and March 1961, p. 76.

45. SHPCH, December 1958, pp. 54–55.

46. SHPCH, January 1962, p. 82.

47. SHPCH, 7 January 1956, pp. 26–27.

48. SHPCH, 29 June 1966, p. 111.

49. *Recuerdo Histórico, Santo Angel Parish, El Paso, Texas* (privately published, 1946), p. 14.

50. Buchanan, *The First 100 Years*, pp. 39–43, 51–58, 62–65.

51. Michael Miller, "Women of Strength Provide Bond of Culture," *New Mexico* 71, no. 3 (March 1993): 20–27.

52. Simmons, *Anglo Americans and Mexican Americans*, pp. 84–91, 158–59.

53. Cited in Simmons, *Anglo Americans and Mexican Americans*, p. 89.

54. Stephen A. Privett, S.J., *The U.S. Catholic Church and Its Hispanic Members: The Pastoral Vision of Archbishop Robert E. Lucey* (San Antonio: Trinity University Monograph Series in Religion, 1988), pp. 3–4.

55. Ibid., pp. 4–9.

56. Ibid., pp. 10–15.

57. Ibid., pp. 15–21.

58. Ibid., pp. 27–44.

59. Ibid., pp. 129–36.

60. Ibid., pp. 34–36, 162–64.

61. Ibid., pp. 60–65.

62. Ibid., pp. 114–16.

63. Ibid., pp. 74–75.

64. Ibid., pp. 110–17, 52–64.

65. Ibid., pp. 157–66.

66. Ibid., p. 218.

67. Ibid., p. 220.

68. Information on the Cursillos de Cristianidad for this section was compiled from Carlos Mántica, *Para cambiar en Cursillos de Cristianidad* (Dallas: National Ultreya Publications, 1979); El Secretariado Nacional [de Cursillos] de Venezuela, ed., *Ideas Fundamentales del Movimiento de Cursillos de Cristianidad* (Dallas: National Ultreya Publications, 1974); *Programa Conmemorativo* [celebrating the 300th Cursillo in the San Antonio archdiocesis] (San Antonio: privately printed, 1978); and interviews with Mr. Raul Mata, Rev. Roberto Peña, Rev. Rogelio Martínez, and Rev. Baltazar Janacek.

PART II: THE MEXICAN CATHOLIC COMMUNITY IN CALIFORNIA

1. Establishing the Mexican American Catholic Community in California: A Story of Neglect?

1. Quoted in David F. Gómez, *Somos Chicanos: Strangers in Our Own Land* (Boston: Beacon Press, 1973), p. 157.

2. Manuel Servín, *The Mexican Americans: An Awakening Minority* (Beverly Hills: Glencoe Press, 1970), p. 148.

3. Douglas Monroy, "Mexicans in Los Angeles, 1930–1941" (Ph.D. diss., UCLA, 1978), p. 223.

4. Richard Romo, "Mexican Workers in the City: Los Angeles, 1915–1930" (Ph.D. diss., UCLA, 1976), p. 188.

5. Paul Sedillo, quoted in Antonio Soto, "The Chicano and the Church in Northern California, 1848–1978: A Study of an Ethnic Minority within the Roman Catholic Church" (Ph.D. diss., University of California, Berkeley, 1978), pp. 151–52.

6. Archives of the Archdiocese of San Francisco (hereafter referred to as AASF), McGucken Files. Rev. Augustine O'Dea to Archbishop Joseph McGucken, January 8, 1978.

7. "A Sad Story of Neglect," *San Francisco Monitor*, September 20, 1913, p. 1.

8. Editorial, *San Francisco Catholic*, April 1988, p. 1; cited in Terry Norton, "The Mexican-American Gift to the Catholic Community" (M.A. thesis, Franciscan School of Theology, Berkeley, 1988), p. 1.

9. Juan Hurtado, *An Attitudinal Study of Social Distance between the Mexican American and the Church* (San Antonio: Mexican American Cultural Center, 1975).

10. Quoted in Beatrice Griffith, *American Me* (Boston: Houghton Mifflin, 1948), p. 89.

11. "A Sad Story of Neglect," p. 1.

12. *Dedication of San Salvador Parish, Colton, California*, copy in the Archives of the Diocese of San Bernardino (hereafter referred to as ADSB).

13. AASF, "Report of the Priests' Conference for the Spanish Speaking for the Archdiocese of San Francisco, November 6, 1949."

14. Margaret Clark, *Health in the Mexican American Community: A Community Study* (Berkeley and Los Angeles: University of California Press, 1970), p. 98.

15. See Leonard Pitt, *The Decline of the Californios: A Social History of the Spanish Speaking Californians, 1846–1890* (Berkeley and Los Angeles:

University of California Press, 1966), and Rodolfo Acuña, *Occupied America: The Chicano's Struggle toward Liberation* (San Francisco: Canfield Press, 1972).

16. Quoted in Moisés Sandoval and Salvador E. Alvarez, "The Church in California," *Fronteras: A History of the Latin American Church in the USA since 1513* (San Antonio: Mexican American Cultural Center, 1983), pp. 218–19.

17. Warren S. Thompson, *Growth and Change in California's Population* (Los Angeles: The Haynes Foundation, 1955), p. 70.

18. See Soto, "Chicano in Northern California," pp. 59, 63, 96.

19. "Lo que puede y necesita la raza española en San Francisco" (San Francisco, 1871). Copy in Bancroft Library.

20. Michael Neri, "Hispanic Catholicism in Transitional California: The Life of José González Rubio" (Ph.D. diss., Graduate Theological Union, Berkeley, 1974), p. 110.

21. Francis Weber, *California's Reluctant Prelate: The Life and Times of the Right Reverend Thaddeus Amat, C.M.* (Los Angeles: Dawson's Bookshop, 1964), p. 56.

22. Father Blas Raho, quoted in Neri, "Hispanic Catholicism," p. 174.

23. Kevin Starr, *Inventing the Dream: California through the Progressive Era* (New York: Oxford University Press, 1985), p. 14.

24. Soto, "Chicano in Northern California," p. 80.

25. Neri, "Hispanic Catholicism," p. 136.

26. Richard Griswold del Castillo, *The Los Angeles Barrio, 1850–1890: A Social History* (Berkeley and Los Angeles: University of California Press, 1979), p. 17.

27. Francis Weber, *The Old Plaza Church: A Documentary History* (Hong Kong: Libra Press, 1980), p. 182.

28. See Albert Camarillo, *Chicanos in a Changing Society: From Mexican Pueblos to American Barrios in Santa Barbara and Southern California* (Cambridge, Mass.: Harvard University Press, 1979), p. 78.

29. Castillo, *The Los Angeles Barrio*, p. 168.

30. Camarillo, *Chicanos in a Changing Society*, p. 63.

31. Soto, "Chicano in Northern California," p. 63.

32. Moisés Sandoval, *On the Move: A History of the Hispanic Church in the United States* (Maryknoll, N.Y.: Orbis Books, 1990), p. 47.

33. For background information see Robert Quirk, *The Mexican Revolution and the Catholic Church, 1910–1929* (Bloomington: Indiana University Press, 1973), and Jean Meyer, *The Cristero Rebellion: The Mexican People between Church and State, 1926–1929*, trans. Richard Southern (Cambridge: Cambridge University Press, 1976).

34. Camarillo, *Chicanos in California: A History of Mexican Americans in California* (San Francisco: Boyd and Fraser, 1984), p. 33.

35. This section relies on a number of works including Albert Camarillo, *Chicanos in a Changing Society*; Albert Camarillo, *Chicanos in California*; George Sánchez, "Becoming Mexican American: Ethnicity and Acculturation in Chicano Los Angeles, 1900–1943" (Ph.D. diss., Stanford University, 1989); Richard Romo, *East Los Angeles: History of a Barrio* (Austin: University of Texas Press, 1983); Antonio Ríos-Bustamante and Pedro Castillo, *An Illustrated History of Mexican Los Angeles, 1781–1985* (UCLA: Chicano Research Center Publications, 1986); Norman M. Klein and Martin Schiesl, *Twentieth Century Los Angeles* (Claremont, Calif.: Regina Books, 1990).

36. See Sánchez, "Becoming Mexican American," and Camarillo, *Chicanos in California*, p. 37.

37. Allan F. Deck, *The Second Wave: Hispanic Ministry and the Evangelization of Cultures* (Mahwah, N.J.: Paulist Press, 1989), p. 13.

38. Statistics from Carlos Cortes, "Mexicans," in Stephan Thernstrom, ed., *Harvard Encyclopedia of American Ethnic Groups* (Cambridge, Mass.: Harvard University Press, 1980), pp. 697–719.

39. Sánchez, "Becoming Mexican American," p. 66.

40. Camarillo, *Chicanos in California*, p. 48. See also Abraham Hoffman, *Unwanted Mexican Americans in the Great Depression: Repatriation Pressures, 1929–1939* (Tucson: University of Arizona Press, 1974).

41. Camarillo, *Chicanos in California*, p. 75.

42. José Villareal, *Pocho* (Garden City, N.Y.: Anchor Books, 1959, reprint 1970), p. 16.

43. Carey McWilliams, *North from Mexico: The Spanish Speaking People of the United States* (New York: Greenwood Press, 1968, original 1948), p. 169.

44. These statistics are derived from the works cited in note 35.

45. Rodolfo Acuña, *Occupied America*, p. 159.

46. Villareal, *Pocho*, p. 31.

47. Camarillo, *Chicanos in California*, p. 34.

48. Romo, *East Los Angeles*, p. 116.

49. Ibid., p. 117.

50. Cletus E. Daniel, *Bitter Harvest: A History of California Farmworkers, 1870–1941* (Berkeley: University of California Press, 1910), p. 64.

51. Camarillo, *Chicanos in California*, p. 73.

52. See Camarillo, *Chicanos in a Changing Society*.

53. Sánchez, "Becoming Mexican American," p. 199.

54. Ríos-Bustamante and Castillo, *Illustrated History*, p. 126.

55. Lawrence Mosqueda, *Chicanos, Catholicism, and Political Ideology*, (Lanham, Md.: University Press of America, 1986), p. 94.

56. Robert Alvarez, Jr., *Familia: Migration and Adaptation in Baja and Alta California, 1800–1975* (Berkeley: University of California Press, 1987), p. 59.

57. Gloria E. Miranda, "The Mexican Immigrant Family: Economic and Cultural Survival in Los Angeles, 1900–1945," Klein and Schiesl, *Twentieth Century Los Angeles*, p. 41.

58. Evangeline Hymer, *A Study of Social Attitudes of Adult Mexicans to Los Angeles and Vicinity* (Master's thesis, University of Southern California, 1923; reprinted San Francisco: R.E. Associates, 1971), p. 44.

59. See Sánchez, "Becoming Mexican American," p. 34.

60. Villareal, *Pocho*, p. 61.

61. Mario Barrera, *Beyond Aztlan: Ethnic Autonomy in Comparative Perspective* (New York: Praeger, 1988), p. 13.

62. Camarillo, *Chicanos in a Changing Society*, p. 154.

63. Hope Mendoza Schechter, "Oral History," Regional Oral History Office, Bancroft Library, Berkeley, p. 10.

64. Clark, *Health*, p. 98.

65. Ibid., p. 40.

2. Catholic Ministry in the Era of the "Mexican Problem," 1910–1943

1. Colman Barry, "German Catholics and the Nationality Controversy," in Philip Gleason, ed., *Catholicism in America* (New York: Harper and Row, 1970), p. 69.

2. 1961 Report: Bishops' Committee for the Spanish Speaking, quoted in Albert López Pulido, "Race Relations within the American Catholic Church: An Historical and Sociological Analysis of Mexican American Catholics" (Ph.D. diss., University of Notre Dame, 1989), p. 80.

3. Ibid., p. 80.

4. Ríos-Bustamante and Castillo, *Illustrated History*, p. 165.

5. Quoted in Jacques Levy, *Cesar Chavez: Autobiography of la Causa* (New York: Norton, 1975), p. 84.

6. Leo Grebler, Joan Moore, Ralph Guzman, et al., *The Mexican American People: The Nation's Second Largest Minority* (New York: Free Press, 1970), p. 457.

7. Thomas O'Dwyer, "The Mexican in Our Midst, "*Proceedings of the Fifteenth Session of the National Conference of Catholic Charities, 1929* (Washington, D.C., 1929), p. 195.

8. 1920 Report of the Associated Catholic Charities of the Archdiocese of Los Angeles. Copy in the Archives of the Archdiocese of Los Angeles. (Hereafter referred to as AALA.)

9. For an outstanding discussion of assimilation and Americanization see Philip Gleason, "American Identity and Americanization," in Thernstrom, ed., *Harvard Encyclopedia*, pp. 31–58.

10. Laurence Forristal, "The Mexican Problem in an American Diocese," *Proceedings of the National Catechetical Congress of the Confraternity of Christian Doctrine, 1940* (Paterson, N.J.: 1941), pp. 483, 486.

11. Ibid., p. 484.

12. Ibid., p. 487.

13. Augustine O'Dea, "The Mexican Problem and Its Latin American Background," copy in AALA, p. 59.

14. AALA, John J. Cantwell, "Report to His Excellency [Amleto Cicognani] the Most Reverend Apostolic Delegate on the Spiritual Care of Mexican Immigrants in the Dioceses of Los Angeles and San Diego" (1936).

15. Cantwell quoted in Francis Weber, *Century of Fulfillment: The Roman Catholic Church in Southern California, 1840–1947* (Mission Hills: Archival Center, 1990), p. 491.

16. Grebler, et al., *The Mexican American People*, pp. 460–61.

17. Archives of the Diocese of San Diego (hereafter referred to as ADSD), Charles Buddy, "Response to the Memorandum on Religious Assistance to the Spanish Speaking Catholics in the United States" (12/30/1947).

18. AALA, Bishop Joseph T. McGucken to Apostolic Delegate Amleto Cicognani, December 29, 1947.

19. AALA, Our Lady of Perpetual Help Parish File, 1957: Father López to Bishop Manning, November 20, 1957.

20. AALA, OLPH Parish Files, Sister Marie Helene to Bishop Manning, October 19, 1957.

21. Griffith, *American Me*, p. 185.

22. Camarillo, *Chicanos in California*, p. 37.

23. Manuel Gamio, *The Life Story of the Mexican Immigrant: Autobiographical Documents* (New York: Dover Publications, 1971 reprint; original 1931), p. 41.

24. Quoted in ibid., p. 46.

25. Francisco Balderrama, *In Defense of La Raza: The Los Angeles Mexican Consulate and the Mexican Community, 1929–1936* (Tucson: University of Arizona Press, 1982), p. 68.

26. McWilliams, *North from Mexico*, p. 214.

27. Quoted in Mary Lanigan, "Second Generation Mexicans in Belvedere" (M.A. thesis, USC, 1932), p. 71.

28. Quoted in Romo, *East Los Angeles*, p. 147.

29. Camarillo, *Chicanos in California*, p. 77.

30. Sánchez, "Becoming Mexican American," p. 295.

31. AALA. All quotes taken from correspondence in bound parish files of St. Frances of Rome, Azusa.

32. AALA, 1923 Report, Associated Catholic Charities.

33. Leroy Callahan, "A New Missionary Field in California," *Missionary Catechist* 7 (January 1931): 1, 10.

34. Agnes Kozla, "Busy at the Camps," ibid., p. 10.

35. "El Hogar Feliz," *Los Angeles Tidings* (1910 Christmas edition), p. 80.

36. Michael Engh, "Mary Julia Workman: The Catholic Conscience of Los Angeles," California History 72 (Spring 1993): 2–10.

37. Ibid., p. 2.

38. Romo, *East Los Angeles*, p. 90.

39. See Stephen A. Privett, *The U.S. Catholic Church and Its Hispanic Members: The Pastoral Vision of Robert E. Lucey* (San Antonio: Trinity University Press, 1988) and Saul Bronder, *Social Justice and Church Authority: The Public Life of Archbishop Robert E. Lucey* (Philadelphia: Temple University Press, 1982).

40. Weber, *Century of Fulfillment*, p. 486, 493.

41. *Mexicans in California: Report of Governor C. C. Young's Mexican Fact Finding Committee* (San Francisco: R and E Associates, 1971, reprint of 1931 edition), pp. 192–93.

42. Robin F. Scott, "The Mexican American in the Los Angeles Area, 1920–1950: From Acquiescence to Activity" (Ph.D. diss., USC, 1971), p. 122.

43. "Our Diocesan Charities," *Los Angeles Tidings*, December 26, 1919.

44. AALA, 1924 Report, Associated Catholic Charities.

45. Callahan, "Missionary Field," p. 1.

46. AALA, 1919 Report, Associated Catholic Charities.

47. AALA, Bishop Cantwell to Father Silva, May 5, 1929, San Miguel, Watts Parish File.

48. Weber, *Century of Fulfillment*, p. 484.

49. Dennis Burke, "The History of the Confraternity of Christian Doctrine in the Diocese of Los Angeles, 1922–1936" (Master's thesis, Catholic University of America, 1965), p. 18.

50. Privett, *Lucey*, pp. 7–9.

51. Weber, *Century of Fulfillment*, p. 484.

52. Elizabeth Ann Clifford, O.L.V.M., *The Story of Victory Noll* (Victory Noll, Ind.: Victory Noll Sisters, 1981).

53. Ibid., p. 125.

54. These examples were drawn from Clifford, *Victory Noll*, and files in the ADSB and ADSD.

55. Clifford, *Victory Noll*, p. 196.

56. Ibid., p. 144.

57. Linna Bresette quoted in Weber, *Century of Fulfillment*, p. 487.

58. Romo, *East Los Angeles*, p. 143.

59. Oral history interview, Rev. Albert Vásquez, C.M., July 1, 1991 at the Old Plaza Church in Los Angeles.

60. AALA, Francisco Gómez to Chancellor, January 25, 1982, Our Lady Queen of Angels Parish File.

61. AALA, San Conrado Parish Files, 1947.

62. Leo Politi, "Las Posadas at the Old Mission Church," *Script*, December 1947.

63. AALA, Bishop Joseph T. McGucken to Most Reverend Amleto Cicognani, December 29, 1947.

64. AALA, Mexican File.

65. "Los Angeles Now Second Largest Mexican City," *Los Angeles Tidings*, May 18, 1928, p. 6.

66. Ibid.

67. *The Story of a Parish: Its Priests and People* (Anaheim: St. Boniface, 1961).

68. Gilbert Cadena, "Chicanos and the Catholic Church: Liberation Theology as a Form of Empowerment" (Ph.D. diss., University of California, Riverside, 1987), p. 66. See also Our Lady of Guadalupe Shrine, Riverside Parish Files, ADSB.

69. See Robert Delis, *The Grand Lady of Boyle Heights: A History of St. Mary's Church, Los Angeles* (Los Angeles: St. Mary's, 1989), pp. 26–27.

70. "Our Lady of Soledad, Coachella," *Los Angeles Tidings*, February 8, 1929, p. 39.

71. Oral History Interview, Monsignor John Coffield, July 3, 1991.

72. O'Dea, "The Mexican Problem," p. 52.

73. ADSD, Bishop Charles Buddy to Monsignor José Núñez, 11/4/39.

74. ADSB, Rev. Julio Oliva to Bishop Buddy, Coachella Parish File.

75. Francis Weber, *John Joseph Cantwell: His Excellency of Los Angeles* (Hong Kong: Cathay Limited Press, 1971), p. 125.

76. Cantwell, "Report to Apostolic Delegate," 1936.

77. AASF, Ralph Duggan, "Report of the Priests' Conference on the Spanish Speaking for the Archdiocese of San Francisco November, 1949."

78. AASF, "Petition for a National Parish," November 16, 1950.

79. Archives of the Diocese of San Jose (hereafter referred to as ADSJ), José Manterola, S.J., to Chancellor, July 13, 1955.

80. AASF, 1960 Report on the Spanish Speaking.

81. Deck, *Second Wave*, p. 58.

82. Pulido, "Race Relations," p. 26.

83. Soto, "Chicano in Northern California."

84. Deck, *Second Wave*, p. 60.

85. Ibid., p. 61.

86. AALA, John Coffield to Bishop Manning, October 17, 1949.

87. Deck, *Second Wave*, p. 58.

88. AALA, Memo to Eastside Pastors, November 12, 1952.

89. AALA, Sister Marie Helene, O.L.V.M., to Bishop Manning, October 19, 1957.

90. This section relies heavily on the work of Albert López Pulido, "Race Relations Within the American Catholic Church: An Historical and Sociological Analysis of Mexican American Catholics" (Ph.D. diss., University of Notre Dame, 1989). The section is also based on research in the Archives of the Dioceses of San Diego (ADSD), and San Bernardino (ADSB).

91. Pulido, "Race Relations," p. 43.

92. Ibid., p. 42.

93. Ibid., p. 40.

94. Ibid., p. 44.

95. Ibid., p. 45.

96. Ibid., p. 47.

97. ADSD, letter from four parish committees to Apostolic Delegate Amleto Cicognani, September 25, 1939.

98. ADSD, John M. Hegarty to Buddy, March 30, 1940.

99. ADSD, Buddy to David McAstocker, S.J., November 11, 1939.

100. Pulido, "Race Relations," p. 48.

101. Ibid.

102. ADSD, Buddy to Joseph Scott, February 27, 1940.

103. ADSD, Matthew Thompson to Buddy, February 22, 1940.

104. Pulido, "Race Relations," p. 54.

105. ADSD. While we do not have Torres Hurtado's letter, we do have Buddy's response to it. Buddy to Apostolic Delegate Pietro Fumasoni-Biondi, April 10, 1940.

106. ADSD, Testimonies of William Bresnahan, March 30, 1940, and Peter H. Vanderburg, April 10, 1941.

107. ADSD, Buddy to Apostolic Delegate Vagnozzi, September 21, 1939.

108. ADSD, Buddy to Fumasoni-Biondi, September 21, 1939.

109. ADSD, Buddy to Cicognani, December 7, 1939.

110. ADSD, Buddy to Cicognani, March 29, 1940.

111. Buddy to Cicognani, December 7, 1939.

112. ADSD, Buddy to Fumasoni-Biondi, April 10, 1940.

113. Ibid.

114. For more on Bishop Charles Buddy see R. Bruce Harley, and Catherine Louise LaCoste, C.S.J., *Readings in Diocesan Heritage*, Vol. XI: *Most Reverend Charles Francis Buddy, First Bishop of San Diego, 1936–1966* (San Diego: Diocese of San Diego, 1991).

115. Weber, *Century of Fulfillment*, p. 491.

116. Buddy, "Response to 1947 Memorandum."

117. Weber, *Century of Fulfillment*, p. 495.

118. See Weber, *Cantwell*.

119. Mike Davis, *City of Quartz: Excavating the Future in Los Angeles* (New York: Verso, 1990), p. 337.

120. Soto, "Chicano in Northern California," p. 142.

121. AALA, Eastside Committee File, n.d. (1967?).

3. Spirituality and Clergy

1. McWilliams, *North from Mexico*, p. 213.

2. Richard Rodríguez, *Hunger of Memory—The Education of Richard Rodríguez: An Autobiography* (New York: Bantam Books, 1982), p. 86.

3. Clark, *Health in the Mexican American Culture*, p. 98.

4. Sánchez, "Becoming Mexican American," p. 208.

5. Allan F. Deck, personal notes to the author, November 11, 1991.

6. Geronima Marquez quoted in Soto, "The Chicano in Northern California," p. 130.

7. Virgil Elizondo quoted in Deck, *Second Wave*, p. 54, and Cadena, "Chicanos and the Catholic Church," p. 18.

8. Cadena, ibid., p. 65.

9. Rigoberto Caloca-Rivas, "U.S. Hispanics and the Catholic Church," *Oakland Catholic Voice*, September 26, 1983, p. 18.

10. Hymer, *Study of Social Attitudes*, p. 48, and Clark, *Health*, pp. 34–35.

11. Griffith, *American Me*, p. 97.

12. Clark, *Health*, p. 38.

13. Hymer, *Study of Social Attitudes*, p. 48.

14. Gamio, *Life of the Mexican Immigrant*, p. 28.

15. McWilliams, *North from Mexico*, p. 213.

16. Rodríguez, *Hunger*, p. 87.

17. AASF, Report of Priests' Conference for the Spanish Speaking, March 10, 1949.

18. Oliver Lynch, personal notes, Archives of the Diocese of Oakland (hereafter ADO).

19. Ibid.

20. Cited in Alfredo Mirandé, *The Chicano Experience: An Alternative Perspective* (Notre Dame: University of Notre Dame Press, 1985), p. 123.

21. Rodríguez, *Hunger*, p. 85.

22. AALA, Santa Clara, Oxnard Parish Files, 1938.

23. Moisés Sandoval, *On the Move: A History of the Hispanic Church in the United States* (Maryknoll, N.Y.: Orbis Books, 1990), p. 43.

24. Deck, *Second Wave*, p. 64.

25. AALA, Santa Clara, Oxnard Parish Files.

26. Rodolfo Acuña, *A Community under Siege: A Chronicle of Chicanos East of the Los Angeles River, 1945–1975* (UCLA: Chicano Research Center Publications, 1984), p. 27.

27. Davis, *City of Quartz*, p. 331.

28. Recuerdo de solemne Procesión, December 3, 1944 (Santa Ana, 1944).

29. AALA, "Solemne Procesión del Corpus Christi," June 19, 1938.

30. Deck, *Second Wave*, p. 65.

31. Ibid.

32. Clark, *Health*, pp. 102–8.

33. Rodríguez, *Hunger*, pp. 90–91.

34. Quoted in Jean Meyer, *The Cristero Rebellion: The Mexican People between Church and State, 1926–1929*, translated by Richard Southern (Cambridge: Cambridge University Press, 1976), p. 44.

35. Deck, *Second Wave*, p. 64.

36. Davis, *City of Quartz*, p. 333.

37. Ibid.

38. "Mexicans of South to Erect Shrine to Our Lady of Guadalupe," *Los Angeles Tidings*, June 9, 1928, p. 1.

39. Balderrama, *In Defense of La Raza*, p. 75. Much of the story is taken from Balderrama's account.

40. Ibid., p. 76.

41. Ibid., p. 77.

42. Ibid., p. 78.

43. Davis, *City of Quartz*, p. 331.

44. "40,000 in Holy Name Union Demonstrations . . ." *Los Angeles Tidings*, December 14, 1934, p. 1.

45. "Mexican Consul Tries to Stop Religious Parade," *Los Angeles Tidings*, December 28, 1934, p. 2.

46. Balderrama, *In Defense of La Raza*, p. 81.

47. Ibid., p. 87.

48. Quoted in Gamio, *The Life Story of the Mexican Immigrant*, pp. 43, 48.

49. "Man Desecrates Mexican Parish Church of Los Angeles," *Los Angeles Tidings*, December 14, 1934.

50. Deck, *Second Wave*, p. 42.

51. *Los Angeles Tidings*, March 1, 1935, p. 1; March 8, 1935, p. 1.

52. Acuña, *Community under Siege*, p. 15.

53. Deck, *Second Wave*, p. 64.

54. ADSD, Calexico Parish File.

55. Finian McGinn, O.F.M., "The Mexican Male and the Church" (1965), unpublished paper in the Archives of the Diocese of Oakland.

56. ADSD, José Gutíerrez to Buddy, November 10, 1939.

57. Soto, "Chicano in Northern California," p. 174.

58. AALA, Cantwell to Nativity Parish, February 28, 1930.

59. Quoted in Josephine D. Kellogg, "Ministry, Hispanics, and Migrants: The San Francisco Mission Band 1949–1961" (unpublished revision [1985] of Master's thesis, Franciscan School of Theology, Berkeley, 1974) copy in AASF, p. 46.

60. AALA, Nativity, El Monte Parish Files, 1943.

61. AASF, R. Hayburn to Leo Maher, November 30, 1959.

62. Brawley Parish Files, ADSD, Layton to Buddy, December 7, 1937.

63. Clark, *Health*, p. 105.

64. Ibid., p. 100.

65. O'Dea, "The Mexican Problem," pp. 97–98.

66. Cited in Sánchez, "Becoming Mexican American," p. 211.

67. See McGinn, "The Mexican Male and the Church," ADO.

68. ADSD, Bishop Charles Buddy to Cardinal Fumasoni-Biondi, April 10, 1940.

69. Camarillo, *Chicanos in a Changing Society*, p. 187.

70. Harry Morrison, "Before the Sulpicians: Formation of Priests in Early California," *Patrician*, Spring 1992, n.p.

71. Quoted in John Dwyer, *Condemned to the Mines: The Life of Eugene O'Connell* (New York: Vantage Press, 1976), p. 150.

72. Delis, *Grand Lady of Boyle Heights*, pp. 26–27.

73. Ibid., p. 27.

74. ADSB. See Our Lady of Guadalupe, San Bernardino, Parish Files.

75. Mary Haas, "The Barrios of Santa Ana: Community, Class, and Urbanization, 1850–1947," (Ph.D. diss., University of California at Irvine, 1985), pp. 87–88.

76. AALA, McGucken to Cicognani, December 29, 1947.

4. A New Era: World War II and After

1. McWilliams, *North From Mexico*, pp. 229–31.

2. Quoted in Camarillo, *Chicanos in California*, p. 66.

3. Ibid., p. 65.

4. Quoted in Soto, "The Chicano in Northern California," p. 160.

5. Quoted in Sanchez, "Becoming Mexican American," p. 359.

6. Monroy, "Mexicans in Los Angeles," p. 222.

7. Lanigan, "Second Generation Mexicans," p. 15.

8. Coffield interview.

9. Miranda, "The Mexican Immigrant Family," p. 56.

10. AASF, Priests' Conference for the Spanish Speaking for the Archdiocese of San Francisco, November 6, 1949.

11. Griffith, *American Me*, p. 181.

12. Lanigan, "Second Generation Mexicans," p. 28.

13. ADO, Oliver Lynch, "The Religion of the Mexican American Church," personal papers.

14. ADSB, letter to Bishop Buddy, June 2, 1948, Our Lady of Guadalupe Parish File.

15. Patrick McNamara, "Mexican Americans in Los Angeles: A Study in Acculturation" (Master's thesis, St. Louis University, 1957; rpt. San Francisco: R and E Associates, 1975), p. 41.

16. Griffith, *American Me*, p. 185.

17. Ibid., p. 175.

18. Weber, *Century of Fulfillment*, pp. 484–86.

19. Deck, notes to the author.

20. AALA, Our Lady of Guadalupe, Parish File.

21. ADSB, Bishop Charles Buddy to Rev. José Núñez, November 4, 1939.

22. AALA, Pedro Penamil to Bishop McGucken, November 29, 1947; OLG Rosehill Parish File.

23. See Mary I. Zotti, *A Time of Awakening: The Young Christian Worker Story in the United States, 1938–1970* (Chicago: Loyola University Press, 1991).

24. AASF, Richmond Young Christian Students Guide.

25. Coffield interview.

26. Scott, "The Mexican American in the Los Angeles Area," p. 250.

27. Griffith, *American Me*, p. 296.

28. AASF, Duggan, Priests' Report, March 10, 1949.

29. Grebler et al., *The Mexican American People*, p. 459.

30. Acuña, *Occupied America*, p. 196.

31. Mosqueda, *Chicanos, Catholicism, and Political Ideology*, pp. 65–66.

32. Ibid., p. 66.

33. Grebler, *The Mexican American People*, p. 460.

34. AALA, 1958 Survey, Mexican File.

35. ADSD, Calexico Parish File.

36. AALA, James Dessert to Cardinal McIntyre, October 9, 1961, St. Mary's Parish File.

37. Quoted in Camarillo, *Chicanos in California*, p. 79.

38. Griffith, *American Me*, p. 187.

39. P. David Finks, *The Radical Vision of Saul Alinsky* (New York: Paulist Press, 1984), p. 39.

40. Acuña, *Occupied America*, p. 209.

41. Acuña, *Community under Siege*, pp. 94–95.

42. AALA, Cardinal McIntyre to Fidencio Esperanza, March 4, 1957.

43. Ibid.

44. Coffield interview.

45. AASF, Louis Kern, S.J., Priests Meeting, Archdiocese of San Francisco, February 10, 1949.

46. Moisés Sandoval, *On the Move*, p. 44.

47. Archbishop Edward Hanna quoted in "Hanna Hits Free Entry of Mexicans," *San Francisco Chronicle*, March 10, 1926, p. 4.

5. Migrants and Braceros

1. Kathryn Cramp, "A Study of the Mexican Population in Imperial Valley, California" (New York: Council of Women for Home Missions, 1926). Mimeographed copy in Bancroft Library, Berkeley.

2. ADSB, Coachella Parish File.

3. Cited in Kellogg, "Ministry, Hispanics, and Migrants," p. 53.

4. ADSD, Thomas O'Toole to Buddy, Calexico Parish File.

5. AALA, José Cumplido to Bishop Cantwell, July 6, 1939, El Monte Parish File.

6. Quoted in Rodolfo Acuña and Carlos Navarro, "In Search of Community: A Comparative Essay on Mexicans in Los Angeles and San Antonio," in Klein and Schiesl, eds., *Twentieth Century Los Angeles*, p. 196.

7. Deck, *Second Wave*, p. 84.

8. ADSJ, Holy Family Parish File, 1943.

9. AASF, Bracero File, Report, May 16, 1951.

10. AASF, Thomas McCullough, May 16, 1951, Report.

11. Soto, "Chicano in Northern California," p. 164.

12. Ernesto Galaraza cited in Pulido, "Race Relations," p. 84.

13. ADSJ, José Peña, S.J., "One Year of Work Among the Mexicans in San Jose," September 26, 1944.

14. Carlos Gonsalves, O.F.M., *Franciscan Annals for the Santa Barbara Province* 27 no. 2 (May 1965), p. 97.

15. Soto, "The Chicano in Northern California," p. 164.

16. Victor Salandini Papers, Stanford University.

17. Peña, "One year. . . ."

18. AASF, Anthony Ochoa, "Report on Braceros," 1948.

19. AASF, "Resolution of the First Annual Bracero Priests Conference," Sacramento, February 12, 1957.

20. AASF, Ronald Burke Oral History Interviews.

21. Much of the discussion on the Spanish Mission Band has relied on the work of Josephine D. Kellogg, "Ministry, Hispanics, and Migrants: The San Francisco Spanish Mission Band."

22. AASF, John García, "Five Year Report, 1955."

23. Ibid.

24. Kellogg, "Ministry, Hispanics, and Migrants," p. 39.

25. John Duggan, "My Mind to Me a Kingdom Is: An Autobiography" (unpublished manuscript, June 1984: copy in AASF).

26. AASF, Charles Philipps to Archbishop Mitty, November 22, 1952.

27. Soto, "Chicano in Northern California," p. 183.

28. "Our Lady of Guadalupe," *Franciscan Annals of the Province of Santa Barbara* 26, no. 4 (December 1964), p. 257.

29. Quoted in Grebler et al., *Mexican American People*, p. 483.

30. AASF, Bishop Donahoe to Donald McDonnell, April 6, 1954.

31. Joan London and Henry Anderson, *So Shall ye Reap: The Story of Cesar Chavez and the Farm Workers' Movement* (New York: Thomas Crowell, 1970), p. 94.

32. AASF, Donald McDonnell, "Report, 1956."

33. "Legend of Pancho Sánchez," copies in AASF.

34. Henry Anderson, "Ballad of Christ the Bracero," copies in AASF.

35. Kellogg, "Ministry, Hispanics, and Migrants," p. 94, and Duggan, "My Mind . . . ," p. 28.

36. AASF, 1958 Report, Bracero File.

37. AASF, William Rogers to Buddy, 1961.

38. Burke Oral History.

39. Sandoval, *On the Move*, p. 97.

40. Kellogg, "Ministry, Hispanics, and Migrants," p. 110.

6. The Mexican-American Catholic Community Comes of Age,
1960–1965

1. Soto, "Chicano in Northern California," p. 199.

2. Deck, *Second Wave*, p. 67.

3. Soto, "The Chicano in Northern California," p. 199.

4. Ibid., p. 201.

5. Ibid., p. 202.

6. AASF, "Report of Catholic Council for the Spanish Speaking, January 16, 1962."

7. Soto, "Chicano in Northern California," p. 205.

8. Acuña, *Occupied America*, p. 177.

9. Grebler et al., *Mexican American People*, p. 467.

10. ADO, Oliver Lynch notes.

11. Leo Mahon, "A Plan for Religious Instruction of the Spanish Speaking in Chicago," 1964. Copy in AASF.

12. See Jeffrey M. Burns, "¿Qué Es Esto? The Transformation of St. Peter's Parish in San Francisco," in J. Lewis and J. Wind, eds., *American Congregations* (Chicago: University of Chicago Press, 1994).

13. AASF, Archbishop McGucken to Rev. Timothy Hennessy, St. Peter's Parish File.

14. AASF, McGucken to Hennessy, July 15, 1964, St. Peter's Parish File.

15. AASF, Hennessy to McGucken, February 8, 1966, St. Peter's File.

16. AASF, McGucken to Hennessy, February 9, 1966, St. Peter's File.

17. ADSB, Núñez to Buddy, July 31, 1963, Our Lady of Guadalupe Parish File, San Bernardino.

18. Sister Noreen Murphy, "Sister María de la Cruz Aymes" (unpublished paper, copy AASF).

19. ADSJ, Holy Family Parish File, 1965.

20. ADSJ, McGucken to Antonio Soto, July 9, 1962, Our Lady of Guadalupe Parish File.

21. Deck, *Second Wave*, p. 61.

22. ADSJ, Holy Family Parish File, 1965.

23. Deck, *Second Wave*, p. 58.

24. AALA, Denis J. Gerity, "The Spanish American Question, December, 1949," Nativity, El Monte Parish File.

25. ADSJ, John Dwyer, "Report on St. Mary's, 1968," St. Mary's, Gilroy Parish File.

26. See Burns, "¿Qué Es Esto?"

27. AALA, Our Lady of Lourdes Parish File.

28. ADSJ, Soto to McGucken, February 15, 1965, Our Lady of Guadalupe Parish File.

29. ADSD, El Centro Parish File, 1962.

30. Burke Oral History.

31. ADSD, Letter to McGucken, June 17, 1964.

32. ADSJ, Dwyer to McGucken, March 21, 1963.

33. Joan Johnson, "In Stockton, a Mission to Migrants Moves Forward," *San Francisco Monitor*, October 12, 1962, p. 7.

34. Quoted in London and Anderson, *So Shall Ye Reap*, pp. 143–44.

35. Levy, *La Causa*, p. 91.

36. Daniel, *Bitter Harvest*, p. 223.

37. Victor Salandini, "The El Centro Lettuce Strike of 1961" (Master's thesis, St. Louis University, 1965).

38. César Chávez, "The Mexican American and the Church," *El Grito*, p. 2.

39. James Vizzard, S.J., quoted in McGinn, "The Mexican Male and the Church."

40. Levy, *La Causa*, p. 107.

41. National Conference of Catholic Bishops, *The Hispanic Presence: Challenge and Commitment* (Washington, D.C.: USCC, 1984), p. 3.

PART III: THE CATHOLIC CHURCH AND THE MAKING OF
MEXICAN-AMERICAN PARISH COMMUNITIES IN THE MIDWEST

Abbreviations

AAD: Archdiocese Archives of Detroit

ACA: Archdiocese of Chicago Archives and Records Center

UNDA: University of Notre Dame Archives

The Center for Chicano-Boricua Studies of Wayne State University provided assistance for travel and research in the early stages of this project. Moisés Sandoval, Mary Kay Vaughan, and Marc Zimmerman offered valuable comments on drafts.

1. Midwestern Catholicism and the Early Mexican Parishes, 1910–1930

1. Dennis N. Valdés, "*Betabeleros*: The Formation of an Agricultural Proletariat in the Midwest, 1897–1930," *Labor History* 30 (Fall 1989):

551, 556, 560. For an overview of Mexican Americans in the Midwest see Juan García, ed., *Mexicans in the Midwest* (Tucson: Mexican American Studies and Research, 1990).

2. Valdés, "Betabeleros," pp. 557, 561; George Edson, "Mexicans in the North Central States" (1927), in García, ed., *Mexicans in the Midwest*, pp. 106, 109, 111.

3. Paul S. Taylor, "Chicago and the Calumet Region," *Mexican Labor in the United States*, ed. Carlos E. Cortés (Berkeley: University of California Press, 1932; rpt. Salem, N.H.: Ayer, 1970), vol. 2: 226, 229, 279–280; Taylor, "Migration Statistics," in ibid., pp. 48–49.

4. Taylor, "Chicago and the Calumet Region," pp. 34, 77, 226, 229.

5. Dennis N. Valdés, *Al Norte: Agricultural Workers in the Great Lakes Region, 1917–1970* (Austin: University of Texas Press, 1991), pp. 11–24.

6. The national structure of Protestant churches usually followed a few typical patterns. The Methodist Church, highly centralized in organization, was divided into separate conferences for Anglos and Mexicans, each having its own ministers, administration, and parishes supported from an independent fund. Baptists, on the other hand, had no separate Anglo and Mexican conferences and local churches received little financial help from the regional and national organizations. They enjoyed greater independence in selecting ministers and remained under the control of the local Anglo church to a greater degree than the Methodists. The Pentecostals, relatively weak in terms of organization, were nevertheless the only church fully financed and administered by Mexicans themselves; Douglas E. Foley, *From Peones to Políticos: Class and Ethnicity in a South Texas Town, 1900–1987* (Austin: University of Texas Press, 1988), p. 106.

7. On Americanization and assimilation, see Edward G. Hartmann, *The Movement to Americanize the Immigrant* (New York: AMS Press, 1948); James R. Barrett, "Americanization from the Bottom Up: Immigration and the Remaking of the Working Class in the United States, 1880–1930," *Journal of American History* 79 (December 1992); and Philip Gleason, ed., *Speaking of Diversity: Language and Ethnicity in Twentieth-Century America* (Baltimore: Johns Hopkins University Press, 1992).

8. Dennis N. Valdés, "The New Northern Borderlands: An Overview of Midwestern Chicano History," in García, ed., *Mexicans in the Midwest*, pp. 8–10. For the rise of mutualistas in Mexico see Reynaldo Sordo Cedeño, "Los Sociedades de Socorros Mutuos, 1867–1880," *Historia Mexicana* 38 (July–September 1983).

9. For an examination of the centrality of parish life see Jay P. Dolan, ed., *The American Catholic Parish: A History from 1850 to the Present* (New York: Paulist Press, 1987), vol. 2, and Jay P. Dolan, *The American*

Catholic Experience: A History from Colonial Times to the Present (Garden City, N.Y.: Doubleday, 1985, rpt. Notre Dame, Ind.: University of Notre Dame Press, 1992).

10. Diocesan priests had been particularly ineffective in converting and exacting tithes from Indians during the early years of the Conquest, and mendicant religious orders often encouraged the adaptation and melding of folk religion elements for purposes of mass conversions. See, for example, Bernard R. Ortiz de Montellano, *Aztec Medicine, Health, and Nutrition* (New Brunswick: Rutgers University Press, 1990), 12–14.

11. Migration chains from Mexico to Kansas are discussed in Judith F. Laird, "Argentine, Kansas: The Evolution of a Mexican–American Community 1905–1940" (Ph.D. diss., University of Kansas, 1975), pp. 105, 224. For earlier periods see Victor S. Clark, "Mexican Labor in the United States" (1908) in Cortés, ed., *Mexican Labor in the United States.* See also Stanley A. West and Irene S. Vásquez, "Early Migration from Central Mexico to the Northern United States" and Gilbert Cárdenas "Mexican Migration to the Midwest," in Stanley A. West and June Macklin, eds., *The Chicano Experience* (Boulder, Colo.: Westview Press, 1979).

12. Francis C. Kelley, *The Book of Red and Yellow: Being a Story of Blood and a Yellow Streak* (Chicago: Catholic Church Extension Society, 1915), p. 6.

13. Kelley, *Book of Red and Yellow,* p. 36.

14. "Protest of the Mexican Catholic Hierarchy to the 5 February 1917 Constitution, February 24, 1917," in Colman J. Barry, ed., *Readings in Church History* (Westminster, Md.: Newman Press, 1965), p. 324.

15. "Protest of the Mexican Catholic Hierarchy," p. 325.

16. Francis C. Kelley, *The Story of Extension* (Chicago: Extension Press, 1922), p. 128.

17. Moisés González Navarro, *Historia Moderna de Mexico: El Porfiriato* (Mexico City: Editorial Hermes, 1956), vol. 4: 475–76; Jean Pierre Bastián, *Protestantismo y Sociedad en Mexico* (Mexico City: Casa Unida de Publicaciones, S.A., 1983), p. 181; Deborah J. Baldwin, *Protestants and the Mexican Revolution* (Urbana: University of Illinois Press, 1990), p. 452.

18. Jean A. Meyer, *The Cristero Rebellion: The Mexican People between Church and State, 1926–1929* (Cambridge: Cambridge University Press, 1976), pp. 48, 53, 75, 178–79; Ramón Jrade, "Counterrevolution in Mexico: The Cristero Movement in Sociological and Historical Perspective" (Ph.D. diss., Brown University, 1980), pp. 6, 159; Robert E. Quirk, *The*

Mexican Revolution and the Catholic Church, 1900–1929 (Bloomington: Indiana University Press, 1973), p. 3.

19. Kelley, *The Story of Extension*, p. 128.

20. Ibid., pp. 237–39.

21. "Immigration," in Bureau of Immigration, National Catholic Welfare Council, *Official Year Book* (Washington, D.C.: National Catholic Welfare Council, 1928), 1.

22. American Board of Catholic Missions, "Minutes of Meetings of May Twelfth and Thirteenth, 1927, with the Bishops of the West" (Chicago: American Board of Catholic Missions, 1927), p. 7, Madaj Collection (hereafter MC), ACA.

23. Laird, "Argentine, Kansas," 44–47, 66. Other studies relating to Mexican Catholicism in Kansas include Larry G. Rutter, "Mexican Americans in Kansas: A Survey and Social Mobility Study, 1900–1970" (Master's thesis, Kansas State University, 1972); Socorro M. Ramírez, "A Survey of the Mexicans in Emporia, Kansas" (Master's thesis, Kansas State Teachers College, Emporia, 1942); Marian F. Braun, "A Survey of the American-Mexicans in Topeka, Kansas" (Master's thesis, Kansas State Teachers College, 1970); and Robert Oppenheimer, "Acculturation or Assimilation: Mexican Immigrants in Kansas, 1900 to World War II," *Western Historical Quarterly* 16 (October 1985).

24. Michael M. Smith, "Mexicans in Kansas City: The First Generation, 1900–1920," in García, ed., *Mexicans in the Midwest*, pp. 30, 37.

25. Ibid., pp. 42, 43, 48.

26. John T. Duncan and Severiano Alonzo, *Guadalupe Center: 50 Years of Service* (Kansas City, Mo.: private printing, 1972), pp. 28–30.

27. Church Committee of Sacred Heart Church, *Official Publication and Year Book* (Ottawa, Kans.: Church Committee of Sacred Heart Church, 1918), p. 159.

28. Ibid., pp. 151, 155.

29. Ibid., pp. 165, 173, 177.

30. Ibid., p. 173; "Abbelen Memorial and Letters of Bishops Keane and Ireland," in Colman J. Barry, ed., *The Catholic Church and German Americans* (Milwaukee: Bruce, 1953), p. 294.

31. Hector Franco, "The Mexican People in the State of Kansas" (Master's thesis, University of Wichita, 1950), pp. 73–77; Duncan and Alonzo, *Guadalupe Center*, p. 23.

32. Paul M. Lin, "Voluntary Kinship and Voluntary Association in a Mexican-American Community" (Master's thesis, University of Kansas, 1963), pp. 31–33, 36, 38–40.

33. Laird, "Argentine Settlement," pp. 363–64.

34. Smith, "Mexicans in Kansas City," pp. 43–44.

35. Lawrence A. Cardoso, "La Repatriación de Braceros de Epoca de Obregón—1920–1923," *Historia Mexicana* 109 (April–June 1977): 576, 581; Laird, "Argentine, Kansas," pp. 73, 74.

36. Duncan and Alonzo, *Guadalupe Center*, pp. 28–30; Laird, "Argentine Settlement," pp. 363–64. The Sister Servants of Mary, familiarly known as the "Spanish Sisters," settled in Kansas City, Kansas, in 1917 after having been exiled from Mexico and living for three years in New Orleans. Five of them assisted the Sisters of the Poor of St. Francis and the Sisters of Charity in caring for the sick. New recruits came thereafter from both Mexico and Spain, and in 1926 the order moved into new quarters near Our Lady of Mt. Carmel; see Duncan and Alonzo, *Guadalupe Center*, pp. 12, 27.

37. Smith, "Mexicans in Kansas City," pp. 42, 43, 48.

38. Kelley to Mundelein, December 18, 1918, *MC*.

39. Eunice Felter, "The Social Adaptations of the Mexican Churches in the Chicago Area" (Master's thesis, University of Chicago Divinity School, 1941), p. 36; Robert C. Jones and Louis R. Wilson, *The Mexican in Chicago* (Chicago: Commission of the Chicago Church Federation, 1931), pp. 19–21, 24–27.

40. David S. Weber, "Anglo Views of Mexican Immigrants: Popular Perceptions and Neighborhood Realities in Chicago, 1900–1940" (Ph.D. diss., Ohio State University, 1982), pp. 64–65.

41. Ibid., p. 65.

42. January 1, 1925, Robert Redfield Diary, Box 59, Robert Redfield Papers, University of Chicago Special Collections, p. 78.

43. Cited by Redfield in English copy of typescript of "Those Who Deny Their Country," from *Mexico*, February 7, 1925, Redfield Papers, pp. 1–2.

44. Jane Addams, *The Second Twenty Years at Hull House: September 1909 to September 1929* (New York: Macmillan Company, 1930), pp. 282–83; Thomas L. Philpott, *The Slum and the Ghetto: Neighborhood Deterioration and Middle-Class Reform, Chicago, 1880–1930* (New York: Oxford University Press, 1978), pp. 283, 284; Anita E. Jones, "Conditions Surrounding Mexicans in Chicago" (San Francisco: R & E Research Associates, 1971; copyright 1928), pp. 43, 51; Weber, "Anglo Views of Mexican Immigrants," pp. 138, 141.

45. January 1, 1925, Redfield Diary, p. 78.

46. January 1, 1925, Redfield Diary, p. 79.

47. Edward Kantowicz, *Corporation Sole: Cardinal Mundelein and Chicago Catholicism* (Notre Dame: University of Notre Dame Press, 1989), p. 74; Charles H. Shanabruch, "The Catholic Church's Role in the

Americanization of Chicago's Immigrants: 1833–1928," (Ph.D. diss., University of Chicago, 1975), pp. 543–45.

48. Harry C. Koenig, ed., *A History of the Parishes of the Archdiocese of Chicago* (Chicago: Archdiocese of Chicago, 1980), pp. 286, 287.

49. Gerald P. Fogarty, *The Vatican and the American Hierarchy from 1870 to 1965* (Stuttgart, Germany: Anton Hersemann, 1982), pp. 229–30, 231.

50. Humbert S. Nelli, *Italians in Chicago 1880–1930: A Study in Ethnic Mobility* (New York: Oxford University Press, 1970), pp. 183, 185–87.

51. Rudolph J. Vecoli, "Prelates and Peasants: Italian Immigrants and the Catholic Church," *Journal of Social History* 2 (Spring 1969), pp. 222–24, 228–30; James W. Sanders, *The Education of an Urban Minority: Catholics in Chicago, 1833–1965* (New York: Oxford University Press, 1977), p. 67.

52. Vecoli, "Prelates and Peasants," 226; Meyer, *Cristero Rebellion*, pp. 59–60, 71.

53. By 1918, twenty-six religious orders, including Franciscans, Augustinians, and Carmelites, administered parishes, schools, and charitable institutions for Italians in the United States. Midwestern Mexicans had no such strictly national counterparts, although those orders, as well as Basilians, Redemptorists, and of course the Spanish Claretians, dominated the administration of their parishes throughout the period under study.

54. James A. Farrell to Msgr. D. J. Sheil, April 9, 1925, *MC*.

55. Shanabruch, "Catholic Church's Role," 544–46.

56. Louise Año Nuevo Kerr, "The Chicano Experience in Chicago, 1920–1970" (Ph.D. diss., University of Illinois, Chicago, 1976), pp. 1–2, 56–58; Edith Abbott, *The Tenements of Chicago, 1908–1935* (Chicago: University of Illinois Press, 1936), p. 297; Robert A. Slayton, *Back of the Yards: The Making of a Local Democracy* (Chicago: University of Chicago Press, 1986), p. 148. See also Lizabeth Cohen, *Making a New Deal: Industrial Workers in Chicago 1919–1939* (Cambridge: Cambridge University Press, 1990).

57. Francisco A. Rosales, "Mexican Immigration to the Urban Midwest during the 1920s" (Ph.D. diss., Indiana University, 1978), pp. 92, 93.

58. Cited in Taylor, "Chicago and the Calumet Region," p. 47.

59. Ciro Sepúlveda, "La Colonia del Harbor: A History of Mexicanos in East Chicago, Indiana 1919–1932" (Ph.D. diss., University of Notre Dame, 1976), p. 54.

60. See Ciro Sepúlveda, "The Origins of the Urban Colonias in the Midwest 1910–1930," *Revista Chicano-Riqueña* 4 (Autumn 1976).

61. Cited in Raymond A. Mohl and Neil Betten, *Steel City: Urban and Ethnic Patterns in Gary, Indiana, 1906–1950* (New York: Holmes and Meier, 1986), pp. 95, 96–97. Opposition to a priest's refusing rites because of nonattendance also occurred in areas in Mexico. According to traditional folk Catholicism, one could be religious without attending church services. Indeed, high fees sometimes caused insurrection. See William B. Taylor, *Drinking, Homicide and Rebellion in Colonial Mexican Villages* (Stanford: Stanford University Press, 1979).

62. James J. Divita, "The Indiana Church and the Italian Immigrant, 1890–1935," *U.S. Catholic Historian* 6 (Fall 1987): 326; Rosales, "Mexican Immigration," pp. 183–89.

63. Rosales, "Mexican Immigration," p. 189; Nicolás Kanellos, *A History of Hispanic Theatre in the United States: Origins to 1940* (Austin: University of Texas Press, 1990), pp. 189, 190.

64. Cited in Mary Helen Rogers, "The Role of Our Lady of Guadalupe Parish in the Adjustment of the Mexican Community to Life in the Indiana Harbor Area" (Master's thesis, Loyola University, 1952), p. 28.

65. Santacruz quoted in Jrade, "Counterrevolution in Mexico," p. 138.

66. Jrade, "Counterrevolution in Mexico," pp. 137, 146. Jrade offers a view of priests caught in conflict with forces of modernization, either in revolutionary or cristero *municipios*; Juan R. García and Ángel Cal, "El Círculo de Obreros Católicos 'San José' 1925 to 1930," in James B. Lane and Edward J. Escobar, eds., *Forging a Community: The Latino Experience in Northwest Indiana, 1919–1975* (Chicago: Cattails Press, 1987), pp. 100–101.

67. Arthur Shumway, "Gary, Shrine of the Steel Goddess: The City That Has Everything, and at the Same Time Has Nothing," *American Parade* 3 (January–March, 1929): 23–26, 30.

68. Bishop Herman J. Alerding to Father John De Ville, July 18, 1920, J. B. De Ville Collection, UNDA; Mohl and Betten, *Steel City*, pp. 113, 164–65.

69. Mohl and Betten, *Steel City*, p. 115; Ruth Hutchinson Crocker, "Gary Mexicans and Christian Americanization: A Study in Cultural Conflict," in Lane and Escobar, *Forging a Community*, pp. 125–26.

70. De Ville cited in Manuel Gamio, *Mexican Immigration to the United States: A Study in Human Adjustment* (New York: Dover Publications, 1971; copyright 1930), p. 119.

71. José Gallardo quoted in Gamio, *Mexican Immigration*, 119–20.

72. De Ville to Charles T. Fisher, December 12, 1928, J. B. De Ville Collection, UNDA.

73. Rogers, "Role of Our Lady of Guadalupe," p. 35.

74. Cited in Eduard A. Skendzel, *Detroit's Pioneer Mexicans: A Study of the Mexican Colony in Detroit* (Grand Rapids, Mich.: Littleshield Press, 1980), p. 11. For a perspective on the historical context of race, class, and ethnicity in Detroit before the arrival of the Mexicans see Olivier Zunz, *The Changing Face of Inequality: Urbanization, Industrial Development, and Immigrants in Detroit, 1880–1920* (Chicago: University of Chicago Press, 1982).

75. See Zaragoza Vargas, "Mexican Auto Workers at Ford Motor Company, 1918–1933" (Ph.D. diss., University of Michigan, 1984); Zaragoza Vargas, "Life and Community in the 'Wonderful City of the Magic Motor': Mexican Immigrants in 1920s Detroit," *Michigan Historical Review* 15 (Spring 1989); and Louis C. Murillo, "The Detroit Mexican 'Colonia' from 1920 to 1932: Implications for Social and Educational Policy" (Ph.D. diss., Michigan State University, 1981).

76. Juan Pablo Alanís to Bishop Michael Gallagher, July 25, 1923, Our Lady of Guadalupe Parish File (hereafter OLG), AAD; Alanis to Gallagher, March 11, 1923, OLG.

77. Cited in Skendzel, *Detroit's Pioneer Mexicans*, p. 28.

78. Ibid., p. 29.

79. Murillo, "The Detroit Mexican 'Colonia,' " p. 26.

80. Ralph Janis, "The Brave New World that Failed: Patterns of Parish Social Structure in Detroit, 1880–1940" (Ph.D. diss., University of Michigan, 1972), pp. 86, 169.

81. Father Gabriel Ginard to Msgr. Doyle, March 5, 1926, OLG.

82. "Jacobus" to Msgr. J. M. Doyle, September 14, 1927, OLG, AAD.

83. Vargas, "Life and Community," p. 60.

84. Ann M. Rynearson, "Hiding Within the Melting Pot: Mexican Americans in St. Louis" (Ph.D. diss., Washington University, 1980), pp. 26, 49–50, 109–10; T. Earl Sullenger, "The Mexican Population of Omaha," *Journal of Applied Sociology* 8 (May–June 1924): 290–91; T. Earl Sullenger, "Ethnic Assimilation in Omaha," *Sociology and Social Research* 19 (July–August 1935): 550–51.

85. Jane B. Haney, "To Join or Not to Join: Chicano Agency Activity in Two Michigan Cities," in West and Macklin, *The Chicano Experience*, pp. 256–58; Harvey M. Choldin and Grafton D. Trout, *Mexican Americans in Transition: Migration and Employment in Midwestern Cities* (East Lansing: Michigan State Agricultural Experiment Station, 1969), pp. 380–86.

86. John Gurda, "The Latin Community on Milwaukee's Near South Side" (Milwaukee: Milwaukee Urban Observatory, University of Wisconsin, 1976), pp. 5–7.

2. Depression, Survival, and Fragmented Religiosity, 1930–1945

1. Moisés Sandoval, *On the Move: A History of the Hispanic Church in the United States* (Maryknoll, N.Y.: Orbis Books, 1990), p. 61. For an overview of United States Catholicism during this period see David J. O'Brien, *American Catholicism and Social Reform: The New Deal Years* (New York: Oxford University Press, 1968). See also Debra Campbell, "The Struggle to Serve: From the Lay Apostolate to the Ministry Explosion," and Jay P. Dolan, "American Catholics in a Changing Society," in Jay P. Dolan, R. Scott Appleby, Patricia Byrne, and Debra Campbell, *Transforming Parish Ministry: The Changing Roles of Catholic Clergy, Laity, and Women Religious* (New York: Crossroad, 1989).

2. Laird, "Argentine Settlement," p. 203.

3. Laird, "Argentine Settlement," pp. 173, 191, 200, 204; Duncan and Alonzo, *Guadalupe Center*, p. 20.

4. Dorothy Gallagher, "The Mexican Guadalupe Center of Kansas City," in *Proceedings of the National Catechetical Congress of the Confraternity of Christian Doctrine* (Paterson, N.J.: St. Anthony Guild Press, 1940), pp. 362, 366; Dorothy E. Hoffman, "Services Rendered to Mexican Groups in Kansas City, Missouri, through Guadalupe Center" (Master's thesis, University of Missouri, 1938), p. 30.

5. Duncan and Alonzo, *Guadalupe Center*, pp. 65, 80.

6. Kanellos, *History of Hispanic Theatre*, p. 188.

7. For unofficial policy measures concerning repatriation on the part of Mexican and United States governments see Camille Guerín-Gonzales, "Repatriación de familias inmigrantes durante la Gran Depresión," *Historia Mexicana* 35 (October–December 1985) and George Kiser and David Silverman, "Mexican Repatriation during the Great Depression," in George C. Kiser and Martha W. Kiser, eds., *Mexican Workers in the United States: Historical and Political Perspectives* (Albuquerque: University of New Mexico Press, 1979).

8. Daniel T. Simon, "Mexican Repatriation in East Chicago, Indiana," *Journal of Ethnic Studies* 2 (Summer 1974): 14, 16–17, 19; Mohl and Betten, *Steel City*, pp. 103–5.

9. Rogers, "The Role of Our Lady of Guadalupe Parish," pp. 36, 39, 44–52, 58.

10. James J. Divita, "The Indiana Church and the Italian Immigrant," pp. 336–39; John C. Nowicki, Jr., *Souvenir Album of the Golden Jubilee of St. John Cantius Parish* (Indiana Harbor, Ind.: St. John Cantius Parish, 1956), pp. 24, 25.

11. Rosales and Simon, "Chicano Steel Workers and Unionism in the Midwest," pp. 270–72.

12. "Changes among the Sisters," pp. 1, 4, n.d., ca. 1948, St. John Bosco Settlement House Collection, UNDA.

13. Doris L. Kozlica, "Sister" Felicitas, typescript, pp. 1–2, n.d., ca. late 1970s, St. John Bosco Settlement House Collection, UNDA.

14. Norman D. Humphrey, "Mexican Repatriation from Michigan: Public Assistance in Historical Perspective," *Social Service Review* 15 (September 1941): 497–98, 500–503; John L. Zurbrick, "Memo from District Director of Immigration, Detroit District, to Commissioner General of Immigration, October 20, 1932," pp. 42–44; Ignacio L. Batiza, Consul for Mexico, "To the Mexican Colony," October 13, 1932, in Kiser and Kiser, *Mexican Workers in the United States*, pp. 44–45.

15. Humphrey, "Mexican Repatriation," 505–6.

16. Simón Muñoz et al., "Petition to Bishop Michael J. Gallagher," October 18, 1932, OLG.

17. Petition of the Altar Society to Bishop Gallagher, May 14, 1936, OLG, AAD.

18. Telegram from Mexican Committee to Bishop Gallagher, July 13, 1927, OLG, AAD. Complaints against Castillo dated back to 1927, his first year as pastor at Our Lady of Guadalupe, when petitions circulated for and against his stewardship. Muñoz had a longtime feud based on financial and other disagreements with Castillo; see Castillo to Msgr. S. Woznicki, October 23, 1931, OLG. Castillo's supporters later included several concerned Anglos outside of the parish; see "Friends of Luis Castillo to Bishop Gallagher," November 17, 1936, OLG. For patterns elsewhere in the Detroit Archdiocese, see Leslie W. Tentler, *Seasons of Grace: History of the Archdiocese of Detroit* (Detroit: Wayne State University Press, 1990), pp. 424–25.

19. "Church Committee Candidates, Presented by Father Alanís to Bishop Gallagher," 1923–1926, OLG, AAD; "Church Committee Candidates, Submitted by Luis Castillo to Monsignor J. M. Doyle," 1928, 1930–1932, 1934–1935, OLG, AAD.

20. Norman D. Humphrey, "The Mexican Peasant in Detroit," (Ph.D. diss., University of Michigan, 1943), pp. 145–47; Skendzel, *Detroit's Pioneer Mexicans*, pp. 32–35.

21. Humphrey, "The Mexican Peasant in Detroit," pp. 211–13.

22. James Gleason, *Apostolic Blessing: On the Occasion of the 100th Anniversary of Holy Redeemer Parish, 1880–1980* (Detroit: Holy Redeemer Church, 1980), p. 44.

23. María Magaña Alvizu quoted in Margarita Valdez, ed., *Tradiciones del Pueblo: Traditions of Three Mexican Feast Days in Southwest Detroit* (Detroit: Casa de Unidad Cultural Arts and Media Center, 1990), p. 10.

24. Weber, "Anglo Views of Mexican Immigrants," pp. 143, 249; Louise Manning, "The Mexican Immigration: An Over-all Study of Ninety Mexican Families Living in a Particular Chicago Area," (Master's thesis, Loyola University, 1947), pp. 3, 16.

25. Cohen, *Making a New Deal*, pp. 268–69; O'Brien, *American Catholicism*, p. 182.

26. Jane Anne Evans, "Mexicans Naturalized in Chicago" (sociology class paper at the University of Chicago), Latin American Project, n.d., Immigrants Protective League Papers, Chicago Historical Society, Box 7, f. 83, 4.

27. Frank X. Paz, "Mexican Americans in Chicago: A General Survey" [Typescript, January 1948], Welfare Council of Metropolitan Chicago, Chicago Historical Society, p. 8; Taylor, "Chicago and the Calumet Region," pp. 118, 222–23; Slayton, *Back of the Yards*, p. 113. Mexican American service in the armed forces during World War II smoothed over previously uneasy and sometimes violent relations in several other locations as well. In 1944 the same American Legion Post in northwest Indiana that twelve years earlier had cooperated in the repatriation campaign organized a homecoming celebration for a Mexican–American Marine sergeant who won several decorations in the Pacific. Later it staged a "Latin American Night"; see Francisco A. Rosales and Daniel T. Simon, "Chicano Steel Workers and Unionism in the Midwest, 1919–1945," *Aztlán* 6 (Summer 1975): 275.

28. Felter, "Social Adaptations of the Mexican Churches," pp. 45–47; Jones and Wilson, "Mexicans in Chicago," p. 12; Weber, "Anglo Views of Mexican Immigrants," pp. 45–47, 202–3.

29. Slayton, *Back of the Yards*, pp. 183–84.

30. Koenig, *History of the Parishes*, pp. 444–46.

31. Kerr, "The Chicano Experience in Chicago," pp. 86–88; for a comparative perspective focusing on the ideologies of European immigrants see John Bodnar, *The Transplanted: A History of Immigrants in Urban America* (Bloomington: Indiana University Press, 1985).

32. Navor Rodríguez, "Síntesis Histórica de la Colonia Mexicana de Joliet, Ill., USA," in García, *Mexicans in the Midwest*, pp. 162–64; Fabian Donlan to Robert E. Lucey, October 14, 1952, Bishops' Committee for the Spanish Speaking Correspondence, reel 13, Robert E. Lucey Collection, UNDA.

33. Foley, *From Peones to Políticos*, pp. 84–88.

34. Valdés, *Al Norte*, pp. 54–55, 99. For descriptions of the hardships of Tejanos going north see Carey McWilliams, "Mexicans to Michigan," *Common Ground* (Autumn 1941), reprinted in Wayne Moquín, ed., *A*

Documentary History of the Mexican Americans (New York: Praeger, 1971). See also Carey McWilliams, *Ill Fares the Land: Migrants and Migratory Labor in the United States* (Boston: Little, Brown, 1942).

35. Foley, *From Peones to Políticos*, pp. 32–33.

36. For an interpretation of Mexican folk religion and folk medicine see Bernard Ortiz de Montellano, "Syncretism in Mexican and Mexican–American Folk Medicine" [Working Paper No. 5] (College Park, Md.: Department of Spanish and Portuguese, 1989).

37. James M. Reardon, *The Catholic Church in the Diocese of St. Paul: From Earliest Origins to Centennial Achievement* (St. Paul: North Central Publishing Company, 1952), p. 591; Lorraine E. Pierce, "Mexican Americans on St. Paul's Lower West Side," *Journal of Mexican American History* 4 (1974): 3–4; Valdés, *Al Norte*, pp. 29–32.

38. Cf. Joseph Cada, *Czech-American Catholics, 1850–1920* (Chicago: University of Chicago Press, 1964), pp. 32, 33. Rosales, "Mexican Immigration to the Urban Midwest," pp. 229–31.

39. Barbara J. Macklin, "Structural Stability and Culture Change in a Mexican-American Community" (Ph.D. diss., University of Pennsylvania, 1963), pp. 64–65.

40. Macklin, "Structural Stability and Culture Change," p. 64; Lawrence A. Mossing, *History of the Diocese of Toledo*, vol. 3: *Northern Ohio, West Central Section, Toledo, and Lucas County* (Toledo: Diocese of Toledo, 1985), pp. 31, 32, 68.

41. Andrés G. Guerrero, *A Chicano Theology* (Maryknoll, N.Y.: Orbis Books, 1987), pp. 96–99, 109. See also Eric R. Wolf, "The Virgin of Guadalupe: A Mexican National Symbol," *Journal of American Folklore* 71 (1958). The Virgin of Guadalupe became inseparable from Mexican Catholicism after the 1531 vision of the Indian peasant Juan Diego on Tepeyac Hill, the site of the shrine to Tonantzín, Aztec mother of the gods. Thereafter, millions of Indians became Mexican Catholics. La Virgen Morena symbolized strength and protection, permitting survival in hostile environs.

42. Valdés, *Al Norte*, pp. 84–85.

43. Father Peter T. Fiexa, speech at Ste. Anne's Church, September 18, 1939, cited in Humphrey, "The Mexican Peasant in Detroit," p. 157.

44. Valdés, *Al Norte*, pp. 89–94.

45. Devotional symbols of folk Catholicism expanded outside parish boundaries and even into the workplace. One study incorporating interviews with Mexican American women who had worked in a midwestern wartime munitions plant revealed that most of them displayed pictures on their lockers of La Virgen de Guadalupe alongside

those of their families; see Richard Santillan, "Rosita the Riveter: Mid-western Mexican American Women during World War II, 1941–1945," in García, *Mexicans in the Midwest*, p. 126.

46. Louise Año Nuevo Kerr, "Mexican Chicago: Chicago Assimilation Aborted, 1939–1954" in Melvin G. Holli and Peter D'A. Jones, eds., *Ethnic Chicago* (Grand Rapids, Mich.: Eerdman's, 1984), pp. 274–76, 290.

3. Parish Growth and Barrio Diversity, 1945–1965

1. James A. Hickey, "Report from James A. Hickey, Director, Mexican Apostolate, Saginaw Diocese, to Robert E. Lucey," July 8, 1953 (Austin, Texas), 3, Reel 13, Bishops' Committee for the Spanish Speaking Correspondence, Lucey Collection, UNDA (hereafter BCSS).

2. Macklin, "Structural Stability and Culture Change," pp. 32, 36, 186.

3. Duncan and Alonzo, *Guadalupe Center*, pp. 84, 85, 99–100.

4. Lin, "Voluntary Kinship," pp. 56–67.

5. Ibid., p. 85.

6. Cited in ibid., p. 38.

7. Franco, "Mexican People in the State of Kansas," p. 1; J. Neale Carman, *Foreign Language Units of Kansas*, vol. 1, *Historical Atlas and Statistics* (Lawrence: University of Kansas Press, 1962), p. 316.

8. Cited in Franco, "Mexican People in the State of Kansas," pp. 4, 8.

9. Valdés, *Al Norte*, pp. 156, 157.

10. Kerr, "Chicano Experience in Chicago," pp. 167, 173, 179. See also William Kornblum, *Blue Collar Community* (Chicago: University of Chicago Press, 1974).

11. Jorge Prieto, *Harvest of Hope: The Pilgrimage of a Mexican-American Physician* (Notre Dame: University of Notre Dame Press, 1989), pp. 67–68.

12. Kerr, "Chicano Experience in Chicago," pp. 7, 8, 204; Dominic A. Pacyga and Ellen Skerrett, *Chicago, City of Neighborhoods: Histories and Tours* (Chicago: Loyola University Press, 1986), pp. 251–52; Cardinal's Committee for the Spanish Speaking in Chicago, *Report for 1961* (Chicago: Cardinal's Committee for the Spanish Speaking, April 10, 1962), pp. 1–3.

13. Cardinal's Committee, *Report for 1961*, p. 3.

14. Robert Reicher, "Programs for Migrants in Illinois," in *Catholic Council for the Spanish Speaking* (Ninth Regional Conference, San An-

tonio, Texas, August 15–17, 1958), pp. 62–65, UNDA; Koenig, *History of the Parishes of the Archdiocese of Chicago*, pp. 1002–3, 1078, 1080.

15. Edwin Maldonado, "Contract Labor and the Origins of Puerto Rican Communities in the United States," in Lane and Escobar, *Forging a Community*, pp. 201, 203–4.

16. Cardinal's Committee, *Report for 1961*, p. 3; Koenig, *History of the Parishes of the Archdiocese of Chicago*, p. 278.

17. Kerr, "Chicano Experience in Chicago," p. 175.

18. Cardinal's Committee, "Report for Mexican Community," in *Report for 1961*, p. 1.

19. Julian Samora and Richard A. Lamanna, *Mexican-Americans in a Midwest Metropolis: A Study of East Chicago* [Advance Report 8, Mexican-American Study Project] (Los Angeles: Regents of the University of California, 1967), pp. 33-4, 23, 39, 44–45,

20. "Movimiento por la Parroquia de Ntra. Señora de Guadalupe," September 30, 1948, vol. 2, *El Mutualista*, pp. 48–49, in Rodolfo J. Cortina and Federico Herrera, eds., *El Mutualista (1947–1950): A Facsimile Edition of a Milwaukee Hispanic Newspaper* (Milwaukee: University of Wisconsin, Spanish Speaking Outreach Institute, 1983), pp. 48–49; Avelardo Valdez, "The Social and Economic Integration of Mexicans and Puerto Ricans in Milwaukee" (Milwaukee: University of Wisconsin, Spanish Speaking Outreach Institute, 1988), pp. 18, 20; Gurda, "The Latin Community on Milwaukee's South Side," p. 21. See also Leo Rummel, *History of the Catholic Church in Wisconsin* (Madison: Knights of Columbus, 1976).

21. Carolyn W. Matthiasson, "Acculturation of Mexican-Americans in a Midwestern City" (Ph.D. diss., Cornell University, 1968), pp. 18, 19, 51–52.

22. Cited in Humphrey, "Mexican Peasant in Detroit," p. 60.

23. Grand Rapids Diocese, *The Catholic Church in the Grand River Valley* (Grand Rapids: Diocese of Grand Rapids, 1961), pp. 366–67.

24. Gumecindo Salas and Isabel Salas, "The Mexican Community of Detroit," in David W. Hartman, ed., *Immigrants and Migrants: The Detroit Ethnic Experience* (Detroit: New University Thought Publishing Company, 1974), p. 379.

25. Skendzel, *Detroit's Pioneer Mexicans*, p. 41.

26. Clement H. Kern to William F. Kelley, Director, Social Action Department, Diocese of Brooklyn, November 23, 1952, uncatalogued, Holy Trinity Rectory Files, Holy Trinity Church.

27. Kern to Kelley, p. 2.

28. "Irish Hail Their Patron Saint," *Detroit News*, March 17, 1956, p. 1; "A Man for All People," *Michigan Catholic* (August 19, 1983),

pp. 10–12; Genevieve M. Casey, *Father Clem Kern: Conscience of Detroit* (Detroit: Marygrove College, 1989), pp. 20–21, 22; Tentler, *Seasons of Grace*, p. 394.

29. Clement Kern to Joseph Breitenbeck, April 18, 1947, Holy Trinity Parish File, AAD.

30. Vice Chancellor, Detroit Archdiocese to Miguel Mazatán Racegas, October 20, 1955, Holy Trinity Parish File, AAD; Clement Kern to Monsignor of the Detroit Archdiocese, October 17, 1955, OLG, AAD.

31. George M. Foster, *Tzintzuntzán: Mexican Peasants in a Changing World* (Prospect Heights, Ill.: Wavelength Press, 1967), pp. 203, 207, 228, 319; see also María Hernández de Alcalá quoted in *Tradiciones del Pueblo*, p. 19.

32. Josefina González quoted in Valdez, ed., *Tradiciones del Pueblo*, p. 19.

33. Clement Kern, "The Migrant in the North," in *Catholic Council for the Spanish Speaking*, p. 51.

34. Kern, "The Migrant in the North," pp. 51–52.

35. Hickey, "Report from James A. Hickey," p. 3.

36. Valdés, *Al Norte*, p. 102.

37. Hickey, "Report from James A. Hickey," p. 2.

38. "I've Seen Them Work," *Carmelite Review* 9 (January 1950): 3; James A. Hickey to Robert E. Lucey, October 15, 1952, pp. 1, 2, BCSS.

39. Sister Mary E. Thomas, "A Study of the Causes and Consequences of the Economic Status of Migratory Farm Workers in Illinois, Indiana, Michigan and Wisconsin, 1940–1958" (Ph.D. diss., University of Notre Dame, 1960), pp. 267–68; Joseph H. Crosthwait, "Excerpts from Report of Field Trip to the Northern States," October 1957, p. 5, UNDA.

40. Crosthwait, "Excerpts from Report of Field Trip to the Northern States," p. 2; Crosthwait, "Excerpts from Report of Field Trip to the Western States," 1957, p. 5, UNDA.

41. Bishop of Grand Island, Nebraska, to Robert E. Lucey, October 28, 1952, BCSS.

42. José Garibí Rivera to Robert E. Lucey, August 30, 1952, BCSS; Robert E. Lucey to José Garibí Rivera, November 21, 1952, BCSS; Bastián, *Protestantismo y Sociedad en Mexico*, p. 13; Stephen A. Privett, *The U.S. Catholic Church and Its Hispanic Members: The Pastoral Vision of Archbishop Lucey* (San Antonio: Trinity University Press, 1988), pp. 102–5. The Conference of Archbishops and Bishops, in its landmark meeting of 1945, discussed the Mexican question in the context of the West and Southwest. Its departments centered on four archdioceses—Los Angeles, Santa Fe, Denver, and San Antonio. The Bishops' Committee

for the Spanish Speaking traces its roots to a 1943 meeting of bishops in the spirit of Good Neighbor Diplomacy and with the support of the American Board of Catholic Missions, the National Catholic Welfare Conference Social Action Bureau, and the Church Extension Society. Archbishop Lucey led the program which resulted in the formation of the Bishops' Committee to enhance the presence of priests and women religious familiar with the Spanish language and Mexican culture. The Bishops' Committee, which survived in modified form through the mid-1960s, concentrated its early work almost exclusively in Texas, leaving midwestern venues beyond its reach before Operation Migratory Labor began in 1953.

43. Robert E. Lucey, "Analysis of Report by Father Radtke Concerning Migrant Mexican Workers in the North Central States," October 15, 1952, pp. 1, 2; Robert E. Lucey letter to Bishops and Archbishops concerning shortage of priests due to service of army chaplains during World War II, March 8, 1945, Box 19, BCSS Correspondence (hard copy file), Robert E. Lucey Papers, UNDA; Saul E. Bronder, *Social Justice and Church Authority: The Public Life of Archbishop Robert E. Lucey* (Philadelphia: Temple University Press, 1982), p. 76; A. V. Ulanowicz, "Use of Priests from Mexico," in *Catholic Council for the Spanish Speaking*, pp. 36, 37.

44. Hickey, "Report from James A. Hickey," p. 2.

45. Ibid.

46. Crosthwait, "Excerpts from Report of Field Trip to the Northern States," pp. 6–7.

47. Ibid., pp. 7, 9.

48. Edward A. Fitzgerald to Robert E. Lucey, October 9, 1952, BCSS.

49. Foreword by Robert E. Lucey, *Catholic Council for the Spanish Speaking*, pp. 5–7; Privett, *The U.S. Catholic Church*, p. 110.

50. Joseph H. Crosthwait, "The Status of Our Spanish-Speaking People," in *Catholic Council for the Spanish Speaking*, p. 10.

51. Crosthwait, "Excerpts from Report of Field Trip to the Northern States," pp. 6–7.

52. Moisés Sandoval, "Church Structures for the Hispanics," in Sandoval, ed., *Fronteras: A History of the Latin American Church in the USA since 1513* (San Antonio: Mexican American Cultural Center, 1983), pp. 420–22; Bishops' Committee for the Spanish Speaking, *Annual Report 1966* (Washington, D.C.: National Catholic Welfare Conference, 1966), p. 2.

53. Victor Cardin to Robert E. Lucey, October 21, 1952; "Spanish Education Program Statistics 6–5 to 7–31–52," Diocese of Crookston, BCSS.

54. Edward G. Baumgartner to John A. Donlan, Chancellor, Archdiocese of Detroit, May 28, 1954, Sacred Heart Parish File, Imlay City, AAD.

55. "Migrant Agricultural Workers in the Archdiocese of Detroit," *Michigan Catholic*, July 30, 1959, cited in Lucey to Fathers Juraschek and Wagner, August 10, 1959, BCSS.

56. Rogers, "The Role of Our Lady of Guadalupe," p. 70.

57. Samora and Lamanna, *Mexican Americans in a Midwest Metropolis*, pp. 5, 7, 60, 118, 152.

58. Albert Hamilton, *The Catholic Journey through Ohio* (St. Meinrad, Ind.: Abbey Press, 1976), p. 72.

59. James A. Ward to Robert E. Lucey, October 27, 1952, BCSS.

60. Norman S. Goldner, "The Mexican in the Northern Urban Area: A Comparison of Two Generations" (Ph.D. diss., University of Minnesota, 1959), p. 56; T. Allen Caine, "Social Life in a Mexican Community" (San Francisco: R & E Research Associates, 1974), p. 49; Lorraine E. Pierce, "Mexican Americans in St. Paul's Lower West Side," *Journal of Mexican American History* 4 (1974): 11, 13.

61. June Macklin and Alvina Teniente de Costilla, "La Virgen de Guadalupe and the American Dream: The Melting Pot Bubbles in Toledo, Ohio," in West and Macklin, *The Chicano Community*, pp. 119, 126–27, 133; Macklin, "Structural Stability and Culture Change," p. 68.

62. Mossing, *History of the Diocese of Toledo*, pp. 32, 69; John A. Soto, "Mexican American Community Leadership for Education" (Ph.D. diss., University of Michigan, 1974), pp. 15, 90–91; Macklin, "Structural Stability and Culture Change," 209–10. Cultural and attitudinal differences between clergy and Mexican Americans sometimes combined to provoke misunderstandings. The pastor of St. Mary's Church in Joliet, Illinois, wrote in 1952, "I sincerely believe, Your Excellency, that our big problem with the Mexican people is to get them acclimated to a regular Sunday schedule of attending Mass and devotions. We find that our major difficulty with them here in Joliet is a lack of loyalty to the Sunday Mass because of their great social activities on Saturday," Fabian W. Donlan to Robert E. Lucey, October 14, 1952, BCSS; Navor Rodríguez, "Síntesis Histórica de la Colonia de Joliet," p. 150.

63. Julie Burns, *Viva Cristo Rey* (Lansing: M-R Publications, 1980), pp. 7, 13–14; Haney, "Migration, Settlement Patterns, and Social Organization," p. 230; Carol Berry, "A Survey of the Holland Spanish-Speaking Community" (East Lansing: Michigan State University Department of Sociology and Institute for Community Development, 1970), p. 17.

64. See, for example, Antonio M. Stevens-Arroyo, ed., *Prophets Denied Honor: An Anthology of the Hispanic Church in the United States* (Maryknoll, N.Y.: Orbis Books, 1980), p. 176.

65. Valdés, *Al Norte*, pp. 186, 189, 195; Kay D. Willson, "The Historical Development of Migrant Labor in Michigan Agriculture" (Master's thesis, Michigan State University, 1978), p. 125. For secular leadership among Mexican Americans in the Midwest see Richard Santillán, "Latino Politics in the Midwestern United States: 1915–1986," in F. Chris García, ed., *Latinos and the Political System* (Notre Dame: University of Notre Dame Press, 1988).

66. Bishops' Committee, *Annual Report 1966*, p. 104; Privett, *U.S. Catholic Church*, p. 117.

67. Macklin, "Structural Stability and Culture Change," p. 218; Ortiz de Montellano, "Syncretism in Mexican and Mexican-American Folk Medicine," pp. 16–19.

68. June Macklin, "Three North Mexican Folk Saint Movements," *Comparative Studies in Society and History* 15 (1973): 91, 105; June Macklin, " 'All the Good and Bad in This World': Women, Traditional Medicine, and Mexican American Culture," in Margarita B. Melville, ed., *Twice a Minority: Mexican American Women* (St. Louis: C.V. Mosby Company, 1980), pp. 127, 128, 130, 136–40, 142.

69. June Macklin, "Curanderismo and Espiritismo: Complementary Approaches to Traditional Mental Health Service," in West and Macklin, *The Chicano Experience*, pp. 207, 209–10, 214; Sandoval, *On the Move*, p. 88; *Tzintzuntzán*, pp. 195, 203; George M. Foster, *Empire's Children: The People of Tzintzuntzán* (Mexico, D.F.: Smithsonian Institution, Institute of Social Anthropology, Publication No. 6, 1948), pp. 202–3, 221–22; Norman D. Humphrey, "The Cultural Background of the Mexican Immigrant," *Rural Society* 13 (September 1948): 251–52.

70. Crosthwait, "Excerpts from Report of Field Trip to Western States," p. 8.

71. Ibid., p. 5.

72. Ninety-nine parishes throughout Chicago had Sunday Mass in Spanish in the Chicago Archdiocese by the 1980s. The Detroit archdiocese, with the next largest Mexican-American population in the Midwest, offered fewer than a dozen; "Parroquias con Misas en Español," n.d., ca. 1985, in Office of Hispanic Affairs File, AAD; *Catholic Directory*, 1985, p. 123.

73. In 1964 the American hierarchy created a new committee to supervise the work of both offices and designated the one in San Antonio as the national office for the Spanish speaking; Privett, *U.S. Hispanic Church*, pp. 87, 117.

CONTRIBUTORS

David A. Badillo is an urban historian specializing in comparative Latino Studies and Assistant Professor of Latin American Studies at the University of Illinois at Chicago.

Jeffrey M. Burns is Archivist for the Archdiocese of San Francisco and is associated with the University of San Francisco and the Graduate Theological Union at Berkeley.

Jay P. Dolan is Professor of History at the University of Notre Dame and former Director of the Cushwa Center for the Study of American Catholicism.

Gilberto M. Hinojosa has taught and written books and articles on Texas, the Southwest, and Mexican-American history for over two decades. He is currently Dean of Humanities and Fine Arts at Incarnate Word College in San Antonio.

Index